I0128750

GRASSROOTS ACTIVISMS

INTERSECTIONAL RHETORICS
Karma R. Chávez, Series Editor

GRASSROOTS ACTIVISMS

PUBLIC RHETORICS IN LOCALIZED CONTEXTS

Edited by Lisa L. Phillips,
Sarah Warren-Riley,
and Julie Collins Bates

THE OHIO STATE UNIVERSITY PRESS
COLUMBUS

Copyright © 2024 by The Ohio State University.
All rights reserved.

Library of Congress Cataloging-in-Publication data available online at https://catalog.loc.
    gov
LCCN: 2023040881
Identifiers: ISBN 978-0-8142-1559-3 (hardback); ISBN 978-0-8142-5898-9 (paperback); ISBN
    978-0-8142-8329-5 (ebook)

Cover design by Alexa Love
Text composition by Stuart Rodriguez
Type set in Minion Pro

CONTENTS

PART 3 • PEDAGOGIES FOR GRASSROOTS ACTIVISMS

ILLUSTRATIONS

FOREWORD

OCTAVIO PIMENTEL AND MIRIAM F. WILLIAMS

Over the past few years, we have faced immense struggles, ranging from the COVID-19 pandemic, to mass shootings, to hate crimes against Asians and members of the Jewish and LGBTQIA+ communities, to police violence against Black people, to caging Latinx children, to "building walls" and closing borders to Muslims, to food insecurity and climate change, to misinformation about elections and science, to conspiracy theories, to insurrections, to courts limiting women's rights and Black voting rights, and so much more. Some of these issues may not be new, but witnessing them at the same time has been exhausting. Still, as we doomscroll social media, we know that grassroots activists are working diligently to build coalitions, to find solutions, and to implement changes to address not one but all of these problems.

If we have learned anything over the past few years, it is that our institutions will not save us and in many cases work purposefully to oppress multiply marginalized communities. The editors and authors in *Grassroots Activisms: Public Rhetorics in Localized Contexts* acknowledge that we cannot count on the checks and balances within institutions to combat the many institutional failures we have witnessed (and in some cases finally acknowledged) over the past few years, but we must instead seek efforts from grassroots activisms within our local communities. The editors wisely divide this comprehensive collection into three categories: (1) grassroots activisms from resistance to institutions, (2) sites of grassroots activisms, and (3) pedagogies for grassroots activisms. This organization is important, because the authors of the chapters cover much ground in this comprehensive and groundbreaking collection. It is rich with stories of coalitions, collectives, connections, and communities, all working to resist and dismantle inequalities across sites and purposes.

This excellent collection shines light on problems that we have faced throughout history, but especially over the last several years. At the foundational level, the goal of this edited collection is to highlight examples of grassroots activisms, which can be defined as the policy or action of using vigorous campaigning to bring about political or social change. And to no surprise, this is what scholars in this collection achieve. The authors demonstrate strategies to dismantle negative discourses and practices in health and medicine, immigration, human rights, environmental justice and land rights, and so much more. After living in such foggy and unpredictable times, this collection shows the undeterred labor of those grassroots activists, often BIPOC or guided by the knowledge of BIPOC, who worked for social change from the comfort, or in the danger, of their own homes. There is no doubt that the readings found in this edited collection will plant seeds of knowledge for many and consequently instill hope in lands where hope is greatly needed.

ACKNOWLEDGMENTS

This edited collection would not be possible without the tireless, innovative, and inspirational efforts of grassroots activists. Beyond that, we thank the contributors to this collection for their thoughtful and motivational research and trust in our collaborative efforts to bring this collection into the world in a moment of unusual precarity. We also thank the two anonymous reviewers who helped shape the collection through their careful review. Thanks also to Tara Cyphers and Karma R. Chávez for their vision, editorial assistance, and support of the project.

This project was supported by the Humanities Center and the Office of the Vice President of Research at Texas Tech University and the Department of Writing and Language Studies and the College of Liberal Arts at the University of Texas at Rio Grande Valley. Finally, we are delighted that our collection is the first edited collection to be included in the Intersectional Rhetorics series.

ACKNOWLEDGMENTS

Valuing, Learning from, and Amplifying Grassroots Activisms

SARAH WARREN-RILEY,
JULIE COLLINS BATES, AND LISA L. PHILLIPS

When we first conceived of the call for proposals that led to the edited collection you are reading now, we felt an urgency to bring attention to the difficult, often thankless activist efforts unfolding around us in response to so many localized exigencies. We were energized by the activist efforts we had been part of or witnessed in our communities and were committed to producing an edited collection that focused on these efforts and highlighted their important work. Then, right before we released the call for proposals (CFP), life shifted. First, the initial wave of the COVID-19 pandemic in the United States brought swift and unexpected lockdowns, travel restrictions, and fear. It was March 2020. As we grappled with changes to our own lives and work situations and concerns about our and our families' health and safety, we also remained keenly aware of how economic and health care disparities were leading already marginalized communities to bear the brunt of the risk. We initially paused this project, both as a reflection of our own situations and also in recognition of how poor the timing seemed for sending out a call for proposals given all of the stress and uncertainty during that period.

Fast-forward a few months to when we again planned to release the CFP for this collection. There were even more shifts. Protests against racial injustices were spreading across the country in response to the deaths of George Floyd, Breonna Taylor, Ahmaud Arbery, and so many other Black Americans at the hands of primarily white police officers. Joe Biden was about to secure the Democratic presidential nomination at the same time that President Donald Trump forcefully cleared peaceful protestors from Lafayette Square in Washington, DC, for a staged photo op outside St. John's Episcopal Church. Our concerns for environmental justice had not abated after nearly four years under President Trump, during which time countless environmental protections were rolled back and drilling and pipeline projects were green-lighted left and right. The construction of a border wall between the United States and Mexico—billed as the means of keeping out "unwanted" migrants—continued. We could go on. All of this led us to contemplate another pause on this project.

Yet it was the awe-inspiring work of localized efforts in response to these moments that gave us hope during this difficult time. When the COVID-19 pandemic resulted in lockdowns and mass unemployment, grassroots activists organized to stock food banks and distribute essential aid to those in need. People mobilized local networks to reach out to and take care of the elderly and immunocompromised, willingly giving their time and risking their own health and safety to do so. Despite the pandemic, grassroots activists organized local protests against racism and police brutality, both in large crowds in liberal places where they were cheered and in small groups in rural conservative areas where they faced backlash. Local efforts also ensued to educate migrant children detained in border camps in Mexico and to support newly arrived immigrants by showing up at bus stops with shoelaces, food, phone numbers, and more. In all of these cases, whether the issues that galvanized people and moved them to action were "widespread" in the sense that they affected people across the world or "limited" in that they affected fewer people in a specific place, the results of these responses illustrate how grassroots activisms can move beyond individual concerns and emphasize how people work collectively toward social justice. This realization deepened our commitment to putting together a collection that specifically focused on interrogating and celebrating the work of localized grassroots activist efforts toward social change.

We recognize that the contexts this book was conceived and compiled within are specific to the current moment and, as such, reflect the issues and grassroots activisms that seem important to highlight right now. Yet we hope the work of this collection remains useful for years to come. Every day, across the country and world, people gather to intervene and advocate for themselves in response to everything from seemingly mundane localized concerns to major social justice movements. It is too early to predict how historians will one day describe this particular moment, but we predict that the many activist actions unfolding online and in local communities across the country will figure prominently into any discussion of this time.

Of course, the relevance of activism and its role in social progress is not a new topic of study. So many decades in American history have been associated with different forms of activism—from the late nineteenth- and early twentieth-century rise of organized labor movements to the civil rights movement of the 1950s and 1960s and the women's rights, gay rights, disability rights, and environmental movements of the 1960s, 1970s, and 1980s. These movements are relevant many decades later and, in new iterations, these topics remain at the forefront of numerous activist efforts unfolding today in different (sometimes—though not always—more inclusive) ways.

Contemporary activist efforts have much in common with the activism of decades past. Many of the techniques that have marked activism for generations are regularly employed to garner attention and make movement on social injustices—think rallies and protests, boycotts and strikes, petition signing and letter writing. Yet we'd be remiss not to acknowledge that today's activist efforts also differ in striking ways, fueled in large part by social media and the internet. As the available means of persuasion have shifted, so too have approaches to activism. Even the naming of so many current activist efforts includes social media hashtags—think #BlackLivesMatter for racial justice, #MeToo to raise attention to sexual harassment, or #FridaysForFuture in response to global climate change.

Clearly, activism is not a new topic of study, nor are the many ways activists take up the issues they care about. Research into such activism also isn't new. Scholarship on activism has been a focus of study across many fields—sociology, history, political science, philosophy, communication, media studies, and environmental studies, to name but a few. Plenty of it exists in our own fields too (specifically rhetoric, writing studies, and technical communication). In fact, a number of recent collections, particularly both volumes of *Activism and Rhetoric,* edited by JongHwa Lee and Seth Kahn, and *Unruly Rhetorics,* edited by Jonathan Alexander, Susan C. Jarratt, and Nancy Welch, have taken up studies of activist efforts in their many forms. *Activism and Rhetoric* seeks to study what specifically counts as activist rhetoric, through analysis of a wide range of political and rhetorical struggles. The scholarship in both volumes of *Activism and Rhetoric* lays important groundwork for analyses of activist rhetorics with a focus on (primarily) large-scale activism, advocacy work, and community organizing. *Unruly Rhetorics,* on the other hand, delves into the intersections of activism, political protest, and public assembly, with contributions to the collection targeted specifically to "unruliness" as it manifests in a variety of recent and historical social justice protests. And yet here we are, trying to persuade you to read this collection on grassroots activisms specifically. Why?

MAKING THE CASE FOR STUDYING
GRASSROOTS ACTIVISMS

From large-scale national and international marches, boycotts, protests, and social media hashtag movements, to smaller localized demonstrations, petition drives, and sewing, knitting, making, or "die-in" sessions, people employ a wide range of activist methods to raise awareness and attempt to bring change in the face of injustice or oppression. We often witness how such activisms unfold in powerful ways in mass settings as they are covered by global media (such as #BlackLivesMatter, the Arab Spring, the Occupy Movement, #MeToo, Women's Marches, and climate strikes). It's less common to recognize, much less celebrate, how such activisms unfold in smaller scales in local contexts (for example, activisms that take place in city halls, homeless shelters, church basements, living rooms, border camps, and schools) in response to global or local exigencies. Local grassroots activist efforts are, despite their powerful and innovative measures, often overlooked as sites of and for critical analysis. The overshadowing of smaller-scale, localized activist labors may unintentionally obscure the important rhetorical tactics enacted by people who attempt to make change in their own communities. As a result, this collection specifically focuses on what might be learned and shared by examining instances of local grassroots activisms.

Certainly, understanding the complexities of activisms on any level can be a confounding rhetorical problem. Learning how people take up activisms at the local level allows us to present examples that parse the complexity into manageable sites of analysis, yielding insights that might not be recognized in examinations of larger-scale movements. It also allows us to highlight how activisms are carried out and composed in localized public and private spheres in ways that allow others to join in or undertake coalitional work that meaningfully supports such actions when the need arises. In this context, such efforts draw on Karma Chávez's (2013) conception of coalition as "a present and existing vision and practice that reflects an orientation to others and a shared commitment to change. Coalition is the 'horizon' that can reorganize our possibilities and the conditions of them" (p. 146). Such coalitional work, as Rebecca Walton, Kristen Moore, and Natasha Jones (2019) assert, requires "redressing inequities, pursuing justice" and supporting practices that include and strengthen marginalized perspectives (p. 10).

Through this edited collection, we hope to contribute to understandings of how social change is enacted, by focusing on how these efforts take shape on the local level. To do so, the collection includes chapters that illustrate how global and local exigencies are engaged within specific communities. We also include studies that offer not only discussions of "successful" activist efforts but also examples where "success" is indeterminate, incremental, or perhaps not readily apparent at all. We believe it is crucial to amplify the work of community activists and learn from their savvy, locally and culturally situated rhetorical tactics, so we have encouraged contributors to center activists' work and ensure efforts are represented faithfully. Furthermore, although the larger field of rhetoric and writing studies has been widely complicit in injustice and marginalization, particularly in its citation practices and perpetuation of patriarchy (as discussed by many technical and professional communication scholars such as Haas, 2012; Itchuaqiyaq, 2020; Walton, Moore, & Jones, 2019; Williams & Pimentel, 2014), this collection recognizes that scholars can and should do more to engage with social justice and expand what we value and whose work we deem worthy of study.[1]

As such, this collection seeks to build upon the work of many who have sought to highlight the rhetorics of activisms in a variety of spaces and places (Alexander, Jarratt, & Welch, 2018; Blair & Nickoson, 2018; Chávez, 2013, 2021; Foust, Pason, & Zittlow Rogness, 2017; Hesford & Kozol, 2005; Lee & Khan, 2010, 2019; Walton, Moore, & Jones, 2019), by focusing explicitly on how localized contexts both shape and constrain activist responses, with a particular emphasis on how those constraints affect and are navigated by marginalized communities. Although several collections have included chapters that highlight localized activist efforts (e.g., Ackerman & Coogan, 2013; Hesford, Licona, & Teston, 2018; Williams & Pimentel, 2014), and many other important collections focus on how social justice might be integrated into our pedagogies (e.g., Haas & Eble, 2018; Walton & Agboka, 2021), there has not yet been a collection in rhetoric and writing studies that focuses entirely on analysis of grassroots activisms, let alone one that pays attention to efforts that are historically marginalized or disregarded.

Ultimately, we see *Grassroots Activisms: Public Rhetorics in Localized Contexts* as contributing to conversations about activism by providing more

---

1. Throughout this edited collection, you will see us breaking a common American Psychological Association (APA) citation "rule," which requires shortening in-text citations with three or more authors so only the first author's last name is listed followed by "et al." Other citation styles used within our field(s) have similar rules. Spelling out all authors' names on each reference is an intentional practice that we believe aligns with our intersectional feminist approach to citation, in that we wish to call attention to the labor and contributions of all named authors of publications. This is particularly important because in our field(s), the order of names listed on a publication does not necessarily mean the first author deserves more credit than the rest of the authors listed. We hope that in the future other scholars citing the important contributions of the authors included in this edited collection might consider listing all of their names when citing them as well.

diverse perspectives, stories, and approaches for thinking about, theorizing, and acting on grassroots activisms. When inviting contributors to join this collection, we have sought to focus less on the large-scale social movements (though certainly some of the chapters herein touch on those) and more on local experiences, local concerns, and local efforts. We hope readers can glean new insights into how social change occurs. In particular, we were interested in collecting studies, stories, and examples of activism by and with marginalized communities. We sought to direct sustained attention to the specific, localized contexts in which activism happens, to make tangible the sometimes incremental but no less important change that occurs when people join together around a common cause. Moreover, we hope readers also recognize that "solidarity and social change manifest through the daily practice of fundamentally redistributing power and resources, not through the balms of awareness and attention" (Schuller, 2021, p. 32). While awareness and attention are acceptable places to start, activism cannot end there.

In the sections that follow, we seek to make apparent the scholarship and theoretical influences that are foundational to this work and pull apart the conceptions of key terms that are central to this collection. However, what really matters here are the stories of grassroots activisms featured in the contributors' chapters.

HIGHLIGHTING OUR COMMITMENTS

The editors and contributors to this collection are committed to narrative and storytelling as important means of knowledge-making. Women of color technical communicators Laura Gonzales, Josephine Walwema, Natasha N. Jones, Han Yu, and Miriam F. Williams (2021) write that "our stories *are* our data, our tools, and our strategies for surviving, transgressing, and thriving" (p. 17). What's more, Aja Martinez's (2020) discussion of "counterstory as methodology" and as "method" illustrates how stories, particularly from historically marginalized communities, can "empower the minoritized through the formation of stories that disrupt erasures embedded" in other methodologies (p. 3). Although not every contribution to this collection focuses on the stories of activists from historically marginalized communities, wherever possible, we seek to draw attention to grassroots activists' own stories in their own voices.

The critical feminist approach we, as editors, all in different ways take up in our own work also dictates that we explicitly state our positionalities and commitments. In the foreword to *The Trouble with White Women* (2021), Black feminist teacher and writer Brittney Cooper notes that "white women" pose a "perennial challenge" to "cross-racial" and other feminist solidarities when they do not acknowledge the "threats" to intersectional solidarity and how to face those threats head-on (p. 10). We understand that "considering simultaneous positions of privilege is one of the most challenging tenets of intersectional feminist rhetoric" because it requires us to consistently interrogate our actions and approaches to whatever we do in coalition with others (Soto Vega & Chávez, 2018, p. 324). Furthermore, we recognize, as Kyla Schuller (2021) notes, that intersectional feminism emphasizes a "praxis of care and coalition" and seeks to "[dismantle] systems and [invent] solidarities anew" (p. 33). Thus, in this section we briefly discuss our own positionality, power, and privilege (Walton, Moore, & Jones, 2019) and how that has shaped this collection as well as how we prioritize social justice and intersectionality throughout this project.

Acknowledging Positionality, Power, and Privilege

All three of us are white, straight, cisgender, middle- or upper-middle-class, relatively able-bodied women in tenure-track and tenured professor positions who recognize the power, privileges, and opportunities these positionalities afford us. At the same time, we all are committed to activism, advocacy, and social justice work in our personal and professional lives and believe strongly that we have a responsibility to support the important social justice efforts we see occurring in our own institutions, communities, country, and world in any way we can. In particular, we seek to amplify the work of activists who are marginalized, dominated, and devalued because of their race, gender, class, sexuality, citizenship status, disabilities, and more. Professionally, this support comes in small ways through our own teaching, our scholarship, and now through our work with this edited collection, though we recognize there is so much more we could and should do.

Being Accountable

We wish to pause here to explicitly acknowledge that we are three white women who are not multiply marginalized serving as the editors of a collection that seeks to amplify the efforts of multiply marginalized activists. We have worked to bring together many multiply marginalized contributors—both scholars and community activists—in this collection and also actively sought out Black, Indigenous, and persons of color (BIPOC) scholars to write both the foreword and afterword of this collection. And yet, where are the BIPOC editors to help shape this collection alongside us? We openly acknowledge they are absent and should not be.

Our call for proposals for this collection went out in mid-June 2020, as racial justice protests occurred across the United States and just after many BIPOC scholars in the field put out calls for their white peers to do more. For instance, Association for Teachers of Technical Writing (ATTW) president Angela Haas wrote in a June 2, 2020, letter that was widely distributed, "I call on our non-Black membership to mobilize our (proximity to) white privilege and use our rhetoric and technical communication skills to redress anti-Blackness in our spheres of influence." Haas called white scholars to prioritize Black voices "and center and amplify their work when doing yours." Furthermore, in "The Just Use of Imagination: A Call to Action," Natasha Jones (ATTW vice president at the time) and Miriam Williams (an ATTW fellow) acknowledged how tired Black folx are and stated, "Dismantling white supremacy requires your work. How might you make a difference?"

At the time, we saw our multiply marginalized BIPOC friends and colleagues faced with many stresses and burdens—caring for themselves and loved ones, all disproportionately affected by the COVID-19 pandemic; angry, traumatized, and worried for their own safety and the safety of loved ones in the midst of George Floyd's murder and so many other senseless acts of violence; and being asked to do a great deal of important but also overwhelming scholarly and pedagogical labor because of their positionalities. As Walton, Moore, and Jones (2019) argue, "by centering the experiences of multiply marginalized individuals, we become better at recognizing how our daily, mundane practices contribute to the marginalization, exploitation, and powerlessness of others" (p. 139). We knew there were many things we needed to do personally and professionally to make a difference, but we saw the edited collection we were already envisioning as one of the scholarly contributions we could make. We could support, amplify, and cite while not adding to the burdens our multiply marginalized friends and colleagues already faced. As a result, we chose to proceed with the trio of editors who were already collaborating, while prioritizing including as many diverse voices as we could (among both the contributing authors and the activists whose work we shared). While this seemed the best approach at the time, we recognized through the process of developing the collection that not including another editorial collaborator from a marginalized community was a mistake. In hindsight, we would have done things differently and prioritized diverse perspectives on our editorial team, which could have strengthened the collection overall. But we hope that this does not take away from your experience with this collection and the important attention it directs toward a wide range of grassroots activisms and diverse scholars.

Attending to Social Justice and Intersectionality

We are committed to attending to social justice and intersectionality, which are key values guiding this collection. All three editors were committed to different social justice concerns and causes prior to our pursuit of doctoral degrees, and in the course of our graduate studies we all realized we could not separate our commitment to social justice from our scholarly and pedagogical interests in rhetoric, writing studies, or technical communication. Fortunately, all three of us had benefited from strong feminist mentors who modeled the ways social justice, scholarship, and pedagogy can intersect and whose work continues to inspire and motivate us. Although we share many intersecting and overlapping interests and approaches, even the three editors of this collection do not engage in grassroots activisms from the same theoretical lenses—nor would we want to or expect the contributors of this volume to do so. So rather than laying out a theoretical framework that guides this entire collection, we instead focus on articulating shared values embedded throughout the collection, though they are taken up in different ways by different contributors.

The work of this collection responds to Natasha Jones's (2020) call to bring together rhetoric, writing studies, and technical communication as we work to "be more inclusive and attuned to the multiply marginalized" (p. 515). Expanding on the book *Technical Communication after the Social Justice Turn: Building Coalitions for Action* by Walton, Moore, and Jones (2019), in "Coalitional Learning in the Contact Zones: Inclusion and Narrative Inquiry in Technical Communication and Composition Studies," Jones (2020) advocates for technical communication and composition studies to collaborate and learn from one another by "integrating innovative, inclusive, and decolonial pedagogies, epistemologies, and methodologies" (p. 516). Our collection brings together scholars from not only composition studies and technical communication but also rhetoric, communication studies, and other fields in an effort to build one of the "relational, dynamic configurations that are attuned to issues of power, privilege, and positionality while actively pursuing options for addressing and redressing inequities and oppressions" for which Jones advocates (p. 519).

To that end, this collection is explicitly concerned with issues of social justice and focuses on the efforts of specific marginalized communities that seek change. Such an emphasis requires attending to intersectionality and recognizing the "overlapping and conflicting dynamics of race, gender, class, sexuality, nation, and other inequalities" (Cho, Crenshaw, & McCall, 2013, p. 788). The notion of intersectionality central to this collection originates in Kimberlé Crenshaw's argument that to expand the possibilities for social justice, conceptions of identity must account for the multiple, intersecting axes of oppression faced by people—particularly by women—of color. Intersectionality, according to Crenshaw (1991), has the potential to result in the formation of coalitions designed to address multiple forms of oppression. More than a theoretical lens, intersectionality has become a means of practice and a political intervention embraced, in particular, by women of color who fight for social justice (Luft & Ward, 2009).

A number of scholars, drawing on social movement history, argue for the potential of intersectionality in coalition-building, particularly among multiply marginalized community members (Nash, 2008, p. 9). For instance, Anna Carastathis (2013) argues that coalitions—defined as "internally heterogeneous, complex unities constituted by their internal differences and dissonances and by internal as well as external relations of power"—may result in "creative acts" that enable the formation of political alliances and the pursuit of "liberatory politics of interconnection" (p. 944). Or as Karma Chávez (2013) explains, "politically, 'coalition' refers to unions, fusions, and combinations designated for certain kinds of action. Often coalitions are understood as temporary and goal-oriented" (p. 7). Such coalitions do not encompass all dimensions of community members' identities, clarify Jennifer Jihye Chun, George Lipsitz, and Young Shin (2013), and yet they do help community members "invent and inhabit identities that register the effects of differentiated and uneven power, permitting them to envision and enact new social relations grounded in multiple axes of intersecting, situated knowledge" (p. 917). Intersectionality serves as a starting point for acknowledging and learning from fluid, changing, overlapping, and even conflicting experiences with and conceptions of inequalities including race, gender, class, sexuality, disability, and nation (Cho, Crenshaw, & McCall, 2013). In grassroots organizing, sometimes what unfolds is not a fully developed coalition so much as a "space of convening that points toward coalitional possibility" (Chávez, 2013, p. 8). This edited collection features the efforts of grassroots activists just beginning to convene these coalitional possibilities, as well as examples of fully formed coalitions in response to local injustices. Both examples illustrate how members of a community come together, not because they all face the same forms of marginalization or oppression or are in complete agreement, but because they recognize the exigency for protecting their bodies, families, homes, careers, and communities. Thus, throughout this collection, intersectionality helps direct attention to the activists in marginalized communities who draw on and integrate their multiple forms of knowledge and multiple identities as they form political coalitions (Carastathis, 2013), even when faced with myriad oppressions and uneven power relations. Importantly for this collection, as Chávez (2013) argues, "coalition enables a different understanding of activists' rhetorical invention as they discover and innovate responses—creative and sometimes mundane—to predominant rhetorical imaginaries" (p. 7).

DEFINING KEY CONCEPTS

In laying the groundwork for this collection, we are less concerned with whether the examples of activism included in the chapters fit specific definitions. Rather, we are interested in amplifying local instances of activism in whatever form they take and recognizing how particular people seek and make change in specific localized contexts. At the same time, we believe it is helpful to have a starting point in thinking about key concepts relevant to this work. So, here, we begin with our interpretations of some of the most common concepts found throughout this collection and then also point readers to chapters in which contributors may take up these concepts in similar or different ways.

Grassroots Activisms

The trouble with trying to delineate a precise definition of "grassroots activisms" lies in teasing out the complexity of the dynamic between the local and the global, which becomes particularly difficult in this kairotic moment where the internet and social media blur boundaries in ways that never quite existed before. Do activist efforts *always* start from the bottom up, meaning from local people engaging with issues that are pertinent to their own lives and communities? Or do people in a given location engage with more global issues that affect them personally and politically, attempting to frame those issues rhetorically within the contexts of their own communities? Perhaps, more importantly, how do people engage with issues within the unique local material, social, and political dimensions of a particular place? These distinctions seem important for the fields of rhetoric, writing studies, and technical communication to engage with. Ultimately, in this collection we seek to better understand what drives people to get involved in activism on a personal level.

What causes anyone to engage to make movement on pressing social issues? In terms of "grassroots activisms," there is a long-understood definition that these works start from the bottom, literally, from the "roots." Simply put, an uncomplicated view of grassroots activism implies that people engage and attempt to intervene when and where it affects them most, working from the bottom up to make change in larger institutions and systems. Of course, that seems easy enough to understand, but the idea gets muddled when information and ideas are widely shared across the internet and social media platforms. If we truly want to delve into a greater understanding of "grassroots activism," we need to understand how other scholars and practitioners have talked about it.

Perhaps the earliest mention of grassroots activism came in 1912, when Senator Albert Jeremiah Beveridge of Indiana said that the Progressive Party had "come from the grass roots. It has grown from the soil of people's hard necessities" (as cited in Rainey & Johnson, 2009, p. 150). The word *root* becomes particularly important in grassroots activisms, whether we are thinking about such actions playing out in local communities (where people are rooted or where their roots are) or as being rooted in local social issues. And it means starting from the ground, not only physically in a specific community but also in terms of how grassroots organizations are formed and led. As social worker and community organizer Lee Staples (2016) explains, "The community provides its own leadership for the change effort. The operative assumption is that effective leadership should and will emerge from within the community, rather than from the outside" (p. 3). Staples goes on to explain that community organizing is not a top-down endeavor and that grassroots organizing is "predicated on the power of numbers, but committed, competent indigenous leadership is needed to provide vision, critical analysis, inspiration, direction, and modeling for the full membership" (p. 3).

The term *grassroots* has, nearly since its inception, been considered radical. As Angela Davis wrote in *Women, Culture, & Politics* (1990), "we must get to the root of our oppression. After all, *radical* simply means 'grasping things at the root'" (p. 14). When we first think about grassroots activisms, it is often the radical resistance actions that spring to mind—protests, graffiti, the sort of image events (DeLuca, 1999) that garner immediate attention and publicity, from which people cannot easily look away. Often, the "radical" in grassroots activisms is read as the unruliness that is the focus of Alexander, Jarratt, and Welch's (2018) edited collection, *Unruly Rhetorics*. Such unruliness, the introduction of that collection argues, "breaks out spontaneously, driven by existential conditions" but also can be "staged as a rhetorical tactic" (p. 12). Political scientist Todd C. Shaw (2009) underscores that not all grassroots activisms are about protest or unruliness: "Not every moment is ripe for protest; nor can every conflict be resolved by citizens politely waiting for politicians to hold public hearings. The acute activist properly reads the signs of the time and chooses" (p. 2).

Yet we believe that even moments when activists undertake tactics that do not *appear* to be radical *are* still radical. For example, a queer Black woman who responds to a localized exigency—say advocating for more inclusive sex education for LGBTQIA+ folx at a majority-white school in a conservative rural area—may interact with a kairotic moment in order to affect change. The act of speaking at a public school board meeting becomes a radical act, because the person incurs personal and relational risk. In this way, we take up Chávez's (2013) rhetoric of "radical interactionality" built on "women of color feminist notions of intersectionality" (p. 51). As Chávez explains, the rhetoric of radical interactionality "is a form of rhetorical confrontation that begins critique from the roots of a problem or crisis and methodically reveals how systems of power and oppression interact with one another in ways that produce subjects, institutions, and ideologies and that enable and constrain political response" (p. 51). We see activists throughout this edited collection enacting a rhetoric of radical interactionality in how they draw on their (and others') embodied, lived experiences of oppression as they seek to carry out "possibilities for creative and complicated responses" to that oppression (Chávez, 2013, p. 58).

It's important to draw a clear distinction between those who advocate on behalf of a community but are not a part of the community and those who are members of a community advocating on behalf of themselves. The former, Staples (2016) argues, cannot be grassroots community organizing, because "organizing is a bottom-up philosophical approach to social change, not simply a method to achieve it" (p. 2). And yet sometimes this perception leads to the argument that grassroots activisms are enacted only by individuals rather than organizations or even companies. What role, then, do local nonprofit organizations or civically and socially minded local companies play in grassroots activisms? It depends, but we argue (and many chapters in this collection illustrate) that we cannot overlook the vital role local organizations can play in grassroots activisms. As Shaw (2009) points out in his study of Detroit's Black politics and grassroots activism, grassroots activisms may occur in local interest-group systems such as community-development organizations, or they can be what Shaw calls "more insurgent" (p. 4). Both forms of grassroots activisms play important roles as activists engage in "the broad repertoire of collective actions" (Shaw, 2009, p. 2). The grassroots environmental justice movement in particular illustrates how a loosely structured activist movement can still rely on different forms of organization, in that often local grassroots environmental justice efforts are sparked by a small group of people directly affected by environmental injustice, who then form a local community organization but may be supported by or work in concert with regional or statewide coalitions and national organizations (Freudenberg

& Steinsapir, 1992). In other instances, as studies such as Claus and Tracey's (2020) have found, organizations can "stimulate grassroots activism," and such collective action "can then take on a life of its own, with growing numbers of activists operating independently of the organization that helped spawn it" (p. 966). Such actions are present in this collection (see, for instance Lukowski and Gross, Novotny, Jones, Mayberry, and Wills) and are worthy of attention and study even alongside those insurgent examples that originate with individuals seeking to make change.

In terms of sussing out the specific nature of grassroots activisms, here's what we do know, from prior research and from the works in this collection: (1) grassroots activisms always start with people who inhabit specific communities or sites, meaning they are always already rooted in local places; (2) these local activist efforts are complicated by specific material, political, and, therefore, rhetorical affordances and constraints; and (3) these localized grassroots activist interactions are worthy of our attention precisely because they highlight individualized and unique responses to specific material, political, and rhetorical contexts that enable or constrain movement on social issues. In what follows, we delve a little further into these facets.

1. Grassroots activisms always start with people who inhabit specific communities or sites, meaning they are always already rooted in local places. Grassroots activisms are responses to exigencies that are unfolding within a specific community and are organized and galvanized by members of said community. Grassroots efforts are "driven by the residents of a community— at the local level. Residents of the local community participate in the social action" to address local issues (Rainey & Johnson, 2009, p. 150). The exigency to act may originate in injustices specific to a given community or awareness that wider social injustices are occurring within that local community. What makes activisms specifically grassroots is that local people are doing the work and the work takes place at the local level. The goal of grassroots activisms, then, can be understood to be making change within local communities.

2. Local grassroots activist efforts are complicated by specific material, political, and, therefore, rhetorical affordances and constraints. Because grassroots activisms are rooted in localized settings, they are complicated by the specific and contextual material, political, and rhetorical affordances and constraints of individual communities. The influence of these factors cannot be understated. People working to make change within their own communities face risks. As Emma J. Rose and Alison Cardinal (2021) explain, "activism attempts to dismantle inequality, rather than work within the boundaries set by institutions. Activism carries more risk, since by definition activism requires putting oneself on the line" (p. 78). These risks can result in material effects on multiple levels, including physical, emotional, financial, legal, and psychological. It is physically tiring and emotionally exhausting to engage in activism and work to change others' perspectives on issues. There is also the risk of alienating friends, family members, and other members of the community with different perspectives, which can take a toll. Legal risks also add to the complexity of the material dimension of grassroots activisms—there may be ramifications (fines, arrests, jail time, lawsuits, etc.) for engaging in such work. Beyond this, there are potential financial repercussions from missing work to engage in activist efforts or participating in activisms that may not be sanctioned by employers. In smaller communities, what happens when those who are self-employed or own businesses engage in activist work that might lead to a loss of business?

The political dimensions of localized activisms are equally complicated, requiring navigation of specific legal, bureaucratic, and interpersonal power dynamics within a given community. Different settings may require permits to protest or may impose "gag" laws that penalize activists' efforts, depending on the context. Who the decision-makers are, what their political persuasions are, and even access to these people also affect activists' ability to make change on issues within local communities. Beyond physical access (meaning the availability to meet with decision-makers), systemic inequalities and power structures in place can prevent people from engaging with a message. Power and privilege within specific, local communities is itself political: certain positionalities, embodiments, and literacies have more influence than others.

Engaging with decision-makers and persuading change at the local level is also complex rhetorical work. Success in a given community can often rely on an understanding of local history (what's been done, who's tried what), the knowledge of who can enact the changes needed and how to influence them (who is in charge, what you need to do or say to persuade them, who else you need to have on board). This is deeply rhetorical work that is situated within the specific contexts of a given community.

Perhaps most importantly, the material, political, and rhetorical dimensions of grassroots activisms are profoundly interconnected, overlapping and converging in ways that exacerbate the complexity of engaging in such work. This is messy, complicated, difficult, and sometimes risky. Yet activists engaging in grassroots efforts navigate this complicated confluence of material, political, and rhetorical affordances and risks as they seek to make change in their communities.

3. Localized grassroots activist interactions are worthy of our attention precisely because they highlight individualized and unique responses to specific material, political, and rhetorical contexts that enable or constrain movement on social issues. The recognition that grassroots activist efforts are localized and therefore individualized and unique responses to specific material, political, and rhetorical contexts demands acknowledgment of the complexity of this work, which often results in unique, innovative, and imaginative tactics geared toward enacting change within specific local communities. Doing so requires understanding that the messaging or activist tactics that work in one place may not work at other sites, yet it also highlights how the affordances and constraints of localized work are worthy of our attention. We hope this collection helps to move us forward in grappling with the complexities of grassroots activisms and how they are enabled and constrained by local contexts while also further explicating how systematic, systemic, and global issues are taken up, inspired by, and engaged within specific communities.

Activisms and Advocacy

The terms "activism" and "advocacy" often are ill-defined or blurred in both mainstream society and in rhetoric, writing studies, and technical communication scholarship. In this collection, we have chosen to differentiate between advocacy and activism by drawing on the work of Sarah Warren-Riley and Elise Verzosa Hurley (2017), who acknowledge that while the two terms are related, "activism connotes directed and specific action, whereas advocacy simply implies support." Warren-Riley and Verzosa Hurley further argue that there is a need to "complicate and interrogate the assumption that its [advocacy's] work—supporting or recommending a particular cause or viewpoint—implies a conscious choice" (2017, para. 5). In this way, activism can be defined as intentional action in service of a specific cause, whereas advocacy as "public support" can be enacted intentionally or unintentionally.

Importantly, we acknowledge that both advocacy and activism can be enacted in many forms and in service of many causes, some of which we personally do not agree with and find abhorrent (such as white supremacy, anti-LGBTQIA initiatives, etc.). To clarify our definition further, in this collection when we refer to "activism," we specifically refer to actions in service of addressing, alleviating, or eliminating systemic power imbalances and their effects. For example, *any* work that seeks to address or redress systemic racism, classism, sexism, ableism, and so forth—even if that work is simply in the vein of rendering those inequalities apparent—is, to us, a means of enacting positive change via activism. We ultimately seek to amplify value-driven work toward social justice that contributes to the overall social good, by which we mean elimination of oppression and/or oppressive forces.

Like Paulo Freire, we make a distinction between intellectual evaluation of oppression and oppressors, "mere activism," and activism that involves "serious reflection" and "organized struggle for liberation" (Freire, 2000, p. 65). The nexus of reflecting on oppression, undertaking organized activism, and engaging in intellectual work to address unjust situations is *praxis*—thoughtful doing—unfolding in distinctive and diverse ways while taking place in large-scale movements and local grassroots activist efforts alike. Though the form their praxis takes differs, authors contributing to this collection all focus in their own ways on the praxis of local grassroots activisms.

As far as defining what activities count as this type of activism, beyond that it entails direct and specific action toward change in systemic power imbalances, we have chosen not to foreclose any possibilities. In fact, one of the questions we asked contributors to consider was "what counts as activisms?" and we requested that they examine how some types of activist actions are not sanctioned or are erased. We are explicitly invested in recognizing, valuing, and amplifying the unique and varied ways individuals work within and against existing local constraints to make change within their own communities. We view these wide-ranging acts of resistance as distinct acts of activism.

We realize that some readers may approach this collection with preconceptions of what activism is or can be, and we anticipate that the distinctions we draw may not satisfy all readers. In the introduction to the second edition of *Activism and Rhetoric: Theories and Contexts for Political Engagement,* while JongHwa Lee and Seth Kahn express excitement over the expanded attention being focused on activist rhetoric, they also voice concern "about the extent to which the word *activism* itself has been stretched out to include individual acts of advocacy or benevolence, at the risk of setting aside the ethos of democratic mobilization we invoke by using the word" (2019, p. 7). Lee and Kahn further argue for clearer distinctions, noting that "sharply pointed calls to organize and mobilize on behalf of democracy against hegemonic power need to be distinguished from more benevolent calls to 'make your voice heard' or 'do good'" (p. 7).

While we recognize these concerns, we also feel the need to point out how these distinctions aren't as clear-cut as they may seem. Mobilizing against hegemonic power takes many forms and can be enacted at the individual level. Furthermore, not all activist work takes the shape of protests, sit-ins, or letter-writing campaigns. Sometimes activist work entails both "doing good" and working toward democracy and against hegemonic power by helping others navigate the systems that marginalize them and prevent them from reaching their goals. One such example from this collection is when activists help migrant detainees write asylum statements that conform to the standards expected in the United States legal system, as is highlighted in Monica Reyes, Randall Monty, Jorge Camarillo, and Cindy Bernal's chapter. Another example is when graffiti and vandal art demonstrate, perform, and motivate social resistance to oppressive acts, which Angela Mitchell discusses. A third: when a student sees and feels hunger and starts a community gardening club to address it, as Vani Kannan and Leah Johnney describe.

Grassroots Activisms versus Social Movements

Grassroots activisms, as defined in the context of this edited collection, are diverse localized responses to emergent or ongoing social injustices that result in collective action both online and on the ground in a specific community. Importantly, local grassroots activisms respond to specific exigencies and are shaped by individual, particular, and localized constraints. Parsing what counts as "grassroots activisms" versus actions that are part of larger social movements is tricky, because so often social movements start as localized, grassroots efforts for change—and even when a movement becomes large-scale and widely recognized, it often still plays out in specific communities in localized ways. This dilemma has pushed us to delve further into the subject. How do you draw distinctions between activist efforts, some of which engage with larger societal issues (such as racism, sexism, and income inequality, to name but a few) versus those that engage with issues that are site-specific (such as local land management, water quality, zoning issues, and access to education)? And how do you account for the role of the nonprofit industrial complex within grassroots activist work? How localized action takes shape—whether individuals or collectives organize and act organically versus whether they are moved to action by a nonprofit organization—also affects the tactics activists use and the values reflected in the work. We, as editors of this collection, recognize and acknowledge the multifaceted complexities of this definitional dilemma.

We understand that sometimes grassroots activisms build slowly over time for many years or even decades (as in the case of the broader environmental justice movement). Other times, people are thrown into activist roles suddenly without warning when they are faced with a crisis, as with the water contamination in Flint, Michigan, or in the aftermath of many natural disasters, like

Hurricane Harvey. In some instances, what begins as a localized grassroots activist campaign grows much larger, into a wide-scale social movement, even as grassroots offshoots of those movements continue to crop up in different places at different times. One such example occurred on the Standing Rock Sioux Reservation, where Indigenous activists first fought locally against the Dakota Access Pipeline but were quickly joined by activists from across the world. Their efforts have since evolved into a larger movement emphasizing Indigenous rights, water quality, and broader environmental concerns in a variety of places, which, in this collection, Luhui Whitebear, Kenlea Pebbles, and Stephen Gasteyer take up in "Resisting Extraction of the Sacred: Indigenous-Based Grassroots Resistance to Frontier Capitalism."

Many scholars define social movements as "constructed from the collective actions of people or organizations that have come together in order to build alternative understanding about those issues" (Atkinson, 2017, p. 13). Such a definition might lead us to see the grassroots activist efforts we are describing here as social movements in and of themselves. Yet more recently, social movements have been characterized as "networks of interconnected nodes" (Atkinson, 2017, p. 22). Such a conception of social movements leads us to see localized, grassroots efforts as a single node that may or may not be part of a larger, interconnected network.

All of this highlights that it's hard to pin down precisely what counts as "grassroots" activism or at what point something stops being grassroots and becomes more of a mainstream, large-scale movement. The complicated nature of drawing these distinctions is part of what convinced us of the necessity of creating a collection that pulls together various authors and their perspectives—from different spaces, addressing distinct issues—to begin the much-needed work of contending with these definitions and recognitions. Many chapters in this collection do just this. For example, in her chapter, Sweta Baniya examines how a specific localized event, the brutal gang rape of two Nepali women in Kathmandu, sparked a transnational movement called #RageAgainstRape. Similarly, Michael Knievel evaluates the role of individual localized bystander video footage of police brutality alongside local instances of organized citizen copwatching, juxtaposing how local conditions shape resistance strategies and may or may not evolve into larger movements.

Despite the difficulties in clearly demarcating lines between what are grassroots versus activist efforts in the service of mainstream social movements, for the purposes of this collection we employ the term *grassroots* strategically as a frame that helps to focus our attention away from large-scale activist efforts and instead onto the micro level of localized activist work. This helps us to better understand how activisms play out in specific contexts.

Online versus On-the-Ground Activisms

Much of the recent scholarship in our fields and in wider society that focuses on activism emphasizes the efforts that occur online, particularly via social media. Yet we wish to underscore from the outset—and illustrate through the chapters in this collection—that grassroots activisms rarely occur solely online or on the ground.

Certainly, the vast improvement of communication, ease of connection to like-minded others, and availability of distribution of messaging via the internet and social media have brought many changes to general society and, more importantly, to activist efforts. As Ding (2009) writes, social media serves "as one possible entry point into power systems for tactical intervention to challenge or contradict dominant discourses" (p. 344). Despite this and the rightful earned notoriety of the power of many hashtag movements, we approach the subject of rhetoric and technology, and more specifically, how it moves people to action, cautiously in this collection. Certainly, there is no doubt that the affordances of the internet and social media lead to a greater distribution of messaging and much more potential for reception than solely offline activist activities. That said, what we have learned through our study of grassroots activist efforts is that often on-the-ground and online tactics are complementary rather than exclusive.

It seems, at this juncture in history, fairly safe to say that the debate over hacktivism, slacktivism, or armchair activism versus on-the-ground activism no longer holds the weight that it once did. While certainly there remain those who retweet or forward messages online or via social media platforms without taking any additional action offline, what we have witnessed as a collective public in the United States in the last few years suggests that those scenarios are potentially much less common than those in which people act both online and offline. Consider the movement of #BlackLivesMatter from Twitter into widespread street protests across the country (and the globe) or the movement of misinformation regarding the usage of critical race theory from Facebook messages online to on-the-ground work at public school board meetings across the nation. To come full circle with these examples, consider how Darnella Frazier's posting of the video of George Floyd's murder led to widespread protest and demands for social justice. In this case, the video (a grassroots activist effort by one individual to hold police accountable) was taken on the ground and later uploaded to social media, where it ignited a widespread movement that occurred both online and back on the ground.

INTRODUCING THE COLLECTION

Thus far, our introduction to this collection has been focused in our disciplines of rhetoric, writing studies, and technical communication. The collection has value for advanced undergraduate and graduate students and current scholars and teachers in these disciplines. Yet we also see a broader audience for the chapters included herein. Some of the topics and analyses will be of interest to scholars in other, related fields, particularly those studying intersectionality and coalitional approaches to social change. Others will prove useful for grassroots activists working in a range of communities, who might glean tactics to try or find it useful to learn from the challenges others have faced.

Thinking broadly about who could engage with and benefit from this collection was vital to our goals from the outset and led us to request that contributors offer a range of approaches. Hence, you will find shorter profiles, Q&As, and reflective essays mixed in with the longer studies included in the collection. We also find the shorter chapters to be an important way to amplify underrepresented voices and stories with less (though, clearly, still some) mediation from others. As we noted above, we see narrative and storytelling as valuable methods for making meaning and wanted to find as many ways as possible to center the perspectives of grassroots activists in their many forms in this collection.

Another priority from the outset was to ensure that each of our contributors in some way emphasized the larger takeaways, lessons learned, and "so what" moments of the grassroots activisms they were highlighting in their chapters. Many chapters move "past description and exploration of social justice issues to taking action to redress inequalities" (Jones & Walton, 2018) and engage with Haas & Eble's (2019) call to "make social, institutional, and organization change toward equity." Thus, this collection takes up Jones's (2020) appeal to "be explicit about the lessons we are continuing to learn, especially when articulating efforts to create a more just and inclusive field" (p. 523). We hope those takeaways in their various forms will spark ideas, prompt action, or at the very least make readers think about moments of local intervention or activism they might engage with, learn from, or amplify.

Just as the chapters emphasize a wide range of approaches to and conceptions of grassroots activisms, they also illustrate the different research methods that studies of such efforts can employ. Many chapters rely on first-person narratives, interviews, and case studies. Other chapters are built on pedagogical, archival, and participatory research methods. Still others engage in situated, critical, or rhetorical analyses of existing documents including activist activities (such as speeches, writing, and graffiti). Such approaches do not represent all of the possibilities for undertaking research of grassroots activisms, but they certainly help make apparent how such research is accomplished in a variety of contexts.

Despite the varied approaches to research methods and chapter composition, the central goal of the collection remains consistent. That is, we seek to highlight localized responses to social, economic, racial, gendered, environmental, and other injustices and how different groups identify local concerns, organize, collaborate, and assemble to address such situations, drawing on their intersectional identities. In doing so, contributors have taken up at least one—and often many—of the following questions:

- How, when, and why do grassroots activisms take place?
- What emergent, unique, or divergent forms of activisms are at work in localized contexts?
- What "counts" as activisms? What types of activisms are sanctioned? What types of activisms are erased?
- What tactics do local activist movements use to sustain momentum and keep volunteers energized?
- How do positionality and embodied experience affect who participates, leads, and benefits from grassroots activisms?
- Whose knowledges are valued in local activist efforts? Which activist practices (by which bodies) are valued or ignored?
- How do local activists contribute to larger conversations about social, economic, racial, environmental, climate, or other injustices, and how and when do the perspectives of marginalized community members inform those conversations?

EDITED COLLECTION ORGANIZATION

We recognize that there are different ways to arrange a collection like this. Inherently, the arrangement we devised maintains fluidity among the parts even as it reflects a potential path for engaging with the works of this collection based in resistances, sites, and pedagogies of grassroots activisms.

Specifically, we organized the collection into three parts that each contain a mix of longer articles along with profiles of activists and activist organizations. Part 1, "Grassroots Resistances to Institutions," highlights how grassroots activisms take place in response to local exigencies (connected to institutions of different forms). Localized response often involves resistance to different kinds of institutional power, and the chapters in this section illustrate how people take up resistance as activists, as allies, as advocates, and as coalitions. Part 2, "Sites of Grassroots Activisms," spotlights local spaces and places (or sites) where grassroots activisms occur. Sites of activisms can move from the local to the global, but the initial site at the root informs how and why the activism unfolds and how it is shaped by that context. Finally, part 3, "Pedagogies for Grassroots Activisms," emphasizes various pedagogical contexts for grassroots activisms that include and extend far beyond the traditional academic classroom.

Grassroots Resistances to Institutions

The chapters in part 1 of this collection foreground the myriad ways grassroots activists deploy resistances to institutions and their power and work within and against systems to make change. This section opens with Michael Knievel's chapter on copwatching and police reform, which describes the potential for both individual citizen video surveillance and coordinated grassroots copwatching organizational work to contribute to police accountability at a local level and to spark national conversations about policing. Specifically, Knievel draws on incidents of individual video surveillance and his own observations of and involvement with copwatching organizations to illustrate copwatching as an activist practice and how such citizen-driven efforts engage in complex rhetorical activism both online and on the ground. As Knievel explains, "copwatching highlights how local acts—embodied, situational rhetorical activities—have the potential to condition behaviors that, in turn, have the potential to ripple through activist ecologies and ecologies of reform and impact culture."

Law enforcement accountability and resistance to institutionalized brutality is also central to the emergent coalitional actions described in Heather Olson Beal's profile of the Nacogdoches Accountability Coalition (NAC). The NAC formed in response to local police officers' sexist and racially charged interaction with Black women undergraduates at a university. In describing the NAC's efforts to accomplish a short-term goal of advocating for the students and a longer-term goal of proposing a citizens' review board to hold local law enforcement accountable, Olson Beal illustrates both the potential and pitfalls of starting and sustaining small, grassroots community organizations. In particular, this profile highlights how local initiatives can be stalled or sidetracked due to issues beyond activists' control.

The leadership of a Black woman rhetor from the civil rights movement is the focus of Coretta Pittman's chapter on Fannie Lou Hamer, a working-class Black woman who learned firsthand the impact grassroots activism could have on the lives of her neighbors in the Mississippi Delta as she worked to convince Black community members to register to vote despite the potential for retaliation from white people in power. The archival work and rhetorical analyses of Hamer's speeches in this chapter focus our attention on what Pittman calls the "long game" of activism. Pittman's chapter points to the many lessons contemporary activists might learn from reading about or researching historical activists while also highlighting the real, material (physical, economic, and so forth) risks that activists may face when they attempt to make change in institutions run by people hostile to the cause.

Whereas Pittman's chapter focuses on the efforts of one Black woman, Ericka Wills puts the voices of diverse labor activists front and center in her conversation with activists from different regions of the United States who organize workers from diverse demographics, including African American, LGBTQ+, Latinx, and immigrant communities. Organizers share their stories, advice, and successful tactics for addressing systemic discrimination and forming strategic alliances to effectively engage with institutional power centers.

Also concerned with resistance to harmful institutional labor conditions, Rebecca Hallman Martini highlights her own involvement in labor activism at the University of Houston. Specifically, her chapter discusses the efforts of English teaching fellows at the university who fought for improved working conditions and a stipend increase. In their efforts, activists in vulnerable positions joined together via social media and in-person protests to attract the attention of decision-makers who, in turn, could make change for the teaching fellows.

To round off part 1's focus on grassroots resistances to institutionalized power, Maria Novotny emphasizes the effects of "everyday interactions that build stronger coalitions leading to change" in her Q&A with Sara Finger, executive director of the Wisconsin Alliance for Women's Health. Novotny and Finger discuss inequities in maternal health and mortality rates for Black mothers and how rhetorical skills, listening, reflection, and relational practices are vital for encouraging grassroots activisms in state policymaking regarding inequitable reproductive health outcomes and access to services.

Sites of Grassroots Activisms

While resistance to institutional power remains in play, the work included in part 2 of this collection also focuses on specific sites of grassroots activisms and how those localized efforts are always already enabled and constrained by the material, political, and rhetorical dimensions of each site. Bridging the gap between parts 1 and 2, Luhui Whitebear, Kenlea Pebbles, and Stephen Gasteyer's chapter focuses on international Indigenous-based grassroots resistance and activism. The authors highlight the connections between the global and the local as they describe four local sites where Indigenous peoples are disproportionately impacted by the global issue of extractive capitalism. These sites include Standing Rock resistance to the Dakota Access Pipeline, resistance to water privatization in Mexico, Menominee Nation activism against mining, and activism against land colonization in the Jordan Valley in Palestine. Through these stories and sites of Indigenous activism, the authors illustrate the potential for grassroots activists to engage with the 4Rs (relationship, respect, reciprocity, and responsibility; https://4rsyouth.ca/) as they push back against frontier capitalism.

Moving to the site of Lehman College in the Bronx, New York, Vani Kannan and Leah Lillanna Johnney's profile discusses the creation of a gardening club and community garden that originated from a course on food insecurity and social issues. The first-person narrative written by the professor and an undergraduate student in the class emphasizes the potential for community-building offered alongside the fresh, local produce grown in the garden. The profile also offers a unique look into how awareness of a problem within the local community led to direct action centered on listening to and responding to the specific needs of that community.

Emphasizing how large-scale environmental problems are addressed differently in distinct sites, Madison Jones illustrates how grassroots activism for the Florida Springs is a distributed and relational activity that includes a number of different initiatives, including the work of the nonprofit Howard T. Odum Springs Institute, the *Springs Eternal Project* multimodal advocacy series, and the efforts of a local business, First Magnitude Brewing Company. Jones argues that, more than simply seeking to "raise awareness," such efforts illustrate how working in coalition toward a shared goal can build a local activist network for public action.

Next, April Conway offers a site where the benefits of localized organizing shine, in her profile of La Conexión, a grassroots organization that represents the Latinx immigrant population in northwest Ohio. Conway's profile draws on an interview with the executive director of the organization as well as numerous primary source materials to illustrate how community nonprofits engage with unique and situated exigencies as they employ grassroots tactics that respond to the realities of individual communities to address needs that may echo national trends. Drawing on local histories and knowledges, community nonprofits can direct resources to address emergent issues affecting local communities. For La Conexión, this work includes offering interpretation and grant-writing services, partnering with local domestic violence shelters, and engaging in specific local responses to the COVID-19 crisis.

As much as grassroots activisms are rooted in local sites, they also can spark transnational movements. Angela Mitchell's chapter delves into sites of transnational grassroots activisms writ large—literally, in the form of graffiti and vandal art in response to social justice exigencies in Paris, France; Tehran, Iran; and Richmond, Virginia. Mitchell's analysis of what is often considered "illegal" writing and drawing highlights the ways graffiti and vandal art are performative acts that make apparent activists' arguments and visions, which in turn can spark further activist efforts. Additionally, her chapter pushes back against the notion that disruptive or unruly rhetorics cannot be effective.

Sites of grassroots activism can also themselves serve as the impetus for sustained efforts to address long-term goals. Kalie Mayberry's profile features the Urban Affairs Coalition, which traces the long arc of 50 years of organizing within Black and Brown communities in Philadelphia through personal interviews with organization members. The Urban Affairs Coalition was started after the riots sparked by the assassination of Martin Luther King Jr. Today it is a prominent female-led Black organization that offers radical access to many underserved community members.

Like Mitchell, Sweta Baniya considers how a site-specific event can become transnational in her discussion of #RageAgainstRape, a Twitter movement started in response to a 2018 gang rape in Nepal that led to a national and international discussion of gender-based violence. Baniya traces the first three years of the movement and illustrates how such efforts are "shaped by cultural, social, and economic interconnectivities and interactions as well as by cross-cultural mobilizations of power, language resources, and people." Baniya, a founding member of the movement, weaves her own experiences into this case study, highlighting her positionality as an academic activist and advocating for transnational coalition-building across time, sites, platforms, and countries.

Pedagogies for Grassroots Activisms

Chapters in part 3 of the collection take on another dimension of grassroots activisms, as each engages critically with how people learn to "do" grassroots activism. This can be pedagogical in an academic sense, but it also extends to community-oriented contexts like Erica Stone's profile of Organizing for Action (OFA). OFA was a grassroots organization that trained local community organizers about activist tactics and policy processes from 2013 through

2019 and then made materials available online via an open-access archive. Stone shares her own experience with OFA trainings and emphasizes how both community organizers and publicly engaged scholars might use OFA's archive as a resource for teaching new organizers to build capacity through an "ecological and localized approach to storytelling and story listening." Of particular interest is OFA's concept of a "public story," which Stone illustrates as she describes how a specific fellowship project she created emphasized community-oriented and place-based understandings of organizing that discourage hierarchical thinking.

In the longer chapter that follows, Alison A. Lukowski and Jeffrey Gross further delve into the intersections between advocacy and activisms as they describe Writing for Advocacy, a co-taught course they developed that encourages meaningful writing, promotes student agency, and empowers students—particularly underrepresented, multilingual, first-generation learners, many of whom are DREAMers—to advocate for themselves and their communities. Lukowski and Gross make the case for seeing advocacy work as part of the process of enacting grassroots activisms. Specifically, they see writing for advocacy as a grassroots response that exploits the public awareness raised by protests and other on-the-ground activist efforts.

Highlighting another form of grassroots activism pedagogy in action, Molly Appel, Laura Decker, Rachel Herzl-Betz, Jollina Simpson, Katherine A. Durante, Rosemary Q. Flores, and Marian Azab, all faculty and staff at Nevada State College, contribute to a profile of the Anti-Racist Pedagogy Collective they created in response to George Floyd's murder. Each member shares their individual exigency and experiences with the grassroots collective in which they "support, push, learn from, and inspire one another" as they focus on anti-racist, equity-minded practices.

Joe Cirio's chapter engages with the question of what assessment looks like in grassroots activist work. He employs a range of case study methods, including field observations, interviews, experience-sampling methods, and reflective text-based interviews, to describe the structures of vernacular assessment designed and implemented at The Plant, a volunteer-operated, community-driven space where activists and organizers meet. Cirio suggests that assessment should not be confined to formal institutional settings; rather, intentional consideration of the assessment structures of activists and grassroots organizations is vital to the work of activists in a variety of settings. The assessment practices undertaken by grassroots organizers are a sometimes unglamorous yet necessary part of achieving their goals.

Leveraging localized networks of care is central to the grassroots initiative Retórica del Refugio (RDR), which is analyzed in detail by a collective of emergency shelter staff and volunteers from the University of Texas Rio Grande Valley (UTRGV), located on the United States–Mexico border. Specifically, authors Monica Reyes, Randall Monty, Jorge M. Camarillo, and Cindy Bernal describe how volunteers, including faculty, staff, and students from UTRGV, provide support and feedback for shelter staff on professional documents, conduct professional writing workshops for clients seeking to enter the US workforce, and offer writing consultation services for shelter clients as they compose their asylum application narratives. Informed by the tenets of invitational rhetoric (Foss and Griffin, 1995) and new materialist theory (Clark, 2018; Coole and Frost, 2010), the authors outline the networks of care they assembled to create RDR and emphasize the importance of drawing on collaborative storytelling and recognizing the trauma faced by asylum-seekers in such localized efforts.

The diverse range of contributions throughout this collection spans social justice exigencies, approaches, and even countries to highlight the messy, challenging efforts of grassroots activists who seek to build coalitions to intervene in local and global concerns. Despite this diversity, we recognize that our collection is imperfect and missing many marginalized perspectives that deserve to be highlighted. Though our schema of resistances, sites, and pedagogies of grassroots activisms provides readers one path through the collection, we encourage readers to move among the parts as they deem fit and to choose their own reading journey contingent upon their interests and needs. Put differently, while we believe the argument the arrangement makes is strong, the collection doesn't have to read in a linear or hierarchical fashion from start to finish. Rather, like the collection's namesake "grassroots," it can be read rhizomatically or nodally. It is our hope that readers can learn from the myriad grassroots activisms represented here and that they might then be inspired to undertake their own research, writing, and potentially their own local activist interventions. We look forward to learning from such efforts in the future.

PART 1

GRASSROOTS RESISTANCES TO INSTITUTIONS

CHAPTER 1

Copwatching, Police Reform, and Grassroots Action

Positioning Video within Strategies of Rhetorical Intervention on the Street

MICHAEL KNIEVEL

Citizen-captured video of excessive police force has become the most consequential rhetorical artifact in the larger police accountability movement. Footage of the tragic deaths of George Floyd, Eric Garner, and others has captured public attention through mainstream media distribution and social media circulation, playing a critical role in shaping public awareness and understanding outside of institutional framing (Fiore & Gollner, 1991; Helsel, 2015; McLaughlin & Vera, 2020; Sanburn, 2014; Walsh, 2020). Floyd's death at the hands of Officer Derek Chauvin, for instance, captured via cellphone camera by Darnella Frazier, not only put on display Chauvin's seeming disregard for Floyd's life as it slipped away in real time but also made visible an almost unthinkable lack of action on the part of other officers who witnessed the event (Walsh, 2020).

However, video's role in citizen-driven efforts to hold police accountable extends beyond these moments of serendipitous video capture by citizens armed with cellphone cameras. Grassroots "copwatching" organizations—activist organizations focused on regular, systematic monitoring of police activity—expand upon the influential documentary capabilities of digital video, locating cameras, video footage, and the act of recording within a broader strategy of coordinated rhetorical interventions. These interventions, in combination, seek to condition police tactics used during citizen encounters, support citizens in the aftermath of such encounters, and grow public support for police accountability. More specifically, copwatchers systematically combine and integrate video capabilities with education, physical presence, other technology tools, and other socially driven accountability measures to refigure the rhetorical and cultural context of citizen-police interaction.

In this chapter, I outline the role that video plays in copwatching as a form of grassroots activism. Video's capacity to document instances of police brutality is integral to copwatchers' work. Beyond that capacity, though, I wish to show that both the camera itself (as object and symbol) and the documentary artifact it creates—as well as the social pressure and influence they foster—coalesce to impact police accountability efforts in the near and long term within local cultures of policing. After reviewing the role that video footage plays in shaping the public's experiences with police accountability, I outline common elements of copwatching's activist, rhetorical practice. I then describe how copwatching organizations develop multifaceted rhetorical strategies through and around digital video to pursue immediate goals as well as broader activist objectives, drawing, in part, from my own engagement with two copwatching organizations. Finally, I consider implications for pedagogy and activism.

VIDEO, POLICE REFORM, AND ADVOCACY— DEFINING AND DIFFERENTIATING

Citizen-captured video footage has long been a key driver in broader national conversations about police brutality. George Holliday's recording of LAPD officers beating Rodney King during a traffic stop in 1991 remains, perhaps, the most iconic example of such footage, as it circulated widely through media and news channels, inciting public anger across the United States. Peter K. Manning writes of the video, "It apparently fits the reality rules that enable viewers to see a brief video as an instance of real events and become outraged and active" (as cited in Toch, 2012, p. 83). The aftermath of the King beating and officer acquittal was marked by days of protests and riots in metropolitan Los Angeles (Lieberman and Murphy, 1992). But in the bigger picture of police reform and accountability, Holliday's recording offered evidence of long-held, yet marginalized, concerns regarding how police have too frequently wielded excessive force against people of color, particularly Black men. Both then and now, because such encounters often unfold out of view, competing testimonials and counternarratives, whether in the courtroom or in the public arena, are regularly diluted or muted altogether in the face of "official," institutionally sanctioned narratives of policing.

Fueled by now-ubiquitous cellphone and digital recording capability, citizen-captured video like that of Rodney King's beating has become more common and more visible in recent years. For instance, footage of the officer-involved choking death of Eric Garner, the shooting deaths of Walter Scott and Philando Castile at the hands of police, and the death of George Floyd, among others, have had a similar effect on public discourse surrounding police brutality and accountability. For instance, Feidin Santana's video capture of officer Michael Slager shooting Scott five times in the back after a brief foot pursuit featured prominently in both the subsequent public outcry and the court proceedings leading to Slager's guilty verdict on charges of second-degree murder (Edwards and Andone, 2017; Kinnard, 2017). More broadly, a concentration of citizen-captured video (including the deaths of Scott and Eric Garner, among others), along with the unrecorded death of Michael Brown in Ferguson, Missouri, all occurred within a roughly nine-month period in 2014 and 2015, helping to galvanize a nationwide movement by spurring broad conversation and protest in support of both police reform and recognition of Black lives. In the public eye, video's role in the police accountability move-ment has often been most apparent in examples like these—citizen bystanders, oftentimes present and witnessing events by chance, deploy video technology to document police violence, with the subsequent circulation of footage driv-ing public conversation.

Within an organized activist context, however, video's documentary capac-ity expands, with video as both an artifact and as an activity positioned stra-tegically within a broader, ongoing rhetorical practice geared toward change. "Copwatchers," as such activists are oftentimes called, are not alone in seeing the utility and value of video in achieving activist goals. For instance, writing on behalf of human rights organization WITNESS—a significant influence on many copwatching organizations' approach to video use, among other tac-tics—Gillian Caldwell (2005) argues for video's role within advocacy practice, noting its capacity to enable elements of WITNESS's multipronged effort to stop human trafficking and exploitation:

> We recognized that video could elicit powerful emotional impact, connect-ing viewers to personal stories. It can illustrate stark visual contrasts and provide direct visual evidence of abuses. It can be a vehicle for building coalitions with other groups working on an issue. It can reach a wide range of people since it does not require literacy to convey information. It can help counter stereotypes and assist you in reaching new, different and multiple audiences, particularly if broadcast is a possibility. And it can be used in seg-ments of varying lengths for different contexts. (p. 2)

Moreover, Caldwell and others affiliated with WITNESS elaborate the video's role as a "deterrent." Katerina Cizek (2005), for instance, describes how the sheer physical presence of videographers helps to deter illegal activities in human trafficking contexts (p. 40). Such a view highlights the complex nature of video as both a *physical artifact*—here, a camera held by a human being—capable of eliciting a conditioning response and as a *documenting* activity that holds power in its narrative-building potential.

Copwatching and its use of video can be described as a form of street-level, grassroots activism. Joshua D. Atkinson defines activism as "collaborations by people in order to advocate for a position, nurture conflicts in society, or violate or transgress laws or norms in society" (as cited in R. Jones, 2020, p. 26). In a similar vein, copwatching seeks to disrupt norms of deference to police and frequently vacillates between Atkinson's sense of focus—what Warren-Riley and Hurley (2017) describe as "directed and specific action"—and a more macro-level interest in reforming policing practices. This hints at the complexity of copwatching's project, functioning as it does at a local level of specific police/citizen interactions within a neighborhood or municipality while oftentimes aiming for broader (cultural, societal) levels of reform through a rich rhetorical strategy and best practices centered on presence, deterrence, interrogation, education, and challenge in pursuit of social justice.

THEORIZING THE RHETORICAL WORK OF COPWATCHING

Two theoretical lenses help to clarify the ways that video features in the rhetorical work of copwatching: embodied agonistic participation and ecological understandings of rhetoric. I briefly outline each of these here in order to situate video's varied roles within copwatching's broader activist strategy and to highlight how these roles are bound up in both the physical scene of copwatching—the streets—as well as the larger constellation of rhetorical texts surrounding police accountability.

Copwatching is an embodied rhetorical practice rooted in shared physical space—copwatchers observing police with citizens—and the interactions that arise from those conditions. As Mary A. Bock (2016) and Jocelyn Simonson (2016) have noted, respectively, the physical act of monitoring police with cameras in the street leverages aspects of both embodied rhetoric and an "agonistic" approach to politics and policy. As A. Abby Knoblauch (2012) describes it, embodiment comes from "knowing something *through* the body" (p. 52). In such a view, physical, material experience becomes crucial in developing knowledge. In her analysis of copwatching, Bock (2016) notes the significance of being physically present to observe police:

> The storytelling power of a smartphone video is further enhanced by its origins in embodied watching. Creating a witnessing video requires physical presence; it cannot be conjured in discourse and photography's corporeality is part of its credibility and its risk. Their [copwatchers'] monitorial function as government watchdogs is not metaphorical, it is material: Using a camera to document events from a citizen's perspective creates a unique record, one that represents not only the camera's facticity but the body's reality. (p. 26).

Copwatchers' bodily presence as observers, then, helps to constitute the material conditions of the unfolding social performance happening during an observed and documented police/citizen interaction, including the actions police do or do not undertake. Such presence helps enable what Simonson (2016), citing Chantal Mouffe, calls an "agonistic" form of political participation in policing: "Agonism takes an adversarial stance toward practices and ideologies of institutions in power, but it does so through engagement with those institutions rather than withdrawal, by acknowledging intractable differences but respecting the adversary who disagrees" (pp. 435–436). Rather than reject policing as a system or rely entirely on deliberative processes of policy change that rely on government use of citizen input, agonistic copwatchers, according to Simonson, embrace their constitutional rights to engage directly with the execution of policing as it unfolds: through their physical presence, use of video recording, and verbal interaction with police, copwatchers seek to influence the character of police actions.

Such embodied, agonistic aspects of copwatching as a rhetorical practice at the material site of police/citizen interaction is but one part of the broader rhetorical ecology of texts, artifacts, and activities surrounding copwatching and police reform. Ecologically minded scholars in writing studies emphasize ways in which rhetorical acts function within a web of interconnected rhetorical moves and texts that may or may not be immediately related in time and space but that combine to create a rhetorical ecology. Marilyn Cooper (1986) argues, "The ideal image the ecological model projects is of an infinitely extended group of people who interact through writing, who are connected by the various systems that constitute the activity of writing" (p. 372). Such systems "reflect the various ways writers connect with one another through writing: through systems of ideas, of purposes, of interpersonal interactions, of cultural norms, of textual forms" (p. 369). As such, the ecological model of writing attends to the ongoing construction of texts situated in and emergent from these interconnected systems, as well as those texts' capacity to disrupt or reorient the ecology. For instance, Nathaniel Rivers and Ryan Weber (2011) describe the wide range of texts and modalities leading up to, surrounding, and following Rosa Parks's 1955 bus protest in Montgomery, Alabama. These texts—speeches, newspaper articles, street protests, and more—combine to nurture a broader rhetorical ecology that created conditions for Parks's action as well as the reception and integration of Parks's bus protest into the ecology of civil rights going forward (pp. 196–197). Other scholars, such as Brian Gogan (2014) and Jenny Edbauer (2005), emphasize that change happens over time and space and involves widespread articulation of innumerable authors and texts, often unpredictably and in nonlinear fashion, interacting within a broader ecology of rhetorical actions (Gogan, 2014, pp. 543–545).

Copwatchers' rhetorical work contributes in a similar way to the broader ecology of police reform and culture-building, frequently through the act of capturing video footage as police activity unfolds and then shaping subsequent local and, sometimes, societal rhetorical actions through the artifacts it produces. These conceptual frames offer ways of understanding video's role within the work of copwatching, and I return to them below to further examine ways that video features in copwatching's activist strategy.

COPWATCHING:
ORGANIZATION, GOALS, AND ACTIVITIES

As an activist practice, copwatching traces its historical roots to the Black Panthers and police monitoring practices of the 1960s and 1970s during periods of civil unrest and racial tension, most notably in Oakland, California (Nelson, 2016). More recently, Berkeley Copwatch is recognized as the first organized, sustained copwatching group utilizing contemporary technologies and practices, tracing its roots to 1990 when local activists began monitoring police activity in response to claims of ongoing police harassment of homeless people in the community (Berkeley Copwatch, 2020a).

Copwatching centers video documentation within the broader activist practice of monitoring police activity, part of a coherent philosophy of *sousveillance* wherein "the commoners are using cheap, portable technologies to monitor and publicize the behavior of Power" (Bollier, 2008). In doing so, citizens participate in both the monitoring and conditioning of police behavior in the short and long term. Marc Krupanski (2012) lays out elements of practice and the broader philosophy behind organized copwatching as such:

A critical tool for documenting misconduct, seeking redress, and advancing reform efforts is the street-level use of video monitoring by civil society. . . . The monitoring . . . is essential for strengthening the rule of law and democratic governance of police services, for encouraging appropriate reform, reducing violence and improving police-community relations. (para. 1)

Krupanski's account emphasizes "holding security institutions accountable to the people they serve," echoing elements of Berkeley Copwatch's credo: "Berkeley Copwatch is based on the idea that WATCHING the police is a crucial first step in the process of organizing. . . . It is our hope that, one day, mass outrage at police and government violence will increase to a point where fundamental change in the nature of policing becomes inevitable" (Berkeley Copwatch, 2020a).

The organization enumerates the following goals:

1. Reduce police violence by directly observing the police on the street, documenting incidents and keeping police accountable. We maintain principles of non-violence while asserting the rights of the detained person. We provide support to victims whenever possible. We also seek to educate the public about their rights, police conduct in the community and issues related to the role of police in our society.

2. Empower and unite the community to resist police abuse. We will do this by sharing information with the community, conducting "Know Your Rights" trainings, sponsoring rallies, supporting victims and other community based efforts to deal with the problem.

3. Encourage people to solve problems WITHOUT police intervention. We want to explore alternatives to calling the police.

4. Most importantly, we encourage people to exercise their right to observe the police and to advocate for one another. (Berkeley Copwatch, 2020a)

Another copwatching organization, CopBlock (2020), offers the following description of its mission: in part, "CopBlock is a decentralized organization made up of a diverse group of individuals united by their shared belief that, 'Badges Don't Grant Extra Rights.' . . . By documenting police actions with a camera—whether they are illegal, immoral, or just a waste of time and resources—we can work together to show people that 'Badges Don't Grant

Extra Rights.'" Members seek to "promote ways to not only film the police, but to get such content in front of as many eyes as possible," with an eye toward revealing pathologies in policing.

While copwatching organizations differ in emphasis and scope, these two accounts offer some insight into the broader strategy and shared interests that characterize copwatching as an activist practice unfolding at a grassroots level. Copwatching organizations typically hold in common a fundamental emphasis on monitoring police activity through filming or other types of recording, as a means of exposing problematic uses of force and other violations. Beyond monitoring and documenting police behavior, such organizations seek, variously, to nurture broader conversations about institutionalized power, police accountability, citizen empowerment, and support for victims of police-related violence or rights violations, oftentimes by and through building coalitions with like-minded organizations pursuing local social justice goals.

COPWATCHING ON TERRESTRIAL AND DIGITAL GROUND: RHETORICAL ACTIVISM IN MUNICIPAL AND ONLINE SPACES

For copwatchers, video-supported police monitoring and documentation unlock additional potentials, including networking, storytelling, deterrence, and pursuit of other strategic goals. In this section, I further develop my account of copwatching as a rhetorical activist practice by outlining my own brief encounters as a participant observer in two copwatching organizations and positioning that experience alongside other digital and online rhetorical activity that copwatchers engage in to extend and complicate the integration of video in activist strategy.

On the Streets: Observations and Perspectives

For this project, I conducted site visits at three different police monitoring organizations,[1] two of which identify more specifically with regular, organized copwatching; the third is a police-monitoring group that utilizes copwatching intermittently, primarily through the work of a single copwatcher. At each site, I interviewed copwatchers. At the two copwatching-focused sites, I also

---

1. IRB Protocol #20160303MK01113; to encourage subject candor, I chose to protect subject identities as part of the IRB consent protocol.

participated in a handful of copwatch patrols in order to learn more about the nature of the activity. In doing so, I sought to utilize, in part, the approach that Michael Middleton, Aaron Hess, Danielle Endres, and Samantha Senda-Cook (2015) advocate: "Participatory critical rhetoric, because it encourages the rhetorical critic to enter the field and be present in the moment of the rhetorical act, offers the critic access to live(d) rhetorics in their complex intersections between words, places, bodies, and context" (19).

Both of these two copwatching-focused organizations employ a range of often-overlapping strategies, with video featuring prominently in the work of each organization's respective approach. In my observations and interviews, it was clear that the central activity for each group was regular copwatching patrols in minority-majority neighborhoods that were disproportionately subject to police surveillance or entertainment districts where police presence was common. As a member of one organization noted, the reason for copwatching was plain: "Copwatching, obviously, has a very direct impact. The primary function of copwatch is to de-escalate situations and make sure police don't harm people. The police know they are being filmed; they are much less likely to beat, frame, rape, or murder people. And that's, like, our primary focus."

Patrols began after members met in a common space, such as organizational headquarters or a coffee shop. During these meetings, members were given cameras and instructed, as needed, in their use. The group leader would then review ground rules for copwatching, reminding members about basic rules of engagement, how to film for varied information and perspective, and when and where the right to film police is constitutionally protected. One group leader reminded members what to do if a member was arrested while copwatching, sharing the phone number of an allied attorney and encouraging them to use it. Group members (about five of them) then commenced patrolling in a single vehicle, seeking police/citizen encounters, such as traffic stops or calls to residences. During patrols, group members would converse, sometimes to predict where police activity might unfold or to reminisce about previously witnessed incidents. One group played a police-antagonistic playlist (e.g., NWA's "F— tha Police" or The Clash's "Know Your Rights") while patrolling, setting a somewhat adversarial mood. The process of locating scenes of police activity varied. Group members in one organization would scout out police cruiser lights while patrolling and pursue them when spotted. The other group relied on a police scanner to locate addresses where police might be active and then quickly drove to those sites to monitor events.

Upon arrival at a traffic stop, copwatchers would typically identify themselves and communicate their intentions to citizens and officers. Copwatchers would then fan out to create a perimeter of sorts, each member taking a different position vis-à-vis the incident in an effort to capture different perspectives on both time and space, as well as to gather identifying information on vehicles, officers, and precipitating actions. One copwatcher noted the importance of establishing a panoramic view of the scene: "You want to have the context of the before and after. Maybe an officer strikes someone with a baton. Maybe he (the citizen) was sitting there peacefully. But the officer says, 'No, he was resisting.' You want to have the context of 'before' so once the scene escalates, you can prove there was no reason to escalate." Afterward, copwatchers typically offered "Know Your Rights" information and copwatching organization contact information cards to detained citizens after the police engagement ended.

Occasionally, copwatchers would engage verbally with officers on the scene, asking for identification or directly interrogating officers as to why certain tactics were used. Other interactions centered on the right to film or on where copwatchers were positioned vis-à-vis the officer and detained citizen. The tone or mood of these interactions varied, with one copwatching group employing a more confrontational approach, the other a more detached, observational stance. Officers sometimes recognized copwatchers and would occasionally address them with familiarity. Some officers were friendly and professional, while others were brusque and less so, ignoring requests for badge numbers and questions about why or how the citizen was being detained. All copwatchers who were present actively recorded video throughout the police/citizen encounters.

After a shift ranging from three to five hours, copwatching teams would return to download video and debrief about the night's events, reviewing notable footage together. The team leader would then consolidate footage to be archived, deleted, or later edited to circulate via social media, post on the organization's website, or, in one of the organizations, add to a database for future use.

In many ways, the activity of copwatching seemed mundane and routinized for both organizations, in part because it is rooted in laws, ordinances, and best practices, requiring both knowledge and discipline to perform successfully. For instance, one copwatcher was remonstrated by another for filming too close to the scene and risking an arrest for interfering with an officer. Because the organizations I observed were well established within their respective municipalities, the appearance of copwatchers seemed largely taken in stride by officers, but at times, officers evidenced some irritation at copwatchers' presence, impatiently directing copwatchers where to stand, for instance. These moments exemplified the kinds of agonistic engagement described by Simonson (informed by Mouffe), with copwatchers inserting themselves and their vision for policing into the actual physical space and execution of police work. The tension—found, for instance, in the curt commands from officers and the loud assertion of constitutional rights by copwatchers in response— admittedly created a measure of anxiety for me as an outsider-participant. As Middleton, Hess, Endres, and Senda-Cook note, "the bodily experience of rhetoric cannot be separated from the time and place of its creation, meaning that participatory critical rhetoric also attunes rhetorical scholars to the emplaced nature of rhetoric" (24). Indeed, perhaps more than anything, participating, for me, revealed the tension between the mundane act of copwatching and the potential for escalation embedded in that activity, whether that be through interaction between officers and copwatchers or between detained citizens and officers.

Other Uses of Video:
The Digital Online Work of Copwatching

Beyond its role as artifact and activity on the streets, digital video enables sharing of information, cultivation of culture, and support for citizens through its subsequent life online. While a comprehensive examination of copwatchers' online activity is beyond the scope of this project, a brief look at some established organizations' websites and social media suggests how video footage is used, oftentimes as a means of spotlighting problematic or illegal policing practices vis-à-vis copwatchers' efforts to improve accountability and nurture support. Portland Copwatch (2020), for instance, which identifies itself as "a grassroots, volunteer organization promoting police accountability through citizen action," uses video sparingly on its site, favoring other resources (e.g., compilations and reports on police violence, correspondence with officials on related matters, etc.). One video (Peace and Justice Works, 2017) linked from the page, however, includes footage of police officers offering a rough hands-on escort of a copwatcher away from a protest scene. Another individual copwatcher, Oregon Cop Watcher (2017), uses YouTube to post videos of police activity that raise questions about police and protocol, such as one in which he and others are detained by officers and asked for identification without a clear legal reason. Yet another video, posted on Facebook by Seattle Cop Block (2014), shows police officers using explosives in a chaotic street scene and includes a copwatcher's hostile engagement with officers before and after he claims officers used explosives that directly hit him.

Other copwatching organizations sometimes post video on websites or social media to spotlight questionable police behavior toward other citizens.

A video posted, for instance, on the Copwatch Brooklyn Facebook page (Copwatch Patrol Unit-Brooklyn, 2020) shows a bicycle cop riding over a citizen lying on the street. A Twitter video (Copwatch Brooklyn, 2020) from the same organization shows a brief, physical encounter between officers and a citizen in Mount Vernon, New York. Another video posted on the website of the Peaceful Streets Project (2016) of Austin, Texas, shows a brief clip of a horse-mounted police officer seemingly kicking a passing citizen on a crowded street. Other videos are less inflammatory, capturing, for instance, officers' more perfunctory procedural lapses.

Videos on copwatching websites, social media, and YouTube channels often range in quality and can reveal the sometimes complicated motives behind copwatching, especially by individual copwatchers. Some videos represent work by copwatching organizations, while others, even if posted by the organizations, may have somewhat unclear origins, such as those sent to an organization by a like-minded but unaffiliated citizen. Some videos are narrated or captioned to offer interpretation; others feature copwatchers engaging directly with officers to challenge their actions. Video footage is also sometimes edited rhetorically with an eye toward storytelling. For instance, as Karen Hao (2020) notes, a supercut of captured police brutality titled "This Is a Police State," composed of incidents captured on video during summer 2020 protests following George Floyd's death, has attracted a massive online audience, having been viewed nearly 50 million times. Such editing techniques have the capacity to amplify the storytelling power of documented police violence through a kind of rhetorical accumulation and concentration.

Digital Archives:
Video and Sustained or Future Impacts

Another emerging use of copwatching video footage is digital archiving. Rooted in the work of the aforementioned human rights organization WITNESS, some copwatching organizations have sought new ways to create impact with the footage they capture. For instance, Berkeley Copwatch (2020b) recently announced the launch of a database initiative in collaboration with WITNESS, noting that the tool "could be a game-changer for organizers who want to ensure that the everyday abuses committed by police officers are recorded, archived and able to be used to alert our communities when particular officers or police practices threaten public safety." The project resembles work undertaken by El Grito de Sunset Park (2020) as part of the "Profiling the Police" initiative in Brooklyn, New York. While Berkeley Copwatch's database is not exclusively populated by video footage (it also includes images, notes, officer information, incident reports, etc.), video and other media play a significant role in enabling the organization to serve as a resource for the community, with database access offered to citizens and attorneys who might benefit from compiled data illustrating patterns of abuse or who might need specific footage in the courtroom. Both of these projects emphasize aggregating, archiving, organizing, and searching archived footage of police activity. As the El Grito de Sunset Park (2020) project description notes, "our project investigates how video and open source data gathered by local groups can help corroborate incidents of abuse, help communities tell their own stories, and strengthen advocacy efforts for greater accountability and transparency."

Interview subjects at one organization I observed spoke to the power and potential of a database. The leader of the organization, concerned that endless images of police brutality online had led to "diminishing returns," was interested in putting "some power behind our punch" through a database-driven "focus on creation of evidence and what is required to create credible, actionable evidence." Members noted that it was not uncommon to have attorneys or citizens approach the organization when seeking information about a police officer involved in a client case. A database offered a powerful way to organize a vast amount of footage and leverage it, making it searchable and sortable. Having the ability to track incidents and track problem officers enabled the organization to target its activism, organize its assets, and strategically share video in pursuit of social justice goals.

LOCATING THE RHETORICAL WORK OF
VIDEO IN COPWATCHING ACTIVISM

Within the context of copwatching as an activist practice, similar to spontaneous citizen capture of police violence, video is used to document action and promote accountability. As part of copwatching's enduring, organized activist efforts, however, video as act and artifact is further enmeshed in a broader, ongoing strategy to recompose the dynamic space of citizen detention and arrange rhetorical resources for more expansive citizen support. By altering the very conditions of police/citizen interactions, copwatchers and their cameras engage in a kind of embodied, agonistic rhetoric that bears upon the broader ecology surrounding police accountability and the use of force.

One key site of strategic integration is the embodied encounter between police and citizens. By virtue of their physical presence, copwatchers and their cameras become part of the police/citizen interaction, actively participating through verbal exchange with officers and citizens, physical presence, and video documentation. Indeed, the material presence of video cameras and the potentials of video recording have the capacity to condition police behavior and alter the actual content of the "document" of the police/citizen interaction. A copwatching group's presence changes the calculus of citizen detention: assuming the group's advocacy for and alliance with the citizen, the citizen-copwatcher collaboration typically "outnumbers" the officer or officers on the scene, altering perceptions and adding perspectives. Fundamental practices of copwatching—reminding citizens of their rights, asking questions, reminding officers of copwatchers' and citizens' rights, and wielding a camera to enforce accountability—array to reinforce detained citizens' humanity, their power, and their claim on constitutional protections.

Indeed, when copwatching, the camera may capture something noteworthy, but more likely, it will not—most patrols and captured videos are fairly mundane and uncontroversial. But the potentials embedded in this form of sousveillance and the presence of both cameras and citizens alike consciously and unconsciously condition the structure of the police/citizen interaction. As Bock (2016) notes, "the embodied nature of cop-watching and its literal, rather than metaphorical, form of government surveillance distinguish it from other forms of user-generated media" (p. 18). These impacts of embodiment and the presence of video within the material space of detention create conditions for agonistic engagement, which "maintain[s] that change can come through contestation that engages with formal democratic processes" (Simonson, 2016, pp. 435–436). Copwatching may be seen as adversarial by virtue of copwatchers' use of cameras and (sometimes) disposition toward police, yet it remains legal and potentially fruitful through enabling persistent citizen participation and engagement at sites where power is wielded. Simonson (2016) notes, "The control of copwatchers over their own actions, recordings, and participation in formal institutions turns the tables on the traditional control that officers have to dictate the terms of public participation" (p. 435). The presence and capability of video recording within this context confers power and status to both the copwatchers who wield cameras and the detained citizens themselves. Such involvement adds a psychosocial dimension to policing by bringing representatives of the citizenry directly, physically into the scene and act of detention. Simonson notes that copwatchers' agonistic presence and real-time interaction with police enables them to participate in Fourth Amendment interpretation and execution: "Through their presence, they [copwatchers] ask that officers consider the experience of residents of entire neighborhoods with respect to their practices. They ask that police officers consider the dignity of those residents. They bring issues of race and class to the forefront. . . . Indeed, it is the adversarial nature of copwatching—the ability of copwatchers to contest police practices in the moment—that gives the practice the potential to change legal meaning" (p. 427). Interestingly, then, presence and the *act* of recording video have the capacity to alter the very "content" of policing—its practice and outcome—and, consequently, the resulting captured video *artifact*. As Simonson (2016) notes, copwatching organizations "do more than capture videos" with an eye toward deterrence; they also leverage video's capacity for "providing more data points, more perspectives, and less opportunity for police officials to dominate the conversation over what policing can and should be" (p. 434).

However, at the same time, Simonson (2016) recognizes copwatching's potential for introducing conflicting and even negative outcomes for citizens: "Organized copwatching may also intrude on the privacy interests of third parties and those under arrest" (p. 432). The copwatcher quoted earlier in this section ("Copwatching, obviously . . .") seemed aware of the precarity attending the intersectional identities of some citizens in the predominantly Black, economically disadvantaged neighborhoods where the organization frequently patrolled, demonstrating a sensitivity echoing Gilson's (2021) recognition that "individuals do not experience vectors of power only as gendered, racialized, sexualized, disabled, or economized bodies but rather at the intersection of these, and other, positionalities" (p. 180). Indeed, for some citizens, the nexus between and among these positionalities means that copwatching can introduce additional risks by escalating tensions with police or through the recording of a video document that could be widely circulated and used or interpreted differently by different parties. This concern highlights the importance of consent and communication between copwatchers and citizens as part of the broader ethics of such activism and is manifested in the widespread copwatching practice of recording police/citizen interaction to focus on capturing officer identity and behavior while trying not to capture citizen faces or other identifiers.

In its richness and variety, the web of rhetorical activity surrounding policing and police reform is vast, including rhetorical acts enjoying institutional sanction, such as incident reports, press conferences, and embodied performances of police officers and agencies. While it can introduce additional ethical complexity and risk to citizens, copwatching, as an activist rhetorical practice, seeks to expand and add a productive complexity to the broader reform ecology—to include, directly and indirectly, citizen voices and values. Video cameras are key to this, featuring first as a symbol of accountability, but also as a signifying artifact on the streets, indicating copwatcher intention and setting an expectation of accountability for law enforcement. Beyond that, the documentation enabled by the camera as a tool comes to feature in the police accountability ecology. Footage posted on websites circulates via social media, conditioning the broader ecology by infusing new energies and texts while creating possibilities for activism rooted in evolving sociocultural views regarding policing. For instance, as the copwatching database projects mentioned above indicate, video documentation—archived and searchable— offers ways to track and identify patterns of behavior, as well as to manage and make available evidence that can be valuable in the courts. Other copwatching videos represent police behaviors and then move through social media and other channels, conditioning thinking, inspiring protests and other rhetorical actions, and raising questions. As Edbauer (2005) notes, rhetorical acts "concatenate" throughout ecologies, however unpredictably, altering views and spurring conversations (p. 19). The potential here is for the observational and archival functions of copwatching to help in the creation of local knowledge that informs behavior and the local culture of policing.

Copwatching, then, has the capacity to condition the police accountability ecology at the local level of practice while also contributing to broader conversations about policing. Such work takes place across time and space, ranging from direct involvement in the actual detainment of citizens by police, to the aforementioned "Know Your Rights" trainings that position citizens to better navigate those moments with police when copwatchers are not present. In short, copwatching organizations seek to create new opportunities for both deliberate and unanticipated rhetorical articulations that move far beyond the conventional interactions of police, citizens, and copwatchers on the streets.

Conclusion

Copwatching highlights ways in which local acts—embodied, situational rhetorical activities—have the potential to condition behaviors that, in turn, have the potential to ripple through activist ecologies and ecologies of reform to impact cultures—in this case, cultures of policing. While it is difficult to gauge this kind of impact, in the two cities wherein I directly observed copwatching activity and interviewed members, it was clear that each organization saw itself as influencing how the broader community saw and experienced policing. In one city in particular, the copwatching organization's long-term presence meant that it played a leading role in interpreting and framing the narrative around local police initiatives and actions. This sometimes led to tension with police, not surprisingly, but it also meant that citizens' rights vis-à-vis policing and law enforcement policy development were visible and part of the local public discourse in ways that they might not otherwise be. Indeed, this organization's stable leadership and membership, which consisted of local citizens—including, at various times, those who had or were experiencing homelessness, working professionals, activists with police-adjacent interests, university students, and others—engendered a sophisticated interpretive perspective with regard to power and the ways in which policing interfaced with the community's diverse, complex citizenry. Such varied membership and the visibility of the organization's work create ongoing coalitional potentials. Working from Chávez's (2013) notion of coalition as a "possibility for coming together within or to create a juncture that points toward . . . change" (p. 146), Jones, Moore, and Walton define coalitions as "relational, dynamic, configurations that are attuned to issues of power, privilege, and positionality while actively pursuing options for addressing and redressing inequities and oppressions" (as cited in N. Jones, 2020, p. 519). Within such a frame, coalitions might be said to function as grassroots sites of invention characterized, in part, by possible articulations of subjectivities, lenses, and perspectives that offer new capacities. For local copwatching organizations, such relations among varied, shifting membership and local allies and partners can sharpen attunement to the complexity of policing as institutionalized power within the community, illuminating new possibilities for reform.

Copwatching emerged as a rhetorical practice because police/citizen interactions so often happen out of sight, making it difficult for many citizens to have their voices heard and their experiences taken seriously. Accountability for police actions, particularly excessive force, was and is elusive. However, the simplicity that now attends video capture in a society wherein the great majority of citizens carry a cell phone capable of recording video footage makes anyone a potential participant in police accountability. The camera, enmeshed in the material scene of copwatching out in the streets, becomes a way to condition policing itself as an unfolding performance. While no one would mistake a video camera's capabilities for those of a firearm, the camera alters the rhetorical dynamics of policing, enabling citizen participation in both the use of force and in developing subsequent narratives of force that bear upon the unfolding story of police accountability as it plays out in local contexts.

For students and researchers interested in activism that focuses on accountability and government institutions, examining the multifaceted use of video within the rhetorical practice of copwatching can be instructive in other related and unrelated settings. Perhaps most obviously, the range of uses and rhetorical impacts that the camera creates invites consideration of possibilities for applications and raises related questions: how can the use of video advance activist goals? How might video cameras' mere presence in public or private spaces encourage (or suppress) thoughtful discussion or gainfully condition activity? How might video be used to shape broader conversations and local cultures by and through coalitional activity and affordances? What role might archiving play in shaping policy or empowering citizens? What other ethical questions attend video-centered activism? Students and teachers interested in activism and public-facing writing may well find these and other questions to be urgent and instructive, especially in an increasingly visual culture engaged in the development and circulation of texts to pursue strategic social justice goals.

CHAPTER 2

Nacogdoches Accountability Coalition

Challenges to Grassroots Organizing in Deep East Texas

HEATHER K. OLSON BEAL

THE IMPETUS FOR THE ORGANIZATION

One evening in April 2019, a group of Black female undergraduate students in Nacogdoches, a small town in Deep East Texas, casually gathered in an apartment complex parking lot, chatting and making plans about the evening ahead. An off-duty, plainclothes police officer approached them in his unmarked vehicle and began yelling at them, causing them to disperse. He chased after those who had walked away, pinning one of the women to the ground and shoving her face against the pavement. Onlookers screamed and begged him to stop. Two uniformed officers arrived at the scene, guns drawn, and helped the off-duty officer further subdue the girls. The entire melee, which lasted 4 minutes and 30 seconds, was recorded on multiple phones and went viral on social media.

Just days later, two of the young women were arrested and charged—one with criminal trespassing and the other with assault of a public servant and resisting arrest. Several protest marches took place in the community. But then, just like that, it seemed, the spring semester ended, most of the college students went home for the summer, and our little town began settling into its sleepy summer routine.

STARTING OFF STRONG

In May, I was invited to attend a meeting to discuss community action in response to this racialized incident of police violence. I did not know what to expect at the first meeting, but I knew, or knew of, everyone there. Eight people attended the first meeting, including one Black former student, two Black moms, three white young adults, one white emergency room physician, and me (a white professor and mom).

The young Black man who called the meeting started off by sharing details of the incident. We quickly agreed that we wanted to act. After much discussion, we decided on a short-term goal of advocating for the students harmed in the incident and a long-term goal of drafting a proposal to create a citizens' review board to hold local law enforcement accountable. Tasks were quickly delegated. We settled on a name—Nacogdoches Accountability Coalition (NAC)—and created a logo, a Facebook page, and a private Facebook group for internal communication.

A palpable sense of urgency prevailed at the next meeting, which 19 people attended. We created informal committees (e.g., community outreach, policy) and something resembling a leadership team. In its first few months, NAC held a benefit concert and raised $2,000 to help the students obtain legal representation, held a meeting to get buy-in from local Black pastors, organized community members to speak at city council meetings about issues related to community policing, and hosted a Know Your Rights event. It felt like we were moving at a fever pitch.

HOMING IN ON THE
CITIZENS' REVIEW BOARD PROPOSAL

After the fundraiser, the three-person policy committee began drafting a proposal to create a citizens' review board to hold local law enforcement accountable. We continued to meet every week to work on the proposal, to discuss issues related to the ongoing cases against the students, and to discuss other related ideas. While there were sometimes 12 to 15 people at weekly meetings, a smaller core group consistently attended meetings and worked on the proposal between meetings. Often, a community member that none of us knew would show up to our meetings. They had stories to tell about confrontations they had had with local law enforcement. Their stories, which included interactions between local law enforcement and undocumented people or people from the queer community, highlighted the intersectional nature of challenges with local law enforcement. Sometimes a new person or two would show up and get excited about a particular issue. There were two people attending meetings for a few weeks, saying they wanted to work on a podcast that would highlight some of the many stories we were hearing about local law enforcement as well as the experiences of people of color in local jails. We spent some time discussing the possibility of conducting oral history interviews of local people who had experienced police violence. We chased these ideas for short periods of time, but never to their implementation. We often lacked enough consistently involved people to head up these projects.

After weeks of wordsmithery, the policy committee met with Dora,[1] a supportive city council member who offered advice regarding how to pitch it to the city. The committee brought drafts to weekly meetings, where we painstakingly parsed words, trying to strike a balance between the assertiveness the proposal demanded and the deference we needed to get it approved. In early November, Dora volunteered to set up a meeting between the city manager and our policy committee about including the proposal as an agenda item at a city council meeting. The Thanksgiving holiday came and went, and everyone got bogged down by year-end work expectations and holiday happenings. The city manager, who we believed tentatively supported the idea, announced that he planned to retire in January and that an interim city manager would be appointed while they completed a search for a permanent city manager.

On January 21, 2020, our citizens' review board proposal was included on the regular city council meeting agenda. We were elated and shocked. The proposal was presented, and the city council agreed to discuss it further. No action was taken. We met again on February 4. The city manager retired and the chief of police was appointed as the interim city manager, an unwelcome change for our cause. Early March came and we were distracted again by spring break.

STALLING OUT

In mid-March, COVID-19 hit, and things started shutting down. Our university went remote, which meant my job as a professor became exponentially more difficult overnight, as did the lives of the students in our group. Several NAC members had kids at home trying to do online school. Everyone was scared. We turned our attention to surviving—hunkering down at home, scavenging for toilet paper, making homemade masks, and wiping down our groceries.

---

1. A pseudonym.

After a couple months of no real dialogue, I asked in our private Facebook group whether we should get back to work on the proposal. One coalition member responded: "It's definitely time to get back on it." Another reached out to Dora, who had recently given birth, to ask about the status of the proposal. She felt we should wait until a new city manager was appointed, so that we could get "buy-in from the get-go." She also explained that COVID-19 was really taxing on city staff resources.

As the pandemic dragged on, one NAC member lost her job due to the economic collapse. One graduated in May but was unable to secure gainful employment in a pandemic. Another relocated to a bigger city where she felt her children's educational needs would be better supported. Several struggled with mental health issues. Our ragtag group of four to five people who had been so proud of our collective progress and so enthused in November, when we seemed to be on the cusp of achieving our primary objective, was individually and collectively spent.

LESSONS LEARNED

What went wrong? How did we start so strong and end up faltering? What can we learn about grassroots activism from our organization's experiences? Some of our stumbling blocks were within our control while others were not.

Within Our Control
Our Organization's Leadership Was Too Thin

While there were sometimes 12 to 15 people at weekly meetings, a core group of just 4 to 5 people did the bulk of the coalition work. We would have been wise to thoughtfully and strategically work on growing coalition membership, cultivating relationships with people who attended meetings and developing a stronger formal leadership structure. We initially attempted to do some of this but never got to the point where the work could be sustained if one or more coalition leaders stepped back.

Our Organization Was Too Independent

Early on, we opted not to associate ourselves with existing local, state, or national organizations (e.g., NAACP, Democratic Party), because we believed our goals were nonpartisan and extended beyond the scope of most larger organizations. However, if we had invested more time in identifying places where our objectives aligned with those of extant organizations, we might have been able to leverage existing human or financial resources to help achieve our mutual goals.

Our Workflow Was Not Sustainable Year-Round

Our ability to accomplish concrete actions toward achieving our goals was not sustainable long-term. As a professor, fewer teaching and university service obligations during the summer enabled me to dedicate about 15 hours a week to coalition work for most of June and July. Summertime also meant greater flexibility and free time for the mothers in the group. However, we were not able to sustain that kind of work once the regular school year routine started again. Holiday breaks (e.g., a week off at Thanksgiving, two weeks off during December) also caused us to lose momentum that we struggled to regain.

Our Organization Was Overcommitted

The collective anger and enthusiasm that inspired us to start the coalition also led us to commit to too many things. At one point, we were investigating the legal ins and outs of the cases against the young women, planning for the meeting with Black local pastors, planning the benefit concert, hosting a Know Your Rights event, creating social media accounts and content for the accounts, working on drafting the citizens' review board proposal, brainstorming about how to involve local high school students in our work, developing a means through which we could collect oral histories of local citizens' experiences with law enforcement, and even creating a podcast. In short, we were too few people working on too many things.

Outside Our Control
Changes in City Personnel

Changes in city personnel contributed to successes and challenges. We were initially fortunate because we had personal connections to Dora, who was sympathetic to our cause and responsive to our queries, and the city manager was tentatively supportive. However, those advantages were quickly erased when the city manager retired and an interim city manager was appointed.

A Global Pandemic

Lastly, the COVID-19 pandemic laid waste to our initial plans and dramatically constrained members' free time and energy. The economic collapse led to unemployment and mental health problems. University and pre-K–12 school shutdowns increased our professional workload such that some of us felt we had nothing left to give to the organization, even though we remained committed to the cause. COVID-19 safety protocols kept us from meeting together in person and some coalition members did not have access to the technology or broadband necessary to meet virtually.

LOOKING FORWARD

We began this work several years ago and our city still does not have a citizens' review board—an admittedly discouraging reality. However, expanding our definition of success helps elucidate the value in what we did accomplish. We raised money to assist a young woman with a legal battle. We created and nurtured relationships with people in our community. For five to six straight months, we regularly called the attention of the mayor, city council, and larger community to police brutality and law enforcement accountability. We educated the community about their rights when detained by law enforcement. We showed people in the community that there are local people who care about the safety and rights of people of color. We demonstrated to our own and to each other's children that working on local grassroots organizing projects is worthwhile.

Two days before this essay was due, I received a text from one of the early coalition leaders that said, "Hey, Dora reached out and wants to meet . . . about continuing with the community relations board. You wanna do it?" I immediately texted back, "Yes!" We now have a new mayor, one new city council member, and a new city manager. The protests in honor of George Floyd that took place across the country during summer 2020 called desperately needed attention to citizens' review boards. We are all vaccinated against COVID-19 and can gather together in person again. And we still have all of our previous work on the citizens' review board. Perhaps we will achieve our original goal after all.

CHAPTER 3

Behind the Still Life Image

The Word *and Fannie Lou Hamer's Activist Impulses*

CORETTA M. PITTMAN

Well-known Black men and women in the Black liberation struggle are often memorialized during January and February, particularly its most visible figures, including Dr. Martin Luther King Jr., Rosa Parks, and Malcolm X. Focusing on these iconic figures at a time when there is a national spotlight highlights their contributions to America. In taking on these cultural acts of recognition, the danger lies in codifying particular moments in time, like the images captured of King marching for voting rights from Selma to Montgomery, Alabama; Parks's 1955 mugshot; or the myriad images of a pensive-looking Malcolm X. Images like these emblazoned in our collective memories can be helpful. They remind us that Black Americans have forced America to reconcile both its democratic ideals and its actual practices. Yet those iconic moments erase the work involved in challenging and ultimately changing state and federal laws and dismantling social customs. In other words, such still life images can obfuscate the activist efforts of freedom fighters who fought valiantly for Black people's humanity and for the granting of their inalienable rights.

In this chapter, I highlight another key freedom fighter, Fannie Lou Hamer, who captivated an American society with her testimony to the Credentials Committee at the August 1964 Democratic National Convention (Brooks & Houck, 2011, p. 42). Although Hamer's national profile rose after her testimony, she is also too often memorialized by the images of her captured on that day in a "plain dress," recorded speaking with a regional accent while using African American vernacular English. Yet Hamer's journey to the Democratic National Convention was hard-fought. She had been a timekeeper on a Southern plantation in Mississippi but was fired when her white employer, Mr. Marlow, learned she had tried to register to vote. She and her husband, "Pap" Hamer, were forced to leave the house provided by Mr. Marlow, because she dared to exercise her citizenship rights. She had even been forced into exile for a short time because she wanted to be recognized as a first-class citizen. Hamer recalls being first politicized at a mass meeting in 1962. Immediately thereafter, Hamer became a local grassroots activist helping to register Black rural Mississippians.

This discussion of Hamer's activist impulses is an attempt to peel back the most iconic still life image of her in that plain dress to lay bare her work as a fieldworker for the Student Nonviolent Coordinating Committee (SNCC). Moreover, I expound on the ways Hamer as a working-class Black woman learned how powerful grassroots activism could be in the lives of the disenfranchised, specifically in the Mississippi Delta but also throughout the United States. While Hamer became a national figure in the 1960s and 1970s, it is my hope that an analysis of her grassroots activism can provide inspiration and paths forward to contemporary activists and activist scholars hoping to engage in meaningful work around social justice.

One way to see behind the still life images of Hamer in the cultural imagination is to focus on key aspects of her rhetorical methods. The first is her masterful use of what Molefi Kete Asante (1998) conceptualizes as *the word,* including her ability to employ signifying as a rhetorical tool, and the second is her mastery of the African American jeremiad. Evidence of Hamer's rhetorical methods are embodied in the songs she sang, the speeches she delivered, and the testimonies she gave. While SNCC and other activists and volunteers as well as scholars have highlighted the importance of Hamer's singing as a rhetorical tool used to lead and provide sustenance and energy to a weary people, I have instead chosen to focus on other activist efforts she engaged in as a SNCC fieldworker, particularly while canvassing and speaking at rallies and mass meetings, that were used to teach poor Mississippians the benefits of voting, to demonstrate how to register to vote, and, once they were registered, to encourage them to vote. Hamer was well-suited for the role of a grassroots activist, given how she felt about local people's ability to lead in their communities. She describes grassroots activism this way: it "ha[s] to be with the people, for the people, and by the people" (as cited in Brooks & Houck, 2011, p. 97).

Fannie Lou Hamer joined an activist tradition in Mississippi that "reflects another tradition of Black activism, one of community organizing, a tradition with a different sense of what freedom means and therefore a greater emphasis on the long-term development of leadership in ordinary men and women" (Payne, 2007, p. 3). The idea that ordinary working-class and poor rural citizens could be at the center of their own liberation was born out of the work of Septima Clark and Ella Baker. Both women believed that leadership could be developed from the Black working classes who were often talked about but rarely asked to talk for themselves about how to improve their lives. Clark and Baker also understood that local people were in the best position to solve local problems. Charles M. Payne (2007) describes their philosophy in this way: "all three [including Myles Horton] espoused a non-bureaucratic style of work focused on local problems, sensitive to the social structure of local communities, appreciative of those communities" (p. 68). SNCC leaders in Ruleville, Mississippi, found in Hamer the kind of local leader who had the capacity and verve to become a leader among her own rural people. Keisha N. Blain (2021) describes Hamer's grassroots impulses: "during the 1960s and '70s, Hamer made the case for empowering ordinary individuals to advance the fight for social justice" (46). Indeed, Hamer's leadership skills—combined with her approach as an "ordinary" citizen with a grassroots philosophy and genuine care for the Black underclass in Mississippi and beyond—eventually catapulted her to the national stage as a freedom fighter. In many ways, Hamer was part of a grassroots movement that was changing the politics of the Mississippi Delta and the nation.

Recognizing her leadership qualities provided SNCC leaders such as Charles McLaurin, James Forman, and others a golden opportunity to take advantage of two moments. One, at 44, Hamer was ready to be politicized. As she is famous for saying, "she was sick and tired of being sick and tired" (as cited in Brooks & Houck, 2011, p. 57). She was ready to join the Black freedom struggle. Two, she had been immersed in an oral tradition suited for the type of grassroots activist the SNCC leaders needed to encourage Black people in the Mississippi Delta to register and vote. She had watched and listened as her father preached sermons in a Black Baptist church. Like her minister father, it seems, Hamer understood the power of *the word*. Asante ascribes to *the word* in the African and African American contexts an almost ethereal quality. He writes, "the black speaker knows what the ancestors knew with their use of *nommo*: that all magic is word magic, and that the generation and transformation of sounds contribute to a speaker's power" (Asante, 1998, p. 60). This organizing principle of *nommo* explained by Asante accurately describes one of Hamer's rhetorical methods. What Hamer lacked materially to influence the world around her, she more than made up with in *the word*, grit, wit, and grassroots work. Embedded in her *word*, Hamer also adapted signifying to great effect. Geneva Smitherman (1977) writes, "Signification . . . refers to the verbal art of insult in which a speaker humorously puts down, talks about, needles—that is, signifies on—the listener. Sometimes signifyin . . . is done to make a point, sometimes it's just for fun" (pp. 118–119). One can see and hear evidence of signifying in Hamer's speeches when she is in front of people in rural Mississippi, in urban centers, or giving testimonies.

In addition to Hamer's astute and audacious use of *the word* in both formal and informal settings, she also was gifted in her deployment of the African American jeremiad in speeches she gave at rallies and mass meetings organized around voter registration. Adapted from the American jeremiad, which is defined as "a rhetoric of indignation, expressing deep dissatisfaction and urgently challenging the nation to reform" (Howard-Pitney, 2005, p. 5), the African American jeremiad "has been frequently adapted for the purposes of black protest" (p. 10). In form, the African American jeremiad warns, seeks accountability, and relies on foundational declarations within such documents as the Constitution and the Declaration of Independence to call America to task for failing to live up to its highest ideals, while also arguing fervently that America can be rescued by a chosen people, Black people, to lead it out of its morass of political and moral failings. One can see these rhetorical strategies by reading and listening to some of Hamer's speeches.

THE WORD: CANVASSING AND MASS MEETINGS

As a SNCC fieldworker, Hamer was tasked with a difficult job. She and other fieldworkers had to go from rural town to rural town to convince Black sharecroppers, domestics, cooks, laundresses, and the disengaged that they had a right to vote and that they should do so despite possibly risking life and limb. This was part of their grassroots efforts. Michele Wittig (1996) defines "grassroots organizing [as] a form of collective advocacy on behalf of a shared cause or direct action in the service of achieving a collective goal. It is locally mobilized and primarily single-issue based" (p. 4). Together, they could organize around the shared goal of Black liberation, focusing specifically on voter registration. Although voter registration was the reason Hamer and others canvassed in rural towns, the issues that drew them there were multilayered. Voting was just one step in a process she hoped would ultimately allow Black Americans to be recognized as citizens and to exercise that citizenship to its highest ends. Grassroots work, as Hamer admits, was not easy. She explains her role canvassing in a 1972 interview with Dr. Neil McMillen. She concedes:

> It was rough because we would go to places, go in do voter registration in places, and we talked to people. We would walk the streets in different little

areas and would tell them we were coming back the next day. And by the next day somebody would be done got to them and they wouldn't want to talk with us. (as cited in Brooks & Houck, 2011, p. 154)

Hamer laments that she did not always get the results she wanted during her canvassing efforts. Unfortunately, local whites who did not want Black people to register to vote often interceded by threatening local Blacks or violently making their displeasure known. She tells McMillen, "Some days it would be disgusting, some very disappointing. . . . Then we'd go to churches, and occasionally along, they was burning up churches. These are the kinds of things we faced" (as cited in Brooks & Houck, 2011, p. 154). Though Hamer acknowledges that her canvassing efforts were not as successful as she had hoped, she refused to stop encouraging Black people to register and vote.

Undaunted by her community members' fears, Hamer knew how to talk to the people who dreaded reprisals from white employers and white mobs. Because of her activist work, she had already experienced physical and economic retaliations. For instance, she had been fired from her job of 18 years on the Marlow plantation as a timekeeper for registering to vote and for refusing to withdraw her registration. At one point, someone shot several bullets inside a home where she was living temporarily, and she had been severely beaten in a Winona, Mississippi, jail in 1963 for her activist activities. Hamer had lived the realities some rural Mississippians thought might happen to them. Such fears should not be ignored. They must be acknowledged. Thus, it was important that *the word* was spoken to the people in the Mississippi Delta. The words were steeped in Hamer's experience and authenticity. As Asante makes clear, *the word,* or *nommo,* is experiential. What Hamer reveals while canvassing is then transmuted by *the word.* Hamer could say to them in a profound and personal way why they should register to vote and that it was their constitutional right to vote. She had registered to vote, and they should, too.

Since Hamer had attended citizenship schools that taught her how to understand the Mississippi Constitution, connected the ballot to local and state policies, and ultimately explained why voting mattered, she more keenly understood and could explain to her fellow Mississippians the connection between voting and local and state power. Those who encountered her while she was canvassing and speaking at mass meetings could appreciate that she spoke with "clarity" (Brooks, 2014, p. 29).

Meagan Parker Brooks (2014) acknowledges Hamer's successes:

Her eventual success at the Sunflower County Courthouse and her determination to use the ballot to challenge the white supremacist oppression surrounding her were contagious. The town saw a marked increase in registration hopefuls. "In February 1963 alone," observed historian J. Todd Moye, "400 Ruleville residents traveled to Indianola to take the registration test." (p. 48)

Although Hamer expressed frustration to McMillen, it should not go unnoticed that her work was effective even if the numbers were not as large as she wanted. Despite the daily frustrations experienced while canvassing, Hamer's words to her fellow Mississippians served as both affirmation and inspiration.

A former volunteer in Mississippi recalls the voice and words of Hamer. Robert Jackall, a young professor from the North who volunteered in Sunflower County in 1967, describes how mesmerized local people were by Hamer's words and presence. Before Hamer rose to speak, Jackall recalls that preceding speakers at the mass meeting had been unable to effectively communicate with the people, but when she began to address the audience:

> Immediately, an electric atmosphere suffused the entire church. Men and women alike began to stand up, to call out her name, and to urge her on. . . . She went on to speak about the moral evil of racism itself and the grievous harm it was doing to the souls of white people in Mississippi. . . . When she finished, the entire assembly was deeply shaken emotionally. People crowded around her to promise they would join the struggle. (as cited in Payne, 2007, p. 242)

Jackall emphasized Hamer's "charisma" as rooted in "'her unvarnished, earthy forcefulness, devoid of all pretense; her unshakeable conviction in the justness of her cause . . . [and] her ability to articulate her ideas with a powerful religious rhetoric that had deep resonances for her audience but that had no trace of practiced cant'" (as cited in Payne, 2007, p. 242). Hamer's authenticity, passion, and her righteous cause embodied in *the word* all but ensured she would make a lasting impression. It was her deep connection to the people and the systemic issues that contributed to all of their poverty that linked her grassroots activism to local participatory democracy.

Canvassing was just one part of the work Hamer did on behalf of SNCC. She also spoke at rallies and mass meetings, which called together local leaders like Hamer, some rising stars in the Black freedom struggle such as Medgar Evers and Dick Gregory, student volunteers from the North, and local community members who joined together in common cause. Mass meetings contained several elements. Prayers, testimonies, spirituals, and affirmations as well as the business of civil rights were all part of the mass meeting experience (Payne, 2007, pp. 256–263). Equally poignant, Payne (2007) reveals, were the "mixtures of the sacred and the profane, the mass meeting could be a very powerful social ritual. They attracted people to the movement and then helped them develop a sense of involvement and solidarity" (p. 263). Hamer's early foundation in the church suited her well for the work involved in galvanizing the people at mass meetings. She knew what the people needed to hear to get them motivated to join the fight for liberation, she was a local person who understood their needs, and she knew how to talk to them. All this she learned because she was intimately connected to them. This explains to a large degree why her rhetorical gifts shined at mass meetings. She would signify on the people whom she wanted to inspire and castigate. Moreover, she employed the African American jeremiad to contest white supremacy, encourage the dispossessed to join in the fight for their own liberation, and argue that such battles could be won by Black people, who could bring Black and white America out of the dark wilderness and into the light. For Hamer, delivering *the word* was authentic and part of her grassroots efforts. Todd C. Shaw (2009) aptly outlines how grassroots activism works, "*grassroots activism,* or community organizing, is a form of political action that assumes ordinary citizens can confront maldistributions of power by organizing as communities of geographic or ascriptive identity (race, class, gender) and thus use their indigenous creativity" (p. 15). As a SNCC fieldworker, Hamer joined others in their grassroots efforts as part of a "geographic" community with "ascriptive identity" markers to change rural Mississippians' living conditions.

FANNIE LOU HAMER'S SPEECHES: "I DON'T MIND MY LIGHT SHINING" AND "WE'RE ON OUR WAY"

To understand rhetorically the relationship between *the word* expressed, signifying, and the schematic importance of the African American jeremiad to Hamer's grassroots efforts and communication style, I turn to two speeches, "I Don't Mind My Light Shining" and "We're on Our Way," as points of reference. Although Hamer delivered several speeches, these two early speeches provide a window into what would later become Hamer's signature style as an activist steeped in the Black religious rhetorical tradition. Richard L. Wright (2003) maintains "through the constructive act of doing language, by taking the word and making it their own, African American users of rhetoric have demonstrated that they live as much 'in the word' as they live 'in the world'" (p. 94). Hamer's fieldwork took *the word* to the people. In 1963, she delivered a speech at "a Freedom Vote Rally in Greenwood, Mississippi" (Brooks & Houck, 2011, p. 28). This speech was given 13 months after she first attempted to register to vote and after the brutal beating she endured in a Winona, Mississippi, jail.

During 1962 and 1963, Hamer suffered other indignities but was not cowed even by attempts on her life. Her movement activities had to continue. To that end, she joined others at the Freedom Vote Rally, which was designed "to show that the masses of Negroes did in fact want to vote . . . [and] . . . to mock the legitimacy of the regular election by making the point that the candidates elected did not represent hundreds of thousands of Negroes" (Payne, 2007, pp. 294–295). Oddly, some white Southerners believed Black people did not want to vote; thus, SNCC and the Council of Federated Organizations (COFO) organized a mock election to disprove the myth and to allow Black people to participate in electoral politics without too much risk to their lives (Payne, 2007, pp. 294–295).

THE WORD AND FANNIE LOU HAMER: "I DON'T MIND MY LIGHT SHINING"

Hamer was invited to give a speech at the rally to encourage the attendees to register and vote, to participate in the mock election, and to actively demand their own liberation. The speech "I Don't Mind My Light Shining" reflects how she employed *the word* and reveals her theological convictions and her use of the African American jeremiad. Much of the speech includes biblical verses revealing a theology that is Christ- and justice-centered. Repeatedly, she reminded the audience Christ is on their side. In so doing, Hamer told the audience that they were part of God's chosen people. She began this speech by citing first from Luke 4:18:

> The spirit of the Lord is upon me, because he has anointed me to preach the gospel to the poor. He has sent me to heal the brokenhearted, to preach deliverance to the captive, and recover the sight to the blind, to set at liberty to them who are bruised, to preach the acceptable year of the Lord. (as cited in Brooks & Houck, 2011, p. 4)

The opening verse had dual purposes. First, it reminded the audience that Christ was there to help them, the dispossessed, and second, that Hamer was there, too, to help lead them out of their hopelessness and into their rightful place as full citizens. Because Christ was on their side, they must fight the good fight alongside Hamer and other movement activists. *The word* here, the most sacred of the words, could perhaps compel rural Blacks to actively work for their own salvation and ultimate freedom. *The word* could fortify them against known and unknown risks they were likely to encounter as they sought to gain their citizenship rights. Hamer knew the history of Black people was one steeped in faith. Citing the biblical *word* would be speaking in a language they knew well.

Hamer continued to return to scripture to frame the persuasive intent of this speech. Turning to Jesus's crucifixion, Hamer told the audience that Jesus's death should not be in vain. He suffered and died on the cross so that his believers could live. The biblical story of Simon the Cyrene, who assisted Christ to "carry his cross" (Mark 15:21), helped Hamer emphasize the shared burden of Jesus's cross and the cross Hamer carried as a grassroots activist. Hamer recites the following verse: "When Simon [of] Cyrene was helping Christ to bear his cross up the hill, he said, 'Must Jesus bear the cross alone? And all the world go free?' He said, 'No, there's a cross for everyone and there's a cross for me'" (as cited in Brooks & Houck, 2011, p. 4). Hamer wanted the audience to consider the double burden; thus, she asked: must she carry the cross of activism alone, or will the attendees at the rally carry the burden alongside her to demand their full citizenship rights? Hamer acknowledged that the cross (fighting against voter suppression and racism more broadly) is heavy, but together they must forge ahead to defeat the origins of the cross they all bear. Together, as locals invested in themselves and their communities, they must join forces and work toward common ends that will change their political and economic conditions.

In her role as activist-prophet, sometimes *the word* Hamer employed was direct. One might even say confrontational. She meant for her words to activate within the minds and bodies of her fellow Mississippians a causal and cumulative effect so that her words might eventually bear fruit. As Wright (2003) asserts, "the spoken word (released through human agency) is not merely an utterance skillfully manipulated, but rather an active force and companion to human activity, which gives life and efficacy to what it names or verbally affirms" (p. 6). Hamer's declaration "quit running around trying to dodge death because this book said 'He that seeketh to save his life, he's going to lose it anyhow'" (as cited in Brooks & Houck, 2011, p. 5) is *word,* prophecy, and life force meant to bring *the word* from utterance to action. Thus, trying to escape death is a futile endeavor.

In fact, God sent Bob Moses to help them fight against unjust laws. For Hamer, Bob Moses, the SNCC organizer and fieldworker, embodied the biblical figure Moses sent to free the people from Pharaoh. As Hamer recalled in her speech, "you see, he made it so plain for us. He sent a man in Mississippi with the same name that Moses had to go to Egypt. And tell him to go down in Mississippi and let my people go" (as cited in Brooks & Houck, 2011, p. 5). Just as the biblical Moses freed his people from Pharaoh, so too, were SNCC leaders like Moses, Hamer, and others sent to help free Black people from the hands of white Southerners who refused them their full citizenship rights. For Hamer, *the word* is meant to be active rather than passive. Hamer hoped her words would inspire the attendees to leave the rally and engage in movement activities such as registering, voting, and participating in the mock election.

THE JEREMIADIC *WORD* AND FANNIE LOU HAMER: "I DON'T MIND MY LIGHT SHINING"

For Hamer and the rally attendees, Moses the biblical figure and Bob Moses as an earthly manifestation of the biblical Moses are joined together metaphorically and literally to change the lives of the disinherited. Black people, whose rights were denied to them from Mississippi to New York, could understand the interlocking Moses stories adapted by Hamer. Both Moses figures led their people out of bondage, as Hamer describes it. When Hamer invoked the Moses story, she knew doing so would resonate with her audience. This was rhetorically savvy. As Keith Gilyard and Adam Banks (2018) note, "African American rhetoric is as much about trading in story as it is about the application of schemata" (p. 4). Hamer's choice to invoke the Moses story based on Bob Moses's role in her life and in the SNCC signaled for her God's hand in leading Bob Moses to his people in Mississippi. It is also a story that circulates ubiquitously in the Black religious tradition. Ultimately, Hamer's "trade" in the Moses story to appeal to the attendees' religious knowledge, to draw on their shared experiences, and to encourage them to be led to the promised land is her *word* at work. *The word* then moves from the abstract to the real, exemplifying, as Carla Peterson (1995) writes, "the Word as the productive life force that brings about generation and change" (p. 22). Hamer was always employing *the word* to seek change.

The schemata Gilyard and Banks mention in the formation of African American rhetoric is, in fact, also part of Hamer's rhetorical methods. Hamer's "I Don't Mind My Light Shining" speech is a rhetorical recitation warning and condemning whites for their brutal treatment of Black people. It also demonstrates a belief in the power of Black people to shape their destiny and the shared destiny of the American polity. In the speech, one can hear echoes of the African American jeremiad. Hamer encouraged the attendees to read Proverbs 26:27, which says, "Who so diggeth a pit shall fall down in it" (as cited in Brooks & Houck, 2011, p. 5). In quoting this proverb, Hamer sets out to invert the power differential between the white oppressor and the oppressed Black American. White people had for too long dug literal pits for

Black bodies. Yet the scripture warns the oppressor that the pits they dig will eventually be for them, not for the oppressed as they had designed. Thus, Hamer warns that God will rebuke and punish white people for the terror they have exacted on Black bodies.

Hamer quotes from Matthew 5:18 and Galatians 6:7 to stress her point: "'Before one jot of my word would fail Heaven and earth would pass away. Be not deceived for God is not mocked. For whatsoever a man soweth, that shall he also reap'" (as cited in Brooks & Houck, 2011, pp. 5–6). God will punish the punishers of Black bodies, and God will also punish Black people for not participating in their own liberation. She warns the attendees, "we can come out here and live a lie and like the lie and we going just straight to hell, if we don't do something. Because we got a charge to keep too" (as cited in Brooks & Houck, 2011, p. 6). Christ kept his charge. Now it was time for Black and white people to take on the charge, too. The charge is to be active in the move-ment. Black people should go register to vote, participate in the mock election, and do what is necessary on an individual and communal level to enact real change. White people should stop actively harming their Black brothers and sisters, who are simply trying to enjoy all the rights and privileges guaranteed to them by the Constitution and God's divine order.

Hamer's status as an outsider-insider gives credence to her speech. She is an outsider in the white world, experiencing racial discrimination, and an insider in the Black community, experiencing and fighting against racism for herself and on behalf of her fellow Black citizens, particularly those in the Mississippi Delta. She is maturing in her role in SNCC, yet she remains deeply wedded to her working-class roots. Writing about Hamer's rhetorical meth-ods, Brooks (2011) suggests she embodies an outsider persona that links her witness to the biblical Jeremiah story:

> Her status as an oppressed other sitting outside of, and in opposition to, formalized institutions is something that she repeatedly defines and recon-structs for her audiences during their speaking encounters. What's more, Hamer links this subjugated status to the deeper cultural resonances of the Exodus narrative and its Jeremiadic extension in a manner that transforms the experience of powerlessness into a source of moral authority and expe-riential wisdom. (p. 527)

Jeremiah is called to warn the people to turn away from idolatry and wicked-ness or feel God's continued wrath. If they repent and choose to live a righ-teous life, there is hope for a better day. In the jeremiadic tradition, Hamer warns those who refuse to heed the call to turn away from unjust laws and argues that those who fail to actively seek to change will suffer severe consequences. The one will be in perpetual states of oppression and the other will suffer God's wrath. Yet at the end of the speech, Hamer finds a way out for all. If they turn to righteousness, each group can be rewarded for engaging in acts of liberation. This jeremiadic ending is apropos. It signals that battles, though hard, can be won.

THE SIGNIFYING *WORD* AND FANNIE LOU HAMER: "WE'RE ON OUR WAY" (1964)

One year later Hamer delivered "We're on Our Way," a speech given at a mass meeting in Indianola, Mississippi. The purpose of the meeting was to encourage the attendees to register and vote (Brooks, 2011, p. 46). The location of the mass meeting was ironic, which Hamer addressed early in the speech. She had campaigned earlier in 1964, hoping to win a congressional seat for the Second Congressional District, which included Sunflower County, where Indianola was located. Her congressional bid was unsuccessful. It was also where Hamer had twice attempted to register to vote. She was not successful on the first trip but returned a second time and passed the literacy test. She told the county clerk, "'you'll see me every 30 days till I pass'" (as cited in Brooks, 2020, p. 48). Luckily, she did not have to "make good on that threat" (Brooks, 2020, p. 48).

In the speech, Hamer reveals how difficult it had been to find a church in Indianola in which to hold a mass meeting and one that would open its doors to her while she was on the campaign trail. Unfortunately, and for understandable reasons, local Black preachers were afraid to open their churches to movement leaders. The Citizens Council, a group of prominent white men in counties throughout Mississippi and other Southern states, focused their efforts on directly and indirectly discouraging participation in voter registration. One way they punished Black preachers was to "strip . . . [them] of their tax-exempt status or firebomb [their] [churches]" (Brooks, 2020, p. 49). Thus, it is little wonder that preachers in towns like Indianola did not want to deal with the consequences for acting against whites who were against the civil rights movement. Of course, Hamer was not pleased that fear had interfered with her activism and political hopes. She acknowledged the change in attitude on that September day by stating boldly, "It's good to see people waking up to the fact—something that you should've been awaken to years ago" (as cited in Brooks & Houck, 2011, p. 47). Fortunately, a church was finally made available to Hamer to speak to the people honestly, brazenly, and with a religious intent that would come to be a hallmark of her rhetorical style.

Hamer's open chastisement of her fellow Mississippians is in the African American signifying tradition. This rhetorical method operates, at least the way Hamer employs it in this speech, to settle scores and simultaneously instruct. Thus, in the opening two paragraphs, she on the one hand applauds them for finally inviting her to speak and on the other hand condemns the time it took for the invitation. She told the audience, "We been working across—for the past two years—and Mr. Charles McLaurin worked very hard trying to get a place here during that time that I was campaigning, and he failed to get a place" (as cited in Brooks & Houck, 2011, p. 47). Hamer suggests that in those two years, more movement work could have been done had they opened the doors of the church sooner.

In the second paragraph, Hamer signals to all who are there that she, unlike others, is not afraid of the Citizens Council or anyone else there who might do her harm. For instance, she does this by listing her address as "626 East Lafayette Street in Ruleville, Mississippi" (as cited in Brooks & Houck, 2011, p. 47). All those who did not know, now know where they can find her. "To Signify," as Gates (1998) acknowledges, "is to engage in certain rhetorical games" (p. 48). Hamer here engages in a rhetorical game of wits. In one sense, she wants to outfox the fox. Instead of hiding, Hamer outs herself before anyone else can. Doing so reveals her fearlessness and her rhetorical savvy. In this way, Hamer controls the narrative and possible outcomes. She learned some early and difficult lessons as a first-time voter registrant and as a SNCC fieldworker. When she registered to vote the first time, she was required to list "the date, her full name, and 'to whom [she] was employed' . . . 'mean[ing] [she] would be fired by the time [she] got back home'" (as cited in Brooks, 2014, p. 39). These lessons soon reveal themselves in her speeches as signifying moments. In coded messages, Hamer engages two audiences: the audience there seeking change and the one there to meddle in her activist activities. Gates (1998) explains, "the language of blackness encodes and names its sense of independence through a rhetorical process that we might think of as the Signifyin(g) black difference" (p. 66). Black difference here for Hamer has to do with acknowledging through *the word* that she recognizes all the ways the white power structures mark her as different; however, she takes that difference and subverts it for her own rhetorical purposes. She renames it, signifies upon it, and redefines it. Therefore, she can signify at that mass meeting so beautifully, because it is through *the word* that she can love and criticize the very people she hopes to encourage, at the same time as she rebukes those who want to stop the Black freedom struggle.

Signifying takes on different forms. For Hamer, this also means that her sometimes sharp wit is deployed as a rhetorical weapon. Smitherman (1997) explains that "signifying can be a witty one-liner or a series of loosely related statements, or a cohesive discourse on one point" (p. 121). Several times throughout "We're on Our Way," Hamer identifies certain attitudes and behaviors as absurdist, particularly those exhibited by whites to control Black citizens. This provides some comic relief. In other words, *the word*, rather than remaining heavy and static, is used intermittently to remind the audience that claims to their racial inferiority come from people who behave ridiculously. For example, Hamer describes the time in 1962 when she and the seventeen Black registrants rode on a bus to go to Indianola to register to vote. On their way home back to Ruleville, they were stopped by the police and told to return to Indianola. Their "crime," other than registering to vote, was riding in "a bus the wrong color" (as cited in Brooks & Houck, 2011, p. 47). Hamer explained:

> This is the gospel truth, but this bus had been used for years for cotton chopping, cotton picking, and to carry people to Florida, to work to make enough to live on in the wintertime to get back here to the cotton fields the next spring and summer. But that day the bus had the wrong color. (as cited in Brooks & Houck, 2011, p. 47)

Hamer knows the audience will recognize this absurd ruse used by the police. They were forced to return because the police wanted to harass them. By retelling this odd behavior of the police, she can provide temporary humor amid more difficult realities. Those in the audience audacious enough to register to vote after the mass meeting will need to understand the consequences for participating in their own liberation efforts; nevertheless, they cannot and should not become so fearful that they do not fight for their rights.

There are other witty moments signified in the speech. Hamer needles those Black preachers and teachers who stay out of the Black freedom struggle to ensure they maintain their middle-class status. For instance, she mocks a preacher who claims he does not like to bring politics into the church. Hamer exclaims, "When he says this it make[s] me sick because he's telling a big lie because every dollar bill got a politician on it and the preacher love it'" (as cited in Brooks & Houck, 2011, p. 55). What preacher, Hamer muses, turns away dollar bills so he can stay out of politics? In another humorous moment, Hamer admits feeling intimidated by preachers and teachers, but "since [she] found out that that's the scariest two things we got in Mississippi," she no longer feels nervous around them (as cited in Brooks & Houck, 2011, p. 55). Signifying on fear and status here, Hamer removes the veil of awe that accompanies the sacred and learned and instead shows how a woman of her status, who is part of the Black working-class, can lead the people with her words, actions, and indomitable spirit. These clever moments work in the speech because Hamer can "invoke an absent meaning ambiguously 'present' in a carefully wrought statement" (Gates, 1998, p. 86).

THE JEREMIADIC *WORD* AND FANNIE LOU HAMER: "WE'RE ON OUR WAY"

Hamer again returns to the Exodus story in this speech. Bob Moses, she told the audience, was sent to Mississippi to free his people from bondage, like the biblical figures Moses and Jeremiah, who were called to help lead the people. She also quotes again from Luke 4:18, where Jesus reads from the scroll of the prophet Isaiah: "'The spirit of the Lord is upon me because he has anointed me to preach the gospel to the poor. He has sent me to proclaim and bring relief to the captive'" (as cited in Brooks & Houck, 2011, p. 49). Hamer explains that she and her people are captives who are suffering now but will soon be free. The sacred *word* offers them the truth they know to be active in their lives. To provide additional reassurance, Hamer quotes from Psalms 37:1–4:

> Fret not thouselves because of evildoers
> Neither be thy envious against the workers of iniquity
> For they shall be cut down like the green grass
> And wither away as the green herb
> Delight thouselves in the Lord. (as cited in Brooks & Houck, 2011, p. 49)

Citing from Psalms 37:1–4 allows Hamer to caution a weary audience not to look with envy at the material accumulations of white people. Rather, they should turn to God for strength, and they will be rewarded. Direct allusions to God were not out of place at that mass meeting or others. Aside from speaking inside a place of worship, Hamer understood the kind of people who were in attendance. They were people who would have been familiar with biblical allusions and biblical verses, who needed a healing balm to get them through their rough days. Indeed, Hamer knew this because she was of the people. Out in the corporeal secular world, there were few ways to rest one's weary soul, particularly among Black people. The sacred *word* could provide their souls a temporary respite. As a believer in Christ, Hamer called upon the sacred word to love, scold, and provide laughter when needed. All these rhetorical tools Hamer perfected as a speaker.

As the prophet coming to lead the people out of their fear, Hamer embodies the voice of the righteous crusader to help her people fight the good fight.

In so doing, she hopes to persuade them to register and vote. To provoke this action, she becomes a kind of spiritual guide who leads and tells the truth. She did so within the jeremiadic tradition and spoke those truths to people as both an insider and an outsider or outcast:

> In a jeremiad, the speaker adopts the stance of a prophet-outcast, evoking Old and New Testament prophets such as Moses, Elijah, Jeremiah, and John the Baptist. These prophets went into the wilderness to discern God's voice and returned to communicate that message to the rest of the community. In African American jeremiads, the speaker signals this position of alienation through metaphor and scriptural allusions rather than through social isolation. (Vander Lie & Miller, 1999, p. 87)

As the prophet, Hamer did not go to a literal wilderness to hear God's word and take it back to the people. Her wilderness included her experiential and learned truths based on time in a jail cell, a severe beating, harassment by white people, food and housing insecurity, bus and car rides, singing, and campaigning, all of which allowed her, while canvassing and speaking at rallies and mass meetings, to take back to the people *the word* she hoped would lead them to register and vote and, ultimately, seek full liberation. God was on their side. Christ was sacrificed so they could have everlasting life, and, in that vein, they had to act knowing that in the material world, active engagement would eventually set them free.

STILL LIFE AS REAL LIFE AND PATHS FORWARD

Space does not allow for more analysis of Hamer's two speeches in this chapter. I do, however, hope it is evident that Hamer is more than the still life image of her in that plain dress in 1964 giving her testimony to the Credentials Committee at the Democratic National Convention. Hamer worked hard as a fieldworker canvassing in small rural towns to change the conditions of rural Mississippians. Her activism must not be stilled by still life images. Simply put, the famous image of her must not undercut the work she did to improve the political and economic conditions of Black people in the Mississippi Delta and beyond. Behind that impassioned look on her face and the plain clothes she wore was a middle-aged woman who risked her life so others could live decently. The grassroots work she engaged in at the local level demonstrated her abiding faith in individual and communal agency: local people in the Mississippi Delta with very little money but a righteous cause could alter their material and political conditions. Keisha N. Blain (2021) notes that "in Hamer's political vision, the most effective leaders emerged from the same local space in which they sought to organize. . . . She believed that local people understood, more than anyone else, the challenges in their communities and could articulate how best to address them" (p. 46). As a local leader, Hamer enacted what she believed grassroots organizing truly meant.

In the following section, my aim is to provide paths forward for current activists hoping to adapt some aspects of Hamer's activist goals that make sense for their purposes. First, her life story reveals there is probably a Hamer inside of all of us. She was a local woman in rural Mississippi who was tired of being mistreated and watching others suffer as well. She needed a spark and received it when a family friend encouraged her to attend a mass meeting in 1962 at Williams Chapel in Ruleville, Mississippi. Inspired by the speakers at that mass meeting, such as James Bevel and James Forman, Hamer decided that it was time to act. No one can predict when that moment will come for them, but like Hamer, one must be ready when that moment occurs. When called upon to act after that mass meeting in 1962, Hamer stood up and said she would register to vote. Her life was never the same after that. She would soon come to embody the very definition of a grassroots activist. Along with other SNCC organizers, Hamer traveled around Mississippi to cajole, encourage, and inspire real change. The reality is there are others like Hamer in communities across the nation who have the leadership skills to be led and to lead, like Hamer.

Second, Hamer's role in SNCC and in other organizations reveals that leadership does not belong only to the elites or middle classes. Here was a woman who had to leave school before she turned thirteen to help her family earn money. Yet her activist work and her rhetorical methods were as dynamic as any of the other movement leaders we have come to know. Thus, a layperson sitting on a church pew or working in the local factory, the local librarian, or the scholar writing about the theoretical world of social justice can look to Hamer's maturation process in the Black freedom struggle and know that she has presented a viable path forward. Hamer learned that voting mattered, and she spent the last 15 years of her life dedicated to making sure voting was a central part of her activism. Focusing on a central issue, studying the issue, and joining forces with like-minded community leaders can be the starting point one needs to become active in their community, like Hamer did.

Third, current activists interested in doing grassroots work in their communities can recognize through Hamer that activism is a long game. Hamer started her activist work before 1962. In small ways, she rebelled against Jim Crow. In speeches, she describes moments when she challenged oppressive systems, for instance, by bathing in her employer's bathtub while he was away with his family. She was the first to eat food prepared for her employer's family, because she was told she could not eat at the table with them because she was Black. She wore her employer's wife's clothes when they were not home, because she did not have money to purchase fine clothes, though she worked hard. Then there were more overt acts against Jim Crow that we know of because of her work with SNCC and other organizations. In 1970, Hamer created a Freedom Farm Cooperative, because she recognized that land ownership could give poor Black and white people economic independence. As a poor woman her entire life, Hamer recognized that poverty was an impediment to full freedom. Relying on others, particularly on white plantation owners in the rural South, was and would continue to be financially devastating. Thus, she sought ways to seek the full liberation of her people. Full liberation would take a long time. Likewise, it is necessary for current activists hoping to impact their local communities or the world around them to recognize that change takes time and that one will need patience and perseverance. Even Hamer's activist work was not the end point. Justice work, as well as grassroots organizing in local communities, continues today.

Finally, current activists can borrow some elements from Hamer's grassroots activism. To be successful, activists who are engaged in acts of civil disobedience do not need to frame their causes around a theology like Hamer's or give speeches in the rhetorical style of the African American rhetorical tradition. If nothing else, Hamer's life teaches us that one should use one's gifts as they are. Hamer was of the people, and she used their commonalities to speak to them on their level. What are the important issues in your community? How might you use the gifts you have to connect to people and issues on the local level to enact necessary changes to make the lives of the people in your community better? Despite the difficulties, the work must be done. Ultimately, activists must have strong convictions and a mission, join a group or create one, recognize the short- and long-term consequences, and like Hamer be ready to act when the time is right.

CHAPTER 4

"Creating a Longer Table"

A Conversation about Diversity in Grassroots Labor Organizing

ERICKA WILLS

Just as the strength of a union lies in its members, the power of the labor movement is ignited by the grassroots work that labor organizers participate in every day. Yet, too often, we hear the voices of national leaders more frequently than those of on-the-ground activists. The following collaborative discussion seeks to amplify the diverse voices of grassroots labor activists from different regions of the United States who specialize in organizing workers in diverse demographics, including African American, LGBTQ+, Latinx, and immigrant workers.

Ephrin "E.J." Jenkins works in the steel mills of Gary, Indiana. He established the United Steelworkers' Black Labor Week in Gary, Indiana, and has facilitated the growth of the program in other states and unions. He is active in Black Lives Matter and the American Federation of Labor–Congress of Industrial Organizations (AFL-CIO) constituency group, the A. Philip Randolph Institute (APRI).

Josette Jaramillo is a social worker and member of the American Federation of State, County and Municipal Employees (AFSCME) in Pueblo, Colorado. She uses vacation time to serve in the unpaid position of Colorado AFL-CIO president and is the first Latina and openly LGBTQ+ individual to hold this position. She is involved in multiple types of grassroots labor organizing, including Pride at Work, an AFL-CIO constituency group.

Guillermo Perez is a union labor educator who is also involved with worker centers that represent low-wage immigrant workers through a community-based model that fosters collective action on social and labor issues. He is founder and president of the Pittsburgh, Pennsylvania, chapter of the national AFL-CIO constituency group the Labor Council for Latin American Advancement (LCLAA).

Ericka Wills: Can you share a little about what inspired you to get involved as a labor organizer?

Ephrin "E.J." Jenkins: I felt I was invisible to the larger labor movement as a Black steelworker in the Rust Belt. So the vision to create Black Labor Week started in Gary, Indiana, back in 2012 as an emotion. I was enraged by the stereotypical and racist narrative being talked about by some members of unions. I wanted to create an event that would put the labor movement directly inside of the Black community and contribute tangible resources that benefited organizations, businesses, schools, and residents. I also wanted to, ultimately, create a week that invited white folks to understand the plight of the Black community and workers.

Josette Jaramillo: For me, I want to help create a "longer table" so organizations making decisions for workers look like the workers they represent. Being inclusive is natural for me because I am a member of the LGBTQ family. Because of my union, my employer can't fire me for being gay. But this wasn't the reality for many other workers in the country until Title VII protections were extended to LGBTQ workers across the nation in 2020 with the US Supreme Court *Bostock v. Clayton County* decision. So my organizing started locally, trying to get Pride at Work chapters and educating LGBTQ workers about their rights, as well as getting them involved in labor movement leadership.

Guillermo Perez: I became active with the Labor Council for Latin American Advancement (LCLAA) in the early 2000s when I was working in upstate New York. I was asked to help some workers in a recycling facility, because the union didn't have any Spanish-speaking folks who could communicate with these members. It became obvious early in the discussions with the workers that almost everyone was undocumented. This was the first time I really confronted this idea of undocumented workers being unionized. I then learned that undocumented workers are covered under the National Labor Relations Act, which gives most private sector workers in the US the rights to unionize, and that the union has the duty to represent them. So part of what I have done for the last 20 years is work through unions, workers centers, and LCLAA to organize immigrant workers.

Wills: As you talk about your experiences, each of you focus on diverse constituencies of the labor movement. What methods, actions, or tactics have you found most successful in organizing workers? How do you link your local organizing with national or international structures?

Perez: For organizing immigrant workers, I can't overstate the importance of community-based organizations such as worker centers, because they are directly involved in helping undocumented immigrant workers. While every major union has undocumented members, the overwhelming majority of undocumented workers don't belong to unions. So the best way the labor movement can connect with these workers is to build relationships with worker centers. Then we connect the dots between these local centers and national organizations like the National Domestic Workers Alliance, Restaurant Opportunities Centers United, and others.

Jenkins: For me, the first step needed to organize workers is to talk to them. I try to find common ground and create a comfort zone. I want them to understand that everyone and every idea and vision is important. Afterwards, I allow others to lead, making sure they understand that we won't let them fail. That's at the local level, one-on-one, but as we organize, we expand. Black Labor Week has grown from Gary, Indiana, and the United Steelworkers to other states and other unions.

Jaramillo: As E.J. said, simple as this sounds, it's about making time to talk to people. For Pride at Work, we started recruiting locally, then linked up to the national organization. I'm proud to say that currently, we have six LGBTQ board members on the Colorado AFL-CIO executive board. Like E.J. talked about, I got the Colorado Pride at Work started, recruited leaders, and passed it on.

Wills: As you talk with workers with a goal of increasing diversity in the labor movement, how do you address systemic discrimination? How do your efforts extend out into the community?

Jenkins: Through Black Labor Week, we address racism and discrimination by being unapologetic, direct, and blunt. A lot of folks will say racism doesn't exist, because they haven't experienced it. But some of us address it every day in different ways. So everything we do during Black Labor Week impacts and directly extends into the community. For example, we go inside various schools to educate students in Black labor history. Students hear how the majority of us experience struggles of systemic racism and discrimination, but we have overcome challenges and fight to change those systems. We create hope.

Jaramillo: I am eternally grateful for white folks who step up. The Black Lives Matter conversations were difficult to have because some of our union folks think we shouldn't tackle "social issues." However, our unions have a great history of joining with social movements and helping workers connect the dots between labor and social progress. To do this, it's essential to create a "longer table," because we have so much to learn from each other's experiences.

Wills: Do you think the labor movement forming strategic alliances with social justice groups can facilitate wider cultural change for workers' rights, dignity, and, increasingly, diversity and inclusion? How do we form these alliances in a way where all groups' voices are still heard and respected?

Jenkins: The foundation that labor unions were created on was the fight for everyone to have a better quality of life. One way we can do this is to form alliances with social justice organizations, often run by young people, people of color, and people with new ideas. That's what we need to bridge the gap and make everyone part of this. For Black Labor Week, we teamed up with the National Black Worker Center Project, Black Lives Matter, National LGBTQ Workers Center, 9to5 National Association of Working Women, and others.

Jaramillo: Over the past four years, the labor movement has really put an emphasis on expanding our reach. In addition to partnering with groups like E.J. mentioned, we have formed the BlueGreen Alliance in Colorado and have had some tough conversations about the environment and workers. We want to show up and educate our members about what's going on in our communities and help them participate in ways that feel comfortable.

Perez: If there's something I want people to take away from my part in this interview, it is that immigrants are a net positive. We know that economic data bears that out. We don't just need doctors and computer programmers; we need drywall finishers and dishwashers and roofers and domestic workers. All of this work is valuable and needed. Frankly, we need an immigration system that encourages those folks to become part of our labor movement—to revive and rebuild our labor movement from the ground up.

Ephrin Jenkins, Josette Jaramillo, and Guillermo Perez epitomize the effort to "build a longer table" in the US labor movement. The actions they engage in every day—from having personal conversations while organizing, to facilitating alliances between national groups—foster a socially engaged labor movement that not only recognizes but also celebrates the rich and diverse voices of workers. If the labor movement is to mobilize nationally and internationally, it must integrate workers' interests from diverse, localized contexts.

CHAPTER 5

Engaging the (Counter)Public through Digital Activism

A Case Study of the TFsUnite Protest

REBECCA HALLMAN MARTINI

On April 3, 2013, at 9:00 a.m., I sat with a group of about 20 other English teaching fellows (TFs) at the University of Houston (UofH) on the floor of the university president's office lobby, waiting patiently for a meeting with her to discuss our current working conditions and to request a stipend increase.[1] At the time of the sit-in, TFs had not received a pay raise in 20 years, and the sit-in was the result of a majority vote by the group, which occurred after two previous attempts at communication had been ignored. This group, who named themselves TFsUnite, formed after a particular injustice in fall 2012, when the administration "accidentally" charged graduate students an extra $121.05. This number represented an increase in tuition at the university that was not covered by the Doctoral Student Tuition Fellowships. While the university did refund the students this money, it led to an opportunity to fight for a pay increase. As a graduate student in rhetoric and composition and a TF stretched thin with multiple jobs and not enough money, I decided to join TFsUnite as both a participant and also as a member of the student-led core committee, which handled correspondence and meetings with the upper administration, organized the sit-in and group meetings, talked with the press, and facilitated the circulation of information among English graduate students and our online supporters.

---

1. At UofH, "teaching fellow" refers to the instructor of record, while a "teaching assistant" is someone who aids a faculty member in teaching, grading, or both for a course.

At the time of the sit-in, TF stipends were $11,200 per year for PhD students, who taught two sections of first-year writing each term, working with approximately 54 students at a time; received no health insurance; and paid $1,685.70 per year in student fees. In an attempt to change these conditions, the TFsUnite movement, which made national and local news, consisted of two primary components: the first, respectfully occupying the physical space in the university president's office lobby, where graduate students (and eventually faculty members) sat and worked quietly, waiting for a meeting with the university president; and second, utilizing Facebook and Twitter (social media networks, or SMNs) to recruit participation from the student population, broadcast concerns and progress to an international audience, and share the attention we received from the press. The Facebook page, which eventually received well over 1,000 likes, was referred to during our meetings with upper administration as an "annoyance" and something that needed to be stopped. In particular, we used SMNs to make what is often considered to be private knowledge (information about stipends and working conditions) more public and available to a wider audience. Within a week, we received our meeting with the president, along with a $1 million commitment toward TFs' assistantships, which resulted in a 55 percent stipend increase for all English TFs the following fall 2013 semester. This provided students with an additional $623 every month.

While this particular moment of activism centered around the physical sit-in, the in-person meetings with upper administration, and other kinds of on-site work, part of what made it successful was its online presence: a marginalized and underprivileged group of TFs (which I will define later as a counterpublic) used SMNs as valuable tools for activist work. Through Michael Warner's (2002) concepts of "mere attention," a present audience that is active or passive (p. 87); "reflexive circulation of discourse," timely, interactive, dialogic communication beyond a single exchange in time (p. 90); and "world-making," affective expressivity via language with strangers (p. 114), I will theorize how a particular moment of activism that centered around a physical sit-in was strengthened by TFsUnite's SMN use, which disrupted the greater university public in ways that eventually captured the attention of upper administrators.

In this scenario, it becomes clear how online tools can and should serve a necessary role for counterpublics in creating context-specific, issue-based, small-scale change. This case study provides an example of what Warren-Riley, Bates, and Phillips, in the introduction to this collection, have identified as "grassroots activism," because it is an example of how "people engage and attempt to intervene when and where it affects them the most, working from the bottom up to make change in larger institutions and systems" (p. 12), while also serving as an example of how "on-the-ground and online tactics are complementary rather than exclusive" (p. 20). While stories about contingent labor and university teaching have become increasingly prevalent in public narratives about higher education (Becker, 2016; Edmonds, 2015; The Executive Committee, 2020; Fredrickson, 2015; Ludwig, 2015), as have stories about graduate teaching assistants (GTAs) who strike for higher pay (Asher-Schapiro, 2015; Fricke, 2015; Hussain, 2020; Mahoney, 2020; Mead, 2020; Mulhere, 2014; Rhodes, 2019), the field has not adequately theorized how specific stories and grassroots activist efforts led by contingent teachers of writing are told internally and represented externally, what kinds of stories lead to real change, and what role the larger public may have in moving university administrators to action. Thus, this chapter seeks to critically analyze one successful instance of grassroots activism among English TFs in hopes of highlighting how such work can be done, even by those in vulnerable positions.

In doing so, I will also argue that we must take seriously cautions against relying on SMNs for the creation of, or primary action for, grassroots activism and political engagement (Crary, 2014; Pettman, 2016), as well as resist the desire to equate attention with labor (Read, 2014). Instead, I will show how the TFsUnite protest used SMNs to facilitate the kind of distraction that moved the larger public to participate as "enabler[s] of a politics without being-with" (North, as cited in Pettman, 2016, p. 135), thus attracting the attention of those who make decisions. This analysis will demonstrate how a particular moment of grassroots activism rooted in a physical sit-in, meetings, and other kinds of on-site work was bolstered and reinforced by engagement with the larger public made visible via SMNs. The TFsUnite case study suggests that SMNs have much to offer counterpublics that attempt to mobilize with the intention of creating context-specific, issue-based, localized change.

THE STORY OF TFsUNITE:
A SUCCESSFUL CASE OF GRASSROOTS ACTIVISM

The TFsUnite movement may appear to be intense and brief, starting with a sit-in event and ending with a written commitment to significantly increase pay within a week's time. However, the process actually began early in the fall semester, months before the sit-in took place. The early parts of the movement started with a carefully written letter requesting a meeting to discuss a wage increase. In it, we acknowledged that TFs had not received a cost-of-living increase in over 20 years and were receiving a stipend that was below the national poverty line.[2] When the TFs received no response, they began drafting and circulating a petition, which was sent to university officials in March, before the sit-in began. After being ignored for nearly an entire academic year, the TFs made it clear, especially via the press and SMN messages, that they were not going to stop until the university made a real, numerical commitment to making a change.

Although the SMN activity is the focus of this chapter, another important part of the story's context can be found in the numerous popular press articles that were published throughout the week, two of which explicitly acknowledged TFsUnite's effective use of social media to create change (Gabel, 2013; Brooke, 2013). Along with the details about exactly what TFs were paid and what their working conditions included, the press articles emphasized that these positions technically prohibited external work, which TFs noted was necessary for making ends meet. Casey Michel's *Houston Press* article referred to a survey that indicated that 71 percent of TFs surveyed (n=49) said they did have outside jobs to cover living expenses.[3] Several articles also include official statements from at least two university spokespeople, who all say the same thing: "Teaching fellows are students in the graduate program who receive a stipend as partial compensation for providing teaching support as a part of their education. These stipends are modest and not intended to serve as a living-wage salary—students are here to study, learn, and work with their graduate advisers to help them prepare for their careers" (Burton, 2013; Gray, 2013; Michel, 2013; Patton, 2013). While one instance does not mention the spokesperson by name, two articles mention the above quotation as attributed to either Shawn Lindsey or Richard Bonnin, who are both referred to as the university's director of media relations. Yet this statement is challenged by journalist Lisa Gray in the *Houston Chronicle* and Michael Hardy in *Houstonia,* who note that the English TFs are not providing "teaching support" but are instead appointed as instructors of record, meaning that they are fully responsible for designing, teaching, and grading the students enrolled in their courses. This suggests that the university did not seem to understand the actual working conditions or assignments of the English TFs.

Alongside the university's response, popular press articles also included the voices of supportive faculty members and some of the TFs themselves.

---

2. In 2013, a living wage in Houston was $19,213. The federal poverty line was $11,490. English TFs were being paid a maximum salary (before paying mandatory university fees) of $11,200.

3. There were approximately 70 TFs at the time, so 49 survey participants provides a good sample for understanding the lived experiences of TFs.

Most of the faculty voices included came from creative writing professors who had national reputations that were noted prior to their words. At the time, UofH was among the top five creative writing programs in the country. The professors' focus was primarily on the unethical working conditions. They referred to TFs as "an underclass exploited for cheap labor" (Hoagland, as quoted in Gray, 2013) and the department's long history of trying to increase pay, "This isn't the first year we've done something either. . . . They [TFs] should have gotten a raise 15 years ago" (Boswell, as quoted in Michel, 2013). They also explicitly questioned the validity of the administration's vague promises to take the TFs' concerns seriously, "The administration has said to the students, 'We hear you, trust us, we will take care of you.' But when you haven't had a raise for 20 years, they're [TFs] disinclined to take it on face" (Boswell, as quoted in Patton, 2013).[4] These comments aligned faculty perspectives with those of the students, thus bolstering the students' argument and further alienating and discrediting the position of the administration.

In a couple instances, TFs voiced the same perspective as faculty. For instance, one English TF noted that the current stipend was exploitative: "This is the indentured servitude of literature" (Lyons, as quoted in Gray, 2013). Another described the administration's response as unacceptable and stated their unwillingness to step down without their demands being met: "The goal is to get a pay increase, or at least a range, some kind of number talk, not 'We'll make it a priority later,' when they're all hoping we'll just give up and go away. We're not going anywhere. We're just going to stay until we have a meeting that yields what we've voted on" (Lowe, as quoted in Burton, 2013). Further, TFs expressed that stipends were unlivable and anxiety-provoking: "The stress of not having enough money keeps me up worried. I wake up at four in the morning worrying about where I'm going to get money. It makes it difficult to find time to write" (Mailman, as quoted in Patton, 2013). Fellows also emphasized how reasonable their requests were: "What we're asking for is a living wage. It's nothing impossible" (Lowe, as quoted in Michel, 2013). Gray's *Houston Chronicle* article also noted the lived realities for TFs due to their low stipends, ranging from inconveniences (like Roussouw biking due to the inability to afford a car and Scapelatto eating rice and beans because they are cheap) to serious financial and health-related constraints (like Lyons

---

4. According to a longtime faculty member in the English Department, the only way the TFs had ever received significant changes in their stipends was through some kind of movement or protest. For instance, in 1972 they received $280 per month, in 1980 they received $380 per month, in 1982 they received $539 per month (after a movement), and in 1993 they received $11,200 (after a movement). Thus, no increases had been provided outside of TF protests or movements since 1980.

emptying a retirement account and racking up credit card debt and Stallman choosing between buying food or making co-payments for her multiple sclerosis medication).[5]

THE UNIVERSITY PUBLIC, TFsUNITE AS COUNTERPUBLIC, AND THE USE OF SMNs

As the stories discussed above show, the narratives about TFs as expressed by the university administration conflicted with those posed by the TFs themselves and by supportive faculty members. Thus, we can understand the positionality of TFsUnite within the university as a counterpublic within a larger public. As Michael Warner (2002) defines them, all publics are "intertextual, frameworks for understanding texts against an organized background of the circulation of other texts, all interwoven . . . by the incorporation of a reflexive circulatory field in the mode of address and consumption" (p. 16), and such publics are more than textual; they are also visual and disciplinarily flexible. Habermas's concept of the public sphere is that it's a place open to all for critical-rational debate about common concerns among individuals who have bracketed their differences. Warner, like many other scholars, including Craig Calhoun (1992) and Nancy Fraser (1992), critiqued Habermas's concept and argued that there was never one public, but publics, many of which challenged the seeming social totality of *the public*. These publics that formed in response to the Habermasian notion of *the public* have often been referred to as subaltern publics (Fraser, 1992) or counterpublics (Warner, 2002).

The particular, dominant public—in this case the UofH—functions as a localized, representative public, a microcosm of a much larger national issue: exploitation of contingent faculty, namely graduate students. Most universities project an image of openness, access, and rational-critical debate while simultaneously establishing themselves as places of power that reinforce certain kinds of dominant narratives. However, we might ask: How open and accessible are university administrators to students, faculty, and staff? At UofH, the TFs sent a letter stating their concerns and requesting a meeting, on two occasions within the six months prior to their sit-in, and were ignored both times by the university president, the provost, and the dean. This kind of silencing marginalized the TFs as university employees and students who were not given the opportunity for conversation with the administration

---

5. For more details about the personal toll that being underpaid and participating in this movement took on my own mental health and well-being, see Hallman Martini, 2021.

about their working conditions and concerns, leading to an increased level of self-organization with the goal of acting together in response.

Further uniting the TFs in solidarity as a counterpublic were the increasingly conflicting narratives between the private and personal lives of TFs and the dominant narrative broadcasted by the university. At the time of the TFsUnite sit-in, a kind of discourse associated with the university's somewhat newly recognized "tier one" status was in high circulation. This status, according to UofH's website at the time, was given to universities "known for world-class research, academic excellence, an exceptional student body, and the highest levels of innovation, creativity and scholarship." It was in contrast to this kind of university narrative that the TFsUnite community established its own. Using the language of the dominant power—an approach recognized by both Warner (2002) and Ryder (2010) as one used by counterpublics in order to be heard—TFsUnite posted several photos to Facebook with hashtags that read "HungryTierOneTFs" and "AreWeThePride," calling into question the university's fulfillment of tier one status as well as its recent "You are the Pride" campaign.

This calling out of conflicting narratives was done primarily via social media, with a broad, public audience in mind—namely other graduate teaching assistants and fellows, part-time writing instructors, and other academic people interested in labor issues, as well as local Houston residents who were concerned about the well-being of teachers. Yet most scholarship about online tools and counterpublics concludes that the formation of such groups cannot take place online, or that online participation in activism results primarily in "slacktivism" (Gladwell, 2010). The case of TFsUnite proves that wrong. The appeal of the online space for the development of counterpublics is not surprising, given early assumptions that online spaces created a greater opportunity for democracy. However, this idea has been greatly critiqued, and most scholars recognize the limitations in believing that greater democratic participation can and does take place online (Asen & Brouwer, 2001; Bohman, 2004; Dean, 2009; Milioni, 2009; Wimmer, 2012). Specifically, Dean (2003) and Travers (2003) note how online participation is dominated by middle- and upper-class white males who reinforce the same kind of exclusivity the counterpublic concept works against. Yet, more recently, Ledbetter and Vaccaro (2019) pointed out that this kind of exclusionary practice can happen in any kind of activism, not just in digital spaces. These scholars argue that digital practices can challenge activist movements that are not inclusive of women of color and trans women, such as the 2019 Women's March. While there was some initial tension among English TFs across subdisciplines about how the organization was moving forward and to what extent a larger population of graduate teaching assistants across other departments should be included, TFsUnite was organized and led by three female graduate students, one of color, and both the core committee and the social media facilitators were primarily women.

In addition to acknowledging the danger in assuming that online spaces can function democratically and inclusively, it is also important to recognize that online tools may work best for serving counterpublics that have already formed. Catherine Palczewski (2001) notes the material barriers created by the internet and argues that online spaces function better when existing counterpublic identities have already formed (p. 172). While this may be the case, TFsUnite suggests that the continued formation and expansion of counterpublics does occur online. Furthermore, Palczewski questions the extent to which the internet exists as a safe space because of the ways in which the state (or in the case of TFsUnite, the university) can impose various degrees of surveillance (p. 181). While this was not a problem in the spring of 2013, more recently some colleges are moving toward the supervision of social media use by faculty and staff. This possible change makes Palczewski's concern especially relevant and reinforces the value of students' and graduate students' necessary roles in grassroots activist efforts.

While I agree that we must keep in mind the limitations of online spaces for use by counterpublics, online tools and SMNs can and should be used to aid counterpublic efforts to challenge more dominant publics, and such spaces can result in real change. This is recognized by Palczewski (2001) and McDorman (2001). Both argue for the "progressive potential" (Palczewski, 2001, p. 179) of the internet, especially how it can aid activist work and help maintain it. Similarly, Milioni (2009) argues that the internet provides an online space for connectivity and networking that maintains a degree of collectiveness, which can be used to reinvigorate democratic life. Yet he argues that there is also a risk of empty participation in democracy that could result if we view the online space as *the* public, rather than a space of multiple publics. More recently, scholars have recognized the value of digital spaces in bringing more publicity to injustices in generally (DeVoss, Haas, & Rhodes, 2019; McCorkle & Palmeri, 2014; Stokes & Atkins-Sayre, 2018; Vie, Carter, & Meyr, 2016; Walls & Vie, 2017), as well as how this "hashtag culture" has strengthened and united marginalized communities, including disabled populations, via #CripTheVote (Mann, 2018); the Occupy Movement (DeLuca, Lawson, & Sun, 2012; Penney & Dadas, 2014); #blacklivesmatter and #yesallwomen (Dixon, 2014); the progress of Black studies (S. Jones, 2020; Wourman & Mavima, 2020); and the

Arab Spring of 2011 (Harlow & Johnson, 2011). In many of these cases, as was the case with TFsUnite, on-the-ground organizing, social media, and even the more traditional press were working together.

In looking at how TFsUnite used the online space of its Facebook page to help create a larger counterpublic community, we can see how three key concepts from Warner's definition of counterpublic are furthered by the use of online tools. In his influential 2002 book, *Publics and Counterpublics,* Warner acknowledges that there are seven "rules" that govern how publics and counterpublics work (p. 67). These include:

1. A public is self-organized.
2. A public is a relation among strangers.
3. The address of public speech is both personal and impersonal.
4. A public is constituted through mere attention.
5. A public is the social space created by the reflexive circulation of discourse.
6. Publics act historically according to the temporality of their circulation.
7. A public is poetic world-making.

While all of these rules define how TFsUnite acted successfully as a localized, small-scale counterpublic engaged in grassroots activism via on-site and online work, rules four, five, six, and seven are especially useful. In the sections that follow, these rules will be expanded on and used to analyze TFsUnite as a growing, digital counterpublic.

A Public Is Constituted through Mere Attention

Mere attention depends primarily on having members who are "showing up" or being present and on active uptake; it includes forms of attention that are strong and those that are more passive. Warner (2002) explains that publics "commence with the moment of attention, [and] must continually predicate renewed attention, and cease to exist when attention is no longer predicated" (p. 88). Since participation is both free and voluntary, publics depend on their members' continued attention, even if activity fluctuates over time. For counterpublics in particular, which rarely have a recognized, institutional space or the power associated with one, mere attention is what keeps the community comprehensible. In the case of TFsUnite, there was no recognition of the group by university upper administrators. TFs had no voice or institutional-level attention until they gained a following from a much larger community of people, including individual members of various SMN groups created via Facebook and Twitter as well as the traditional press. This level of uptake would not have been possible had the group maintained solely an on-site, local presence. Especially for small-scale, localized activism, mere attention beyond a single site is absolutely necessary.

In accordance with Warner's (2002) definition of "mere attention" (p. 87), the existence of a public depends on the degree of its members' activity and requires consistent participation to continue. While the TFsUnite Facebook page was created September 1, 2012, it did not receive much attention or development until around March 25, 2013, when the petition that was sent to the university president, provost, dean, and English department chair was shared. This perhaps marks the moment in which the TFsUnite online community became part of the TFsUnite counterpublic. That particular post had a 7,400-person "reach,"[6] with over 1,000 "clicks" and "likes,"[7] and these high numbers continued well into mid-April 2013, up until the exact wage offer was made and budget meetings started. For that one-month period during which the highest degree of text circulation and participation occurred, the online community was part of the TFsUnite counterpublic.

This temporary (yet transformative) action, or what Warner (2002) would call "active update" (p. 87), was key in moving the upper administration to meet with the TFsUnite core committee members and to act fast. Our use of SMNs was mentioned in nearly every meeting we had, and our continued use of it clearly put pressure on the university. TFsUnite used the Facebook page for a variety of purposes, including posts that requested on-site support, shared updates, responded to requests for a reposting of the online petition that members could sign, gave thanks to other groups who gave their support, and shared good news about faculty participation in the on-site sit-in.

While this brevity of activity in terms of time and scope may seem ineffective because it did not create large-scale change on a global level, the involvement and vast extension of circulating texts did lead to concrete, significant change in the lives of the on-site participants and all English teaching fellows at the university. SMNs played a crucial role in maintaining the TFsUnite counterpublic in the promotion of an issue-oriented, event-specific activist agenda. While change on a larger scale is desirable and more permanent, creating change on that kind of scale is incredibly difficult, time-consuming, and

6. Post reach refers to the number of people who "saw" a post, meaning that it appeared on their news feed.

7. When a post is clicked on or liked, the story appears on that person's timeline and may appear in their news feed.

rare, especially for vulnerable groups like contingent laborers in higher education. Thus, we should perhaps consider how small but significant changes in
locally based on-site activism can be supported by counterpublics using SMNs,
with the hope that such instances can serve as models and tools to encourage
similar kinds of site-specific activist work in a multitude of other contexts.

A Public Is the Social Space Created by the Reflexive Circulation of Discourse and Acts According to Temporality of Circulation

In part made possible via mere attention, *reflexive circulation of discourse that
acts historically and according to the temporality of that circulation* acknowledges that a range of texts and voices are necessary to constitute a public and
that the timeliness of those exchanges matter. Circulation requires interactive,
dialogic activity from multiple positionalities across a crowd of strangers that
moves beyond a single exchange in time. In this way, continuity within a public is supported by SMNs that capture conversational exchanges, making and
keeping them visible for other audiences outside of the real-time exchange.
Warner (2002) argues that "politics takes much of its character from the temporality of the headline, not the archive," thus suggesting that even the attention maintained outside the real-time exchange must be timely (p. 97). This in
turn supports the circulation of discourse. While Warner (2002) recognized
nearly three decades ago that when we create printed texts, we do so with not
only our intended and immediate audiences in mind but also with "an awareness of indefinite others," he also argued that we also must recognize the "temporality of circulation" (p. 94). In doing so, he makes the case that circulation
should have a rhythm and be punctual. However, looking at the circulation of
discourse via contemporary SMNs in grassroots activism, the unpredictability
and the ability to provide immediate or in-the-moment updates actually lends
itself to an increase in mere attention, even more so than punctuality and
regularity (Warner, 2002, p. 92). The drama and excitement of activist work
and progress can then be shared more broadly.

Throughout TFsUnite's most active moments leading up to and throughout the four-day sit-in that took place, social media was used to showcase
the offline efforts being made. For instance, figure 5.1 shows one of the many
images of students and faculty sitting in that was posted to the Facebook
page. Another Facebook post showed a poster that was made and scattered
throughout the campus grounds, which said: "A Tier One school where your
English teacher can't pay rent." Yet another post showed a photo of the front
of a T-shirt made and worn by many of the English teaching fellows who

FIGURE 5.1. Image posted on social media of graduate
students and faculty members during a sit-in.

participated in the movement (although not worn during the sit-in itself). These images suggest the centrality of the offline, physical actions that took place. While the pictures and signs were made throughout the movement on an as-needed basis, oftentimes by individual members, they don't necessarily represent the whole on-site and online group. In this way, TFsUnite's Facebook page shows images that suggest an already formed on-site counterpublic and the actions being taken by members of that group. While sharing these images of an already formed counterpublic isn't exclusionary, it does seem to forward an existent, rather than collaboratively formed, initial identity.

While the online TFsUnite community, perhaps best understood as those members (both active and passive) who followed the Facebook page and Twitter feed, did not directly participate in the construction of on-site materials, some members did create or suggest ideas for memes that were eventually circulated via the TFsUnite Facebook and Twitter accounts. These examples of textual circulation (both on-site photographs and those created solely for and by the online community) support Warner's (2002) definition of a counterpublic as one that relies on the reflexive circulation of discourse. Not only does Warner speak to the need for a variety of texts from a variety of voices, but he also suggests that a counterpublic relies on "an ongoing space of encounter for discourse" (p. 90). Thus, Warner suggests that discourse circulation must go beyond any kind of "sender-receiver-reader" model to include greater participation.

One example of how members of the TFsUnite online community participated in the creation and eventual circulation of texts in the way that Warner envisions is evident in Facebook page exchanges where members wrote in response to a post requesting help with creating memes that reads: "A couple projects we could pick up . . . Who wants to help??? How about something like . . . In 1993, Bill Clinton became President, Jurassic Park was on at the movies, a gallon of gas cost $1.16, and the UofH set the salary for your English teacher—in 2013. And then just put your logo underneath it. Just a thought. Others can chime in." In response, other members of the group offered additional ideas.

What seems important to note here is how both online and offline texts were created and circulated via both on-site and online members of the TFsUnite community. While the line between the TFsUnite group (on-site) and its online participants and the work and circulation forwarded by each group is blurry, it seems fairly unimportant to determine who deserves credit for what. This aspect of the TFsUnite larger community also follows Warner's (2002) definition that counterpublics support a "relation among strangers" (p. 74) via participation.

In addition to the circulation and regular participation by both on-site and online TFsUnite members, the frequency and temporality of posts and updates created by the core committee via the Facebook page are worth noting. For instance, over the course of the sit-in, the highest number of posts were made on the first day, April 3 (n=20), followed by two more heavy posting days: both April 4 and 5 had 17 posts each day. April 6 and 7 were weekend days, and the number of posts picked up again on the final day of the sit-in, with 12 total posts. While these figures suggest only a snapshot of the circulation of texts, they do suggest a heavy and regular engagement with the larger, online TFsUnite community.

A Public Is World-Making

This circulation of discourse, then, engages in *poetic world-making* via a performativity that facilitates "volitional agency," enabling members to "deliberate and then decide" (Warner, 2002, p. 115). Yet rather than working from a solely rational-critical position, the poetic aspects of affect and expressivity in language become crucial to counterpublic world-making with strangers, who are "not just anybody . . . [but] are socially marked by their participation in this kind of discourse" (Warner, 2002, p. 120). In the case of grassroots activism, though, there is an awareness of the public's eye and of the possible attention of those outside the counterpublic. Warner (2002) argues that a counterpublic, in particular, also "maintains at some level, conscious or not, an awareness of its subordinate status. The cultural horizon against which it marks itself off is not just a general or wider public but a dominant one" (p. 119). In this way, the greater national public of universities and colleges that employ graduate students and adjunct writing teachers as underpaid laborers—in a sense the institution of higher education—enabled a shared, subordinate status beyond a single institution.

While I want to argue that TFsUnite did participate in world-making via utilizing the online space, I also want to recognize that most of that making resulted in a virtual representation and narrative of the on-site TFsUnite community. In "The 'Popular' Culture of Internet Activism" (2011), Tatiana Tatarchevskiy argues that the internet allows for, and in a sense demands, a variety of symbolic visual representations. In particular, the internet can enable a counterpublic to "shape a public image out of the ordinary, 'everyday world'" (Tatarchevskiy, 2011, p. 298). One way the TFsUnite community used the online space to create this kind of narrative was by making what are often considered to be private problems more public. Warner (2002) explains that oftentimes when people are in public, they are expected to "filter" or "repress" (p. 23) that which is considered to be private or belonging to the domestic sphere. Specifically in terms of work, Warner argues, "private labor is unpaid, is usually done at home, and has long been women's work" (p. 37). Although Warner is most likely referring to domestic work in terms of household chores and child-rearing, any kind of work that takes place primarily at home can be considered private labor. Thus, we have to recognize the ways in which the teaching of composition fits this definition of private labor, especially because of the field's history of being feminized and consisting primarily of female teachers whose time in the classroom may be as little as a couple days a week, when actual time spent working (preparing, teaching, grading, etc.) is close to 40 hours per week. Part of the argument that the TFsUnite group wanted to make was that we were putting in many hours of work as teaching fellows and not being compensated for that amount of time fairly, which led many of us to illegally take on extra outside jobs. These external jobs were private in that we had to hide them and complete them without acknowledging them more explicitly among our graduate support networks, namely faculty mentors and teaching supervisors. Thus, some members decided to make

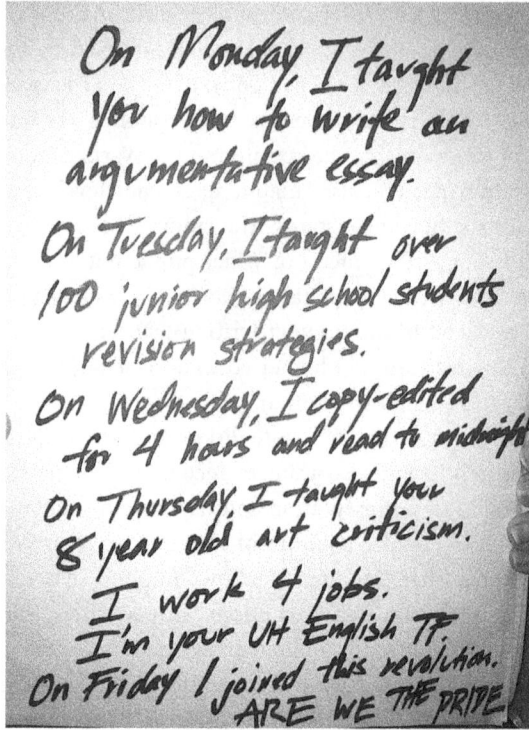

FIGURE 5.2. Photograph of a UH teaching
assistant's individual private lives poster.

their private financial and working circumstances more public through poetic
world-making in the SMN environment.

One way members did this was by composing individual, handwritten letters explaining specific details of their weekly lives and working conditions.
Perhaps the most startling personal letter came from one teaching fellow who
writes about her difficulties living off of such a small stipend as a woman with
multiple sclerosis who must support herself and pay for medicine that she
needs in order to function. This letter, like the one shown in figure 5.2, was
made public on the Facebook page.

These handwritten, rather than typed and posted, lists call attention to the
material work of writing and teaching writing, as well as to the human performing that labor. The handwriting itself personalizes each account. These
were posted as separate images; read together, they engage in world-making
that concretizes the labor realities of English TFs at UofH. The work includes
both the tasks directly related to being a graduate student and meeting the

teaching demands of the position as well as external jobs that are primarily kept private. By accruing these stories, their reality becomes more the norm than the private exception. They challenge the notion that the stipends provided via the teaching fellowships are livable by showing that they are, in reality, not.

ENGAGING IN SUCCESSFUL GRASSROOTS ACTIVISM: SUGGESTIONS FOR SUCCESS

On April 8, 2013, a group of four TF core committee members and five supportive English faculty members met with UofH's president, dean of Arts and Sciences, and provost. According to the minutes kept by a representative of the core committee, the president began the meeting by saying "help me learn" and listened to the TFs explain their concerns. As the meeting progressed, the president asked the dean and provost why she hadn't been made more aware of the issues and did a lot of listening. She claimed, "I respectfully accept your discussion and value students and graduate student success." As someone relatively new to the position, only five years in, she sympathized, "I am personally distressed as well. I don't know how it's possible you haven't got an increase in 20 years." Eventually, she promised to set aside $1 million to increase TF stipends and support teaching in the core curriculum and added that this would provide more support for all TFs and TAs across the College of Arts and Sciences. In addition, she committed to setting up a university task force on graduate assistant success, "not just for you [TFs], but for me to look out for our university." The president left it up to the dean and provost to determine how the funding would be divided, and a 55 percent wage increase was awarded to all English TFs.

Once the $1 million commitment was made and confirmed, a member of the core committee said that they wanted to "bring to social media that stipends will be increased. . . . We would like to bring that information to the 60,000 people tuning into us." In response, the president said, "I'm not doing this because of press. I'm doing it because it's the right thing to do." While this claim and her ongoing sympathy throughout the meeting are admirable, the fact that the letters and petition—all of which were sent to her along with the other upper administrators—were not on her radar at all until the sit-in and this particular meeting suggests otherwise. It suggests that, without the SMN and press attention, she likely would not have even known about the concerns, let alone acted according to what seemed to be "the right thing to do."

Counterpublics and grassroots activists need to tap into online spaces and SMNs as resources to aid in their activist work and make their causes and injustices public. Prior to and around the time of the TFsUnite movement, Hands (2011), Wimmer (2012), and Franklin (2013) argued that we need to think beyond old versus new paradigms and past what Franklin (2013) calls "ongoing polarizations between those 'for' or 'against' the web and its cyberspace as constitutive and so formative of today's sociopolitical realities" (p. 13). Similarly, Hands (2011) acknowledges how digital activism opens up new avenues for protest, both online and in real-time, because of the ways it complicates and extends notions of activism, dissent, resistance, and rebellion (p. 3). More recently, scholars have noted the value of creating digital counterpublics connected to Dutch animal welfare (Wonneberger, Hellsten, & Jacobs, 2020); to support race and gender justice (Jackson, Bailey, & Welles, 2020); and to support social movements over time (Hill, 2018). When looking at the locally based, issue-specific context of the TFsUnite movement as counterpublic and at its success via the temporarily active engagement of its online members, we can see how online spaces can be used to create real change in big ways, even if small in scale.

While grassroots activisms are localized and context-specific, this case study analysis of TFsUnite does provide some suggestions for how similar groups can organize and fight for change. These are particularly useful for similar kinds of labor-based issues within an institutional setting, but they may be applicable in education more broadly beyond the university setting. Further, part of why we were successful was because of our involvement specifically with teaching core curriculum courses and the broader impact those courses had on hundreds of students. Although there rarely seems to be a "right time" to engage in grassroots activism, the below strategies lend themselves well to localized movements.

1. **An on-site, core committee of participants and leaders formed with a clear plan for in-person activism.** The strength of the movement did not depend on the larger, online community; it was merely strengthened by it. The in-person work—the unwillingness of activists to go away—was crucial to getting a response.

2. **SMNs were used to publicize the on-site work, reach out directly to the press, and share stories about TF working conditions that had previously been kept private or primarily within the departmental community.** While I certainly cannot claim to know the entirety of the TFsUnite online community, I do know that those who followed along included other English graduate students and contingent faculty members in similar kinds of positions; local, city, and state community members who were interested in the life of the university; journalists writing for the popular press; and eventually the university administration.

3. **The timing was right, and we moved past lower-level administration.** After going through the official channels via respectfully submitted letters and petitions, TFs were ignored. At that point, we did not wait to hear back from lower-level administrators but decided to call on the university president. There was some exigency to the work, given that the sit-in began in April and the end of the semester was fast approaching.

4. **The TFs used SMNs to maintain attention, circulate discourse, and engage in world-making.** The TFs engaged regularly with a broader community, bringing them into the TFsUnite counterpublic. Regular updates about what was happening on-site, invitations to create and share memes that poked fun at the larger university, and direct acknowledgement of other local groups either showing support or engaging in similar kinds of fights helped to build relations among people who were otherwise strangers.

CHAPTER 6

Mobilizing Grassroots Rhetorics for Reproductive Justice

A Q&A with Sara Finger, Executive Director of the Wisconsin Alliance for Women's Health

MARIA NOVOTNY

Reproductive Justice is "the human right to maintain personal bodily autonomy, have children, not have children, and parent the children we have in safe and sustainable communities."

—SisterSong

The US Supreme Court's decision in *Dobbs v. Jackson* to effectively end a person's right to an abortion has led to an influx of national (e.g., NARAL), regional (e.g., Midwest Access Coalition), and state-based local (e.g., Women's Medical Fund) organizations working to ensure abortion access. The Supreme Court decision underscores the exigence for this edited collection, devoted to examining the often disregarded and marginalized labor involved in grassroots organizing, and invites further scholarly inquiry to consider how our academic labor may amplify and work in coalition with the many grassroots activists fiercely fighting to secure reproductive rights for bodily autonomy. Further, as a legal decision with implications that vary across state lines, the Dobbs decision invites scholar-activists to consider how studying grassroots organizing on a local level may lead to other community collaborations, which may reimagine the products of our academic labor beyond institutional forms of merit.

Acknowledging the contemporary urgency for grassroots organizing, this piece serves as a snapshot into my conversations with a self-appointed "advocacy doula" who has devoted her professional career to ensuring women's access to reproductive health care in Wisconsin. Even prior to the Dobbs decision, inequities concerning reproductive health in Wisconsin were persistent. For instance, a 2018 Wisconsin Department of Health Services report states that approximately 25 Wisconsin women die each year during or within one year of pregnancy. The pregnancy-related mortality rate for Black mothers is five times the rate of white mothers, illustrating systemic inequities. Black infants die at unprecedented rates, with a recent report concluding that "African-American babies born in Wisconsin die before age 1 at a higher rate than any other state in the nation" (Mills, 2018, para. 1).

Despite these statistics, the Wisconsin state legislature has failed to pass legalization addressing such crises. This inaction extends to other issues of reproductive injustice. To date, Wisconsin law allows the shackling of imprisoned women during labor and delivery, and Act 292 permits the state to jail adult pregnant women suspected of abusing drugs, as an effort to protect the fetus. These examples highlight the Wisconsin legislature's repeated failure to protect the mental, emotional, and physical well-being of its childbearing citizens. Many Wisconsinites are angered by the legislature's inaction. Yet partisan logjams remain, preventing the passage of legislation that would improve the reproductive safety for Wisconsinites. In response, this profile features current organizing efforts facilitating legislative action around the health and well-being of childbearing Wisconsinites.

The Wisconsin Alliance for Women's Health (WAWH) is an organization committed to ensuring that every Wisconsin woman at every age and every stage of life is able to reach their optimal health, safety, and economic security. To achieve that goal, WAWH works to inform, involve, and inspire individuals to be effective advocates for positive change. Founded in 2004 by Sara Finger, WAWH believes that state and local policy should happen *with* instead of *to* Wisconsin women.

In what follows, I offer a contextualized conversation between Sara and I as we discuss the specific challenges to improving reproductive healthcare and legislative policymaking in Wisconsin. It is my hope that the profiles of local advocacy organizations like WAWH illustrate how rhetorical skills are critical to fostering grassroots activism in state policymaking.

Maria Novotny: When situating the exigency of WAWH, you often share that 7 percent of Wisconsinites do not know who their state legislators are and how this lack of awareness enables a sense of no accountability amongst elected leaders. Can you explain how that statistic informs the grassroots operations of WAWH?

Sara Finger: If Wisconsinites don't know who their elected leaders are, they cannot connect to them, inform the policymaking process, and hold their leaders accountable. WAWH is proud to serve as an advocacy "doula" organization, helping interested individuals come off the sidelines and empowering them to engage in the policymaking process. We connect people to the information and opportunities related to women's health policy.

Novotny: The metaphor of situating WAWH as an advocacy doula organization is really appealing. If other organizations wanted to embrace this metaphor, what are some tools you'd suggest to do similar work?

Finger: Honestly, listening. When I started WAWH, I conducted 65 listening sessions around the state with various communities—communities of faith, the business community, the health care community, rural women, and women of color. Through these conversations with a variety of stakeholders, I was able to center the voices and experiences of others often not heard in the policymaking debate.

Novotny: It seems like your initial experience at these listening sessions was quite formative. I'm wondering, though, how did these sessions propel you to launch WAWH?

Finger: Through these listening sessions, I quickly realized that a women's health movement in Wisconsin could not be a one-size-fits-all movement. We needed to hear and appreciate where a variety of Wisconsin women were coming from and to meet them where they were.

I also came to appreciate that a new "table" needed to be set in Wisconsin that recognized the intersectionality of the array of issues that impact women's health, safety, and economic security. While a variety of specialty organizations existed focused on specific areas of women's health, like breast cancer, domestic violence, reproductive health care, and mental health, we truly couldn't improve women's well-being until we connected the dots and tackled the related policy threats and opportunities holistically.

Novotny: Listening, then, became a useful methodology informing WAWH. As rhetoricians, we also use listening to guide our work, especially community work. But listening can be challenging when put into practice. I am wondering if you encountered challenges when listening?

Finger: Yes, absolutely. The act of listening can be viewed as a privilege that requires significant time and energy. While I was afforded nine months to conduct these initial listening sessions as a key part of the development of WAWH, I find now, after 16 years, I often don't have the time or capacity to actively continue the valuable listening process. This lack of time and funding to support active listening is such a deficit in the world of advocacy, because so many critical learning moments result from hearing the stories and experience of everyday women in our state.

Novotny: Given the lack of time and money to support listening, does WAWH still employ listening as a practice?

Finger: Well, I'm lucky in that I've been doing this work now for 16 years, which has helped me develop a network and a trusted ethos in the world of Wisconsin women's health. Today, 99.9 percent of my work requires that I sit at the tables where policy ideas are being discussed. In listening to those conversations, I find myself listening in a different way, asking: Are the communities these policies are trying to help represented at this table? Whose voice is being valued? Whose knowledge and best practices are being put forward? In asking these questions, I've been able to make space for other stakeholders to come to that table and advocate for their communities. So, I'm trying to use listening to be more community-driven and community-led. This means communities drive the conversation and solutions, not the experts.

Novotny: Do you have an example of this in practice?

Finger: Sure! Over the past decade, I have watched millions of dollars be thrown at our African American infant mortality crisis in Wisconsin but, frustratingly, have seen Wisconsin persist as the worst in the nation. While communities have been engaged and efforts have been made to intervene, we have continuously failed to center the voices and experiences of those closest to the problem.

For instance, money will be spent on billboards to encourage breast-feeding. However, little funding invests in actually understanding all of the nuances that keep a woman in Wisconsin from breastfeeding, such as having a lactation consultant that looks like you, not having paid medical leave, not having a dignified place to pump. These are challenges that could be addressed through better policymaking in Wisconsin.

Novotny: What would a community-driven approach look like in this example?

Finger: For starters, paying the community members. Many of the experts sitting at the table making these decisions are paid to be at these meetings. Meanwhile, community members are not being compensated for their time. There needs to be more critical integration and value of community perspectives regarding these community-based health initiatives. Right now, it's too "one and done"—a.k.a. "let me check your pulse, and then let me decide what to do with that."

Novotny: Community-driven initiatives are clearly vital to successful localized change. But I'm wondering how embodied positionality factors into this work. For instance, as a white woman, how have you, and WAWH broadly, been able to work with Black and Brown women who are often talked *about* and not *with* at these sessions?

Finger: It's taken so many years of building trust and proving myself. Much of this happens by building strong relationships with other women and proving to them that I'm in it for the long haul and that I can check my privilege. It's not something that has a simple formula.

Novotny: Your frankness with "there is no simple formula" is refreshing and I think underscores how the location, politics, and stakeholders often dictate the terms and approaches to community-driven change. Knowing also that this work takes time and the ability to tap into networks, how can academics be of service to this work? How may they use their access to institutions and resources to support community-based reproductive justice work?

Finger: Studies capturing the experiences of negative policymaking related to women's reproductive health is important. Publishing that information in peer-reviewed journals is also important, because it creates an exigency around the topic. But where so many academics fail is in the ability to translate that data into action.

This is not to criticize academics but to critique how many grant-funded research projects fail to support research-based policy initiatives. We need academics to encourage funders not to be afraid about supporting projects that are connected to policy. Otherwise, we will continue research to report findings about the correlation between experiences and policies, without any actual change.

KEY TAKEAWAYS

My conversation with Sara Finger reveals three takeaways for rhetoricians interested in grassroots advocacy and reproductive justice. The first relates to a feminist rhetorical practice: listening. Sara's interview speaks in many ways to Krista Ratcliffe's (1999) definition of rhetorical listening, which calls for *understanding* as *standing under* by "consciously standing under discourses that surround us and others" (p. 205) and listening not *for* intent but *with* intent, which allows us "to understand not just the claims, not just the cultural logics . . . but the rhetorical negotiations of understanding as well" (p. 205).

Doing so leads to the second takeaway: reflection. Considering—when listening with intent—how one's own positionality shapes the conversation. Remaining vigilantly aware of those who are talked about but not invited to the table. Reflection evokes critical listening, which in turn can lead to the third takeaway: advocacy as a relational practice.

Advocacy is a relational practice that asks us to listen to others so that we can support future next steps of action. As a relational practice, advocacy requires assembling together many stakeholders, sometimes with various or even competing motives. That said, grassroots activisms may not be measured by large-scale advocacy but rather through everyday interactions that build stronger coalitions leading to change.

PART 2

SITES OF
GRASSROOTS ACTIVISMS

CHAPTER 7

Resisting Extraction of the Sacred

Indigenous-Based Grassroots Resistance to Frontier Capitalism

LUHUI WHITEBEAR, KENLEA PEBBLES,
AND STEPHEN P. GASTEYER

Increased extractive activities and violation of the sacred connection between land, water, and people has heightened the need to honor and protect those who are on the frontlines of resistance to these violences. This chapter discusses localized projects while connecting them to global issues related to extractive capitalism, including the number of global murders of water and land activists by cartels, corporations, and governments and the expulsion of peoples from their homelands by government actors and nongovernmental interests. These examples show how frontier capitalism (Laungaramsri, 2012; Patel & Moore, 2017) is conducted by multiple players and resisted by multiple communities.

Using a comparative analysis, we discuss the underlying rationale for takings associated with extractive capitalism—the treatment of land and water as a resource to facilitate accumulation of financial assets and territory. Through stories of Indigenous resistance, we build on a growing literature that describes frontier capitalism as a process that threatens life itself (Bacon, 2019; Dunlap, 2020). Given that frontier capitalism is the continual expansion of extractive activity for capital gain, we agree that "an anticapitalist critique fundamentally entails a critique of the operation, discourse, and values of capitalism and of their naturalization through neoliberal ideology and corporate culture" (Mohanty, 2003, p. 9). By using an anticapitalist critique of frontier capitalism, we center local resistance to exploitation of lands, bodies, and waters. We then weave in stories of activists who have mobilized as water and land protectors in multiple contexts: recognized and unrecognized Indigenous communities, urban communities, and displaced peoples. We discuss not only the strategies and tactics employed but the use of ceremony to facilitate both local and international solidarity. By using ceremonies and community-building activities to bridge place and space, we explore how relationship, respect, reciprocity, and responsibility on the grassroots level in communities can push back on frontier capitalism.

All of the grassroots movements discussed display an adherence to the underlying pieces of the 4Rs (respect, reciprocity, relevance, and responsibility; https://4rsyouth.ca/), even if they do not use these exact terms in their resistance. Deviation from the 4Rs serves as a motivating factor in each of the activist responses discussed. *Respect* is necessary for the people, lands, and waters to be treated in ways that are not exploitive—literally and figuratively. *Reciprocity* is about relationships with all life and living in balance. Understanding that reciprocity builds upon respect in not taking more than needed is in direct opposition with the extractive exploitation discussed in this chapter. *Relevance* helps ground approaches to a reciprocal relationship in ways that are relevant in the local context. Each of the grassroots movements discussed follows different sets of protocols that are based in their local Indigenous contexts, epistemologies, and ontologies. Out of respect for the communities these protocols are used in, and in recognition of the continued exploitation of Indigenous ceremonies, the protocols are not discussed in depth in this chapter. *Responsibility* lies in the assurance that the relationships between people, lands, waters, and other beings continue in a balanced way, following respect, reciprocity, and relevance. Following the 4Rs serves as a healing point for the frontline communities impacted by frontier capitalism and the extractive exploitation it relies on. This healing and restoration of the 4Rs, guided by local Indigenous-based leadership, benefits all people and can be a connecting point of shared healing through solidarity with broader communities outside of Indigenous communities.

We rely on the 4Rs as a guide to bring these stories together (4rsyouth.ca, 2020; Cull, Hancock, McKeown, Pidgeon, & Vedan, 2018; Kirkness & Barnhardt, 2001; Pidgeon, Archibald, & Hawkey, 2014). Additionally, we discuss how breakage of the 4Rs carries on the lineage of violences through frontier capitalism. These attacks on bodies—of water, land, and humans—have resulted in international calls for solidarity through social media (Duarte, 2017; Gilio-Whitaker, 2019; Kino-nda-niimi Collective, 2014). The use of hashtags as a rhetorical tool of resistance allows frontline activists to call for external support as needed (Alexander, Jarratt, & Welch, 2018). While the violence continues beyond these moments of attention and social sharing, the resistance also continues, even if hidden from public awareness. The moving in and out of the public consciousness through social media brings people together in resistance on a global scale while simultaneously creating awareness about the necessity of holding cartels, corporations, and governments accountable for these violences (Duarte, 2017). As such, it is critical to support Indigenous communities, who are fighting day-in and day-out. Solidarity is needed to support the daily work of those on the frontlines of resistance to frontier capitalism.

SETTLER CAPITALISM, FRONTIER CAPITALISM, AND THE THREAT TO LAND, WATER, AND PEOPLE

The role of capitalism in settler colonialism is as a tool of colonization. While colonization exists in other empires (e.g., socialist, communist), capitalism is a primary tool to further colonization. Settler colonialism completely disrupts existing systems and relationships with lands and waters. It is through ongoing occupation that "settlers make Indigenous land their new home and source of capital," causing "the disruption of Indigenous relationships to land [that] represents a profound epistemic, ontological, cosmological violence" (Tuck & Yang, 2012, p. 5). This violence, as the following examples demonstrate, is felt daily by Indigenous people and is a threat to lands, water, and people. Settler capitalism and frontier capitalism, separate yet related tools, become a means to further this violence and assert settler control. Settler capitalism is used in established settler states (Dunlap, 2020), while frontier capitalism involves pushing to new frontiers to extract more wealth (Patel and Moore, 2017), both serving as direct means of breaking the 4Rs.

Settler capitalism is a system in which Indigenous lands, bodies, and waters are exploited for capital gain. Alexander Dunlap (2020) describes this capitalism as part of the "Genocide Machine"[1] (p. 1) that situates capitalism "as a structure of perpetual conquest" (p. 7). Capitalism constantly expands in search of new resources to exploit. Colonial settler states support capitalism through encroachments on the sovereign territories of Indigenous peoples.

---

1. Dunlap (2020) discusses Robert Davis and Mark Zannis's concept of "the Genocide Machine" as a "genocide-ecocide-nexus" in which "the post-liberal approach recognizes the evolving and generational processes of genocide/ecocide; the various (insidious) modalities of killing (e.g. social death, deprivation/starvation, assimilation/self-management); the economization of control and its productive and energy conscious technologies geared towards regimenting/harnessing life as opposed to direct extermination" (p. 4).

The settler state continually pushes Indigenous people to "frontiers," creating conflict as it treats them as less sovereign and conquerable, and views Indigenous lands and waters as capital assets. Laungaramsri (2012) asserts that the location of land and water capitalization is not a coincidence but rather a strategic choice in which existing land practices are viewed as backward to progress. When recognition of this tactic is coupled with Smith's (2012) argument that the tension created by the "denial of humanity" to Indigenous people by settler states "demonstrate[s] palpably the enormous lack of respect which has marked the relations of [I]ndigenous and non-[I]ndigenous peoples" (p. 125), we find that the strategic choice is also based in violence.

Frontier capitalism is a violent and continual cycle in which new spaces are sought for capital gain. Patel and Moore (2017) describe the capital gain as made possible by cheapening, which is "a strategy, a practice, a violence that mobilizes all kinds of work—human and animal, botanical and geological—with as little compensation as possible" (p. 22). It is through the severing of relationships and the resulting continual cycles that settler capitalism expands toward new, albeit increasingly limited, frontiers. Fields (2017) argues that the underlying justification for this continual violence is in a definition of land as valuable only when "enclosed" as property and with its resources extracted as market commodities (p. 1). This ideology fuels a strategy of enclosure for continuing settler colonial expansion onto Indigenous lands both in North America and Israel-Palestine (Fields, 2017).

Extractive technologies that use settler capitalism and frontier capitalism to exploit natural resources rely on the continuing disruption of relationships of Indigenous people with lands and waters. This disruption is made possible through erasure—both literally through acts of genocide and metaphorically through the settler imaginary.[2] Dunlap (2020) describes this combined process as lived erasure, asserting that, "in practice, lived erasure is experienced by never knowing who or what previously lived and flourished in environments where one lives, visits or passes through" (p. 2). Lived erasure makes exploitation of natural resources possible. The lack of understanding and honoring sacred connections to lands and waters by settler systems further serves to erase Indigenous connections. Even in environmental conservation efforts, adhering to settler ideologies and practices replicates this erasure (Bacon, 2019). As a result, Indigenous-led grassroots resistance to these systems is necessary in restoring the relationships that have been disrupted.

---

2. Lynch (2014) describes settler imaginaries as narratives of the attributes that conform to certain idealized depictions of place to encourage settler colonization in the American West. We use this term to describe narratives of valuation and justification of violence against Indigenous people, land, and water, as necessary for continued prosperity and security.

Canada's 4Rs Youth Movement describes the disconnect of both non-Indigenous people's and Indigenous peoples' relationships with lands and waters as "fractured" and as something Indigenous youth inherited from previous generations. Participants in the 4Rs Youth Movement rely on the 4Rs (respect, reciprocity, relevance, and responsibility) as a framework to restore these relationships as well as to serve as a reminder that we are on Indigenous lands. As with the other movements discussed in this chapter, the 4Rs Youth Movement recognizes that disrupted relationships must be restored. The 4Rs provide an interconnected, adaptable framework that works across communities, one that is grounded in Indigenous systems and practices necessary in restoring the connections between communities, lands, and waters. The 4Rs Youth Movement reminds us that while there is no magic formula and that adaptability is needed to meet the needs of each community, the 4Rs help provide necessary components that can create action for change through grassroots resistance.

SCHEMATIC FOR GRASSROOTS RESISTANCE

Grassroots resistance relies on organic mobilization of communities based on firsthand experiences with injustice. This chapter weaves together analyses of grassroots resistance, drawn from the personal experience of the authors, with the understandings of the systems of oppression that threaten land, water, and people. As outlined previously, these perpetual systems have created unsustainable relationships between lands, waters, and peoples, ignoring finite limitations of extraction. Grassroots resistance seeks to interrupt these systems as a localized effort, oftentimes with nonlocal support and solidarity.

Globally, land and water defenders are often targets of violence and criminalization. To understand the depth of this targeting, Global Witness (2020) released the only publicly compiled global report with known murders of land and water defenders. The report states that in 2018 alone, more than three murders occurred each week—167 for the year. The largest sector in which these killings occurred was mining resistance, with 43 deaths. Additionally, Global Witness noted that water conflicts were a rising sector. Media silence plays a role around these murders, in the lived erasure discussed previously while also supporting settler and frontier capitalism—a reflection of the media's own systemic connections and contributions in perpetuating settler control. The combination of the use of frontiers to stay out of the public eye through media and the use of media to report these violences as isolated events further serves to fracture the relationships between settler exploitation and the violence it brings. Therefore, local, grassroots organizers must rely on their own messaging and rhetorical devices to get the word out about what is happening, both in relation to the murders and what is being resisted and, in that sense, caused their deaths.

As we outline in the remainder of this chapter, grassroots resistance comes in many forms and looks different depending on the needs of the local communities. Alexander, Jarratt, and Welch (2018) assert that activism and protest are "a complex mix of bodies, technologies, discourses, and even histories that need to be considered collectively so as to guide a new understanding of contemporary rhetorical interventions within and across numerous spaces" (p. 4). We bring in social media, popular press, hashtags, imagery, anonymous presence, and direct storytelling as part of grassroots resistance rhetorical devices. Oftentimes, movements are compared with each other in effectiveness and in their approaches. For the purposes of this chapter, grassroots approaches are examined comparatively, but in a manner that discusses the rhetorical methods and devices that address the same systems of oppression: settler and frontier capitalisms.

Each grassroots activist response discusses localized projects of extractive capitalism as well as the rhetorical devices used to resist these projects. Our goal is not to tell the story of these resistance movements in their entirety but to focus on the extractive capitalist projects, the local responses, and the solidarity that was developed by their rhetorical choices. We chose to focus on Indigenous responses to extractive capitalism, as they are the frontline communities impacted the most, with sacred lands and waters at stake.

GRASSROOTS RESPONSE TO EXTRACTIVE CAPITALISM

In North America, Indigenous communities have faced colonial intrusion to lands and waters for over 500 years. While the impact has been felt longer in some areas than others, the continual occupation of North America has relied on settler determinations of appropriate land and water management that deviate from the 4Rs. The breakage of the 4Rs is the underlying cause of conflict between settler colonial actions and Indigenous resistance to these actions as related to lands and waters. Colonialist land and water *management* approaches contrast with Indigenous-based land and water *relationships*. The effects can best be described by Dina Gilio-Whitaker's version of environmental deprivation. Gilio-Whitaker (2019) asserts that environmental deprivation "refers to actions by settlers and settler governments that are designed to block

Native peoples' access to life-giving and culture-affirming resources" (p. 39). This historic process of breaking all 4Rs is relived in current times, most notably through extractive capitalism and the threat to water—the source of all life.

Indigenous Resistance to Pipelines—NoDAPL

In the United States alone (a country that is about 2,800 miles from coast to coast), there are at least 2.4 million miles of extractive pipelines running through the earth and across waterways, more than anywhere in the world (Gilio-Whitaker, 2019). These pipelines are not well regulated and routinely leak into waterways. In 2016, one of the largest Indigenous occupations in recent history took place in resistance to the Dakota Access Pipeline. Much like the Idle No More Movement that emerged out of Canada, what became known as the NoDAPL (No Dakota Access Pipeline) called attention to environmental injustice toward Indigenous communities and treaty rights with Tribal nations. Both movements relied on a combination of grassroots activism and social media use through Indigenous-based journalism and the use of hashtags (Gilio-Whitaker, 2019; Kino-nda-niimi Collective, 2014).

The NoDAPL movement centered on local leadership from Standing Rock women and youth. At the heart of the matter was protection of the water source to the Standing Rock community and of the Missouri River more generally, as well as adherence to the Treaty of Fort Laramie (Gilio-Whitaker, 2019). While the City of Bismarck was used as a reason to move the location of the pipeline to avoid threatening the drinking water source of this predominantly white city, from the early stages of conversations, the Standing Rock Sioux Tribe was not afforded the same consideration, despite opposition to the pipeline crossing their lands and waters. The two most common hashtags associated with the efforts are #NoDAPL and #WaterIsLife. Other hashtags were used, but these two in particular allowed activists and allies to connect quickly via social media and develop an international movement in resistance to the extractive pipeline. The hashtags allowed for quick updates through social media. They trended across social media platforms during the fall of 2016 especially. Through livestreams of frontline resistance, ceremonies, arrival of allies (Indigenous and non-Indigenous), attacks on water protectors, and more, the hashtags were circulated on social media by individuals, environmental organizations, Indigenous-based media, and celebrities. Others shared these livestreams quickly with their networks, as they were occurring and afterward. Additionally, imagery through photos and activist art became widespread through the use of these hashtags. For example, in addition to photos of frontline resistance and people physically tied to extraction machines with tape using sacred colors, art that included Indigenous people fighting black snakes or black snakes being cut into pieces was among the most shared. The black snake imagery symbolized the Lakota Black Snake prophecy, in which a black snake would come to destroy the world and the peoples on it (Gilio-Whitaker, 2019, p. 1). The resistance to the black snake through NoDAPL activist art reflected a resistance to both the pipeline itself and the destruction the black snake carries in the Lakota prophecy, an embodiment of all of the 4Rs but most notably relevance and responsibility. While it is impossible to describe the entirety of the NoDAPL movement in this chapter, the impact of the movement continues to be felt.

Despite past-president Trump giving the final approval for the pipeline to be completed, as one of his first executive orders in 2017, the resistance continues. This sense of continued responsibility to protect the water and people who rely on it was further fueled when the pipeline leaked into the Missouri River as predicted. The continued efforts of grassroots activists beyond the several thousand who occupied the unceded treaty territory has led to litigation in favor of the Standing Rock Sioux Tribe. In June 2020, the pipeline was ordered to be shut down until it could be shown that the environmental impacts on the Missouri and potential harm to the Standing Rock people were not present. As of the writing of this chapter, the ongoing legal battle through the appeals process is expected to last several more years.

Resistance to Water Privatization—México

While corporate interests in the United States often control much of what happens in terms of threats to water sources, this reach is not limited to geopolitical borders, nor is it limited to corporate entities. In México, the negotiations of water access and rights is political. Treaties from 1906 and 1944 between the United States and México determine how water from the Rio Grande River along the geopolitical border is distributed between the two settler countries (Feleb-Brown, 2020). The tension between settler nations, local communities, and organized crime for access to water is significant. With little regard for the local farmers and Indigenous communities, the negotiations between the United States and Mexican governments relies on the sharing of water rations, in which debts in the form of water as currency are paid by both countries. This capitalization of water leaves local farmers to rely on organized crime in order to access stolen water, as the needs of corporate agriculture businesses are prioritized with what is left to ration out in México. Additionally, the control of lands and waters for the cartel-controlled avocado trade creates further threats to local communities' access to water.

In the fall of 2020, local activists and farmers took over La Boquilla Dam in Chihuahua over water debts to the United States ("Mexican farmers," 2020). Utilizing a public demonstration by physically blocking access to the dam with their bodies allowed the people to draw attention to the water crisis beyond their local communities, but it did come at a cost. One woman, although she participated in an unarmed, peaceful protest, was killed by the Mexican National Guard, her name likely added to the growing list compiled by Global Witness. Taylor (2003) discusses public demonstration as part of performing a public record. Further, she explains that "the transmission of traumatic memory from victim to witness involves the shared and participatory act of telling and listening associated with live performance" (Taylor, 2003, p. 167). Much like the livestreaming that happened at Standing Rock during the NoDAPL movement, the news coverage of the dam takeover helps the viewer transmit the traumatic memory, along with what the resistance is about, to others—in adherence with the R of responsibility in protecting the water. The transmissions of these memories through recordings may have been different than with the NoDAPL movement, but the result is the same. The arrests, pepper-spraying, and death are part of what people remember about the movements, a representation of how violent the breaking of the 4Rs can be. It is vital that those following these stories do not separate themselves from the issues being faced but rather remember they are now connected to the story with a *responsibility* to help carry the stories forward for change.

The tensions over water due to its privatization in México and the strain on access to this vital resource for all people are not only reflected in this most recent takeover but also in earlier grassroots resistance to water privatization and in advocacy for better water infrastructure. In 2010, the Yaqui water crisis was brought to social media via YouTube when a group of Yaqui young men posted themselves being beaten by Mexican military (Duarte, 2017). Duarte (2017) further explains how safe water is largely inaccessible for the Yaqui people because of the impacts of dams on Río Yaqui, industrial waste contaminants from corporations such as Nestlé, and private land development. The 2010 beating resulted in the use of further rhetorical devices such as #JusticiaYaquis and flash mobs modeled after the Idle No More movement. Duarte (2017) points out the "distinction that the Rio Yaqui Activists asked long-haul truckers and tractor drivers to park their vehicles as blockage posts, rather than using human chains and prayer rallies" (p. 7). Given the heightened threats of physical violences against Indigenous water activists in México, this decision highlights the adherence to the Rs of relationship, respect, and responsibility to both water and people. The reciprocity of the truckers and tractor drivers is reflected in their decision to offer protection to the bodies of people protecting water they also rely on.

Theft of water continued, from the Río Yaqui and in other areas of México as well. For example, in 2014, it was reported that 40 percent of water supplied in Ciudad de México alone was sold illegally one year after national privatization (Páramo, 2014). The lack of adequate water infrastructure to homes in the cities and villages created even more water scarcity. The continual cycle of water theft not only interrupted the 4Rs, it also threatened people's ability to live in some areas, resulting in a type of forced migration. Resistance and standing up against extractive capitalism is a necessary part of continuing to exist connected to ancestral lands, as seen with the Río Yaqui water activists. Adhering to the 4Rs framework through Indigenous resistance does not come without cost, particularly in México and Central America.

Water activists who speak up are targeted and issued arrest warrants (Duarte, 2017; Pearson, 2017) a reflection of oppressive settler colonial tactics. These types of threats make it harder to utilize some of the tactics seen in the NoDAPL movement, such as livestreaming from personal social media accounts and publicly recognizing identities in the media and on social media, because they put activists at risk of being identified. However, water activists' ability to network behind the scenes and use the popular press anonymously allows them to gain further support outside of their immediate communities. The Ejército Zapatista de Liberación Nacional (EZLN), described as the Zapatistas, are widely known as a resistance group that used both anonymity and digital tactics as a rhetorical device to help spread their messages about neoliberal and corporate threats to Indigenous lands, waters, and peoples in México (Duarte, 2017). The Zapatista reliance on digital tactics continues to present times and has moved across various platforms and digital means as media becomes more accessible online. They served, and serve, as inspiration for additional forms of resistance using similar tactics, as seen with the water activists described in this chapter. Despite threats from governments, cartels, and corporate entities, water activists continue to work on behalf of their communities and the earth. There may not always be a single person to cite or to use as an example, but their work remains a powerful force even as they make the rhetorical choice of anonymity.

Resistance to Mining—Menominee Nation

The Menominee Indian Tribe of Wisconsin is a nation that sits on the border of Michigan's Upper Peninsula and Wisconsin and encompasses the Menominee

River. At one time, the Menominee resided on over 10 million acres of land, but congressional termination of federal recognition of the Menominee Tribe of Wisconsin in 1954 resulted in a major loss of their remaining land. Months later, in 1955, the duration of mineral and grazing leases was extended by the Indian Long-Term Leasing Act, enabling agriculture, mining, and lumber companies to buy the land they wanted. These purchases meant that when the Menominee were reinstated by the federal government in 1973, the nation no longer had access or ownership over these lands, leaving the Menominee with 2.5 percent of the land they had occupied.

Many Indigenous nations face a lack of federal recognition, and if national status goes unacknowledged (despite it being recognized in earlier national treaties), respect and the acknowledgment of relationship is missing. Only with the reinstated federal recognition of the Menominee Indian Tribe of Wisconsin could respect and relationships start to be rebuilt. Reinstatement was the beginning of reestablishing respect and relationship, but responsibility and reciprocity are left unaddressed thus far. Since the 4Rs are interdependent upon each other for functionality, there is much work to be done.

Federal and state government interactions with the Menominee Indian Tribe of Wisconsin and the permits being granted to the corporate conglomerate owners of the Back Forty Mine act as a reminder of the violations that occurred during the Indigenous nation's termination. Aquila Resources Inc. is a conglomerate that wants to renew the mining on and near the land that was previously leased through the Indian Long-Term Leasing Act. However, in order to do so, Aquila needs permission from the State of Michigan (as an actor for the federal government). Yet, while Aquila seeks this permission to create the Back Forty Mine, the community remembers who the land belongs to and still lives with the long-term environmental effects of previous mining excursions. As a result, activists continue to explore effective strategies that have been used by a network of activists in similar communities and challenges.

The actions of Aquila are an extension of the extractive frontier capitalism that has affected the Menominee nation. The rhetorical choices the Menominee have made and continue to make are numerous. One strategy used by activists is to disseminate direct and simplified reasoning for their opposition to the mine to a community that has suffered toxic runoff and water quality issues due to previous mining activity. These simplified informational documents explain the rhetorically vague, jargon-laden public reports buried under multiple web links by Aquila.

Aquila's planned open-pit mine would process gold, zinc, copper, silver, and other minerals at a site that is only 150 feet from the banks of the Menominee River in Lake Township, Michigan. As rivers in this area freeze in the winter and often flood in the spring (and on occasion in the summer or fall), it is not a matter of if the toxic chemicals will enter the river, but when.

The dissemination of this information on the No Back 40 Mine website (noback40.com), which is linked to the Menominee Indian Tribe of Wisconsin home page and includes the tribal seal, allowed the information to be easily understood by local activists and helped build a strong network of organizations that were part of the Native American and the non-Native communities. The information posted on the No Back 40 Mine website has an easy-to-follow outline of the data—presented in an accessible arrangement that includes visuals showing clear comparative structures of the depth, width, and placement of the mine.

The No Back 40 Mine website uses specific rhetorical strategies that put the measurements of the open-pit mine into distinctly American frames: "The open pit portion of the proposed mine would measure over 750 feet deep and approximately 2,000 feet wide. That's 2.5 Statue of Liberties deep and the width of over 5.5 football fields—end zone to end zone." By putting the measurements into this comparative structure, the activists did a few things: made the measurements culturally accessible for their audiences, aligned themselves with American culture and identity, and expressed these ideas in concrete terms serving as touchstones that unite them with their audience. This is just one example of the multilayered rhetorical structures activists used in their materials, community outreach, letter-writing campaigns, and attendance at state-run public hearings and community meetings. This clear messaging was effective and was used to expand the activist network to include local, national, and international organizations such as EcoWatch, the Sierra Club, and American Rivers (many of these organizations used the internet and community outreach to convey this information to their own audiences).

Additional rhetorical structures centered around culture and ceremony can be seen on the website as well as in the social media and networking connections of the activist movements. The No Back 40 movement website discusses the importance of the Menominee River and its ecosystem, and the "Culture" section tells the sacred Menominee creation story. This provides a way for nontribal members to gain insight into why and how the local land and water are sacred and encourages support from empathetic audiences interested in building allyship and solidarity. Broader community inclusion in ceremony—such as sharing some of the Menominee stories in open, inclusive activist meetings (which two of these authors have attended) and the water walks (as both ceremony, practice, and a rhetorical tool to increase awareness of the movement)—means that clear explanation of the cultural significance of this practice and ceremony is necessary. This expanded inclusion also allows for more interconnection, and the cultural significance of shared experiences of the sacred—even if from differing perspectives—is conveyed to build the activist base.

Even while facing traditional protest methods, the mine sought permits from the Michigan Department of Environmental Quality (MDEQ; now known as Michigan Department of Environment, Great Lakes, and Energy) to enact the extraction next to the Menominee River. Despite the clear internal protests of engineers within the MDEQ (Matheny, 2019a), these permits were granted, with the final permit being granted in an off-the-record meeting (Matheny, 2019b). Aquila Resources pursued—and was granted—governmental approval for the mine. However, this was not the end of this ongoing case.

On January 16, 2020, the Menominee Indian Tribe of Wisconsin passed a resolution that recognized the inherent rights of the Menominee River (often referred to as the Rights of Nature). The Tribe acknowledged the right of the river to exist and flourish; this includes the connected and recharging water systems (both groundwater and surface water), the right for the river's ecosystem to function without interruption, and the right for the river's water to be "abundant, pure, and unpolluted"—all the way to Lake Michigan (Menominee Tribal Legislature, 2020). Likewise, the Menominee Indian Tribe of Wisconsin filed a case against the EPA in 2020 with Earthjustice representing them in court (Clancy & Pierson, 2020). The rhetorical strategies used in this judicial resolution and to build the as-yet-undecided case have grown and expanded the rhetoric of the activist movement. The Rights of Nature is a rhetorical and judicial tool that is building and growing not just on a national scale but on a global one—giving more rights to the lands we live on and recognizing that our relationship to it must be built on respect, reciprocity, and responsibility. It builds on the cultural sovereignty of Indigenous peoples and uses the respect, relevance, and reciprocal relationships that this activist movement expanded and sustained through the unification of activists and interests. As this case goes to court, we are searching for acknowledgment that all our relations have rights and that we must respect them to have a healthy relationship with our environment.

Resistance to Land Colonization—Jordan Valley, Palestine

The settler colonial "genocide machine" is not limited to attacks on Indigenous communities in North America. Settler colonialism is an international phenomenon (Veracini, 2015). The "genocide machine" (Dunlap, 2020) and its associated "eco social violence" (Bacon, 2019) against Indigenous communities

is evident in multiple places globally. We now turn to the struggle of Palestinians against the expansion of Israeli settler colonial expansion into the Jordan
Valley. The Jordan Valley is an elongated depression that runs along the Jordan River and Dead Sea from the Sea of Galilee (Lake Tiberias) to the Gulf
of Aqaba in Israel, the occupied Palestinian West Bank, and Jordan. We deal
here with the portion of the Jordan Valley in the West Bank. While the valley
is low, hot, and dry, it is also the drainage basin for significant groundwater
and surface water, with multiple springs and water sources that make the area
a valuable site for agricultural production—especially for crops such as coun-
terseasonal vegetables and fruits but also for valuable oasis crops such as dates
(Al-Haq, 2013; Trottier, Leblond, & Garb, 2020).

The potential economic value mentioned above, combined with religious
symbolism and strategic value, has long made the Jordan Valley a target of
Israeli territorial expansion. It is, after all, not only the site of the historic city
of Jericho, located on the banks of the Jordan River and the famous Dead Sea,
but it also has strategic value on the border with the Hashemite Kingdom of
Jordan. Soon after Israel occupied the West Bank in 1967, it implemented the
Allon Plan,[3] which placed state-sponsored "settlements" that were rational-
ized as a civilian frontline outpost. The numbers of Israeli Jewish settlements
and settlers have grown since 1967—but more importantly, the Palestinian
population has decreased due to efforts to expel Palestinians (Al-Haq, 2018).
The 1995 Oslo II Accord divided the West Bank into jurisdictions: Area A (full
Palestinian Authority control, 18%), Area B (Israeli security control, Palestinian control over service delivery, 21%), and Area C (full Israeli control, 60% of
the West Bank). Ninety percent of the Jordan Valley is designated as Area C.
There are currently a little more than 65,000 Palestinians in the Jordan Valley
and roughly 11,000 settlers.

Increased efforts since 2006 to eliminate some 50 Palestinian communities in the Jordan Valley have broken the principles of respect and reciprocity (B'Tselem, 2017). Most inhabitants of these communities are Palestinian
Bedouins who settled in the Jordan Valley when their transhumance route
was cut off following the establishment of the Israeli state in 1948 and the
occupation of the West Bank by Israel in 1967. Israel has never recognized the
title to Bedouin village land holdings (Heneiti, 2018). Rather than respecting
the efforts of Bedouin communities in the Jordan Valley to maintain their
way of life and their tie to a small portion of the land that they have long
utilized seasonally, the state of Israel has progressively moved to expel the

---

3. The Allon Plan is well known as one of the types of Israeli colonial settlement in the
occupied Palestinian West Bank—others being more ideological. For two discussions of the
plan, see Elmusa (1996) and Newman (1984).

Bedouin people, claiming that lack of legal title to the land justifies expulsion. Israeli, Palestinian, and international jurists note that this is a violation of international law, as Israel, the military occupier of the Jordan Valley, has a responsibility to ensure the well-being of the population under occupation. Instead, Israel acts to destabilize and displace people and simultaneously to settle Israeli civilians—whose colonial settlements use up all available water sources—in the area (Al-Haq, 2013; B'Tselem, 2017). This also breaks the principle of reciprocity—the Israeli military and civilian settler movements aim to take and transform but not to reciprocate benefits to displaced Bedouins or indeed to the ecological system to which the Bedouin claim a millennial bond.

The Netanyahu government most recently, during the Israeli election in 2019 and again through 2020, declared intentions to annex the Jordan Valley, with the open support of the United States under the Trump administration, although the government had to walk back those declarations due to international pressure. This has not stopped actions to seize territory—including, significantly, land in proximity to springs and other water sources. Palestinian and international monitoring organizations documented increasingly aggressive land confiscation and expulsion of Palestinian inhabitants from confiscated land in the second half of 2020 (Jordan Valley Solidarity, 2020; WAFA News Agency, 2020).

Two Palestinian organizations—Jordan Valley Solidarity (JVS) and Good Shepherd Collective—are examples of mobilized resistance. They have livestreamed, primarily on Facebook, resistance to expulsion from land and demolitions—including protests, which involved women who marched with songs proclaiming their attachment to the land and confrontation with the military. In one recent case, they filmed the events surrounding the shooting of a resident (Harun Abu Aram) who tried to protect his family's electricity generator after their home and animal shelter were destroyed. They also livestreamed follow-up demonstrations at the site of the attack and outside the military court complex.

They have also organized demonstrations of attachment to the land and other forms of steadfastness. For instance, Good Shepherd Collective organized solidarity efforts around tree planting to demonstrate the attachment to the land (Good Shepherd Collective, 2020)—demonstrating respect, relevance, and the principle of reciprocity to the land. JVS organized volunteers to provide extra labor to support local Palestinian farmers so they could maintain production on the land—protecting their land from a declaration of abandonment and from designation as state land. Under the Ottoman-era land law that has been adopted by the Israeli authorities in the West Bank, Israel can occupy and settle abandoned land (Jordan Valley Solidarity, 2020). The effort demonstrated the principle of respect for the labor engaged in maintaining land title through production on the soil as well as the principle of reciprocity, as volunteer labor was rewarded (as is traditional in Arab culture) with a meal shared. The strategy has also involved explicitly reaching out to allies (both in Palestine and internationally) to assist financially and as participants in demonstrations and actions—including calls to help residents rebuild demolished structures and to assist in protests of demolition orders and actions (Soliman, 2022). The calls for support, and the response, are examples of recognition and relevance—the importance of the work of many to protect the tie of the Palestinian people to the land—but also a reconciliation between the people of national governments such as the United States and Canada that have long supported Israel's attempts at expulsion and shielded the government from international criticism, and the Palestinians of the Jordan Valley.

THE 4Rs AS A FRAMEWORK FOR GLOBAL GRASSROOTS RESISTANCE

The core of the grassroots activist responses discussed in this chapter is based on ancestral connections to lands and waters coupled with the ancestral teachings of their specific communities. These cultural and community understandings of how to live in balance with the earth is amplified through the use of rhetorical devices that make sense in the context of their relationships with the settler state. These strategic rhetorical choices are part of their activism in communication with broader communities, oftentimes on a global scale, to help subvert settler systems and constructs.

In the NoDAPL, México water rights, and Jordan Valley movements, social media is key in helping raise awareness of these ongoing struggles. Duarte (2017) explains that

> Indigenous uses of social media support visibility of Indigenous social movements and issues, promote solidarity for particular struggles and views, foment Freirian processes of consciousness-raising, and enforce the government-to-government trust underlying peace agreements and treaties. Indigenous uses of social media also intentionally disrupt and destabilise participatory processes of oppressive governments. (p. 10)

The Menominee Nation's resistance to mining relied less on social media and hashtags, but disruption of oppressive government processes was present. As with the NoDAPL movement, the Menominee use of US federal legal infrastructure was a core component of their resistance to extractive exploitation. Additionally, in the Jordan Valley and México, we see resistance to the extractive exploitation grounded in restoring connections to lands despite settler disregard for those ancestral connections.

The grassroots movements discussed in this chapter are part of a much more extensive global struggle to protect the sacred and, in many cases, life itself. The rhetorical choices discussed here are examples of similar choices being made in other activist movements that reflect the 4Rs in their approaches. The responses are all connected to a larger resistance to frontier capitalism and exploitation. By understanding the power of their rhetorical methods and the connections to the 4Rs in their choices, we can follow this framework in following the global relationships in protecting lands, bodies, and waters. The sharing of resources and information based on cultural protocols can help "provide a more sustained critique of the practices of states and corporations" (Smith, 2012, p. 109). The path forward can be strengthened by incorporating the 4Rs and cultural protocols that come with this framework.

WHERE DO WE GO FROM HERE?

It is impossible to discuss in depth in a single chapter the power of these grassroots movements as a collective, global story of resistance. It is our intention to understand the rhetorical choices made by a few local activist responses to frontier capitalism and to provide a framework of resistance that is based on the 4Rs. Further discussion in the future will help create even more connections between Indigenous resistance movements globally.

The violence connected to frontier capitalism continues to rely on the exploitation of the sacred. The 4Rs can continue to serve as a reflection of decolonial efforts to intervene in the violence enacted by the settler state. Since decolonization relies on the return of lands, and relationships with those lands under the guidance of Indigenous ways of knowing, the 4Rs remain a strong component of decolonization. The impacts of frontier capitalism are not going away soon, and neither is resistance to its exploitation. As we move forward on a global scale, we can continue to rely on local Indigenous leadership for guidance in understanding how to heal the negative impacts of frontier capitalism as well as understand what resistance can look like.

CHAPTER 8

Community Gardening, Food Insecurity, and Writing Pedagogy

Connecting Classroom, Campus, and City

VANI KANNAN AND
LEAH LILLANNA JOHNNEY

FOOD INSECURITY AND WRITING PEDAGOGY

In fall 2019, Vani taught a class titled "Writing and Social Issues" and assigned the CUNY Food Insecurity Report, which indicated that as many as one in five CUNY students have experienced food insecurity (Healthy CUNY, 2019, p. 1). Food insecurity—along with housing insecurity—dramatically impacts college students' well-being and academic success, particularly students of color (Adamovic, Newton, & House, 2020; Campaign for a Healthy CUNY, 2011). However, an overwhelming majority of CUNY students were unaware of campus resources like food pantries[1] or preferred fresh foods to the canned and boxed foods stocked in the pantries (Healthy CUNY, 2019, pp. 1–3). As a complement to reading the report, Vani took the class on a field trip to the Lehman College campus gardens and facilitated a writing exercise that asked students to think about their relationships with food and land. Like the whole campus, the gardens are on unceded Lenni-Lenape territory, which shapes our relationship to the land and demands a critical historical understanding of it.

---

1. For example, in our survey, students identified family, SNAP (Supplemental Nutrition Assistance Program), and churches as possible sites to address food insecurity. Only one individual mentioned the campus Student Life building, where the campus food pantry is located. Respondents noted that more information on food resources is needed on campus.

In the discussion that followed the writing exercise, many students reflected on family members' gardens, particularly in the Caribbean, and commiserated about the lack of access to green space in the Bronx. For example, Leah wrote about gardening at a young age with her Caribbean family. The class picked carrots, tomatoes, mint, and peppers, and sampled fresh carrot-ginger-coconut soup made with garden vegetables in the campus's industrial kitchens. The following class, students shared photos of the homemade salsa and stir-fry they made with the produce they picked. The trip to the gardens taught us that working to address food insecurity can be a positive community-building event that gives us a sense of autonomy over our food.

The formation of the Gardening Club was part of a larger network of interconnected struggles across the City University of New York (CUNY) system to address food insecurity. Students at Hunter College were pushing the CUNY administration to open a food pantry, while the administration instead installed a Starbucks at the proposed location (Klein, 2020). Kingsborough Community College activists were fighting to preserve its urban farm, which produced thousands of pounds of produce each year to feed students and the community (Save KCC Urban Farm, 2020). An activist coalition of students, faculty, and staff across the 25 CUNY campuses, called FreeCUNY!, was part of a citywide struggle to protest transit fare hikes, policing in schools and subways, food insecurity, and gentrification. Around the same time, local green spaces, including the New York Botanical Garden, were partnering with developers to take part in redevelopment and rezoning plans (Cruz, 2020); local activists feared this would exacerbate gentrification, policing, and food insecurity in the area.

With COVID-19 came additional food shortages, exacerbated by the long history of redlining and other forms of deep-rooted structural racism and economic inequity. In addition, essential workers were getting sick from a lack of safety protocols. The links among food, redlining, and worker safety came into the national spotlight when workers at the Bronx's Hunts Point produce market, the largest produce-distribution center in the world, went on strike. Local food justice organizations like Woke Foods were cooking and distributing free meals "that highlight natural, organic foods that are plant-based, culturally relevant, and familiar to our communities through Afro-Caribbean recipes and flavor" (Woke Foods, 2020). Mutual aid networks formed to distribute food from central locations and to provide door-to-door deliveries to those who could not leave their apartments.

This context sheds light on the need to address student food insecurity in tandem with larger structural injustices. On Lehman's campus, there was (and remains) a need for both student engagement around food insecurity and access to fresh high-quality foods. The formation of the Lehman Gardening Club demonstrates the possibilities for linking writing pedagogy with students' food literacies and the food needs of our local communities.

THE JOURNEY TO THE GARDENING CLUB

Leah grew up in the Virgin Islands (VI), where food was not as accessible to all, but the community worked together to make sure everyone was fed. As a high school student, she worked with the Student Government Association (SGA) to propose a school community garden to grow produce for the school kitchen and engage students. After volunteering in the VI delivering food to unhoused people, Leah's passion for community work grew, and she learned the importance of food in sustaining relationships and well-being. When she moved to New York City, she began volunteering at soup kitchens and learned the term "food insecurity." Her interest in the community-building impact of food and gardening work deepened in her Writing and Social Issues class in a discussion about community control, which the Movement 4 Black Lives (2022) policy platform defines as "a world where those most impacted in our communities control the laws, institutions, and policies that are meant to serve us—from our schools to our local budgets, economies, police departments, and our land—while recognizing that the rights and histories of our Indigenous family must also be respected" (para. 1). Leah decided to dedicate her class project to forming the Gardening Club and pushing the Lehman administration to expand the campus gardens out of a desire to increase the control the student community had over the issues directly affecting them, including food.

Leah learned that the Lehman College gardens (one of which is shown in figure 8.1) were student-run and had initially been born out of a collaboration between the Health Sciences and Adult Literacy programs to help adult language-learners learn English literacy and numeracy skills (National Literacy Directory, 2022). She learned that this community-building impact of gardens is substantiated by research showing that community gardening not only reduces food insecurity but also strengthens relationships (Carney, Hamada, Rdesinski, Sprager, Nichols, Liu, Pelayo, Sanchez, & Shannon, 2012). Based on her research, she created an infographic arguing that the library should create a green roof to expand the campus gardens, emailed campus officials to share her research and advocate for expanded gardens, and attended committee meetings to push for expanded campus gardens. Through these efforts, it became clear that it would take the collective effort of students to make real change.

FIGURE 8.1. Serrano pepper garden on Lehman campus
after cleanup. Photo courtesy of Leah Johnney.

Leah approached several students about starting the Gardening Club. Together, they imagined a space where students would learn to grow their own foods, cook them together, and donate produce to the campus food pantry, which in return would offer students healthier eating options. Club members cited a range of reasons for getting involved, including a love of gardening, a desire to grow things with a community, and an interest in showing "how calming gardening is." One student made ties to family: "Most women in my family garden and my grandfather on my father's side has a farm that he used . . . to grow things like potatoes and garlic." Students who joined the club had experience growing a range of fruits, vegetables, and flowers; they expressed an interest in expanding the gardens to grow a diversity of food sources including carrots, corn, quinoa, and legumes.

The club kicked off with a fall garlic-planting event (since garlic would survive the winter) and cleanup events focused on the white-picket-fenced garden and the small hot pepper garden. As students cleaned up the gardens and planted garlic, they learned about gardening from those who had taken care of the garden previously, and they were able to pick leftover vegetables to take home. At the end of the cleanups, they donated several bags of organic waste to the campus composting station.

Students in the club drew strong connections between this on-campus work and the food insecurity and environmental justice issues that activists were working to address across New York City. One biology and environmental science major noted that they "learned to test soils and what are nutrients that crops need in order to grow and produce a yield of goods." This skill set is crucial for community gardening efforts when soil may be polluted with lead and other industrial wastes. Several students noted that food insecurity and lack of access to fresh foods exacerbate the health problems associated with environmental racism. To end food insecurity, students proposed a range of interventions, from planting small gardens in apartment kitchens and "more active efforts to disseminate information about food banks" to increased access to food through "planting fruit trees in parks and other public spaces." Students also expressed a desire for affordable farmers markets carrying produce from local gardeners. These survey responses indicate the multiple scales along which food insecurity must be addressed and illustrate the food system literacies the Gardening Club has begun to foster.

FOSTERING FOOD LITERACIES THROUGH
WRITING PEDAGOGY AND CAMPUS WORK

Throughout their journey to form the Gardening Club, Leah and the other members learned more about structural food insecurity and the community benefits of gardening. As we wait to return to campus in the context of COVID-19, the Gardening Club has supported local work on food insecurity and green spaces, including the North Bronx Collective's mutual aid work, weekly food distributions, and soil remediation work at a location called Tibbett's Tail near campus (North Bronx Collective, 2020). For example, students helped make small kitchen-windowsill herb planters out of soy milk cartons at a community cleanup and political education event held by the North Bronx Collective. While the club's on-campus work was temporarily stalled by COVID-19, its work suggests that community gardening has the potential to support student engagement in writing courses by forging connections with students' food literacies and modeling concrete campus- and community-based work. Community gardening also emerges as a concrete site of convergence for classroom, campus, and city social justice work.

CHAPTER 9

The Energy of Place in
Florida Springs Activism

MADISON JONES

Florida is a state of water. Surrounded on three sides by coastline, its numerous beaches are an iconic vacation destination. Florida's karst landscape of springs and sinkholes connects distant places across the state. Beneath the ground, the state sits atop the vast Floridan aquifer, a hydrological network that spans the entire state as well as parts of Alabama, Georgia, Mississippi, and South Carolina. Such a large body of water links numerous jurisdictions, and as such, protecting the watershed requires a confluence of local action across city and state lines. While bringing communities together is a difficult task, made more so in today's fractured political climate, Florida's iconic bodies of water have become a focal point through which environmental organizations make environmental degradation visible and actionable for local communities across state and political lines. For many Floridians, the crystal-clear freshwater springs are important sites of connection with the natural world, through what Kenneth Burke (1969) terms "identification," describing the ways that individuals and groups form relations in the act of persuasion. In the summer heat, local residents flock to the springs, which flow out from the aquifer's depths at a steady average of 72°F.

Yet, as I elaborate on below, the springs are under threat from a host of interwoven environmental problems, from groundwater overpumping to saltwater intrusion to nitrate pollution. Such large-scale environmental problems are so vast that they are often difficult to meaningfully frame at the local level

(M. Jones, 2019). While environmentalist groups across the world work in various ways to document environmental destruction, these projects do not always translate to action at the local level. Furthermore, as the editors discuss in the introduction to this collection, such local and grassroots activism is a less common site for analysis and scholarship. As places of community value that are visibly changing as a direct result of these problems, the Florida springs provide a powerful location for activists to connect large-scale problems to local action and for environmental communicators to learn from their activism. By harnessing the fluid nature of the springs through visual messaging and digital media, advocacy organizations and grassroots activists work together to make Florida's water crisis meaningful to local residents. As different organizations participate in the translation process of large-scale to local activism, they practice coalitional work in promoting environmental stewardship (Chávez, 2013; Walton, Moore, & Jones, 2019). Drawing upon what I refer to in this chapter as the "energy of place," these organizations promote grassroots environmental activism by mobilizing the affective circulation of messaging relaying issues impacting iconic bodies of water throughout the state across digital networks and localized contexts. Before discussing the energy of place, it is useful to explore the important situated contexts that powerfully shape the ecologies of Florida water activism.

BACKGROUND

With well over 700 documented freshwater springs bubbling out of its underwater caves, more first-magnitude springs than any other state or nation in the world, numerous karst windows and spring-sink combinations, and 19 state parks named for its springs, Florida sits atop a vast network of water (Schmidt, 2004), as shown in figure 9.1. Though the state is undeniably defined by its numerous beaches (Dobrin, 2015), the freshwater springs were the first tourist destinations in the state. Silver Springs was a popular tourist destination before the Civil War, and its popularity increased with the glass-bottom boat tours starting in the late 1870s (King, 2004). The clarity of the spring water has provided sundry literary tropes, including in the colonial myth of Ponce de León and the Fountain of Youth;[1] the early Florida tourist articles of Harriet Beecher Stowe; the writings of American naturalist William Bartram, which

---

1. Florida's freshwater springs were likely not sought by Ponce de León for magical youth-restoring properties but instead to support the material needs of colonization by supplying potable water for ships. The myth of the rejuvenating waters likely originated in Asia (Olschki, 1941) and was probably not the real exigence that led to the "discovery" of Florida.

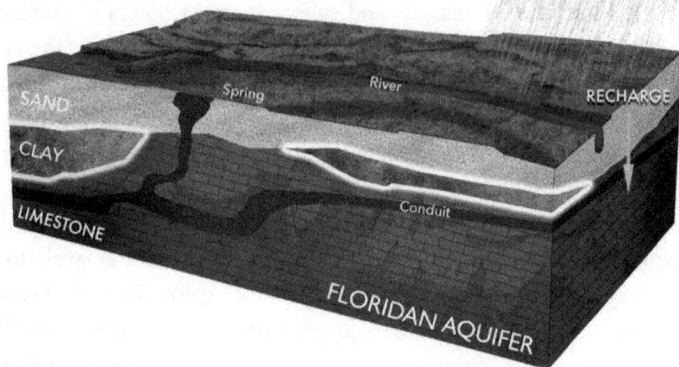

FIGURE 9.1. Floridan aquifer recharge model. Model by Haley
Moody, courtesy of the Florida Springs Institute.

inspired British Romantics like Samuel Taylor Coleridge and early American
environmental ethics (Sivils, 2004); the circulation of water between the segregated boundaries of Silver Springs and Paradise Park; and the representations
of racial identity as water in Zora Neale Hurston's *Seraph on the Sewanee*.[2]
The ethereal clarity of the spring flow made it a perfect backdrop of "pristine
nature" for films like *Tarzan the Ape Man* (1932) and *Creature from the Black
Lagoon* (1954). The closed dimensions of the spring also provided the perfect
conditions for ecosystems ecologist Howard T. Odum's groundbreaking (1957)
study, which first visualized trophic ecological structures. In each of these
examples, the clarity and steady flow of the water provides a powerful image
that mediates ecological values to the community.

The sociohistorical capital of the springs, in tandem with their popularity
as recreational places, help make them important sites of community value
that activists draw upon to motivate the public to get involved and take action
to protect the springs. If Odum were seeking a place to conduct his study
today, Silver Springs might no longer be such an ideal location. The Florida

2. Lu Vickers and Cynthia Wilson-Graham's (2015) *Remembering Paradise Park: Tourism and Segregation at Silver Springs* connects the iconic location to the work of novelist and
anthropologist Zora Neale Hurston and other important African American writers. Their book
traces the rhetorical lives of the springs, from the segregated park to the water that circulated
independently of these boundaries.

springs are experiencing degradations in both clarity and flow as a result of a range of anthropogenic impacts on the landscape. While these changes are extremely destructive, they are also increasingly producing sites where human environmental impacts become visible not just to scientists but to activists and to the local community as a whole. As human impacts produce visible changes in the landscape, they offer spaces to activate public interest in environmental protection. Because the spring water has always participated as an affective visual image for "pristine nature," the water clouding or slowing its flow has become an important tool for Floridians to understand and reimagine their relationship with the environment. Environmental scientists, activists, and educators work together to persuade residents to make changes at the local level, such as joining in springs cleanup events, rethinking traditional approaches to lawn care and fertilizer, and working toward policy-level changes in the agricultural and water industries. As nitrate runoff fuels excessive algal bloom, and overpumping by bottled water companies reduce spring flow, the springs take on new rhetorical energy, transforming from a crystal-clear viewing pane to a clouded mirror reflecting human impact.

This chapter understands grassroots activism for the Florida Springs as a distributed and relational activity by examining the interconnected work of a nonprofit organization, the Howard T. Odum Springs Institute (hereafter "Springs Institute"); a multimodal advocacy series, the Springs Eternal Project (hereafter "Springs Eternal"); and a local business, First Magnitude Brewing Company (hereafter "First Magnitude"). These groups work together to raise awareness of the threats facing the springs, promote public engagement with science, and motivate the community to take action for springs protection. While the Springs Institute works through science education and outreach, Springs Eternal deploys multimodal strategies combining art, advocacy, and science to reach the public through participatory installations and events across the state. In concert with these efforts, First Magnitude offers a locus for the springs activist community through its messaging and philanthropy and by hosting a wide range of events, from academic lectures and documentary film screenings to river cleanups, fostering a space for community engagement with science and environmental activism.

While their efforts are not primarily aimed at cultivating what Alexander, Jarratt, and Welch's (2018) *Unruly Rhetorics* refers to as "radical" or "unruly" political action, I argue that these overlapping efforts go well beyond merely "raising awareness" of the springs for the public, which at best often reinforces a deficit model for science communication (Druschke & McGreavy, 2016) and at worst results in outright greenwashing. Such negative outcomes of public advocacy work play a role in producing what Jenny Rice (2012) refers to in *Distant Publics* as "the exceptional subject," which describes "one who is related to the public through a feeling of awayness just as much as towardness" (p. 67). This discursive mode prevents meaningful change by cultivating a public subjectivity of apathy and despair. At the same time, sites of damage are often locations from which publics emerge. Rice demonstrates how environmental and antidevelopment rhetorics in Austin, Texas, formed through various more-than-human exigencies and how exceptional subjects "occup[y] a precarious position between publicness and a withdrawal from publicness" (p. 5). These subjects imagine themselves as part of a public by feeling or emotion rather than action. Rice (Edbauer, 2005) also illustrates the complex and fluid circulations that form in a "wide ecology of rhetorics" (p. 20). These organizations respond to the kairos of watershed degradation by encouraging coalitional and participatory public action in the form of stewardship, activism, and environmental citizenship.

Through rhetorical energy, I extend Rice's (2012) claim that "messages, as they accrete over time, determine the shape of public rhetorics" (p. 20) to include the buildup of nitrates that fuel algal growth and the siphoning off of water for distant municipalities like Jacksonville. One of the locations Rice discusses in *Distant Publics* as a site for the production of antidevelopment rhetorics in Austin is Barton Springs, a beloved place for swimming threatened by the Circle C Ranch, which sought to develop "an all-inclusive community" including "not only . . . neighborhoods but also its own schools, country clubs, and shopping areas" (p. 70). Rice carefully documents and unpacks the emergence of injury claims as "well-worn patterns of response from both pro- and anti-development forces" (p. 72) and demonstrates how the springs became a topos, a locus for a diverse range of discourse, from those who swam at the springs, those who saw the springs as sacred, and those who believed the springs could be put to use for the betterment of the community. Similar debates abound about the fate of Florida's springs. Two particular environmental threats are familiar topoi in these debates: cloudy water (from excess nutrients) and low flow (from overpumping of the aquifer). These are not the only threats to the springs, and all threats are deeply connected across the scales of watershed and aquifer.

Likewise, degradation in water quality is also an issue of social justice, or in Crenshaw's (1991) terms, "multilayered and routinized forms of domination" (p. 1245), which require coalitional work to meaningfully address. The degradation of the watershed is part of what Rob Nixon (2011) terms "slow violence," referring to the ways that environmental degradation affects marginalized communities to a greater degree. The Florida springs function as what Jenny Rice terms a "site of injury," a location where subjects are cultivated and publics are produced. This is especially true for the iconic Silver Springs, a site familiar and important to Floridian identity. The threats facing the springs connect the impact of individuals (such as overdevelopment and fertilizer runoff) to global ecological issues (like sea-level rise and population growth). Their importance to the local communities, especially in north-central Florida, make them an important place for fostering grassroots participation from the ground up (Staples, 2016) and in ways that connect the local community to larger coalitions at the state, multistate, and national levels (Freudenberg & Steinsapir, 1992). While this work fosters important connections between large-scale and small-scale activisms, the primary goals of their social action are situated within the local community (Rainey & Johnson, 2009).

Rather than taking a top-down approach, these groups function as what Natasha N. Jones (2014) refers to as an "activist network" by building infrastructure for public action, fostering actionable coalitions, and producing meaningful social change (p. 48). Jones argues that "activism, in its most basic form, centers on people and how they communicate and behave in order to promote the accomplishment of goals" (p. 58). As recent studies suggest, environmental decision-making is "not only shaped by rational considerations, but also influenced by how communities define themselves, by historic or fictional narratives and collective memories" (Holzhausen & Grecksch, 2021). As such, this chapter examines the place-based elements of springs activism and, through a case study of Florida springs activism, demonstrates how the springs function as rhetorical topoi for publicly engaged activist rhetoric, an extension of what Caroline Gottschalk Druschke (2013) refers to as the "watershed as common-place," cultivating a sense of community and "common responsibility" for the springs (p. 84). By making visible the degradation of the springs over geological, or "deep," time (Butts and Jones, 2021), and drawing upon the socio-affective circulation (Gries, 2015; Jones, Beveridge, Garrison, Greene, & MacDonald, 2022) of springs iconography, these organizations deploy a fluvial rhetoric which engages with place as an emergent, choric network (M. Jones, 2018). The collaborative and interdisciplinary efforts aimed at protecting the springs reveal the ways that the relationships between people and environment are never fixed and are always in flux and that place is a fluid, emergent, and ecological wellspring for activist discourse.

This study demonstrates how these organizations draw upon the affective "energy of place" to visualize complex environmental problems in ways that are meaningful to public audiences at the local scale and thereby increase public action on environmental problems. As they say on the "Love Our Springs?" page of the Springs Eternal Project website (springseternalproject.org), "We are all part of the problem. Together, we can work to ensure effective and ethical solutions." By connecting large-scale problems to rhetorical circulation within local places, activists make big problems meaningful to the local community. The resulting analysis suggests an array of strategies that activists use to engage local communities through digital and visual storytelling, but it also demonstrates how local activism cannot always be scaled up, revealing place to be both a wellspring and a constraint for activist rhetorics. These tensions point to the productive ways that water and other "wild blue media" (Jue, 2020) unsettle fixed rhetorical notions of local and global in activism. Beyond these limitations, this study ultimately demonstrates some of the important challenges and considerations activists should consider. In the following sections, I discuss the networked activism of three complementary groups to highlight how they draw upon the energy of place to accomplish the overlapping goal of engaging the community in springs protection. Ultimately, this study demonstrates how grassroots organizations can use place-based strategies in concert with visualization to engage local communities in activism.

THE RHETORICAL ENERGY OF PLACE

Sites of sociohistorical value like the Florida springs are a wellspring of rhetorical potential, places where environmental degradation becomes visible, meaningful, and actionable. As activists draw upon visual tropes to promote springs activism, they utilize the rhetorical energy of place. Energy allows us to map the affective circulations of place from environmental science to the image events (DeLuca, 1999) that shape public engagement with activism (Ackerman & Coogan, 2013). In rhetorical terms, "energy" refers to vigorous or vivid expression. While the rhetorical concept of energy has something of a complex and convoluted history,[3] it provides a useful way to understand how springs activists harness the rhetorical, sociohistorical, and affective value of the springs by visualizing the springs' degraded clarity over time. Rhetorical energy helps illuminate why the hydrographic visual tropes of water clarity can circulate from technical science to become iconic in popular culture and public discourse. Likewise, energy sheds light on the role of potentiality (*dunamis*) and actuality (*energeia*) in activism. As activists draw on place-based

---

3. As recent rhetoric scholars like Jason Helms (2017) and Chris Ingraham (2018) demonstrate, *energy* offers a useful, if not convoluted, means to put into practice the new materialist rhetorical theories which have been broadly defined by scholars such as Byron Hawk (2007), Diane Davis (2010), and Thomas Rickert (2013). For an in-depth tracing of the "relative and absolute ambiguities of energy" that further complicate the "historical predicament of energy today," see Marder (2017, p. 2).

strategies to move people to act, they actualize the potential energy of specific places and sociohistorical contexts. In this way, energy presents a useful category through which to distinguish grassroots activism from other forms of advocacy, by indexing the ways that place becomes actionable at the local level. In doing so, this analysis follows Sarah Warren-Riley and Elise Verzosa Hurley's (2017) contrasting of the two terms, with "activism [connoting] specific action" while "advocacy implies support" (para. 5). Before turning to specific examples of the place-based activist strategies deployed by the Springs Institute, the Springs Eternal series, and First Magnitude, it is important to understand how rhetorical energy is tied directly to the social history and contemporary ecological exigency of the Florida springs.

Here, I build from Druschke's notions of "situated analysis" (2013) and "trophic rhetoric" (2019) to understand not only how the concept of energy circulates within our understanding of place but also how the springs as a place have come to shape our notion of energy. As the location for H. T. Odum's landmark "Silver Springs study" (1957), the springs played a crucial role in the development of ecosystems ecology. Odum mapped trophic flow through the springs, positioning energy circulation as a central method for understanding environments. His macroscopic methodology allowed ecologists to holistically map environments and helped shift the field from theoretical to quantitative approaches. As part of this work, Odum later coined the term "emergy," a portmanteau of "embodied" and "energy." Emergy, for Odum, is the energy required to sustain an ecosystem. Through Silver Springs and other sites, Odum (1973) demonstrated how energy moved through various sources and at various levels of scale and complexity, ranging "from dilute sunlight up to plant matter, to coal, from coal to oil, to electricity and up to the high quality efforts of computer and human information processing" (p. 224). Because of their steady flow, the springs offered closed dimensions through which to measure the movement of energy through a system. As such, the spring flow participates in shaping the rhetorical concept of energy, and in turn, trophic mapping has made energy a central concept for understanding the environmental threats facing the springs today.

Just as Odum's "emergy" concept lays bare how the springs participate as a conduit between energy and place, so does George Kennedy's concept of the "rheme" help produce circulation points with rhetoric, science, and activism. Bridging from Odum to Kennedy, rhetorical energy helps us understand the move from identification with place to actualizing activism for and with place. In understanding place-based activism through the rhetorical concept of energy, I build from Chris Ingraham's (2018) work that situates the term within its expansive intellectual history and as part of a constellation of other contemporary concepts, including affect theory, new materialism, and ecological rhetorics. Ingraham positions Kennedy's (1992) article "A Hoot in the Dark: The Evolution of General Rhetoric" as pivotal to our contemporary understanding, not just of energy, but of each of the aforementioned rhetorical concepts. Kennedy argues for a definition of rhetoric built on the concept of energy, suggesting that it is "perhaps a special case of the energy of all physics" (p. 13) and even going so far as to suggest the "rheme" as a "unit of rhetorical energy" (p. 2). Extending these two theories, I understand the rhetorical energy of place as the affective embodiment of rhetorical relationality. While this study primarily focuses on the human nodes in the network of exchanges, energy offers a way to map rhetorical circulation across the human/nonhuman divide, just as trophic mapping did for Odum's work at Silver Springs. Studying the energy of place helps us to understand both the potential that places have for activism and the ways that potential is actualized through activism. Having briefly mapped these points of connection through the Florida springs, I now apply rhetorical energy to understand the networked activism of three local organizations dedicated to engaging the public in springs protection.

CIRCULATING SCIENCE

Founded in 2010, the Springs Institute is a 501(c)(3) nonprofit organization dedicated to springs protection through quantitative science and public education. Named for Howard T. Odum, the Springs Institute works to build a "scientifically defensible baseline of ecological data" in order to provide "recommendations for individuals, businesses, and state government agencies on how they can better protect Florida springs" (Florida Springs Institute, n.d.). Through a wide range of reports, outreach events, and multimedia tools, the Springs Institute works both to develop quantitative data and to make that data visible and meaningful to the public. For instance, their Blue Water Audit project (bluewateraudit.org) offers interactive maps that visualize nitrate runoff and groundwater withdrawal, and their Aquifer Footprint Calculator helps residents understand how they are impacting the springs. Building from Bruno Latour's (1999) notion of "circulating reference," I argue that these projects endeavor to circulate (rather than merely translate) science through place as an energetic conduit, branching from in situ data to multimodal design and back to the public through maps that make complex data visible, understandable, and actionable.

FIGURE 9.2. Florida Springs Institute's citizen science program, Wekiva Springs Watch, conducting monthly water quality sampling. Photo courtesy of Florida Springs Institute.

Through their multimodal digital projects and public engagement, the Springs Institute works to actualize the energy of place, making ecological data visible and actionable for the local community. As a cadre of scientific communication scholars have argued, multimedia communication offers ways to persuade audiences to view and interpret information in certain ways (Dyehouse, 2011) and to make arguments about complex problems (Walsh, 2015). As the Springs Institute works to educate and motivate the public, they draw from both scientific and social interpretations of the energy of place. For example, their citizen science project, SpringsWatch, brings together volunteers from the local communities across the state with Springs Institute staff to collect water quality data for the Springs Institute and state agencies, monitor environmental conditions, and observe human and wildlife interaction (see figure 9.2). The goal of the project is not only to collect important data that informs springs protections and to help produce behavioral changes in the local community through outreach and experiential learning but also to start to cultivate a dynamic reciprocity between scientists and citizens that effects positive change by producing a "give-and-take" (Cushman, Powell, & Takayoshi, 2004, p. 150) from a "shift from observation of users to participation with users" (Salvo, 2001, p. 273).

By participating in sampling, monitoring, and observing, local citizens become participants in the research process. However, involving local residents in research alone doesn't necessarily meet the latter goal of activating the kind of dynamic and reciprocal relationship that might cultivate grassroots activism, nor does it necessarily disrupt existing hierarchies between scientists and citizens. As Caroline Gottschalk Druschke and Carrie E. Seltzer (2012) demonstrate in their pilot study of a citizen science project, participation does not necessitate engagement. From their study, they argue that citizen science projects "can potentially do as much harm as good" (p. 185). In order to foster more successful engagement, coordinators should "attend to their citizen scientists and not just their data" (p. 185). While the Springs Institute offers a rich, multifaceted outreach program that works to achieve many of the goals Druschke and Seltzer outline in their criteria for successful citizen science projects, this chapter understands the overall success of their project as a larger relational activity that is distributed across a vast network of advocacy and activist projects focusing on springs protection. In this case, citizen science is a node in the network of Florida watershed activism. While the Springs Institute works to activate the rhetorical energy of place by focusing on the circulation that occurs between citizens and scientists, the following sections examine affiliate organizations that draw upon the social and historical dimensions of the springs to further foster grassroots environmental activism.

VISUALIZING PLACE:
THEN AND NOW

The multimedia project Springs Eternal is an evolving series created by Florida nature photographer John Moran with artist Lesley Gamble and visual designer Rick Kilby to document the degradation of the springs and advocate for their protection. This project assembles "a diverse community of springs scientists, researchers, artists and advocates" in order to

> inspire Floridians to value our springs and the diverse ecosystems they support as fundamental to the health and wellbeing of us all, human and non-human; to redefine these relationships in socially just and ecologically sustainable terms; and to work collaboratively to conserve, restore and protect Florida's precious waters for our children and theirs, for generations to come.

Through a combination of art and visual and digital storytelling, the project harnesses the rhetorical energy of the springs to visualize and document their degradation and call the public to act on protecting the springs through participatory exhibits throughout the state. Springs Eternal functions as a kind of anthology of the transdisciplinary and multimodal projects led by its individual partners. For example, John Moran's before-and-after photographs of the springs document the drastic ecological changes that have taken place over the last few decades.

Along a larger temporal frame, Rick Kilby's book and museum exhibit *Finding the Fountain of Youth: Exploring the Myth of Florida's Magical Waters* reveals the colonial history and mythology of the Florida springs, which echoes today through "Ponceabilia." Lesley Gamble's project *Urban Aquifer: Vehicles to Think With* combines performance art with visual media from local artists to place representations of the springs on Regional Transit System buses in Alachua County, Florida. Through these interconnected multimedia projects, partners make large-scale environmental problems affecting the springs visible at the local level.

These individual projects converge in Springs Eternal to create a multifaceted and multimodal project that calls public attention to the threats facing the springs, provides outreach for engaging the community in valuing the springs, and offers actionable steps that can be taken at the local level to effect change. The project website's home page claims that the first step toward revitalizing the springs "is to listen to the springs themselves, to their many intricate languages: visual, biological, hydrological, geological" (para. 6). Through these various projects, the organization reaches communities across the Southeast and makes these large-scale environmental problems visible and actionable at the local level. Combining artwork and storytelling, the project celebrates the springs as places of wonder and beauty. Through statewide traveling exhibits, Springs Eternal documents the environmental degradation of the springs "Then & Now," revealing the springs as places of value that are under direct and immediate existential threats. This project channels the sociohistoric energies circulating through the springs of place to encourage residents across Florida to make individual changes to the ways they relate to water, such as using less water, taking part in river cleanups, growing native plants instead of lawns, supporting farmers who use responsible water and fertilizer practices, spending time with friends and loved ones at the springs, and taking part in organizations devoted to protecting them. At the larger scale, these projects also encourage citizens to vote, as well as to organize and contact elected officials to bring about meaningful changes to industry and politics at the state level.

Springs Eternal functions as a micronetwork of activism, combining the individual efforts of local artists, educators, scientists, and advocates, and it also participates as a node in the larger decentralized network of Florida springs activism that includes the other organizations discussed throughout this chapter. While these are but a few of the many groups dedicated to saving the springs, their work brings a particular focus on how channeling the energy of place can serve as a conduit for environmental activism. Jessica Holzhausen and Kevin Grecksch (2021) note the "strong connection between places and identities" and argue that "a historical perspective to existing discussions about climate change . . . can help us understand why and how these self-perceptions and collective identities have developed and what this means for climate change adaptation" (p. 2). As such, learning from these place-based strategies employed by Springs Eternal can help environmental advocates better understand how place shapes grassroots activism.

The Then and Now campaign by Springs Eternal draws from the visual rhetoric of the before-and-after photograph to establish the historic degradation of the springs and to counteract the problem of shifting baselines, which typically prevent us from noticing their gradual decline. The clarity and flow of the water at Silver Springs has long been an inspiration for scientists, writers, filmmakers, artists, advocates, and activists. By engaging with social histories of place, these images of the springs rhetorically function as a collective environmental icon, or what Sean Morey (2014) terms an "econ" or "ecotype," which "taxonomizes a way of identifying and theorizing those environmental images that become iconic across mass audiences and symbolic of environmental issues and situations beyond any econ's individual . . . concerns" (p. 1). Morey cites examples of econs that circulate at national and global scales—such as the bald eagle and the giant panda—which he compares to what he refers to as a "Florida econ," or images that achieve a more localized circulation, citing examples like the brown pelican, American alligator, and Florida panther. Examples like these circulate over visual and digital media through a process that Sid Dobrin and Sean Morey (2009) refer to as "ecosee" (building from Killingsworth's *Ecospeak*), which Morey (2014) claims "subscribes to a way of seeing nature that is not seeing nature" but is instead a visualization (pp. 16–17). In describing how ecosystems can become "econic," Morey points out that it is "difficult to visualize water pollution, especially when it occurs in a marshy area rather than in clearer water such as springs" (p. 10). This partially explains the success of Springs Eternal's Then and Now campaign and exhibit, which places images of the springs from the 1970s through 1990s alongside more contemporary images taken in the same place.

In these images, the energy flowing between humans and nature is rendered visible through algal overgrowth, fueled by excess fertilizer runoff and other groundwater contaminants. These images show how an excess of emergy transforms the idyllic, crystal water murky and clouded. Images of iconic springs like the Ichetucknee evoke a powerful sense of identification with local residents, conducting powerful connections with place through localized forms of concepts like childhood and nature. These images draw upon the sense of energetic systems as they visualize excess nitrates in the system. As human activity destructively transforms the springs, they become a locus for environmental activism in the public sphere.

Such locations of disaster and destruction are places where identification can be traced and constructed. As the springs dry up and cloud with algae, they become visible, affective topoi for environmental rhetoric. For instance, sites like the White Springs bathhouse have become a trope in local environmental discourse. Once a popular tourist destination, White Springs ceased flowing in the 1980s and now serves as an example of what might happen to Silver Springs (and other iconic springs) if water management policies are not changed.

These sites all are places where complex cultural histories converge with uncertain environmental futures. In the next section, I turn from the springs as sites of activism to understand how First Magnitude is making a place for grassroots springs activism in the local community.

PUB(LIC) RHETORICS

As a major sponsor of Springs Eternal and the Springs Institute, as well as a longtime advocate and supporter of local watershed restoration, First Magnitude—a local brewery in Gainesville, Florida—incorporates this social history into their ethos through visual design and practices that support, and make space for, local activism. First Magnitude draws upon the energy of place, not only to craft visual storytelling in their logo and beer label designs, but also to create a place for springs activism. While the mermaid figure on their logo, "Maggie," refers to Florida's iconic first-magnitude springs, First Magnitude goes beyond the "branding" traditionally affiliated with industry practices of greenwashing by serving as a site where various nodes of springs advocacy and activism meet.

For example, First Magnitude regularly provides a no-cost space for activists to host river cleanups, screen documentaries about the springs, and hold fundraising events like their annual 7.2-kilometer Springs Run. As a company, they are also dedicated to practicing what they advocate, becoming the first carbon-neutral brewery in the Southeast, minimizing water and energy use, and donating proceeds from sales to springs protection initiatives. In their storytelling, advocacy, and industry practices, First Magnitude further circulates the energy of local activism by organizations like Springs Eternal and the Springs Institute. As they circulate this energy, the brewery also fosters a space for the community to connect with springs activism. In doing so, First Magnitude demonstrates how place is more than just a wellspring for activism. Place is also shaped by and created through the ongoing grassroots efforts of activists.

As a brand, First Magnitude meaningfully builds from and extends the place-based network of storytelling and activism that works to protect the Florida springs. As such, they deploy ethos in the traditions of the Victorian public house (or "pub"). According to Ben Clarke (2012), pubs in the 1930s became centers of community for members of the middle and working classes, combining "the notion of general admission and belonging" (p. 39). Rather than simply serving alcohol and promoting mass alcohol consumption, negative associations Clarke traces to Victorian attitudes, pubs functioned as a "communal space" that offered "an opportunity to experience an inclusive, equal society" for those who could not afford membership in elite clubs (p. 40). Pubs became spaces that fostered a sense of local community. In *Craft Obsession,* Jeff Rice (2016) builds from Walter Benjamin's (1968) work with storytelling and craft to tell the story of craft beer as well as of "rhetoric and, in particular, the rhetoric of social media" (Rice, 2016, p. x). "These stories," Rice demonstrates, "affect taste, consumption, behavior, political affiliation, and other activities for the ways that they frame overall interests" (p. 2). Jeff Rice refers to his own relationship to craft beer as a "networked terroir" (p. xiii) and (drawing from Jenny Edbauer) "an ecology of place," which includes Gainesville (though Rice notes he lived there before it experienced the craft beer renaissance currently underway) as part of his aggregate lived experience with crafting place (p. 77). Like yeast metabolizing sugars into energy, producing carbonation and alcohol in beer as a by-product, place cannot be reduced to separations of living/nonliving, human/nonhuman, nature/culture. Jenny Rice (2012) refers to place as "a space of contacts, which are always changing and never discrete" (p. 10). Put simply, the friction of these changing contact spaces produces the circulating energy of place.

Casey Boyle and Nathaniel Rivers (2018) draw from the intersecting history of the coffee shop and the public sphere to illustrate the ways that locative media are changing our public spaces today. Just as "the stimulating effects of caffeine and open room–styled cafés" shaped our contemporary public as we know it, so are emerging mobile technologies changing our public today (p. 83). They "trace a public in circulation" as they argue that communicators must "place circulation in rhetorical practice" (p. 84). Through their digital and visual storytelling practices, as well as their direct financial support and promotion of local springs activism, First Magnitude embodies the traditions of the public house and extends those traditions into the "augmented" public sphere by building space, both online and on the ground, for grassroots community activism. Like Odum's trophic mapping of Silver Springs, their storytelling practices help materialize the energy of place. For instance, the Miami Blue Bock beer was one of the first augmented reality (AR) beer labels.

The Miami Blue Bock was created to raise awareness of the endangered Miami blue butterfly and support conservation efforts by the Florida Museum of Natural History (FMNH). The FMNH created the free AR (augmented reality) application, which, when the beer can is scanned by a smartphone, reveals a 3D animation of the butterfly to help make the endangered species visible to the public.

Of the numerous beers First Magnitude has since brewed in collaboration with the FMNH, their recent Bartram Blonde (released April 2018) draws upon Bartram's writings to tell a story with the Bartram's scrub-hairstreak butterfly. These designs draw upon the rhetorical energy of Florida history to promote identification with iconic (or "econic" in Morey's terms) local species and to directly link consumer behavior with environmental protection. These images rhetorically tie together place, advocacy, and First Magnitude's brand. As such, their storytelling practices engage place and combine science, art, and popular culture as they foster public engagement with advocacy.

Through place-based craft storytelling, First Magnitude promotes activism and fosters identification with Florida environmental icons and their own ethos through social media and emerging technologies. For example, their logo, "Maggie," as well as beer label designs like that of the Siren Blonde Ale refer to underwater mermaid shows—a roadside tourist attraction featuring performers wearing fish tails and breathing through underwater oxygen tubes—which have taken place at Weeki Wachee Springs since 1947. Today, these professional performers are also "among the activists standing in opposition to politically powerful industries and an industry-friendly state government they feel is practically giving away its publicly owned water supply" (Corral, 2021). In drawing upon this history and contemporary activism, First Magnitude's visual and digital storytelling practices build on the iconic circulation of Florida springs imagery and history to produce an energetic link between activism, place, and ethos. Here, the springs function as what Morey calls a local econ, one which has a more restricted circulation within a regional group. While it is unlikely that these images will become global environmental icons, they circulate within the context of north-central Florida as the part of the circulation of placemaking. In crafting brand identification with econs in their Florida springs ethos, First Magnitude embodies the traditions of the public house, creating a space for community identity and crafting identification with the environment and activism. In its storytelling practices and direct support for springs activism, First Magnitude actualizes the energy of place to persuade audiences to act. As such, First Magnitude moves beyond symbolizing activism to materializing, and fostering a space for, action.

CONCLUSION

This chapter performed a situated analysis of examples of local activist projects aimed at protecting the Florida springs. Using the concept of rhetorical energy, I argue that activists can draw upon the circulation of place to deploy communication strategies and help create spaces for activism. As an activist network, the organizations I highlight work together to foster public engagement with science and build community around saving the springs. They promote grassroots activism by drawing rhetorically upon the circulating energy of place, moving from visualizing environments as icons and symbols to networking within ecologies of activism and action. Through this study, I have demonstrated some of the ways that activists draw upon the sociohistorical and affective dimensions of place to connect communities with action.

The energy of place suggests important considerations for researchers, advocates, and educators. However, it also presents limitations for grassroots activisms. Just as place offers important sites for the production of activist networks, so can it constrain those networks to specific locales or regions. Likewise, emphasizing sites of sociohistorical value risks ignoring places that lack richly documented social histories, public interest, or qualities traditionally associated with "nature." Furthermore, such an emphasis may promote negative elements of "toxic tourism" (Pezzullo, 2009) by exploiting some sites of damage and ignoring others. Such dangers are further exacerbated by slow violence, as environmental degradation affects marginalized communities to a greater degree and in ways that are gradual and often ignored and erased from public discourse. Still, as Pezzullo demonstrates, these places, too, provide spaces of community resistance and activism. While this chapter has contributed to the rhetorical energy of place in grassroots environmental activism, further research might seek to understand how regional activisms can work to achieve or inform larger-scale activism and how place-based activisms are taken up from Indigenous perspectives and in global contexts. Working to include these important concerns and building from future studies expanding on the energy of place from a diverse range of perspectives and regional contexts will lead to a richer understanding of the role of place in grassroots activism.

CHAPTER 10

La Conexión

Advocating for Latinx Immigrants in Northwest Ohio

APRIL CONWAY

La Conexión's origin story begins in Bowling Green, Ohio, with residents who wanted to create an organization to represent the growing Latinx population in the region. The group's first goal was to assess the needs of the community, which included knocking on doors to survey their neighbors. La Conexión's executive director, Beatriz Maya, said she even went up to people speaking Spanish in the grocery store to learn how they experienced life in the area (B. Maya, personal communication, October 23, 2020). As group members demonstrated with their initial outreach, living in the community one serves and focusing on community needs are indicators of a grassroots ethos La Conexión repeatedly shows.

In this organizational profile, I use primary source materials, particularly my interview with Maya, to analyze the work of La Conexión, a nonprofit that advocates for Latinx communities in Northwest Ohio. The organization's activism is one of coalition, because despite limited funds, the group is always oriented to others and committed to change (Chávez, 2013). In responding to COVID-19, for instance, the organization demonstrated its rhetorical acumen by pivoting to community needs further exacerbated by the public health crisis. As a researcher and a volunteer with the organization, I am amplifying La Conexión's work to illustrate how nonprofits like this one utilize grassroots tactics that respond to localized realities echoing national trends.

ORGANIZATIONAL GOALS AND RESOURCES

La Conexión's rhetorical acuity is rooted in a multidimensional response to myriad exigencies, like those unearthed by Maya when speaking with community members in the grocery store. According to its website, La Conexión offers "programs (that) focus on capacity building, immigrant integration, and social change" (La Conexión, 2020). This includes helping members establish small businesses, build credit, and learn English. To achieve these goals, the nonprofit has expanded its resources over time. La Conexión accomplishes a lot on a limited budget because of the monetary, partnership, facility, and skill-based resources negotiated and generated by members.

One example of how La Conexión manages to do critical work while safeguarding resources is through interpretation services, which support the organization's immigrant integration focus. Interpretation is crucial for La Conexión as the organization seeks access for those it serves. These services came about because, as Maya said, "there was no interpretation, anywhere" (B. Maya, personal communication, October 23, 2020). Initially, La Conexión's interpreters—whose hourly wages are covered by the nonprofit—translated for La Conexión members and the institutional staff they interacted with, such as doctors, school staff, and the police. However, these institutions receive federal funding to provide interpretation. Adjusting their approach, La Conexión researched and recommended a global language service company that many of these institutions now use, thus freeing La Conexión's interpreters to work in situations when federal funding cannot be applied. This is what local activism looks like: showing up for community members, learning of local practices that thwart or ignore national policies, then instituting changes that benefit everyone in the region who relies on translation services.

Maya is keenly aware of how to secure and safeguard resources due, in part, to her grant-writing experience. La Conexión primarily receives grants from private foundations, especially those focused on social justice. These are "not the richest or wealthiest foundations," so La Conexión also receives money from individual donors, churches, interpretation services, and T-shirt sales (B. Maya, personal communication, October 23, 2020). The group also hosts dinner dances (as shown in figure 10.1) that serve as fundraisers and opportunities to build community within the Latinx community or across the broader public, thus underscoring how community support can include a mix of social, entrepreneurial, cultural, and educational efforts.

In 2014, La Conexión developed a partnership with a local domestic violence shelter. According to Maya, this partnership "is a model of how things should be done" because the shelter recognizes the necessity of working with

FIGURE 10.1. Community party to celebrate National Hispanic Heritage Month. Marsha Olivares, former president of La Conexión's board of directors, is shown here at the community party in September 2019. Photo by the author.

knowledgeable and trusted advocates from survivors' communities (personal communication, October 23, 2020). La Conexión's ability to work with allies who are committed to similar outcomes is another grassroots tactic that benefits members while also establishing additional networks that strengthen the community at large.

Another allyship is with the La Conexión Immigrant Solidarity Committee (LC ISC), an internal program founded in 2017 to educate the broader public about immigration. La Conexión and the LC ISC responded to national policies like Immigration and Customs Enforcement (ICE) family separation and detention by delivering letters to congressional representatives (DuPont, 2019) and holding protests in front of ICE detention centers. They also responded to localized occurrences, including a racially motivated hate crime that resulted in a multipartner effort to train local businesses in de-escalation and reporting. When President Donald Trump announced his intention to end the Deferred Action for Childhood Arrivals (DACA) program, local DREAMers (minors who migrate to the US) needed to pay the reapplication fees, so LC ISC raised the necessary funds. This resulted in the establishment of the Direct Support Fund, which is reserved for families affected by immigration enforcement. Sometimes when allyships form in response to immediate exigencies, the payoff can include long-term solutions, such as the Direct Support Fund and a dedicated bank of volunteers working steadily or ready to rally around the next crisis.

RESPONDING LOCALLY TO A GLOBAL CRISIS: COVID-19

One such crisis was COVID-19 and its impact on the community. Early in the pandemic, Maya said, "we realized that it was very important that we didn't shut down contact with our members" (personal communication, October 23, 2020). The outreach staff began surveying members' health concerns and employment status via phone calls. Because undocumented essential workers and "mixed status" families were unable to receive federal pandemic relief funds in 2020, La Conexión provided personal protection equipment, advocated for students to receive free internet hotspots from local school districts, and distributed Visa gift cards to 162 farmworker families (McLaughlin, 2020). The staff also recruited families to make home videos with simple messages about how to take care of oneself during the pandemic. In one video, children demonstrated how best to wash hands. Other videos relayed messages about the need to stay at home and to wear masks. All videos were posted to Facebook. This was a great experience, Maya said, because the kids had fun and parents felt like they were doing something for the community. Although La Conexión is member-centered, presenting opportunities for families to create meaningful content underscored the fact that members are more than recipients of aid or employees. Rather, the videos emphasized that members are part of the engine that runs the organization.

Because of their continued involvement with members after the statewide COVID-19 shutdown, when many industries were ordered to close, La Conexión staff learned that workers at a local food plant were not informed about an internal COVID case. La Conexión staff and members called the health department and, as a result, the plant instituted COVID precautions. Due to this victory, Maya said, there was an effort to unionize the plant, because "a momentum for further organizing" was initiated (personal communication, October 23, 2020). Experiences such as this demonstrate the tactic of people power, or grassroots mobilization, where La Conexión members wanted to permanently formalize better working conditions, an action that would benefit all plant employees. Actions such as these serve as conduits that can have ripple effects in the local industry and reflect the efforts of national labor movements.

COMPREHENSIVE COMMUNITY IMPACT

La Conexión responds to crises and opportunities as they arise, while also building on what is gained in response to these exigencies. By forging numerous partnerships, La Conexión accumulates resources and creates networks that impact not only the local Latinx community, but also many people in the region. La Conexión's activism is one of coalition-building, for it positively alters local institutions and opens pathways for individuals and groups to work collectively.

CHAPTER 11

Off the Wall

The Performance of Graffiti and
Vandal Art in Grassroots Movements

ANGELA MITCHELL

INTRODUCTION:
UNRULY GRAFFITI AND PROTEST ART

The graffiti and vandal art that sometimes occurs in demonstrations or marches may be troubling to grassroots activists seeking peaceful protests. Yet this chapter explores the ways that protest graffiti and vandal art represent performative acts that have the potential to ignite and sustain local grassroots movements. Although ephemeral by nature, graffiti and vandal art constitute aggressive acts of social resistance that can work to reshape public spaces and set the stage for change. Through analysis of activist work in Paris, France; Tehran, Iran; and Richmond, Virginia, I will argue that illegal writing and drawing constitute enabling performances that offer audiences opportunities to encounter and act on activists' claims, views, or visions. In extraordinary circumstances, these performances can even generate long-term change in the space itself, creating places that represent those made invisible through political, cultural, or economic oppression. This kind of sustained impact depends on how the writing or art transforms the space by including the bodies of those who have been excluded from it—either literally or symbolically.

The "unruly" rhetorical strategies (Alexander, Jarratt, & Welch, 2018) that graffiti writers and vandal artists use allow local grassroots movements to write their ideas into city spaces that have largely discounted them. These rhetorical strategies, ranging from complicated satirical tropes to simple acts of "tagging," or naming, operate to claim spaces and provide sites of inspiration for change in social, political, or economic relations. By definition, graffiti and vandal art constitute illegal vandalism, as they can be characterized as noncommissioned writing and involve marking on public and private property. In fact, it is their illegality that really defines them. In "At the Wall: Graffiti Writers, Urban Territoriality, and the Public Domain," Andrea Brighetti (2010) claims, "Illegality is regarded by writers as one of the crucial characteristics that differentiate writing from other practices or visual products in the urban landscape" (p. 318). Graffiti and vandal art operate as unruly forms of public rhetoric in their illegality and in their demand to be read, to be seen, to be made visible. Regardless of any individual purpose, graffiti writers and vandal artists cut through the illusions that govern particular social systems. Their inscriptions work as disruptions to the spaces in which they write and to the powers that govern those spaces. It is my argument that protest graffiti writing and vandal art can create the opportunity to turn public spaces into contested places and allow discounted bodies to matter in those spaces.

Henri Lefebvre's (1991) key idea in *The Production of Space* is that bodies and the spaces they inhabit are inextricably connected: "each living body is space and has its space: it produces itself in space and it also produces that space" (p. 170). What bodies do in a space, how they move or perform, and the traces they leave behind can transform the social relations in that space. Further, unruly actions by bodies in that space can act as disruptions to how that space has been used in the past. According to Lefebvre, space constructs social relations but also allows for the possibility of bodies inhabiting that space with different rules. "Itself the outcome of past actions, social space is what permits fresh actions to occur, while suggesting others and prohibiting yet others" (Lefebvre, 1991, p. 73). Activist writers and artists can seek to rewrite the rules of those spaces—to mark them for their own purposes and people. Lefebvre's analysis recognizes how space can be marked physically (through signs, tags, and so on) so that it becomes symbolic. According to Mark Halsey and Alison Young (2006), "illicit writers inhabit spaces haptically instead of optically—that for particular kinds of bodies a surface is never just 'looked upon' so much as it is felt or lived" (p. 296). A graffiti writer's tags or an artist's screen print represent texts to be read and experienced haptically and bodily as the artist-writer both performs in the space and then leaves behind evidence of existence for others to witness. Passing through that space, witnesses become accountable to seeing and responding to the invitation to act. As Halsey and

Young (2006) argue, graffiti writing represents "an affective process that does things to writers' bodies (and the bodies of onlookers) as much as to the bodies of metal, concrete and plastic, which typically compose the surfaces of urban worlds" (pp. 276–277). In fact, the affective domain may be where graffiti and vandal art truly harness their power. This affective impact comes from the interaction of the audience with the graffiti's writing or image and the emotive power they evoke in a particular space. Truly experiencing graffiti and vandal art requires an exploration in the spaces that the writers and artists have created through their illegal performances—spaces that are physical and social but also dynamic and reimagined. These imagined potentialities can allow witnesses to see what perhaps they had not, to consider the space (and how it is used or named) differently. It is in this regard that the rhetorical context inherent in the illegality of graffiti and vandal art offers something that cannot be found in other visual representations (such as banners, posters, or T-shirts) associated with activist movements.

Although many grassroots activists seek peaceful protests, the destructive and aggressive denunciation that graffiti and vandal art creates offers an opportunity to communicate in a world where civility no longer seems possible. As Seth Kahn and JongHwa Lee (2010) claim, while "democracy and civic engagement have been a part of the rhetorical tradition for centuries," activists need more than "deliberative democracy" or "consensus-building frameworks" (p. 1). Activism requires dissent, law-breaking, and strategies for public protest. Further, Kevin Mahoney (2018) argues against seeking consensus, because it "is an ineffective tactic if the strategy of civility has broken down— or has yet to be established" (p. 154). Indeed, according to Deborah Mutnick (2018), unruly rhetoric should "first be understood in relation to exploitation, state and other violence and the denial of civil, economic, and human rights" (p. 219). Unruly rhetoric, such as protest graffiti, reveals "how speech, action and bodies" may collide in grassroots movements to do the work of political resistance (Alexander, Jarratt, & Welch, 2018, p. 13). These collisions offer the potential for new ways of being. As Halsey and Young (2006) write, "There are countless examples of such writing serving to interrupt our sense of the familiar, our sense of certainty, our sense of the established and proper order of things. And it is these interruptions that contribute to the making of new subjectivities and dispositions" (pp. 297–298). Unlike other art forms, protest graffiti and vandal art can grab viewers' attention, make them uncomfortable, and demand a reaction. The success of protest graffiti or vandal art, however, lies in its ability to create spaces for, in Judith Butler's (2015) words, "bodies that matter." In order to tap into that potentiality, however, writers and artists must engage in performative rhetorical acts.

EXPLORING THE PERFORMATIVE NATURE
OF GRAFFITI AND VANDAL ART

Performativity is a complicated term that has been used by theorists and philosophers in many different ways. For this chapter, I will focus on how performative statements literally allow us to make things happen with words. It is not within the scope of this short chapter to take up "performative activism," which represents a type of posturing on issues without any real action, as seen in celebrity and social media users who "protest" for the Black Lives Matter movement simply by posting a blackout image or quote. In contrast, I seek to analyze the traceable effects of protest graffiti and vandal art through an understanding of performative writing as writing that makes something happen.

As Andrea Lunsford (2015) pointed out, many political texts we read are performative in nature. For instance, the Emancipation Proclamation was an executive order issued by President Abraham Lincoln on January 1, 1863. Through its words, the proclamation made more than three million enslaved people in the southern United States free. Other familiar public documents are also performative in nature—such as the First Amendment to the US Constitution, granting free speech to all Americans, or, as Lunsford points out, the Declaration of Independence, the document that, consequently, began the American Revolution. I find it striking that some of the most important historical documents in the United States are performative in nature and therefore have had a great impact on many lives. Grassroots movements also use performative acts to make things happen. As the Tehranian vandal artist Black Hand (2018) remarked on Instagram, "from dark walls come clear messages." Protest graffiti can act as a type of performative writing that seeks to allow for the potential for change in thought or in action by the audience.

As Christopher Norris (2002) states, "performative speech-acts derive their operative meaning from the fact that they embody *conventional* forms and tokens of utterance which are always already in existence before the speaker comes to use them" (p. 109). Performatives always exist in a larger context of signification and also have the capacity to be repeatable in different contexts. Judith Butler makes this notion of performativity central to her understanding of subjects and subjection. According to Butler (1997), "The illocutionary speech act performs its deed *at the moment* of the utterance, and yet to the extent that the moment is ritualized, it is never merely a single moment" (p. 3). While every communicative act is dependent upon conventional or ritualized performances, the possibility for improvisation and change exists. Further, according to Butler (1997), "performativity has its own social temporality in which it remains enabled precisely by the contexts from which it breaks" (p. 40). Graffiti represents excitable performative utterances that seek to break the power dynamics that govern particular spaces. Protest writers and artists break these dynamics through the ways in which their work inherently questions or destroys the historical or conventional uses of those spaces. As Halsey and Young (2006) note, "Graffiti writers engage in events that do not fit neatly into the binaries marked out by late modernity" (p. 294). In performative writing, the boundaries between words and actions become immediately collapsed. For example, graffiti's tagging—an illegal act of naming—breaks the social contract and demands a response from the witnesses: the graffiti writer's name is made visible by the context from which it breaks.

Since the use of the performative always implies an "audience," the success of the performative depends on how witnesses hold those in power accountable to the act. For example, to state to another person, "I dare you," ostensibly involves not only two people (the one giving and the one receiving the dare) but also relies on the implicit demand for a third person (not necessarily literally present) who acts as audience or witness to the dare (Parker & Sedgwick, 1993, pp. 171–172). In turn, performative public graffiti or vandal art relies on the witness of a third party—one who acknowledges the "act" and holds the writer (and witness) accountable. In *How to Do Things with Words,* Austin (1962) delineates "unhappy" performances as a special property of the performative to account for when "something *goes wrong*" in the performance of a performative (p. 14). An unhappy graffiti or vandal art performance fails to create any obvious change or impact on the audience; it will also be subject to buffing, to erasure, to forgetting, a challenge all illegal writing or drawing must overcome. This erasure begs the question as to how the ephemeral nature of protest graffiti and art allows it to ever achieve its purpose. It is not enough that protest graffiti fuels the demonstration in process. My claim is that protest graffiti must fuel the protest to the extent that it allows for the "taking over" of the space, either real or imagined, by those who have been excluded.

The next three case studies show how graffiti and vandal art can be used to embody a movement and keep its potentialities alive in the imaginations of the witnesses. As Brighetti (2010) notes:

> For a writer, the present, actual wall is an affordance and an invitation, but in itself remains only a part of a larger, virtual wall—it is just a sentence in a continuing conversation. And it is the act of joining your sentences into an ongoing conversation which implies the presence of several voices, that leads you to question the qualities and the properties of this shared, common domain, the public. (p. 329)

In these three case studies, I will show how graffiti and vandal art have the potential to open up spaces to the disenfranchised, but I will also illustrate how they can work to limit the "bodies that matter" in a particular space. In my first case study, I will show how graffiti's potentialities can, in contradictory fashion, both include and exclude bodies that are not represented by the protestors themselves.

The Unhappy Performance of the Yellow Vests

Starting in 2018, transportation workers in France began organizing protests and strikes that called for lower fuel taxes, a reintroduction of the solidarity tax on wealth, and the preservation of the traditional retirement age. The numerous protests, nicknamed for the yellow safety vests worn by protesters, became known as "gilets jaunes." Some protests became riots, resulting in looting, massive property destruction, and even the death of nine protesters. Although initially a grassroots movement, the protests soon included the participation of larger French labor unions. The yellow vest protesters, usually middle-class, white French citizens, see themselves as being pushed out of spaces that the French Left and the French labor movement fought to create in the middle of the twentieth century. Unlike the activists in my other two case studies, the yellow vest protesters did not take over the streets of Paris to enact change but to argue for what was already theirs and to assert the significance of their white bodies. In fact, many protestors wrote their names and messages right onto their vests, becoming human billboards for themselves.

On December 1, 2018, a crowd of demonstrators spray-painted the Arc de Triomphe with easily recognizable slogans such as "The yellow vests will win" and "Macron resign." These writings declare the future the writers desire, but they are unemotive and ultimately ineffectual. These writings do not incorporate the more complex iteration practices common in successful graffiti, such as irony and satire. They simply declare the writers' goal to fight against the neoliberal economic policies taking over France. There is, however, other graffiti on the monument. While it is unclear how all the writings on the monument relate to each other, they probably represent several different writers (as shown in Tessier, 2018). Unlike the earliest declarative statements, these inscriptions operate in disparate ways, for different rhetorical purposes: they use threats, satire, or naming to threaten the system. For instance, one inscription sprayed in bright yellow paint, "Anonymous France: we are here," represents a scare tactic, a rhetorical strategy that involves coercing a favorable response by preying upon the audience's fears. In this instance, the threat involves an allusion to a shadowy international hacking collective, Anonymous, which represents a significant enemy to French computer networks. As a scare tactic, it implies that traditional systems are not safe, whether computer networks or the institutions they support. There is also a Spanish, specifically Chilean, inscription that includes the profane Chilean idiom, "Pico Pa Macron," roughly translated as "Macron suck my dick." Unlike the declarative utterances noted above, this sexualized and demeaning reference to Macron represents an affective response: an emotionally charged and personal attack on the French president. In fact, graffiti's power lies in its potential to open up the affective domain in witnesses: highly charged statements, occurring in places they should not, startle the witnesses and allow them to more fully engage with the message. This is language that is meant to be noticed. There is also, in red paint, the nickname Manu, referencing an incident in July 2018 when Macron chastised a young man for calling him "Manu" at an official ceremony. In a video that went viral, Macron tells the teenager, "No, you can't do that, no, no, no, no . . . you call me Mr. President or sir" (Brock, 2018, para. 3). The nickname quickly became a way to disrespect Macron, to question his power by "tagging" him as Manu and stripping him of his title. Graffiti writers often mock the leaders they take issue with by using nicknames or slurs in sarcastic contexts. However, when a graffiti writer or artist tags their own name, it can also become a powerful rhetorical act for the one that claims a space, while at the same time it shows the writer's lack of inclusion in that very space. As I will show in the final case study, this kind of naming can work powerfully in both a symbolic and literal fashion to include those previously unrepresented in the space.

The yellow vest protests have continued into 2020, but the movement has not had much success in affecting fuel prices or Macron's long-term goals to reduce France's social safety nets. Although the yellow vests' demonstrations briefly take over spaces with bodies, graffiti, or chants, they are weakened because they seek not to rewrite social relations in spaces where they protest but to maintain them. In fact, the protests may have invigorated Macron to continue making unprecedented changes to the conventional French social system, because they reinforced his belief in his economic policies: "In a certain way, the gilets jaunes were very good for me. Because it reminded me who I should be" (McAuley, 2019, para. 17). This reminder not only reinforced Macron's belief in reducing the benefits of the French social system in favor of neoliberal capitalism, it also gave him the ability to speak to the "bodies that matter" to him in France, specifically, white bodies. In 2019 Macron and other far-right political leaders began an attack on the bodies of immigrants as a way to temper the anger of the yellow vests and other middle-class French citizens concerned about maintaining jobs for themselves. They are also, of course, taking advantage of fears about the dangers of religious extremism after the violent attacks in 2001, 2015, and 2020 on the French satirical weekly magazine *Charlie Hebdo* and the beheading of a Parisian middle school teacher in October 2020 for showing a *Charlie Hebdo* comic of the Islamic prophet Muhammad to his students. For these voices from the "ultra right," Macron's economic policies are not France's problem; the "real" problem is that there are nonwhite people taking the white middle-class jobs and privileges. By alienating Black and Brown individuals, Macron caters to traditional French values, including nationalism. "My goal is to throw out everybody who has no reason to be here," he said in an interview in November 2019 (as cited in Onishi, 2019, para. 12). This shocking statement belies the fact that France has long been the home to the largest Muslim population in Europe. It also represents a significant contrast to the gentler approach to immigration seen in Macron's early years. In late 2019, Macron began to eliminate immigrant camps in Paris and create policies that limit immigrants' use of France's social safety nets. Additionally, in April 2021, the French Senate passed a measure that would ban anyone under the age of 18 from wearing a hijab in public. Instead of seeking to change social relations, the yellow vest protests largely represented the desire to maintain the status quo. In their focus on maintaining what they had, they reinforce the othering of those "who have no reason" to be in France. According to Brighetti (2010), graffiti can represent "a radical interrogation of public territories, a questioning of the social relationships that define the public domain" (p. 329). This interrogation may, however, result in the othering of bodies deemed not to matter. While graffiti or vandal art have the possibility of opening up spaces for disenfranchised bodies, they can also operate to deny those spaces to others. The next case study shows how a vandal art collective works in Tehran to find a way to include bodies not acceptable to the theocracy.

Protest Graffiti and Vandal Art in Tehran

Graffiti as a form of protest is an old phenomenon in Iran; before the 1979 revolution, street walls in Iran were used as canvases for slogans against the Shah, the last monarch. Since the revolution, however, Iranian authorities only tolerate state-sponsored graffiti and wall paintings. Murals in Tehran and other Iranian cities usually show martyrs of the eight-year war with Iraq and revolutionary figures. Even these murals, dominated by men, are subject to censorship.

The vandal artist Black Hand arose out of the Arab Spring in 2011. Often resembling the work of Banksy, Black Hand's political street art in Tehran embodies ideas that are not welcome to be represented in an Islamic Republic. Many of their images and writings are very offensive to the state and to some (or many) witnesses on the street—a situation that necessitates Black Hand remaining anonymous. As Black Hand comments in their only interview, in *The Guardian*: "I hide my identity for security reasons. Under the Iranian municipality laws, writing on walls or advertising without official permission is a crime" (Dehghan, 2014). In fact, it's not just graffiti and vandal artists who face censorship and severe penalties. In 2015, after releasing a documentary on Iranian graffiti, *Writing on the City,* on YouTube, director Keywan Karimi was arrested and sentenced to six years in prison and 223 lashes (Associated Press, 2015; "Iranian director," 2015). Consequently, Black Hand only displays images of their work on Instagram, and they do not give interviews. In cyberspace, Blank Hand plays with showing their body in their work. In some posts, they show themselves in a hijab putting up a screen print on a busy Tehranian street; in others they show pictures of their hands with painted nails or petting a black cat. According to Brighetti (2010), "It is the writer's body that makes a territory with his or her own graffiti. . . . A search for identity is a search for a territory, and the body is where it all begins" (p. 327). Nothing speaks to the simultaneous vulnerability and power of the body as much as Iranian vandal artists who risk their personal safety to argue on the walls of Tehran for the freedom of bodies other than their own.

On the street, most of Black Hand's work depicts bodies that Muslim laws in Iran keep hidden: female bodies, LGBTQ+ bodies, handicapped bodies. In fact, Black Hand's activism seems focused on placing bodies (real or imagined) in spaces denied to them by the Islamic state. One of Black Hand's longest-running activist projects over the past decade has been to campaign for Iranian women to attend football matches. Women have been banned from stadiums in Iran since 1981, following the 1979 revolution when women's rights came under attack. One of Black Hand's most compelling images is a screen print that shows an Iranian woman in her country's national jersey (Black Hand, 2014). She is wearing a black head scarf and yellow gloves and is raising dishwashing liquid as a trophy. Her face is scowling and defiant, like most of Black Hand's female subjects, and she looks directly at the viewer in a defiant gaze. This confrontational scowl represents an extraordinary reimagining of Iranian women's bodies. The image is darkly satirical, using sardonic humor to exaggerate the contrast between the "trophies" and revealing the anger many Iranian women have about their exclusion from football matches.[1]

---

1. This image can be seen via various newspaper articles, such as Dehghan (2014).

Over the years, Black Hand has unveiled many similar images to protest the ban on women going to the stadium: depictions of women in jerseys walking to the game or celebrating at games have been splattered with red paint only moments after they were finished. Most were quickly painted over or buffed without a trace; screen prints were quickly peeled away by passersby, leaving only fragments of the original images. In October 2018, after many years spent protesting the stadium ban, Black Hand released an emotional message on their Instagram. They begin by writing that "talking about women's rights is upsetting" because they have not made a "positive influence on my serious audience." They are disappointed in themselves, because even "with all the importance of the subject and the hot street art scene," they have not gotten their point across; they feel they have not had an impact. They apologize to their audience and explain that they are looking for a new way to continue fighting for women's right to go to the stadium (Black Hand, 2018). This outpouring on Instagram shows the emotional pain enacted in a grassroots movement's failure to achieve its goals. Black Hand's campaign for women to attend stadiums has long represented a desire of many Iranian people to allow women into stadiums, but the Iranian government has steadfastly refused, although most other Muslim countries allow women in stadiums. The ban has not been supported by the Fédération Internationale de Football Association (FIFA). In fact, in 2019, under pressure from FIFA, the state allowed a few Iranian women to enter a football stadium for the first time in decades, "after FIFA threatened to suspend the Islamic republic over its controversial male-only policy" (Agence France-Presse, 2019, para. 1). As reported, "as many as 100 Iranian 'handpicked' women entered Azadi for a friendly against Bolivia. But the day after, the prosecutor general warned there would be no repeat, saying it would 'lead to sin'" (para. 10). Consequently, the ban was immediately put back in place. As of the writing of this essay in 2022, Black Hand's vandal art still has not had the desired impact; the ban on women in stadiums remains, seemingly stronger than ever.

Although Black Hand laments what they did not accomplish, they have done work that matters. Graffiti and vandal art operate as interventions into everyday spaces, which as Lefebvre (1991) writes, are always political and ideological. Political and ideological change usually comes slowly, to be sure, and Lefebvre's work provides a framework for analyzing and understanding the complexity of urban spaces and how graffiti and vandal art in those spaces allow for the potential for reclaiming and remaking the city into a more humane and just social space over time. Certainly, Black Hand's October 2018 post reveals that they see their work as an unhappy performative; they have not had an impact on their "serious" audience, and they fear their cause is seen as "superficial," but their imaginative renderings that put "unwanted" bodies into places and spaces does make something happen: witnesses can see women in jerseys going to stadiums even if they do not actually get there. Their attendance exists as a possibility. Notably, these images, long painted over on the street, still exist on Black Hand's Instagram, a platform now considered by graffiti and street art aficionados to be the "wall of the world." Although they do not seem to be putting much new work on the street these days, Black Hand constantly reposts work from the past on social media. Further, the imaginative bodies Black Hand depicts are not "superficial." They remain, symbolically, speaking to the desire for women's freedom in Iran. Black Hand's messages may be diffused spatially onto the virtual landscape, but they remain there, nonetheless, to protest basic human rights issues in Tehran. The message persists and still has the potential to enact change, even if the city's spaces continue to keep women out. Of course, the long-term success of grassroots activism depends on the ability to make significant changes in the social relations within those contested spaces, a possibility, I argue, that may be seen in the graffiti on the Robert E. Lee statue in Richmond, Virginia, following the protests that arose after George Floyd's death.

Black Lives Matter and the Robert E. Lee Statue in Richmond

Reading protest graffiti and vandal art requires an ongoing, dynamic reenvisioning of social relations between the writers, artists, and witnesses who create and recreate symbolic spaces together. Readers can make meaning not just by witnessing but by participating in the space in new and different ways. The Black Lives Matter protest writing on the Robert E. Lee statue works to imagine, and ultimately invent, new ways for Black people to see and be seen in that space. As a specific localized site, the space has been used to celebrate the Confederacy, slavery, and the devaluation of Black life that occurred in Richmond's past. The history surrounding the monument's historical placement, reception, and use by the community creates a rhetorical context ripe for engagement by Black Lives Matter activists. Richmond's history in making space for white supremacy and its contemporary moment in the Black Lives Matter protests combine to set the stage for witnessing the full performative potentiality of Black Lives Matter graffiti.

When local grassroots protests arose out of the Black Lives Matter movement in the days following George Floyd's murder by police officers in Minneapolis at the end of May 2020, protestors vandalized Confederate statues all over the south; however, no other graffitied statue received as much press as the one of Robert E. Lee in Richmond (shown in figure 11.1). Images of the

FIGURE 11.1. Photo of artist Dustin Klein's projection of George Floyd's image on the statue of Confederate general Robert E. Lee. Photo by Reuters / Julia Rendleman in Richmond, Virginia, US, June 18, 2020.

statue covered in graffiti have become a national representation of the Black Lives Matter protests against police brutality.

Unlike the yellow vest protests in France, ongoing challenges to white supremacy in the Richmond park have served both to call for the removal of the racist statue as well as to symbolically and literally rewrite a space that had memorialized slavery. Richmond participants did not just arrive to witness the graffiti. They also joined in to recreate a space beyond simply the removal of the statue. The graffiti they wrote signifies how Black lives suffered in Virginia. Although the statue's visual aesthetics were transformed by graffiti writers, it was the dynamic "takeover" of a space once dedicated to memorializing slavery that truly reconstructed it to honor Black individuals.

This freedom came to an emotional peak on June 18, 2020, when artist Dustin Klein created a heart-stopping and visually arresting projection of George Floyd on the base of the statue. The black-and-white image of Floyd's somber face on top of the graffitied Confederate statue went viral, showing the world how protest art can reimagine a space: in this case, symbolically placing the Black body onto a space that had previously denigrated it. This image made the front page of many newspapers and websites and quickly spread across social media. *National Geographic* used it as a cover for its annual Year in Pictures issue for 2020. It is an indelible image of 2020 and of the Black Lives Matter movement: its symbolic projection on the statue reveals the pain, suffering, and hope of the Black Lives Matter movement.

The space around the statue was quickly changed as well. As reported by Ezra Marcus for the *New York Times,* during the summer of 2020, the statue and its surrounding park became a place for protestors to memorialize their participation in the Black Lives Matter movement and for music, dance, and art to come together to create an ongoing participatory and collaborative space for Black people. Spray paint cans were left on the steps of the statue, and Black families brought picnics and took photos. As with many graffiti memorials, flowers, candles, and stuffed animals could be found all around the bottom of the statue. Participants also left laminated photographs and biographies at the base of the statue to memorialize others who have suffered police brutality, such as Eric Garner. On Juneteenth, hundreds of people attended the holiday celebration and held a candlelight vigil at Lee Circle organized by several local groups (Marcus, 2020).

As the graffiti on the statue continued to be written and rewritten over the summer, the messages changed, often moving from declarative statements to satirical performance. Frank D'Angelo (1974) explores the rhetorical strategies graffiti writers use to achieve their purposes and argues that effective graffiti is satirical in nature. Using satire, graffiti often takes aggressive action: it attacks in order to change opinions, highlighting what is obvious yet often overlooked in plain sight. According to De Angelo, the figures of satire most often seen in graffiti include allusions, puns, irony, alliteration, rhyme, antithesis, parallelism, apposition, and parody. All of these figures could be seen on the monument on June 15. In looking at Terry Kilby's (2020) 3D reconstruction of the statue as it looked that day, one can see alliteration and parallelism in slogans such as "No Justice No Peace," "Just Want Justice," "Cops are Creepy," and "Let's Heal the Hurt." Readers also see appositions, figures that use opposing concepts to highlight key messages, such as "Divisionism only creates Racism." Allusions to previous American historical events in the civil rights movement or the American Revolution can also be seen in inscriptions such as "Hate is the Enemy of Mankind;" and "Give me Liberty or Give me Death." On one prominent section of the statue, a writer sloppily sprayed a cloaked figure as "KKK" with "Killer" written right next to it. Directly across the statue is a "Welcome" message, an ironic positioning that shows who is welcome and unwelcome in the space. In one instance, "Restitution" appears to be written at the top of one side of the statue, but it was later crossed out in different paint and some of its letters were revised to say: "Revolution." Not surprisingly, "FUCK Pigs" or "FUCK police" show up frequently, as well as many hastily sprayed pig faces. We see the word FUCK perhaps more than any other word, highlighting both the intense anger and powerful resolve to stop police brutality. We also find several inscriptions that seek to denigrate and attack prominent figures who have promoted white supremacy, such as "Trump has Little Hands" and "Lee fucked his Horse." The profanity and sexualized attacks lie alongside the many names inscribed on the statue—tags of writers and artists, but also the names of victims of police brutality. These names exist beside the satiric tropes as claims for identity in the spaces the satire has opened up. Names that matter. Names to remember. It is hard not to feel emotional when viewing the statue. The graffiti and vandal art open up the affective domain to the audience and emotionally illustrate the pain and suffering of Black Americans. Perhaps in the most moving inscription, the words "Imagine being," can be found scrolled along the bottom of the monument, a profound statement on the devaluation of Black existence in America and the concomitant hope that comes from the Black Lives Matter movement.

Unsurprisingly, there are many sprayed tags for "Black Lives Matter." However, this apparently simple declarative statement reveals the real political potential that may arise from these words. According to Judith Butler (2020), there is a transformative value to the utterance "Black Lives Matter":

> The speaking asserts the value, which means that the one who speaks [Black Lives Matter] designates itself implicitly as one who deserves to be valued. The performative act of the self—the speech act—is also a way of asserting that self and its value. When then, a black life claims that it matters, it is not only the speech act but the living self that is performative, and so the performative is not mere show or some kind of fakery. On the contrary, it is a way of really mattering. (para. 7)

The writing on the statue redefines the space visually and conceptually as an information space that holds histories of past white supremacy alongside representations of those excluded or oppressed by that history. Participants are invited to bear witness to the marking of the existence of the performing "Other." As a spatializing practice and performance, Black Lives Matter graffiti creates witnessing opportunities and the chance to encounter not just an/other's claim: "I am/was here," but "I matter."

The Lee statue had been in Richmond Park for 130 years, but Virginia governor Ralph Northam declared in June 2020 that the statue would be removed, prompting lawsuits against the removal of the Confederate monument that cited restrictive covenants from 1887 and 1890. As litigation drew on through the summer and into the fall, activists began speaking about ways to memorialize the protest that occurred in and around the statue. In November 2020, the governor asked the state to fund the creation of a more inclusive public space representing the diversity of Virginia's people (Schneider, 2020). However, legal cases brought by homeowners in the neighborhood delayed the removal of the statue until September 8, 2021. Two weeks after the Lee monument was removed, a new monument commemorating the emancipation and freedom of enslaved people was placed near the James River in downtown Richmond, more than two miles away.

Valuing the Black Lives Matter inscriptions and the projections on the Robert E. Lee statue requires a literacy that sees the rhetorical purpose of the tags and images on the statue as inclusion of the bodies of those that have been excluded. In this way, although the spaces on and around the monument will change, it has already been claimed in history by Black Lives Matter protestors who have asserted their value, their outrage, and their existence on a statue that had previously symbolized their denigration as human beings. The statue will no longer be a place that renders the Black body invisible. The protestors changed this landscape by using the power of graffiti to transform the space into one that memorializes not a hero of the Confederacy who fought to keep slavery but those who have fought and will continue to fight to make Black lives matter.

CONCLUSION:
IMAGINE BEING

Graffiti writing and vandal art represent dynamic, complex productions that have the potential to recreate both literal and symbolic transgressions that may inspire, support, or sustain a grassroots movement. A graffiti writer or vandal artist works within a localized space that operates, according to Lefebvre (1991) as "always, and simultaneously, both a field of action and a basis of action" because human bodies leave traces (like tags or screen prints) that are both "symbolic and practical" (p. 191). Just like a sit-in or march, protest graffiti and vandal art appear and disappear; they inhabit spaces in which their message can easily be erased or forgotten. And yet, these case studies allow us to see how writers and artists can provide the impetus for the audience to become participants and performers in those contested spaces, to take over a space literally, symbolically, or in both ways and actively pursue the possibility for real change in the social relations in that space. Graffiti and vandal art are disruptive because they reveal, as Halsey and Young (2006) note, "the presence (and frustrating absence) of highly problematic if not threatening bodies—namely, writers of illicit graffiti" (p. 295). Those bodies are dangerous because they "interrupt the familiar, the known, the already named" (Halsey and Young, 2006, p. 295). All of the grassroots movements in the three case studies presented above used both literal and symbolic transgressions as strategies to achieve their goals. As of the writing of this chapter, these goals have not been fully realized. The gilet jaunes have not impacted Macron's economic policies. Black Hand has not seen women attending football matches. The Lee statue remains in legal lockdown, sequestered behind a fence in the park until the case is decided by the courts. It would be easy to dismiss these movements as failures, but that dismissal does not account for the potentialities that unruly rhetoric can have.

Urban graffiti, as it first developed in the 1960s and '70s in Philadelphia and New York City, expressed intense anger at the lack of opportunity for marginalized groups in both cities. Tagging their names was a way for writers to assert their existence and to make themselves visible in spaces that did not value them. They tagged the city because they hated the city; they hated its social relations and constructs and hated its lack of justice and inequality. In the decades following, graffiti and street art came to be commodified, like everything else within a capitalist system. However, if and when graffiti writers and vandal artists can operate outside established norms and laws, their unruliness still opens up spaces to see inequality and moves witnesses to consider the potentialities beyond the present moment's realities. As Halsey and Young (2006) note, "graffiti writers are not so much seeking to escape or suspend reality so much as they are willing and knowing participants within various realities" (p. 294). Therefore, graffiti is an interstitial practice in that it is read differently by its incidental audiences. It is always both a criminal activity and an aesthetic one; it operates as resistance and vandalism. Future research on graffiti as an interstitial practice might illuminate the complicated ways graffiti and vandal art could be interpreted and used by different social groups. Research is also needed to more fully articulate how the unruliness of graffiti and vandal art impact the affective domain of their witnesses, so researchers could make more specific connections between writers and their audiences. This work, coupled with a wider range of case studies in various localized landscapes, may allow scholars to reveal more specific rhetorical patterns that lead to change in social relations in contested spaces. This work is crucial to understanding how activists can use the unruliness of graffiti and vandal art to further their causes. If activist writing and vandal art work to take over spaces so they long remain in the imaginations of witnesses (both actual and virtual), they not only encourage participation and identity within a movement but also open up the opportunity for their messages to come down off the wall. In this way, they allow the disenfranchised to move from having to "imagine being" in a space to being in one that fully and resolutely includes them.

CHAPTER 12

Urban Affairs Coalition

Fifty Years of Organizational Organizing in Philadelphia

KALIE M. MAYBERRY

Marginalized Philadelphians find power in coalitions, stemming from the city's grassroot activisms initiated in the 1960s. And while social and economic issues still require persistence and resilience, one organization stands out as having spent more than 50 years organizing, shifting, and adapting to the needs of Philadelphia's citizens through highly localized initiatives and programs set to combat structural inequality, systemic racism, and police brutality.

The 55-year-old Urban Affairs Coalition—a combination of the Philadelphia Urban Coalition and the Greater Philadelphia Partnership—has stood the test of time within a changing city facing the challenges of growth, discrimination, and inequalities common among urban communities. Built from ideals and values of shared resources, the Urban Affairs Coalition created a radical approach to mobilize access by using their own power to strengthen others and uplift marginalized populations.

For over 50 years since its founding, the mission and focus of the organization has remained the same: "UAC is a place that really connects and hopefully inspires dreamers and doers. We are a place where government, business, individuals, and community can come together to work on very important issues and initiatives. Sometimes we lead, sometimes we support. Sometimes we coordinate, but there is very little that goes on in the city of Philadelphia that UAC does not touch in some way" (S. Matlock-Turner, personal communication, November 10, 2020). As the Coalition looks forward to the next 50 years, one thing is clear: wherever UAC goes, there is a movement, not a moment.

MAKING A MOVEMENT

When the news rang out of Dr. Martin Luther King Jr.'s assassination on April 4, 1968, the streets of 125 cities nationwide broke into protest within hours, erupting from heartache that over the next few days teetered toward violence and destruction (Howard, 2016). Cities across the Northeast, including Boston, Baltimore, and Washington, DC, saw a historic turnout of activists, specifically African Americans. Philadelphia was no exception, prompting the mayor to call a state of emergency (Howard, 2016; Kennedy, 1983).

Seeing this unrest in the predominantly Black communities of their city, white executives of three major local banks headquartered in Philadelphia organized a meeting with the established Black leaders on the "frontlines" to discuss the condition of the city (B. Anderson, personal communication, December 2, 2020; S. Matlock-Turner, personal communication, November 10, 2020). However, Black leadership in Philadelphia throughout the 1950s and 1960s was split into two distinct groups: the more politically moderate group, made up of the Black middle class, and the more radical group, taking a militant-style approach against the majority-white political and police leadership (B. Anderson, personal communication, December 2, 2020; Kativa, n.d.). It was the radicals who were those true frontline leaders, and their eventual meeting with the bankers laid the groundwork for a movement, merging two distinct worlds in the city at that time: the white business owners and elites, who held resources and money, and the Black activists and changemakers, who held trust and commitment from their unofficial constituents.

REACTING AND RESPONDING TO CITY NEEDS

Following the 1968 meeting, the first iteration of the Urban Affairs Coalition—then still the Philadelphia Urban Coalition—started to transform from an idea at a table to a fully-fledged 501(c)(3) organization. In the weeks immediately following, the business leaders raised nearly $1 million to fund the organization; appointed lawyer, activist, and prior deputy mayor Charles Bowser as the first executive director; and decided upon a tripartite board leadership—"one [chair] from the community, another from business, and third from government"—to have a space to "properly hash out" solutions to pressing issues (E. Jones, personal communication, November 30, 2020; B. Anderson, personal communication, December 2, 2020).

As for the structure of the organization, the Philadelphia Urban Coalition became a "home for nonprofits," housing smaller grassroots groups under their umbrella and developing a model where these groups could share internal structures—such as accounting and human resources—at a lower cost than through either outsourcing or in-house personnel. These "program partners" could then leverage their representation under the Coalition to work and advocate together, while still operating independently and providing "necessary services" as they best saw fit (E. Jones, personal communication, November 30, 2020). And in a city where years of disinvestment in redlined neighborhoods disintegrated housing and school infrastructure and depleted the lending and employment opportunities of the once thriving Black middle-class, these services needed to fill the economic and social service gaps where no city services were available. Thus, the Coalition began to focus on a three-part approach: "prevention, intervention, integration" to "disrupt poverty, racism, and discrimination" (S. Matlock-Turner, personal communication, November 10, 2020).

One example of an intervention strategy unique to Philadelphia relied on the organization's role as a connector across communities, businesses, and government. The third executive director and a former lawyer, Ernie Jones, saw an opportunity to mediate between the three entities under his jurisdiction when the State of Pennsylvania issued a request for proposals for organizations to help recruit and bring minority companies into the bidding process and provide technical assistance (Devins, 1994; E. Jones, personal communication, November 30, 2020). In response, the Coalition founded their Economic Development Projects initiative, connecting minority and women-led construction businesses with major projects to further wealth-building and economic inclusivity among these marginalized populations. Since 1983, over $9 billion in construction projects have been managed by the Coalition, at sites including the Comcast Center and the Philadelphia Museum of Art. According to Jones, the program was "very, very successful" and put the organization "on the map" as a local advocate, far exceeding the goals established in the federal grant and bringing new resources to the communities involved.

Meanwhile, as the Philadelphia Urban Coalition was attracting attention from every corner of the city, it also underwent a mutual acquisition with the Greater Philadelphia Partnership to strengthen their political capital and expand their leadership potential. The Greater Philadelphia Urban Affairs Coalition (GPUAC) was officially formed in 1988, bringing together the two organizations, their partners, and their boards. As a newly merged organization, GPUAC was then approached by the City of Philadelphia with an opportunity: serve as an intermediary for funds between the city government and grassroots community groups (E. Jones, personal communication, November 30, 2020). This not only allowed GPUAC to further their own localized grassroots mission by connecting more city funding to marginalized communities, but it allowed them to capitalize on their own size and status through grant funding to disburse through their program partners so they could "go out and do what they do best" (E. Jones, personal communication, November 30, 2020; S. Matlock-Turner, personal communication, November 10, 2020).

This radical approach to shared resources has continued to shape the model of the organization as a convener, connector, and doer, as GPUAC was putting actual dollars behind their actions to solve social issues. Over the next ten years, the organization's budget jumped from roughly $2 million to about $20 million. The commitment to building solutions became a defining focus of the first Black female leader of the Coalition, Sharmain Matlock-Turner.

INFLUENCE OF LOCAL LEADERSHIP

One of the greatest strengths of GPUAC has been their dedicated local leaders, who serve as advocates for the distinctive communities they are from. And while each leader has brought both their personal and professional experiences advocating for the rights of Black citizens to the Coalition, it was the rise of Black women in leadership that defined the organization as it entered the twenty-first century.

Running parallel to the growth of the organization throughout the 1970s and 1980s was the "advancement of Black people into elected office" including the city council and state legislature, thanks in part to the Civil Rights Act (B. Anderson, personal communication, December 2, 2020). Among these rising political leaders were prominent Black women, including Ethel D. Allen, the first African American woman elected to Philadelphia's city council in 1972, and Marian Tasco, who served as secretary to first executive director Charles Bowser in the early 1970s, before becoming the first African American city commissioner in Philadelphia and later a city council member in 1987 (Terruso, 2015). Tasco later became a mentor to a young Sharmain Matlock-Turner, an activist and advocate from West Philadelphia, who rose to prominence after this initial wave of Black women leaders.

"I'm a poor kid from West Philly. I'm blessed that I came along in the Civil Rights Era," recounts Sharmain Matlock-Turner, current president and

CEO of the Urban Affairs Coalition, fourth leader in the organization's history, and the first woman to hold the title. "[Around that time] people are saying 'maybe we need to hire some Black and brown people to be a part of our workforce.' So I get a chance to be successful because I was a part of that" (S. Matlock-Turner, personal communication, November 10, 2020).

By the time Matlock-Turner was tapped to run the merged UAC in 1999, she had already spent nearly a decade working in state and city politics, including as chief of staff to a state senator, and another six years in the corporate health care sector. And while the city had more Black representation in the city council (including Marian Tasco) and new growth under Mayor Ed Rendell, the Coalition now needed to position itself to take advantage of that growth, building upon a $20 million budget, a handful of programs, and a need for a structured leadership and framework.

COALITION AS FAMILY

After completing an organization assessment during her first few months, Matlock-Turner understood that "the bones of the organization" were well respected: "People definitely look to UAC as a home for other nonprofits, that [narrative] was very, very well established by the work that [former Executive Director] Ernie Jones did" (S. Matlock-Turner, personal communication, November 10, 2020). So she took the existing framework and began to configure "coalition" to become synonymous with "family"—and it stuck.

"I would describe UAC as a family, as a village. I was running around those halls when I was 12 years old," shares Mel Wells (personal communication, December 10, 2020), now president and CEO of One Day At A Time (ODAAT), reflecting on his time growing up within a program partner organization that joined the Coalition back in the early days. Founded by his father Mel Wells Sr., ODAAT serves individuals in recovery from alcohol and drug abuse, along with people diagnosed with HIV and AIDS. "UAC was a village, and Ms. Sharmain became a mother figure to me," Wells recalls.

The motif of the family not only brought everyone—staff, program partners, external connections—together, but it also allowed each of them to maintain their own identities and idiosyncrasies. No one was asked to change when they came to the Urban Affairs Coalition—they were just given the support they needed and connected to resources they did not know existed. The model of shared resources extended in the UAC family, drawing together radical access with unconventional appreciation and love not often found in organizational spaces.

"We are family, and I think that's necessary to do this kind of work, because I have to really believe that you have my back," states Robin Ingram (personal communication, December 8, 2020), executive director of Center for Hope, a program partner of UAC that serves individuals facing homeless. Ingram goes on to say: "I think when that runs deep like with family, then you have more confidence to deal with the confrontation we deal with on the front lines. When you're really up against it, family comes together for a common goal, a common good."

CONCLUSION

Under Sharmain Matlock-Turner's leadership, the UAC continues to be a home for "dreamers and doers" of now over 80 nonprofit program partners, who come under the umbrella of fiscal sponsorship and shared accessibility created by the organization, which now has a nearly $60 million operating budget. But UAC also continues to be a place where advocates and community organizers come together to tackle the big systemic and structural issues our cities and country still face—even more than 50 years later. To achieve this, the organization relies on the framework set forth by the original founders of the organization to eliminate racism, end poverty, and "make sure that people have real opportunity to be successful, no matter where they started, no matter what their race, creed or color" (S. Matlock-Turner, November 10, 2020).

CHAPTER 13

#RageAgainstRape

Nepali Women's Transnational Assemblage and Networked Performances against Rape

SWETA BANIYA

In January 2018, the gang rape of two Nepali women in Kathmandu sparked a national debate in Nepal that inspired discourse around gender-based violence. Spontaneously, during this debate, a transnational movement called #RageAgainstRape took place on Twitter. While the issue of gender-based violence, including rape, is not new in Nepal, the brutality in these two rape cases garnered attention and public sentiment that led to this movement. Initiated by Nepali women residing in transnational geographical locations and spaces, this movement challenged the government, the police, and the public to act against the perpetrators of the two rape incidents. Nepali women living, working, and studying within Nepal and beyond (including me) used the affordances provided by the digital platform to network and launch a hashtag movement (Dadas, 2017). Similar to various transnational feminist activist groups from around the world, the #RageAgainstRape activists also looked at the digital space as a productive place for protest against oppressive practices and as a powerful site for demanding change (Ouellette, 2018). In launching this transnational movement, women tweeted using the hashtag #RageAgainstRape, organized rallies, and wrote letters and newspaper articles to combat the state and the Nepali society's silence toward rape. Three years after its inception, this grassroots movement has been successful in raising awareness about rape, in pressuring the government to act and make strict policies against perpetrators, and in making the public more sensitive toward the issues of gender-based minorities.

The movement #RageAgainstRape first started as a "group message" on Twitter. Members of the group, including 50 different Nepali women who were spread across the world, began posting after the two gang rape cases of January 2018. These gang rape cases created two different rhetorics: supporting the survivors and blaming the survivors. Groups like #RageAgainstRape responded by disrupting discourses regarding the gang rapes to stand strong with survivors. The spontaneous launch of this movement is not only an affective reaction to the two rape cases but also a reaction to the historical suppression of women and other gender-based minorities in Nepal, which is rooted in patriarchal traditions that fail to recognize them as citizens. Unfortunately, however, movements like #RageAgainstRape often get overshadowed by larger global movements like #MeToo, as there is less international coverage and attention paid to issues of marginalized women in Nepal. While various feminist rhetoric scholars have focused on global movements, Royster, Kirsch, and Bizzell (2012) remind us that there is much left to do to situate our contemporary feminist rhetorical studies in transnational contexts.

Studying transnational movements like #RageAgainstRape helps in understanding how these movements are shaped by cultural, social, and economic interconnectivities and interactions as well as by cross-cultural mobilizations of power, language resources, and people (Hesford & Schell, 2008; Wang, 2013). Thinking culturally, socially, and politically, #RageAgainstRape emerged as a powerful force to challenge the societal and political violence against women in Nepal. With their presence on Twitter, these women connect the local to the global through "transnational collective action," as articulated by Schell (2013), where these activists mobilize their resources, networks, and time to coordinate a campaign by forming transnational coalitions. By presenting a case study of the #RageAgainstRape movement, including my ethnographic experiences, I argue that non-Western digital social movements initiated transnationally help bring justice to marginalized and vulnerable populations. As a coalitional force conducting hybrid cyber-public activism (Wang, 2020), the #RageAgainstRape group holds an online space with their hashtag #RageAgainstRape and an offline space with their actions that engage with the public and stakeholders. In this chapter, by sharing my experience as one of the founding members of this transnational feminist movement, I illustrate the case study of #RageAgainstRape to showcase the process of the formation of a transnational movement, the ways activism challenges cultural norms, and some takeaways of this movement for global audiences. In what follows, I provide an overview of the movement, describe my theoretical framework, present the two major results of my case study, and conclude with some takeaways.

THE #RageAgainstRape MOVEMENT

The #RageAgainstRape group and its members specifically use digital media for their activism while also working informally in nondigital spaces by meeting various stakeholders like politicians, the media, police, and other government representatives. The work of the activists in the social and cultural context of Nepal intersects with various power relations, capturing the meaning of experience and community for social action (Collins, 2019). The group has an active Twitter handle, a Facebook group page, a blog, and a Google Drive for collaborative work. The group has been actively using the hashtag #RageAgainstRape and has invited many people and stakeholders to participate in the movement. One could argue that this kind of work, spanning time and space and involving many people with layers of expertise and communication, could be classified as "symbolic-analytic" work (Pigg, 2014). The symbolic-analytic work involves working across time and spaces to complete projects, balancing personal and work domains, and using technology like social media strategically to solve everyday problems (Pigg, 2014). This group involves Nepali women (and some male activists) from different careers, social strata, and educational and professional backgrounds who reside across the world. #RageAgainstRape relies on the network of people who come from various organizations, who are leaders in the sociopolitical sector, and who support this movement. Various women leaders like the former National Human Rights Commission representative Mohana Ansari, former election commissioner Ila Sharma, and constituent assembly member Binda Pandey have continuously supported #RageAgainstRape and have been part of this coalition as listeners and advocates. In fact, it was Pandey who helped in taking the online movement to parliament and advocating for formulating the new strict laws against rape in Nepal. For these reasons, #RageAgainstRape and the work of its members consists of symbolic-analytic work.

The #RageAgainstRape movement initially started its work digitally on Twitter through the use of its corresponding hashtag. However, in addition to the digital spaces, it also started at the grassroots level of engaging with various political stakeholders, police administration, and news organizations. The group has utilized digital spaces such as Twitter and Instagram for regular activism with the hashtag #RageAgainstRape and for updates on gender-based violence and rallies. Similarly, they use their website to provide more information about the group and their mission and to share articles group members have written. After using the hashtag #RageAgainstRape for about a month and a half, the group organized a rally in Kathmandu, the capital of Nepal, on March 8, 2018, Women's Day, to protest the government and law enforcement's silence with regards to the two January 2018 rape cases. While group members in Nepal marched with more than 100 people, I wrote an article published in *Republica,* the national daily newspaper, that called on people to join our movement and protest. Recently, on February 12, 2021, some members of #RageAgainstRape in Nepal participated in a large rally organized by various coalitions of women, protesting a rape case as well as the government's new rules that restricted women's free movement to go abroad. The digital rhetorical practices of the group members of #RageAgainstRape are mostly carried out by writing in both English and Nepali on various digital platforms as well as in nondigital platforms such as daily newspapers, weekly magazines, and blogs.

#RageAgainstRape has three long-term goals: (1) preventing crimes like rape, (2) pressuring the government to create strict rape laws, and (3) conducting awareness-raising campaigns and supporting any survivors of rape and gender-based violence. One of the founding members of the group, Hima Bista, says in one of her recent articles, "when we decided to be a part of this global platform, we set some rules: we won't use this movement for personal gain, or to promote a given political agenda, and we will maintain secrecy with information, and if anyone wants to research or write about us, we will talk about the movement as a group" (Bista, 2018, originally in Nepali and translated by the author). With these ground rules, #RageAgainstRape continued their activism on digital platforms like Twitter and Instagram. Members of the #RageAgainstRape movement also specifically mention that one of their goals is "to create pressure on the government (focusing on Ministry of Women, Children and Social Welfare and NWC) to expedite action on cases of violence against women, resulting in a measurable decrease in these cases" (rageagainstrape.wordpress.com). For example, in September 2018 there was another brutal rape and murder case involving a 13-year-old Nepali girl, which also stirred a lot of conversation as the government failed to pay much attention to the case. During that time, aside from #RageAgainstRape, another movement called #JusticeforNirmala was organized in Nepal. Various members of the #RageAgainstRape group also joined this other movement, which further fueled both digital and nondigital activism against rape. Unfortunately, however, more than five years later, the perpetrators of this crime have yet to be found and brought to justice. As a form of protest, the #JusticeforNirmala

page on the #RageAgainstRape website demands justice for Nirmala by sharing information about her rape and murder and a poster with her photo and
hashtag #JusticeforNirmala.

ANALYZING TRANSNATIONAL FEMINIST ACTIVISM

I present the following case study along with my own ethnographic experiences as a member of the #RageAgainstRape movement from its inception
and my continued work with the team. I am one of the initial founding members of this movement. I was in the United States when we started #Rage-
AgainstRape (and I still am). My engagement is mostly remote, where I
participate in discussions via group chats and phone calls. I also write articles, curate information, maintain the movement's social media platforms,
and design slogans for the rallies. Additionally, along with other members
of the group, I spend time tweeting, sharing information, and responding to
internet trolls, or people who purposefully incite division by writing messages
and comments supporting the notion that the issue of rape and gender-based
violence is not important. While my intention is to present the case study so
that it speaks for itself, I believe that including my own experiences, which
are closely entangled in the movement, may provide an additional perspective
that might not have been possible had I been an outsider to the movement.
The ethnographic experiences that I present here consist of self-reflexive rhetoric, which has transformed my identity so that I could become an academic
activist. As an academic activist, I have been able to deeply consider the civic
purpose of my position in the academy, what I can do with the knowledge I
have gained, who I can help with this knowledge, and by what means I can
help (Cushman, 1996).

Along with my ethnographic experiences of working with #RageAgainst-
Rape, what I present here evokes the understanding of transnational feminist activism and how it plays out in spaces where women's voices are not
heard. In the context of Nepal, socially and culturally, the issues of women
and gender-based minorities are not often listened to or are mostly viewed
as unimportant. Nepal's national newspaper reports, "since the beginning
of the lockdown enforced by the government, on an average, two girls were
raped daily in this period" ("Rape cases," 2020). With the rising number of
rape cases, the government has still failed to impose stricter rape laws. This
case study therefore illustrates how female community activists in Nepal and
abroad launched #RageAgainstRape, which allowed them to raise their voices
against such atrocities and establish a discourse by holding space digitally and

nondigitally. I approach this grassroots-level digital activism using a social justice framework mediated by intersectionality to understand how the activists navigate their multiplicity of identities transnationally to achieve justice for the survivors and to pressure the authorities to create better policies for women (Crenshaw, 2006; Walton, Moore, & Jones, 2019). To complement this framework, I use theories of transnational assemblages that I have addressed in my other works (Baniya, 2020, 2021) and the theories of counterpublics (Asen, 2018; Fraser, 1990; Warner, 2002).

Intersectionality works against reductionism and purity, promoting a perspective that accounts for the "differences that make a difference" in how people can maneuver their worlds (Chávez, 2013). The theory of intersectionality, originally articulated by Kimberlé Williams Crenshaw (2006), became one of the major theories that highlighted social changes and inequalities, directing toward a pathway of social change (Collins, 2019). Patricia Hill Collins (2019) defines intersectionality as a critical theory that can address contemporary social problems and call attention to social changes that are needed to solve these social problems by providing a foundation for critical questions, concerns, and analyses. Using this framework helps in understanding how Nepali women's identities, class, and current positions allow them to advocate and shed light on the inequalities. Additionally, as "intersectionality aims to explain the social world, and heuristic thinking" (Collins, 2019, p. 24), it can also provide an accessible route to understand how Nepali women with intersectional identities address the specific social problem in Nepal.

While theories of intersectionality allow us to gain a deeper understanding of activist works, the framework of transnational assemblages and counterpublics will allow us to understand the networked actions' process of formation across time and space. I have argued that transnational assemblages are "collectives of people, organizations, [and] entities, who are connected via online and offline mediums such as phones, computers, and people who gather transnationally to respond to a certain situation of natural or political crisis" (Baniya, 2020). #RageAgainstRape is a collective of Nepali women who have intersectional identities, who are connected via digital networks, and who perform digital activism (Lang, 2019). While working together as a transnational assemblage, activist movements like #RageAgainstRape territorialize spaces, which means they occupy physical and digital spaces, and then deterritorialize them, which means that they disperse from the original group to join other movements or conduct other activities (DeLanda, 2016). Assemblage theory recognizes these two phenomena of territorialization and deterritorialization as an emerging, ever-becoming quality of an assemblage (Baniya, 2020; DeLanda, 2016; Deleuze & Guattari, 1987). Both territorializing and deterritorializing are motivated by affect. Zizi Papacharissi (2015) argues that "we respond affectively, we invest our emotion to these stories, and we contribute to developing narratives that emerge through our own affectively charged and digitally expressed endorsement, rejection or views" (p. 5). Affect motivates the formation and evolution of various assemblages.

Transnational assemblages could also be articulated as a form of counterpublics, as suggested by various theorists (Asen, 2018; Fraser, 1990; Warner, 2002). Michael Warner (2002) defines counterpublics as publics that provide a sense of active belonging that masks or compensates for the real powerlessness of human agents in a capitalist society. The counterpublics are connected via various networks and are in a transformative relationship with people who are located in and across networks, forming new relationships and engagements that critique exclusions, inequalities, and injustices of the dominant publics (Asen, 2018). Karma R. Chávez (2013) and Linh Dich (2016) argue that there are counterpublic enclaves that build community-based coalitions. Social activists use counterpublics enclaves as the "sites to invent rhetorical strategies to publicly challenge oppressive rhetoric or to create new imaginaries for the groups and issues they represent and desire to bring into coalition" (Chávez, 2013, p. 3). The concepts of counterpublics and counterpublic enclaves helps in understanding how activist women who use Twitter create their own space within a patriarchal as well as male-dominated public sphere by forming their own enclaves or transnational assemblages.

To understand how information flows, how communication is made, and how knowledge is created by the #RageAgainstRape group, the triangulation of intersectionality with theories of counterpublics and transnational assemblages is necessary. This framework will also help in understanding the networked participatory actions, digital activism, and operation of the transnational assemblages driven by affective reactions to the issue of rape in Nepal, as well as the intersections of multiplicity in navigating complex situations such as the historical suppression of women and present crime cases of rape.

TRANSNATIONAL COALITION-BUILDING ACROSS TIME AND PLATFORMS

#RageAgainstRape created coalitional actions by forming transnational assemblages (Baniya, 2020) where various women network and communicate to form a stronger force for advocating against the government's silence regarding crimes like rape and gender-based violence. Transnational activism like the one involving #RageAgainstRape moves beyond geographical boundaries and subjective experiences of mobility and creates global interconnections that involve circulation and exchanges of texts, bodies, material, and information flows that provide a sociopolitical condition and motive for coalition-building and cyber-public activism (Dingo, Riedner, & Wingard, 2013; Grewal & Kaplan, 2001; Parks & Hachelaf, 2019; Wang, 2020). The group functions as a form of "counterpublic" that performs "withdrawal" and "regroupment," working as a training space for "agitational activists directed toward wider publics" (Fraser, 1990, p. 68). Withdrawal here means withdrawing from the mainstream or dominant public discourse, and regroupment means coming together as a counterpublic to challenge the dominant public discourse. We can see that #RageAgainstRape is "withdrawing" from the mainstream established bodies like the government and the group of patriarchs who victimize the survivors of rape. While they regroup, the members of the movement openly discuss issues of rape with the hashtag #RageAgainstRape, tweet at each other to start a conversation, retweet each other's posts, and make connections.

While publicly having open discussions about the rape, members of the #RageAgainstRape movement also build a transnational coalition by drawing the attention of various formal and informal networks via numerous platforms, thus forming "counter public enclaves" (Chávez, 2013). The group works behind the scenes to explore where their ideas and arguments divert, or withdraw, from traditional spaces and then create their own space with a community of strangers (Dich, 2016; Squires, 2002; Warner, 2002). This space provides the #RageAgainstRape activist with a place to hold discussions and strategize. These activities can be carried out in private via the group message mobile application and then publicly when members perform their activism via digital spaces like Twitter, Facebook, or their blog. Reaching out to the wider public allows movements like #RageAgainstRape to recruit new allies—both human and nonhuman—to strengthen the transnational coalitions and perform actions against rape (Dingo, 2012; N. Jones, 2016; Spinuzzi, 2008; Wang, 2020). The group includes women of intersectional identities representing transnational spaces and transcultural communities. In launching this movement, these women come together as a transnational assemblage that works through multiple systems, balancing activities on multiple technologies, connecting to various applications and websites, and accessing space through a plethora of devices (Potts, 2014, p. 20). In using varied digital platforms, these activists evoke the sentiment of the people to keep the conversation going outside of the group and move beyond time, space, and geographies to continue their activism via tweets, blogs, and group discussions to create knowledge on rape.

Performing activism and expressing solidarity draws meaning from tweeting, the sharing of stories, and the organization of the activist community through the creation of official and unofficial networks. Completing such efforts shapes social action specific to addressing the issues of rape in Nepal (Chávez, 2013; Collins, 2019; Walton, Moore, & Jones, 2019). This group is creating knowledge on rape, with members working beyond their personal and professional lives toward social justice and toward changing the dynamic of a very patriarchal society. This network has both human and nonhuman actors. Nonhuman actors include devices such as cell phones, blogs, and digital platforms that help these advocates to perform their activism transnationally (Castells, 2010; Dingo, 2012; Potts, 2014). Within this network, the communication flows internally via the private group message and externally via the use of the hashtag #RageAgainstRape. In doing this, group members create discourse and knowledge around the problems and issues of rape and appeal to many others to join in their fight against this crime. This activism in online spaces inspires change and activism in offline spaces too. Some examples of offline activism include bringing the government's attention to an issue and encouraging it to create better policies. Another example of offline activism may involve activists spending their time motivating Nepali newspaper editors to avoid using stereotypes in news articles that may be detrimental to the movement's cause.

The above actions performed on assorted digital platforms are also affective. Papacharissi (2015) argues that digital platforms like Twitter become spaces where affect plays a major role by connecting people around the world and encouraging them to be involved in collective action and to create a collective memory. The members of the #RageAgainstRape group are connected by the sentiment of anger against the crime of rape, against the authorities, and against the societal norms such that their "bodies act in context with each other" (Rice, 2008). The affect created by the two rape cases among Nepali women in transnational spaces invited women to quickly react to this context and work together to perform their activism. Affect is a powerful binding force that creates counterpublics who are "critical oppositional social forces" (Felski as cited in Asen, 2000). #RageAgainstRape participants respond affectively, invest their emotions into sharing powerful stories, and contribute to developing narratives that emerge through affective interactions that are digitally expressed, endorsed, rejected, or viewed (Papacharissi, 2015, p. 5). The movement's major agenda involves advocacy and activism, which requires it to rely on various group members' skills and commitment. For example, a creative group member who has impressive design skills can be tasked with designing banners and T-shirts, and a member who is technologically savvy can be put in charge of managing the movement's Facebook, Twitter, and Instagram accounts. In this platform, countless kinds of activities occur, such as writing, designing, networking, contacting stakeholders, and preparing letters to send out to media houses and police administration. The group members themselves therefore carry out the bulk of the work, which makes them "believe that their contributions matter and [makes them] feel some degree of social connection with one another" (Potts, 2014, p. 15).

#RageAgainstRape not only engages its members in its closed message group, but it also invites participation from stakeholders and other online publics by asking them to become involved and discuss issues of rape and women's public safety. Their networked activism both online and in-person helps in the building of a coalition through personal networks on and off social media, through stakeholders, policymakers, and other state apparatuses. This is where the intersectional approach of the group is showcased: in the realm of social justice, the framework of intersectionality has been advanced to understand the complicated interworking of power that constitutes the situations of people who experience interlocking oppressions (Chávez, 2013). To address the challenge of historical oppression and marginalization, there is the need for a coalition, and this is where the role of #RageAgainstRape forming a coalitional network comes into play. The group mobilizes their network via engagement and by using all of the possible digital and nondigital means to create knowledge, working "across multiple systems, balancing activities on multiple technologies, connecting to various applications and websites, and accessing spaces through a plethora of devices" (Potts, 2014, p. 20). Use of multiple digital technologies and reaching out to the stakeholders both online and offline is the strength of the group. This transnational coalition is constantly working toward addressing social justice for Nepali survivors of gender-based violence and rape.

DIGITAL FEMINIST RHETORICAL
PRACTICES FOR SOCIAL JUSTICE

By carrying out its activism in digital and nondigital spaces, the #RageAgainstRape movement becomes a powerful example of a "global discursive flow" (Appadurai, 2013) that creates an assemblage of various activists who spread ideas, practices, and frames from one country to the other and present themselves as the critical social opposition force (Asen, 2000; Schell, 2013). This global discursive flow is generated on Twitter and invites participants to fight against the dominant narratives about women, stand up against the lack of government attention regarding ongoing rape cases, share stories, and perform socially just actions. This flow created affective reactions and interactions among various people on Twitter, inviting them to participate, share their views, and be a part of the movement and its assemblage (DeLanda, 2016; Papacharissi, 2015). Affect motivates and plays a great role in the formation of assemblages, encouraging the flow of communication, stories, and emotions that lead people to invest their time, energy, and actions in the movement (Baniya, 2021; DeLanda, 2016). #RageAgainstRape makes various strategic rhetorical choices, an essential element to publicly launching a movement. At the heart of #RageAgainstRape activists' digital feminist practices lies the creation of coalitions and a continued use of the movement's hashtag, which helps in developing the movement's own rhetorical ecology (Lang, 2019).

The activism that #RageAgainstRape performs can be regarded as what Walton, Moore, and Jones (2019) suggest as the 4R framework, where activists recognize, reveal, reject, and try to replace unjust and oppressive practices with intersectional and coalition-led practices (p. 133). The formation of #RageAgainstRape could be associated with how women *recognized* the forms of oppression and injustices that were happening around them. For example, the group observed the oppressive discourses that blamed the rape survivors for the crime and saved the perpetrators, also recognizing the lack of attention the state paid to this matter. While the group members recognized these marginalizing practices, they *revealed* these "injustices and systemic oppression" (Walton, Moore, & Jones, 2019) through their rhetorical practices and by using various digital and nondigital platforms, writing in both English and Nepali. In performing these kinds of activities, group members *rejected* the choices made by the state and by various other people who perpetrated violence against women and other gender-based minorities. It is common for activists to encounter opposers who troll them, accusing them of being "Dollarbadi," or women who are being paid by Western countries and organizations to create political turmoil in Nepal, as they conduct their activism. As a core group member, I reject those allegations. I provide this example as a way to explain how the continuous fight to reject and replace injustices also involves fighting trolls who disseminate inaccuracies. One of the biggest achievements of the group was that of *replacing* unjust and oppressive practices with intersectional and coalitional-led practices (Walton, Moore, & Jones, 2019), which is seen in the latest changes in Nepali policies against rape.

The activism of #RageAgainstRape is mostly based on digital media; however, there are various networking (and other) activities that the group does in an offline setting. The members' activism allows for silent voices to be expressed in the form of social media posts. These women want to be heard, and they want the public to empathize and be a part of their movement so that women and women-identifying individuals do not have to suffer through any kind of gender-based violence and crimes in the future. Varied digital platforms have become activists' space to network, to participate, and to connect to organize a larger movement. Pigg (2014) argues that "social media offer[s] a means through which individuals can aggregate people and knowledge or, at the least, learn how existing webs of participation are held together" (p. 70). For these digital feminist activists, digital media has become a space to not only network and collaborate, but also to bring about crucial changes in public opinion about women in a highly patriarchal society. Additionally, other properties of the assemblage include solidarity, personal reasons, and being motivated by the feelings of togetherness that the community produces in members (DeLanda, 2016, p. 57). Members of a movement possess a feeling of solidarity toward their goals and the survivors and victims of rape. To express this solidarity, movement members gather online and offline, therefore creating an assemblage known as a "networked public." Papacharissi (2015) quotes danah boyd in defining "networked publics" as "publics that are restructured by networked technologies and therefore simultaneously are 1) the space constructed through the networked technologies and 2) the imagined collective that emerges because of the intersection of people, technology, and practice" (p. 19).

The following are a list of #RageAgainstRape's digital practices that exemplify the movement's coalition-building and fight against injustice:

- News sharing: Whenever news of a rape is reported, a group member shares it to the rest of the group, and most of the members in the group proceed to share the initial post on their own Twitter accounts with a comment and the corresponding hashtag. They also invite their followers and other stakeholders to respond and discuss the issue of rape with the #RageAgainstRape group. This evokes pain, anger, frustration, and sadness, as Heather Lang (2019) shares when she talks about the #MeToo movement.

- Collective voice: The group uses their hashtag #RageAgainstRape in every conversation they tweet and in every post they make online. The members internally decide on the desired collective voice each post is meant to embody. Group members make sure to support each other. For example, if anyone attacks a group member in the social media sphere, the group makes sure that the member is protected. Unity is important in the fight for the cause.

- Feminist writing: The biggest part of #RageAgainstRape's digital activism involves the written word. Activist writing typically involves tweeting, blogging, publishing in local vernaculars, discussing the movement on Twitter and other online forums, creating an archive of group activity, and so on. These writings are based on feminist values, ethics, and practices. Most of the time, feminist views are challenged and shamed in Nepal. Hence, in challenging those norms, the publications, tweets, and discussions on digital spaces focus on feminist values and ideas.

- Networking and mobilizing networks: Each woman in the #RageAgainst-Rape group comes from a different background, having their own networks, skills, and opinions. These women use their differing backgrounds to mobilize their networks, asking the followers of their social media pages to speak out against rape. On Twitter, these women continuously tag people at a high decision-making level, such as politicians and media personnel, so that their voices can be heard and so that they may draw these powerful people's attention toward the issues they are fighting for.

Digital activism continues to hold space by circulating information, by articulating anger and frustration in digital spaces, and by drawing attention to the issue. While victim-blaming continues in Nepal, challenges to such conversations persist in a demand for justice. Thus, digital activism becomes a powerful tool for users across the world to bring attention to social injustices (Dadas, 2017). Like #YesAllWomen, #MeToo, and others, the #RageAgainst-Rape movement also facilitated, and continues to facilitate, conversations about rape and the creation of communities built on survivors' experiences (Lang, 2019).

CONCLUSION AND TAKEAWAYS

Examining #RageAgainstRape's rhetorical practices shows how these activist women have worked transnationally to fight against the injustices regarding rape and gender-based violence in Nepal. This case study shows how digital activism that is led and performed by women with various intersectional identities continues to work toward bringing about change. As articulated previously in this chapter, movements like #RageAgainstRape do not receive much attention in both the international and national Nepali arenas. This is because movements like the one addressed in this chapter are constantly fighting within their own contexts and against their own governments and societies and the patriarchal rules that are being imposed on them. Transnational movements like #RageAgainstRape can help in understanding the global feminist perspective in our own research as well as our teaching. These female activists spread across the world, connected via the internet, to continue to fight against the social injustices and inequities in their own contexts. With their digital activism, writing, communication, and coordination, these women have created transnational assemblages and been successful in changing Nepali people's perceptions, drawing the attention of stakeholders, and making the government address the issue. The activism of these women reveals that their networked engagement and participation mediated by technologies is challenging the traditional norms and beliefs regarding women and prompting action against social injustice. Thus, with their digital activism, Nepali women on Twitter and elsewhere raised their voices against the heinous crime of rape in their country. This case study reveals that the group's networked engagement and participation mediated by technologies is challenging the traditional norms and beliefs regarding women and is trying to act out against the social injustice in their society.

Feminist rhetorical studies scholars need to closely consider smaller-scale transnational movements like #RageAgainstRape. The implication of this case study goes beyond highlighting grassroots activism, as it creates a space for transnational activism in the field of rhetorical studies. Oftentimes, when larger-scale movements are researched and taught in our classrooms, movements like #RageAgainstRape get overshadowed. This overshadowing creates a lack of representation for the movements and voices of women across the world. Hence, studying and teaching transnational movements like #RageAgainstRape will help in understanding women's issues globally and raising awareness against such atrocities within our own local communities.

PART 3

PEDAGOGIES FOR GRASSROOTS ACTIVISMS

CHAPTER 14

Organizing for Action's Legacy

Building Capacity through
Personal Stories and Local Networks

ERICA M. STONE

Organizing for Action (OFA) was a prolific grassroots issues advocacy organization that trained local community organizers about activist tactics and policy processes from 2013 to 2019. For over six years, OFA fought for progress on issues such as climate change, health care, gun violence, immigration reform, and economic fairness by establishing 154 local chapters and supporting over 30,000 local grassroots activism projects in all 50 states and Washington, DC (Hogan, 2019). Other progressive organizations like Swing Left, Planned Parenthood, MoveOn, Color of Change, and League of Women Voters used OFA's trainings on grassroots organizing tactics to sustain and build their own movements in cities across the country. After its dissolution, OFA published all of its resources (trainings, toolkits, manuals) in an online, open-access archive to continue to support the work of local grassroots activists and organizations (Organizing for Action, 2019b).

From August 2017 to December 2017, I worked as an unpaid community organizing fellow with OFA. During my fellowship, OFA taught me how to engage with my local networks; organize tactical, policy-focused projects; and contribute my voice to the chorus of issue-based organizers who were working to preserve the Affordable Care Act (ACA) under the Trump administration. As a new resident in Kansas City, Missouri, my understanding of community organizing, coalition-building, and capacity work was shaped by OFA's community-engaged fellowship. Their coalitional approach to policy work helped me build connections with other organizers and advocacy organizations, strengthened my work as an instructor of community and public writing, and played a large role in my assimilation into a new home in the Midwest.

As part of OFA's nonpolitical work as a 501(c)(4) organization, their eight-week community organizing fellowships were designed to teach new community organizers about the history of community organizing in the United States and orient them to the art and science of civic engagement, community organizing, and advocacy-based policy work. Fellows met once per week in a 90-minute Zoom meeting, which often included a brief lecture and small group discussions in breakout rooms of approximately 20 fellows. During my fellowship, there were more than 1,500 fellows from 49 states.

The training portion of the fellowship focused on the history and fundamentals of community organizing at the national level and taught new community organizers like myself how to make a difference in our local communities through themed workshops on subjects such as canvasing, phone banking, and advocating for progressive issues (Organizing for Action, 2019a). But it was OFA's training on how to have an effective conversation about an issue by telling a "public story" or "critical incident story" that was the most impactful for me as a new organizer (Organizing for Action, 2019a).

OFA's concept of a "public story" originated with longtime community organizing scholar and practitioner Marshall Ganz. Ganz's (2010) three-part public narrative framework situates storytelling as an inherently relational (and rhetorical) strategy for inventing ethos, defining values, and inspiring action (p. 540). As the first part of Ganz's structured storytelling approach, the *story of self* offers a way to communicate positionality, identity, and "values not as abstract principles, but as lived experience" (p. 541). Next, the *story of us* shares a collective story or common experience that is situated in a particular time, place, or community and builds an ethos (pp. 543–544). Last, the *story of now* "articulates the urgent challenge" in terms of the shared values and common experiences and makes a specific call for action (p. 544).

Throughout our fellowship trainings, paid professional community organizers (mostly located in OFA's Chicago headquarters) taught us how to develop a personal story about a specific policy or issue impacting our local communities. As a result of OFA's training, I helped organize activists in Kansas City around the preservation of the Affordable Care Act (ACA), using my own personal narrative. If I were to share my "public story" in response to the ongoing COVID-19 pandemic, I might share a story like this one:

> **Story of Self:** In July 2015, my partner changed jobs, and we abruptly found ourselves without health insurance. Rather than using COBRA or purchasing an expensive individual policy from Blue Cross, we purchased health

insurance for ourselves through the ACA marketplace, which saved us $343.76 a month in insurance payments. If we hadn't had the ACA available, we would have spent approximately 30 percent of our monthly income on basic health insurance.

Story of Us: Due to many factors, the United States' workforce has changed to largely gig-based and short-term employment opportunities; hardly anyone stays with the same company or organization for 50-plus years. Given this new reality, the US needs an open marketplace available for citizens to obtain health insurance that is not connected to an employer. Until Medicaid is expanded in all states (if ever), the ACA is the only option and should be preserved and, if possible, expanded.

Story of Now: As of 2022, the entire world is experiencing a viral pandemic with many variants, limited access to vaccines, and few options for effective antiviral medications. In 2019 and 2020, COVID-19 tested our entire infrastructure and exposed the cracks in our healthcare system and economy. In January 2021, over 7 million people filed for unemployment in the United States and, I can only assume, were without health insurance for a few days if not longer (United States Department of Labor, 2021). For the ongoing health of the American people, it would be best if we designed a healthcare system that wasn't connected to our jobs, or better, separate from the private sector altogether.

Throughout all of our trainings, OFA used a storied approach, which sometimes aligned with Ganz's framework and other times simply alluded to it. To ensure the fellows' organizing work had an impact on local communities, we were tasked with designing a local community project that would move citizens in our home cities toward a particular action, ideally one that aligned with one of OFA's central issues, like "climate change, health care, gun violence, immigration reform, economic fairness, and creating a more participatory and accessible democracy" (Organizing for Action, 2019b). We were instructed to identify a problem in our local community, research how we might solve it, design the project or special event, implement our solution or hold our planned event, and report back to OFA headquarters about how it went.

As a scholar of community literacy and technical communication, I was interested in understanding what a more ecological and localized approach to storytelling and story listening might look like. For my fellowship project, I designed a community listening project—called Sound Off—that ran from October 2017 to January 2018 at the University of Missouri–Kansas City (UMKC). Community listening is a relatively new term within community rhetorics; it was first defined in the fall 2018 issue of the *Community Literacy Journal*. Offered as an "explicitly feminist intervention into community writing work" by Jenn Fishman and Lauren Rosenberg (2018), community listening is defined as an "active, layered, intentional practice" that is based in praxis and requires its "users" to suspend judgment and take a listening stance that focuses on the value of relationships and their shared knowledge-making practices (pp. 1–3). Sound Off invited Kansas Citians to share stories about issues they cared about, in a listening booth we set up in a communal area during the 2017 Educate-Organize-Advocate (EOA) conference, an annual social justice and activism event at UMKC that is designed to provide community members the space "to engage in meaningful dialogue over challenging topics; to increase advocacy for self and others" and cultivate "civically engaged members of an urban community" (https://info.umkc.edu/eoa/). Sixteen people contributed to Sound Off, sharing stories on the topics of gun violence, marriage equality, immigration reform, climate change, health care, jobs and economy, and standing with survivors of sexual violence. After the conference, the stories were anonymized and transposed onto posters that hung in the entryway of the library for six weeks: "There, in a building readily associated with literacy, we invited passersby to look and to listen to community members' stories and respond on social media using specific project hashtags" (Stone, 2018, p. 18). Contrary to Ganz's largely performative public narrative framework, Sound Off was focused on gathering and listening to stories using a community listening framework (Fishman & Rosenberg, 2018). As both an art installation and advocacy project, Sound Off offered an intersectional and coalitional approach to OFA's three-part "public story" model. Instead of packaging a lived experience into a three-part, action-oriented story genre, Sound Off invited Kansas Citians to be present within denizens' stories about a medical trauma or encounters with gun violence, not just to be called to action for a specific policy but to reflect on their "shared commitment to [the need for] change" (Chávez, 2013, p. 146) and to consider how a collection of lived experiences might serve as a localized, ecological, and coalitional approach to issue advocacy.

When OFA was operational, local community organizers collected stories of their constituents and retold them in public forums in an effort to advocate for progressive causes, as I did for affordable healthcare in this organizational profile. While this kind of performative and rhetorical approach to activism has worked for centuries (as it did for Aristotle, Cicero, and so on), a more systematic documentation and exhibition of stories from a local place has the potential to build networks and establish local knowledge about how stories function within a community as both identity work (N. Jones, 2014) and change catalysts.

After its dissolution, OFA published its resources (trainings, toolkits, manuals) in an online, open-access archive in the hopes that the resources would continue to support the work of local grassroots activists and organizations. While OFA has received frequent study in other fields like community psychology and organizational communication (see Ganz, 2010; Han, 2014; McKenna & Han, 2014; Speer & Christens, 2014), relatively little attention has been given to OFA as a model for public-facing technical communication and a resource for localized, civic-focused community literacy. In this organization profile, I have narrated my experience as a participant observer and community organizer within OFA, but I will close by offering some suggestions for how publicly engaged scholars might use OFA's archive as a resource for building capacity through personal stories, engaging local networks in civic advocacy and community literacy, and studying community organizing as public-facing technical communication.

Building capacity through personal stories. As noted in the introduction to this edited collection, stories and storytelling are important knowledge-making tools. Many of OFA's trainings, toolkits, and manuals describe how and where to use story as a rhetorical strategy for communicating values and encouraging political action. While I believe a more ecological and coalitional approach to storytelling and story listening has the potential for more sustainable and representative advocacy work, I find it helpful that OFA's use of Ganz's public narrative framework offers portable examples for how to share our lived experiences through story and build capacity for change through local relationships. These examples can be used in local community organizing trainings or studied as rhetorical approaches to narrative-based, policy-focused arguments.

Engaging local networks in civic advocacy and community literacy. More often than not, we choose to engage with civic and community literacies during times of crisis (for example, when *Roe vs. Wade* was overturned) or in response to the political cycle (for example, during an election season). OFA's decentralized approach to activist work relies on a community-oriented and place-based understanding of activism where hierarchical thinking is discouraged, resources are shared, and local networks offer a sustainable approach to the labor associated with civic advocacy and community literacy. OFA's toolkits and resources can be used to educate citizens about civic literacies and processes before they need them in a crisis or election cycle.

Studying community organizing as public-facing technical communication. Most technical and professional communication scholarship is focused on privatized or semiprivatized documents (for example, case studies, user interviews). Not only were all of OFA's documents and trainings designed for specific communities or localized publics, they also remain publicly available for further study even after the organization's dissolution. OFA's online, open-access archive provides technical communication scholars, particularly those interested in the intersection of technical communication and public rhetorics, a place to study a group of highly contextualized and public-facing toolkits, manuals, trainings, and documents.

A NOTE ON COALITIONAL POSSIBILITY

To me, OFA's legacy and archive is what Chávez (2013) refers to as a digital "space of convening that points toward coalitional possibility" (p. 8). Do I think I'll write more about OFA in the future? Absolutely. Do I believe that OFA has more than enough documents and stories to sustain inquiries from a multitude of scholars interested in social justice and activist rhetorics? Yep. OFA grew out of grassroots community advocacy, and its rhetorical legacy should be memorialized and examined through a coalition of (ideally) public-facing studies and localized applications.

CHAPTER 15

Kairos, Communities, and Writing for DACA Advocacy in Memphis

ALISON A. LUKOWSKI

AND JEFFREY GROSS

Grassroots activism is the ongoing process in which individuals coordinate and collaborate with others to create social change. Activist rhetoric requires ground-level organizing to amplify the needs and goals of a group. The most visible and obvious form of grassroots activism may be the protest, where individuals gather and march in a public space to demand change. In "Feminist Activism in the Core: Student Activism in Theory and Practice," Katherine Fredlund (2018) describes an upper-division writing course focused on teaching students activist rhetorics. For instance, in her class, students work to "create their own project for change (DIY Activist Rhetoric)" in working with a community partner (p. 477). Such an activism-centered course shares outcomes with the Writing for Advocacy course we describe in this chapter: "The course aims to teach students to solve problems, evaluate the ideas of others, express themselves effectively both orally and in writing, and demonstrate the skills for effective citizenship" (p. 476). In Fredlund's example, the result of the course is an event: the students in the course develop and cohost their university's annual Take Back the Night. In our essay, we're addressing advocacy, which is a part of grassroots activism, but not its entirety.

While protest is an immediate collaborative response to an injustice, advocacy is a longer coordinated effort that builds on the kairotic opening formed by protests. In other words, if we understand kairos as an opening or gap, then writing for advocacy is a grassroots response that exploits the public awareness raised by protests. Advocacy is part of activism, not activism by itself. Advocacy uses the opening created by protest for sustained and specific policy-level work through protest as well as government lobbying, public meetings, and policy research. A statewide agency grant funded the course we designed to engage college students in educational equity coalition–led efforts to lobby and enact change in state policy. We had the opportunity to advertise our course before registration to recruit students who had a passion for activism and social justice, and we aimed to prepare them to intervene in various ways, ranging from protest to policy research.

In this chapter, we provide an overview of our Writing for Advocacy course, which sought to develop possibilities for meaningful writing that promoted student agency and empowered them to participate in academic and advocacy discourses. Responding in real time to an unstable political landscape, the course had a kairotic relevance, but we also viewed the course's relevance in broader terms important to working with underrepresented and first-generation learners. The course met hard and measurable learning outcomes, such as research methods, incorporating sources, and critical reading, along with softer unmeasurable outcomes, such as professional etiquette, social networking, and community building. Combined, our approach promoted student retention and self-efficacy.

For Deferred Action for Childhood Arrivals (DACA) students attending Christian Brothers University (CBU), a private Catholic university in Memphis, Tennessee, the election of Donald J. Trump to the presidency in 2016 was akin to an impending natural disaster. Our university leadership, in partnership with Latino Memphis—our local Latinx advocacy organization—scrambled to keep students apprised of updates on DACA and to provide them with legal advice: Should they apply for DACA renewals? If so, when? Was their personal data at risk and were they identifying themselves to the new administration by reapplying? Moreover, over the course of 2017 and 2018, our students reported increasing deportations, Immigration and Customs Enforcement (ICE) raids on agricultural workplaces and homes, and detentions of immigrants at the borders. Communities of DACA recipients and other Latinx students were shattered—homes emptied, family members sent to jails in other states, and educations threatened by the unknown.

So, when Conexión Américas and the Tennessee Educational Equity Coalition (TEEC) awarded our university a grant to develop a course to teach students to advocate for themselves, we jumped at the chance. The grant asked us to teach a course with a specific focus of advocating for in-state tuition for undocumented students at Tennessee public universities. It specifically required our students to participate in a state coalition conference and lobbying day at the Tennessee legislature. The grantors wanted to capitalize on the perceived momentum of a 2016 bill that fell one vote short of moving from committee to a full General Assembly vote. Based on the belief that change at the state level would come from grassroots activism, the grant called for a course that leveraged student voices in support of future tuition equity bills. As English professors trained in teaching first-year writing, we also wanted to frame the course in rhetoric, which we view as students' opportunity to engage with the past, present, and aspirational future; as their path to understanding policies, politics, and culture; and as their means to interact in our political world and produce new possibilities and opportunities. We designed Writing for Advocacy as two conjoined spring 2018 courses: a section of first-year composition and an upper-division English course.[1] These courses assigned individual reflective writing to define students' positions and stakes, group public writing to stake out and respond to problems, and presentations to advocate for the Latinx community. Students wrote blog posts, op-eds, phone scripts, and congressional one-pagers and researched white papers. The conjoined courses provided mentorship opportunities for the upper-level students and access to experienced students' wisdom for the first-year students.

Our students were fired up about the unfolding attacks on immigrant communities, and we had to channel their anger toward responding to the disastrous effects of the Trump administration's threats and policies. In "Floating Foundations: Kairos, Community, and a Composition Program in Post-Katrina New Orleans," T. R. Johnson, Joe Letter, and Judith Kemerait Livingston (2009) recount the challenges of relaunching Tulane University's writing program after the university's one-semester closure. They were forced to start with new faculty at a university restored to functioning while the neighborhoods around it remained uninhabitable and largely untouched by the complexities of recovery. For Johnson, Letter, and Livingston (2009), "floating foundations" uses the literal idea of rebuilding homes on foundations that float and rise and fall with water as a metaphor for the challenges and opportunities of teaching writing in an uncertain environment. Floating foundations offers them "an excellent metaphor for attunement to a fluctuating present—the architectural equivalent of kairos—and in that sense, the metaphor has important implications for reimagining what community really means: city communities, campus communities, and the communities that we help construct each semester in our writing classrooms" (p. 34). Through

---

1. At the beginning of the semester, the two sections met separately once per week and together for the second session of the week. For the second half of the semester, the two courses met as one course, which in this chapter we will collectively refer to as "Writing for Advocacy" or "the course." For more information on the logistics of the course, see Gross and Lukowski (2020).

collective action from the bottom and for the community, students and faculty can work with grassroots organizations to create positive change.

Building deeper connections to the community and developing a grassroots network to create change, our course was inspired by the work of Johnson, Letter, and Livingston (2009). Through helping students immerse themselves in the environmental and humanitarian crisis in New Orleans, Tulane's writing program allowed students to engage in writing to change their immediate environment. Livingston speaks clearly to the goals of their approach:

> My critical pedagogy was designed to immerse students in rhetoric as I encouraged them to pay attention to the world immediately surrounding them. I sought to open their eyes so that they would witness a community struggling with some of the most entrenched social problems of our culture. This goal coincides with Tulane's public service mandate. It also ties in well with the idea that student writing is strongest when rooted in local interests and individual experiences. (Johnson, Letter, & Livingston, 2009, p. 37)

As our chapter will demonstrate, we, too, believe in the centrality of rhetoric as a means to teach students both to understand and affect their surrounding communities. We understand meaningful writing to emerge from the intersection of personal aspirations, histories, and values as well as community well-being. Founded by the Lasallian Christian Brothers and rooted in Saint John Baptist de la Salle's belief in providing educational access to the socially and economically disenfranchised, our university emphasizes the values of faith, service, and community, all of which can be aspects of how to engage in the surrounding world in advocacy for others, especially through local efforts and engagement.

Writing for Advocacy would be our own attempt at attuning to a shifting sociopolitical landscape, one where immigrants' rights and safety were increasingly at risk. In our case, the "floating foundations" metaphor falls short, as floating is at least grounded in rules of physics. Based on the density of the object, we know if it will float in a certain substance. The unfolding immigration positions of the Trump administration were immediate and remained unpredictable and chaotic, existing seemingly outside any boundaries of humanity or economics. These policies or unofficial statements of intended policy, often first in the form of tweets, do not adhere to any clear principles. Previously, at the least, capitalism had guaranteed some level of protection of immigrant rights due to their unrecognized but indispensable role in the US economy. In early 2018, nothing seemed to float. And each new Trump tweet or mandate amplified anxiety. Yet, with 26 students, many of them DACA recipients, we began our Writing for Advocacy course in January 2018 with the goal of providing opportunities for meaningful writing, foundations of community, and a transformative learning experience.

ATTUNEMENT:
TEACHING CHANGE IN THE WRITING CLASSROOM

Discussions of first-year composition, rhetoric, and higher education, generally speaking, use "transformative" and "meaningful" to describe institutional and instructional goals. Our university, like many, has subcommittees on "transformative learning" as part of our institutional strategic plan. Within the goals of an actual course, this terminology needs to be more clearly defined, especially for how it interrelates with institutional learning outcomes for a course, grantor outcomes for outside funding, and learning that fosters the agency and self-efficacy of our students. Otherwise, "transformative" and "meaningful" are higher ed jargon for the similarly vague "high impact practices" standard. In *The Meaningful Writing Project,* Michele Eodice, Anne Ellen Geller, and Neal Lerner (2016) prioritize agency in the writing course: "meaningful writing projects offer students opportunities for agency: for engagement with instructors, peers, and materials; and for learning that connects to previous experiences and passions and to future aspirations and identities" (p. 4). Writing for Advocacy students worked in multiple directions: with their classmates, the university community, alumni and local activist groups, and the broader statewide education consortium, TEEC. This comprehensive interaction served to develop students' self-efficacy to present to community leaders in one of the course's final assignments so their research could effect change. The public audience and reception of student work made these networks of connection part of the learning process. Eodice, Geller, and Lerner (2016) add that such projects allow students to experience "the power of personal connection, the thrill of immersion in thought, writing and research, and the satisfaction of knowing the work they produced could be applicable, relevant, and real world" (p. 4). Our students interacted with policymakers and professional advocates, and the course enabled students to be members of these networks.

To achieve these goals, we sought connection with grassroots organizations, topical kairos and relevance, and student agency over their lives. We organized the course around the TEEC two-day summit in late February, an event that assembled statewide coalition members and national partners, such as the Education Trust, Data Quality Campaign, and the OpEd Project. Our course readings, writing assignments, research resources, and class activities served to prepare students for summit workshops and meetings. The second half of the semester focused on using the momentum from the summit to continue advocating for change through writing. From the start, we told students that course readings and discussions might change with the legislative landscape. For the most part, they adapted and accepted that we were learning about teaching writing for advocacy in this hostile political climate as much as they were learning how to write for advocacy. We helped students align their political activism and advocacy, something in which they were already engaged through lobbying efforts as part of their scholarship programs and their campus and regional political organizations, with the rhetorical purpose of education. Self-selected and already aligned with the goals of our course, our students had voice and action already. For instance, most of our students were already active in the community and on campus in advocacy programs for immigrants, people of color, and the poor. The course helped them understand the rhetoricity of their positions and actions and how their projects could change reality.

Current events surrounding immigration policies and DACA made Writing for Advocacy especially timely and relevant. The political climate in the country and Tennessee provided an immediate purpose for composition. Johnson, Letter, and Livingston (2009) note that the physical displacement or "floating foundations" provide an apt metaphor for a kairotic response for students—the need and immediacy of displacement requires a response: "Clearly New Orleans is not the only place in America that might benefit from a prolonged immersion in the rhetorical potentials of *kairos*. The ideological separation between the life of 'America' and the realities of life in the Ninth Ward of New Orleans has its parallel in the disconnections between campuses and communities everywhere" (p. 35). For the DACA recipients in our classrooms, the immediate threat of familial deportation required a kairotic response. For instance, a student posted to her group's blog the sense of urgent danger many undocumented immigrants feel: "Since Congress still has not passed a reform bill to help Dreamers, May's son is stuck in limbo, waiting to see what happens next. When I later called her with the news that a federal judge ruled that Homeland Security may have to start taking in new applications, she was filled with joy."[2] While this student interviewed May about her son's uncertain future, she could have turned to her own mother or peers' mothers. Our students' blog posts responded to the current ongoing legislative and legal

---

2. All student names have been changed to protect their identities. Although all group blogs from the course remain online, we have chosen not to include URLs or full citation information, to protect student identities.

battles at the state and national levels. Their writing had relevance and purpose because May's fears were our students' fears.

Additionally, our students enacted kairotic responses to ongoing legislation through specific genres that focused on creating change. For example, in spring 2018 two bills came before the Tennessee General Assembly that directly targeted the well-being of undocumented residents. Tennessee House Bill 2315 (*Prohibiting Sanctuary Policies*, 2018), sponsored by Representative Jay Reedy (R), prohibited any entity within the state from declaring sanctuary status. Another bill, HB 2312 (*Prohibiting Non-State Identification*, 2018), sponsored by William Lamberth (R), prohibited state agencies from accepting any non-state-issued identification, including those issued by consulates. As the bills came up for a vote in April, our students responded. As part of their group blog assignments, students composed phone scripts to help people opposing the bill speak to their representatives and the governor. Although a phone script was not a specifically required genre in the course, the students blogged about proposed legislation and provided the script to advocate against these proposed laws. One group, Welcome Dreamers, posted links on their blog to Governor Bill Haslam's mailing address, email, and Twitter account and provided a phone script:

> Hello, my name is _____ and I am calling to urge Governor Haslam to veto House Bill 2315 and 2312. These bills are inhumane and will lead to nothing but the separation of families and the uprooting of individuals who are an integral part of this nation. . . . As a proud citizen of this state I implore you: Veto House Bills 2312 and 2315.

Unfortunately, both bills passed and were signed into law. However, in the classroom, our students worked together, outlining the rhetorical appeals they thought would best persuade the governor and assembly members. We reviewed the generic conventions of phone scripts and walked through the steps of composition. Participating in grassroots action, students posted the scripts on Twitter and Facebook, garnering an audience and generating support beyond the classroom.

Another way we helped students respond to current events was through our alumni networks. We asked two alumni to visit our classes on separate days. One alumna was a managing editor for a hyperlocal online newspaper, *High Ground News*. During her visit, she handed out business cards and spoke with individual students about writing stories and op-eds for her publication. She encouraged them to have a voice, get involved, and work at a local level. We also invited an alumna who served as director of engagement and advocacy at Complete Tennessee, a nonprofit that supports college access and completion for students from historically excluded populations. She attended the TEEC Summit, visited our classes, and invited some of our students to the Convening of the Complete Tennessee Leadership Institute that met in Memphis. The Leadership Institute included education and policy leaders from across the state, all of whom had the opportunities to hear our students present their experiences in Writing for Advocacy as a model for transformative education that could be emulated and implemented across the state. Students in attendance encountered leaders in Tennessee who came from similar backgrounds. One African American student spoke at length with Gloria Jean Sweet-Love, president of the Tennessee NAACP. Students were impressed that they were able to provide ideas to community college presidents who treated them as experts and asked them questions about their experiences. Without our alumni networks, our students could not have learned about publication and leadership opportunities beyond the classroom and joined real grassroots activities.

Leveraging alumni networks was important for responding kairotically, but also for providing our students with a sense of agency. First-generation students and students of color must learn to create their own professional networks. For many of these students, their existing networks of family and friends cannot help them navigate the complex challenges of doing college, shifting social class, and developing professional ties. For instance, in their study of Latinx students in college, Rios-Aguilar and Deil-Amen (2012) found that although such students leveraged their personal networks adeptly, their ability to use college and professional networks dropped precipitously. They argued that students needed to be trained on how to build networks because "a college degree is required for accessing rewarding jobs, but it is no guarantee. Interactions and ties that provide job guidance and personal recommendations are also critical" (p. 193). Many CBU students lacked familial social ties to help them succeed, so our class tried to provide these ties. But perhaps more importantly, we helped students learn how to forge these connections for themselves in the ecosystem of statewide grassroots organizations and politics.

When we designed Writing for Advocacy, we wanted to provide advanced-standing students with opportunities to lead and mentor first-year students. We recognized that our position as white faculty may not make us a student's first stop for help. Across the country, first-year writing programs provide peer mentors to students to build community, increase retention, and support student learning (Holt & Fifer, 2018; Ward, Thomas, & Disch 2010; Yomtov, Plunkett, Efrat, & Marin 2017). These programs especially help first-generation and students of color whose imposter syndrome may prevent them from asking authority figures questions, as well as those students for whom asking a white authority figure may be perceived as a potentially dangerous or outing experience. We were motivated by research in the field, but also by Alberto Ledesma's *Diary of a Reluctant Dreamer* (2017), a required course text, in which he describes and illustrates his struggle and fear as an undocumented youth and the joy he receives in mentoring undocumented youth at University of California, Berkeley. In our conjoined classrooms, we found that juniors and seniors could steer group work to meet deadlines and more manageable outcomes. That is, their experience helped first-year students work through complex multifaceted, semester-long projects. The advanced students became a resource for basic writing concerns, which allowed the faculty to help students manage more complicated issues around audience and research. Together, the students formed coalitions outside of the writing classroom. Our third- and fourth-year students were established members of campus activist organizations such as HOLA CBU, Voices United, and the campus chapter of the NAACP. By inviting first-year students into these spaces, they extended the rhetorical advocacy of the course to more immediate campus activism opportunities. The grassroots space of the course forged bonds between students to support both event-based activism and sustained policy-level advocacy.

To support the research essential to advocacy, we used a portion of the grant money to purchase materials for CBU's Plough Library. We reviewed major university press catalogs for recent releases in immigration-related topics, rhetoric, and borderlands studies. Moreover, we selected print and film immigrant narratives published in English and Spanish to provide models for the students. Because we saw the work of our course as long-term, we tried to select books we thought students on campus and in the community might use to conduct research about the history of Latinx immigration, immigrant rights, and patterns of southern migration. For our campus and community, as well as for other researchers who could access these resources via reciprocal borrowing or interlibrary loan, we sought to turn our library into a repository of materials pertaining to advocacy and immigration that could support later research, grassroots activism, and coalitional efforts. We dedicated over $3,000 of our grant budget to library acquisitions, which amounted to approximately 85 books and films.

The course was designed to challenge students' assumptions about what advocacy meant, while empowering them to become advocates. Our approach to the course could be defined as rhetorical advocacy. This term captures the goal of understanding and participating in advocacy efforts from a rhetorical perspective, particularly in relation to being thoughtful about the methods, techniques, and genres that could lead to policy change. Rhetorical advocacy differs from protest, another important form of advocacy work in which a number of our students had previously participated. At times, our students were frustrated (justifiably) because they wanted to take to the streets and organize protests rather than doing the slower advocacy work of the class. They felt the immediate threat of the Trump administration and the increased work of ICE in Tennessee required action. In fact, outside of class, many of our students participated in protests and rallies in the community, and they used these experiences in their group blog posts. We used their protest activities to discuss the kairotic nature of advocacy in which both immediate responses (protests) and long-term responses (advocacy) work together to create change.[3] While we felt impotent in the face of these daily injustices, we discussed the "long game" of public advocacy. That is, a march alone does not change an unjust law. Telling students to think long-term is difficult when their friends and family are detained and deported today. We used our grant funding to take the students to the National Civil Rights Museum in Memphis. There, students saw artifacts of the phone networks, flyers, letters, instructions for encountering police, and behind-the-scenes efforts that made possible the large historical events and marches with which they were familiar. They saw the research and rhetorical foundations behind the protest efforts. With history, and even very local history, as a backdrop, we often stressed that the course aimed to provide the theoretical and rhetorical foundations for a wide range of advocacy situations, which sometimes required us to back off and take a broader view.

Asked to see their rhetorical work as the "mediator of change," students had to understand their writing, particularly the work of first-year composition, as foundational to their abilities to make change in the community. The prescribed learning outcomes of critical reading skills, research skills, evaluation of evidence, and effective writing serve the larger goals of advocacy, but students had to see this work, something removed from their previous lobbying or direct activism approaches, as meaningful, even if removed from more in-person forms of action. After all, writing, tweeting, or attending

---

3. While we were happy to see students join local groups and participate in protest movements, we felt an ethical obligation not to participate in rallies as a class. Because many of our students were either undocumented or first-generation college students, we could not, in good conscience, require them to endanger themselves or their career prospects by drawing the attention of local police or immigration officials. Moreover, with so many students of color in the class, we were acutely aware of how dangerous traffic stops or even the most banal interaction with police could be for these young people. Although the university would support coalition-based advocacy work, student participation in protests and the risk of arrest (and, for some, revocation of DACA) would have to be a personal choice.

community meetings is grassroots activism. In order to protest, the community must know what policies or injustices to respond to. For our students, many of whom identified as directly affected by national and state immigration policies, the course was about culture and identity in deeply personal ways: their own DACA statuses existed in limbo, their siblings' abilities to attend college or their own abilities to work were unclear, and increased threats of raid and deportation were felt on the family level. Students had to wonder if getting pulled over for something as simple as failure to signal would mean detainment and deportation. Against the immediacy and proximity of real political threat, the university and its work can feel a world apart, particularly for first-generation and underrepresented student groups (Alvarez & Wan, 2019). While studies note that Latinx students tend to be some of the most engaged students on campus (Pérez, 2015), these same students simultaneously "constantly battle feelings of shame, trepidation, anger, despair, marginalization, and uncertainty. . . . These socially driven emotions often are derived from experiences of discrimination, anti-immigrant sentiment, fear of deportation, and systemic barriers" (Pérez Cortés, Ramos, & Coronado, 2017, p. 37).

In creating the rhetorical opportunity for meaningful writing, we had to break down the separation between academic writing and culture and, instead, demonstrate the significance of writing as engagement with culture, and we provided many opportunities for low-stakes multilingual writing in their blogs (Martín, Hirsu, Gonzales, & Alvarez, 2019). Likewise, Preston (2015) challenges us to think of writing beyond narrow academic terms and, instead, as culture, symbolic action, reality-building, and change-making. She explains:

> To regard the writing space as a dialectical space replete with ambiguity and change is to see writing not as a contribution to culture but culture making itself. The writing space is a layering of attitudes, experience, words, and motivations, a space wherein the writer transects the familiar rhetorics, ideas, and events of the recent and distant past with emergent ideas and fresh encounters, rerouting these resources into moments of interpretation, expression, and consequence. (p. 40–41)

In other words, instead of an ephemeral protest or discussion, student writing has a life beyond the classroom and the immediate crisis. Furthermore, writing a letter, an op-ed, a blog post, or a phone script provides students agency, a way to speak back to those in power and to create meaningful change. In this sort of writing, students have the opportunity to construct the sort of worlds in which they aspire to live.

FUTURE GRASSROOTS LEADERS:
FROM RHETORICAL ADVOCACY TO COMMUNITY ACTION

Much of our success had less to do with actual advocacy or publishing and more to do with orienting students to academic culture and career professionalization, which help them develop the self-efficacy and networks to support their leadership journeys through college and into life after college. For most of our students, the TEEC summit was their first professional cocktail party, formal dinner, and networking opportunity. When we began to outline the agenda for the event one student shot his hand in the air and asked, "Do I need to wear a tie?" A young woman piped up, "Wait, how fancy is this? Like high heels fancy?" Faculty unaccustomed to working with first-generation students might find these questions off-putting, but we had prepared to talk with the students about correct apparel. Several scholars (Rios-Aguilar, Kiyama, Gravitt, & Moll, 2011; Rios-Aguilar & Deil-Amen, 2012) have noted the cultural challenges that face first-generation students as they move from a working-class identity and adapt the taste and style of middle-class cultural norms. For our first-year students, this transition was largely positive. We mitigated culture shock by leaning on the advanced-level mentors to help lead the first-year students. While most of them were first-generation too, they had more work and internship experience and more opportunities to network. Gaining the cultural knowledge and experience is part of the larger rhetorical situation of advocacy.

In addition to the everyday decorum of professional experiences, we developed class activities to support the speaking and presentation skills that are essential to students' advocacy and grassroots organizing. Research has found that first-generation students are reluctant to speak in class because of imposter syndrome (Davis, 2012; Hayes, 1997; McConnell, 2000; Strayhorn, 2007). For students of color, public speaking can be particularly fraught because of their concerns about code-switching and self-outing (Biber, 2006; Greene & Walker, 2004). Moreover, for many Latinx students for whom English isn't their home language, public speaking becomes a site of anxiety and fear of discovery. While we cannot control students' sense of self, we tried to mitigate imposter syndrome through preparation and practice. For instance, before we left for Nashville to attend the TEEC Summit, we discussed the generic expectations for and rehearsed the cadence of their elevator speeches, or 30-second self-introductions. In addition to preparing students for these brief encounters, we provided in-class instruction, readings, and scaffolded development of their team presentations. We spent an entire class period introducing and modeling what makes a good oral presentation and how to design eye-catching slides. We provided students with time during class to work with their teammates on the content of their speech and slides. Throughout their class workdays, we circulated from group to group to answer questions, provide feedback on specific slides, and ask them questions about their research. One week before the final public presentations, to which we invited campus and community stakeholders in education equity and DACA, the student groups rehearsed their speeches in front of the class, mimicking the conditions of the presentation space with a television screen, in a potentially noisy environment, and with difficult questions. We made a conscious decision to provide challenging feedback. In other words, we told the students ahead of time that we would critique every aspect of their presentation to prepare them. They rose to the challenge and during the final presentation event several attendees remarked at how professional and prepared our students were.

Throughout the semester, some of the most powerful moments for our students were seeing themselves reflected in other grassroots leaders and organizers. For instance, during the 2018 TEEC Summit, John B. King Jr., current CEO of the Education Trust and former US secretary of education, spoke to the coalition about the importance of providing opportunities for students of color across the United States. For the CBU students, the content of his speech was more powerful because of the color of his skin. After his speech, Mr. King took photos with the students, who remarked, "I can't believe someone so important is like me!" In another moment at the TEEC Summit, one Latina student gushed, "Everyone here knows how to pronounce my full name correctly!" In fact, in one of their blog posts, a student noted how much he learned from the presenters: "The speaker explained how we need more educators from different backgrounds to inspire students to achieve a higher education. . . . I did [not] have any teachers that looked relatively like me." At the TEEC Summit, they witnessed a pitch for the Tennessee Educators of Color Alliance, an organization committed to promoting, recruiting, and professionally developing teachers of color in Tennessee schools. They also were introduced to Conexión Américas' Mosaic Fellows, a program that brings together and empowers leaders of color in K–12 education in Tennessee. The summit celebrated diversity in real ways, showcasing the work of individuals and organizations who shared cultural backgrounds with our students.

On their surface, these moments may seem unimportant or even trite. However, several studies (Flores, 2017; Griffin, 2018; Milner, 2006) note the importance of seeing teachers of color and leaders of color for the development and self-confidence of young people. For instance, Gershenson, Hart, Hyman, Lindsay, and Papageorge (2018) find that Black students are less likely to drop out and pursue education beyond high school if they have at least one

Black teacher in grades 3 through 5 (p. 2). Seeing people of color in power matters for students' success. For our students, these interactions provided a greater context for the importance of completing their degrees, because college became more than a duty to the family or a need for a job—a college degree became a way to be a leader, a changemaker, and an example for other young people of color. Our students were acutely aware of how much this meant to them and what it could mean for future generations. One student noted that while she was undocumented, her brothers and sisters were all US citizens—her example as the eldest child was essential to her siblings' success: "If I can go to college with a president who hates me, I can do anything."

Three years later, we are still processing the effectiveness of our course. For many students, this experience has opened new possibilities for internships and employment, for collaboration, and for persistence in college. Diana, a student from the first-year composition section of Writing for Advocacy, shared her experiences at the 2019 Tennessee Educational Equity Coalition 2-Day Summit. She stressed how the Writing for Advocacy course shaped her future interests, into her sophomore year as a psychology major, wherein she applied Writing for Advocacy's practice of research and activism to study the difference in attitudes toward mental health treatment between documented and undocumented students in college:

> I wish to continue this mixture of psychological research and advocacy to provide for my community in the mental health field. . . . The Rojas-Flores et al. (2016) study showed how 4.1 million child immigrants in the United States who have had a parent detained or deported are at a much higher risk of developing PTSD. Those kids should not be forgotten. My passion has not dwindled once the class ended. It has only made me realize how I could take the importance of research in advocacy and combine it with the field of psychology.

Diana's story is the best-case scenario. In writing about her own cultural experiences, she found an impetus for further research and leadership, so cultural writing created the self-efficacy to engage deeper in academic work that would have a purpose beyond the university in building and serving a community. She understood research to be a fundamental part of advocacy. Passionate about her community and causes, she may still be a protester. Within the university community, she also developed the information literacies requisite to later academic success. And these successes are leading to a career in which advocacy and grassroots activism are part of her daily life. In May 2021, Diana graduated from CBU and enrolled in a Masters of Social Work (MSW) program at another university in Tennessee.

Making real change is often the culmination of thousands of small acts of courage and dissent. In *Diary of a Reluctant Dreamer*, Ledesma (2017) realizes the necessity of speaking out as the only way to shape the future, even if there is risk involved in sharing his family's story:

> Unless Americans of undocumented heritage break our silence about what it feels like to live undocumented, unless I publish this and other work, the notion that undocumented immigrants are brain-dead parasites incapable of intellectual and ethical reflections regarding their social, political, and historical condition in American society will persist. (p. 44)

Ledesma's writing here is summed up in his next sentence: "But I know what I am worth" (p. 44). Ledesma understands that the act of speaking, in the moment, is required, even if it changes little. Ultimately, it is this sort of rhetorical advocacy our course introduced and, we hope, fostered for our students. In a hostile political environment, particularly on state and federal levels, our students learned to contextualize their thoughts, to challenge their audience, and to make themselves mediators of change through the use of rhetoric. Although the short-term political gains of this work might be difficult to see or even nonexistent, the long-term psychological and educational value of speaking up articulates a sense of worth on individual, educational, and cultural levels, and that was precisely what the moment of our course demanded.

Rhetorical advocacy requires understanding the entire situation: expectations for attire and professionalism; deep research to understand the local situation in broader historical and political contexts, audience, and realistic objectives; and the writing and speaking skills to share this knowledge. The ability to understand and address these challenges represents the "attunement to a fluctuating present" described by Johnson, Letter, and Livingston (2009, p. 34). The writing course teaches students to address a rhetorical situation for effective communication, and grassroots campaigns, localized and specific, require a similarly deep understanding of the localized situation. Faculty and university leadership can provide connections and pathways for this kairotic understanding, especially for students who may live on or near campus for only a few years. Rhetorical advocacy may not result in change during a student's time in the community, but it asks students to think about change as a process, not an event. Viewing advocacy from a rhetorical position offers the step that follows protest: an articulation of policy goals addressed to the appropriate officials. As students leave college, they are prepared for leadership roles in grassroots efforts, and while the situations will change, the skills necessary to address the situation remain stable. For faculty and institutions, such a course expands the engaged network of alumni to mentor the next generation of student activists, and it builds community partnerships from the foundational work of understanding the rhetorical and political situation. The alumni, students, faculty, and university can all be more prepared for the next disaster, natural or sociopolitical, that demands student-led advocacy. Rhetorical advocacy provides a mooring in the ever-fluctuating political realm and a floating foundation for assessing, organizing, and addressing the local situation from a community-based perspective to organize the activist event and the political advocacy policy response—their passion will not dwindle.

CHAPTER 16

Voices from the Anti-Racist Pedagogy Collective

Individual Exigencies and Collective Actions

MOLLY APPEL, LAURA DECKER, RACHEL HERZL-BETZ,

JOLLINA SIMPSON, KATHERINE A. DURANTE,

ROSEMARY Q. FLORES, AND MARIAN AZAB

The Anti-Racist Pedagogy Collective (ARPC) is a grassroots group of faculty and staff from Nevada State College in Las Vegas, Nevada. This chapter presents a few of their voices.

LAURA DECKER, FIRST-YEAR COMPOSITION

Like so many, I felt overcome by the flood of bystander reports after George Floyd's murder and stories about who Floyd had been as a father, son, and community member. Desperate to act, I reached out to my colleague, Molly, and we mapped a plan for the ARPC (Anti-Racist Pedagogy Collective): we'd invite our colleagues from across disciplines to share their stories and to workshop anti-racist teaching and mentoring practices together.

Since our first meeting in June 2020, I have listened to my colleagues' stories and adapted strategies from our workshops that allow me to better hear the stories my students desire to tell. Each month, a different member brings a strategy to the virtual workshop table, and we collaboratively review, critique, and explore how that practice might make our institutional spaces more equitable. While Molly and I do not consider ourselves leaders in the group, as white, tenure-track faculty who have privileges that not all members have, we opted to take on the administrative labor of creating calendar invitations and meeting links, and we offer support to our workshop leaders by creating the shared documents for each meeting.

Our takeaways from workshops are practical. In one meeting, we collectively created a set of community practices we agreed would support our group's intentions. I brought this activity to my students, many of whom identify as Latinx and first-generation college students, who voiced that this process made their experiences seem valued. But our workshop takeaways also point to the messiness of our grassroots work. One workshop focused on encouraging students to sit in a circle and intentionally acknowledge each other as a tool for building self-awareness and mutual respect, but it simultaneously promoted ableism in the classroom through a focus on "seeing" one another. In another workshop, discussions about intersectional members' experiences with oppression sometimes devolved into conversations led by and about white women's experiences, since our group is mostly white women (reflective of our faculty body). Both examples serve as reminders that our grassroots work must be continually reshaped by our local exigencies.

MARIAN AZAB, SOCIOLOGY

Coming from a disabled Arab immigrant woman with a thick accent, talk of privilege and xenophobia may be alienating to some students and perceived as a personal attack. The ARPC introduced me to a group of mostly white women instructors trying to do something about racism; I had an "aha moment." Each of my classes should be an anti-racist collective. In addition to pointing out white privilege, I should empower my students to use their privileges instead of being ashamed of them or denying their existence. My classes should be an exercise in how to create alliances across different groups.

As a result, I changed how I introduce race-related materials in my classes. For example, when discussing privilege using the documentary *White Like Me*, I explicitly pointed out that all of us are privileged in some ways. I am privileged because I can use public restrooms without much thought. A transgender individual might not be able to. When I understand that using restrooms is a considerable challenge to some groups, I will start to think about privilege. Similarly, we study white privilege not to blame individuals but to imagine new ways of achieving racial equality. Through the hands-on workshopping of anti-racist teaching strategies, the collective empowered me to think about tackling racism in my classes instead of merely discussing its existence. In my classes, I witnessed how conversations shifted from students trying to deny their privilege to a discussion of ways to use that privilege to advocate for minority populations.

RACHEL HERZL-BETZ, WRITING CENTER DIRECTOR, AND JOLLINA SIMPSON, WRITING CENTER COORDINATOR

For the Writing Center leadership team, the ARPC became a valuable testing ground for faculty outreach and collaboration and revealed how systems of power and oppression shape rhetorical situations. We co-led one meeting and hoped to share the anti-racist praxis we use in the Writing Center around the rights students have to their preferred language and get feedback from these hopefully open-minded faculty. Our colleagues are often enthusiastic about anti-racism but are unaware of how that work could impact writing assessment.

During the meeting, the participants were uniformly interested in the ways anti-racism can shape writing in their courses, but we also gained three insights that may help those planning their own anti-racist discussion groups. First, *discipline may not matter in the ways we expect.* Our most surprising questions had less to do with disciplinary knowledge about anti-racism and more to do with disciplinary cultures around writing and revision. For example, in some disciplines we couldn't produce examples of scholarly code meshing, while in others, they proliferate. That gap made it difficult for even the most anti-racist instructor to offer discipline-specific models for their students. Second, *apply an anti-racist lens to the preparation process.* Since most of the ARPC are white women, we'd spent a great deal of time mentally preparing for pushback from them as the majoritized faculty. However, that mindset prioritized participants who shouldn't be centered in an anti-racist pedagogy group, and we found the members of color were left out of some of the conversations. In the future, we will more conscientiously center minoritized instructors and allow white participants to adjust accordingly. Finally, *be prepared to respond to microaggressions in real time.* In this kind of group, participants likely know about racism in contexts that may not transfer into new disciplines. Ensure that the community is ready to respond, so the work doesn't fall to marginalized, contingent, or otherwise vulnerable instructors.

KATHERINE A. DURANTE, SOCIAL SCIENCES

The events of 2020 led me to reflect on and recommit my efforts toward social justice in the classroom, a call heightened at a minority-serving institution such as ours. I joined the ARPC because it provides interdisciplinary faculty and staff with a collaborative environment to workshop anti-racist practices for the classroom. It provides a space to hear what our colleagues are doing and to share how we have sought to adapt our courses and pedagogies to integrate anti-racist practices. For example, I've begun to think about the ways grading writing assignments may reinforce racism or xenophobia. The ARPC introduced me to faculty and staff who share my goal of building an academic environment that facilitates equity-minded teaching, learning, scholarship, and service practices.

Faculty often forget the importance of collaboration and reflection for ourselves. Teaching is an ongoing project that should be responsive to our students and communities. The ARPC provides faculty the space to grow together through workshopping ideas and receiving feedback. It embodies the idea that teaching itself is a form of activism—our course content, assignments, and pedagogical techniques are conscious decisions that have a lasting impact on the skills and knowledge our students leave class with. Grassroots groups like the ARPC provide us with a space to think through what we want our students to learn and how to help get them there in a way that integrates anti-racist, equity-minded practices.

ROSEMARY Q. FLORES, TEACHER ACADEMY PIPELINE

As a college student, I struggled to feel as though I belonged on campus. I was one of few women of color in physics and chemistry, the only Mexican woman, and the only married student with two young children. Professors did not know of my goals and dreams; they did not know why I wanted to become a STEM teacher.

I joined the ARPC because I wanted to learn how professors connect with college students in a culturally responsive manner and how race is discussed during times of conflict. Working with mentors of color in the School of Education through a Title V grant designated for Hispanic Serving Institutions—whose missions are specifically focused on supporting Hispanic students, cultures, and languages—I felt responsible to acknowledge the tragic current events and learn strategies to share with our students during our Pláticas (conversations). Our mentors, who mentor high school students of color interested in careers in education, will soon be classroom teachers themselves. This was an opportunity for me to funnel anti-racist teaching strategies to them and help them develop those practices before becoming teachers. Our next step will be for mentors to share what they have learned and implemented with their mentees.

The collective's grassroots nature has been inviting. It is a space free of institutional constraints, but full of opportunities for us to share how we implement strategies and how students are impacted. It is also helpful to witness how we all still struggle with issues of race. In the future, I plan to share the challenges and impacts of the Pláticas and the way the practice has raised culturally responsive awareness for both mentors and mentees.

MOLLY APPEL, COMPARATIVE LITERATURE

We don't usually think of college faculty when we think about grassroots movements. Of course, student movements for equity have galvanized campuses for decades. Faculty who get involved in these movements must often do so as a rupture from our (often uncomfortable) roles as apparatuses of our institutions. We are pressed to embody the fiction that education should be "apolitical." Yet education, like grassroots action, is driven by an investment in community empowerment and is always inherently—crucially—political.

There were already a lot of good reasons for faculty to build coalitions before COVID-19 and the May 2020 racial justice movement. We are living through the neoliberalization of higher education: watching our schools increasingly rely on adjunct labor and instrumentalize "diversity" as a means of regulating the communities calling for proactive measures to dismantle white supremacy. These conditions are features of what Cedric Robinson has called "racial capitalism" (Robinson, 1983, p. 9). Their roots are the same that cultivated the structural violences that brought about the deaths of Breonna Taylor, George Floyd, and too many other Black lives, as well as those that led to nonwhite communities being disproportionately represented among the COVID-19 hospitalized and deceased.

The confluence of these events affirmed that we cannot wait for our institutions to lead us in addressing these injustices. We must support, push, learn from, and inspire one another. The grassroots nature of the ARPC is in our commitment to collectivity: our members shape our space by seeking out practices to workshop; our workshopping leads to our changed practices; we set our own pace and accountability for our work. Protecting our space of dialogue and disclosure from institutionalization will be crucial for our efficacy if we want to remain in opposition to frameworks that are oriented toward white supremacy. Like all successful grassroots movements, we, too, will need purposeful organization and agitation to stay our course as anti-racist educators.

CHAPTER 17

Vernacular Assessment Activity in Local Community Organizing

JOE CIRIO

An intentional consideration of the assessment structures of activist and grassroots organizations is vital to the work of activists. If, as Brian Huot (2001) has claimed, "in literate activity, assessment is everywhere" (p. 62), then certainly such literate activity would also include writing that serves communities and local exigences. However, research into the processes and impact of writing assessment has been primarily focused on assessment located in or designed and administered by various educational institutions (for example, College Board, classroom grades, state testing). This chapter argues that the assessment of writing is also a literate practice in vernacular community contexts that serve particular purposes and have distinct qualities. By drawing attention to the structures of assessment that sustain activist, grassroots organizing, we can better articulate how local actions come together through discourse and collaboration with other organizers.

Drawing attention to the writing assessment structures in activist organizations brings into focus the mundane, often clerical textual work that, as Rivers and Weber (2011) describe, is not always as visible as the more obvious public displays or actions but is "no less necessary for the creation and re-creation of publics" (p. 188). Jason Del Gandio (2008), likewise, advocates for greater attention to such processes in *Rhetoric for Radicals*:

> We continually argue over the look and design of demonstrations and direct actions; the wording of manifestos and speeches; and the usefulness of ideologies, philosophies and analyses. But these debates always seem peripheral to our physical actions and material conditions. This is mistaken and debilitating. Undervaluing the rhetoric of our efforts hinders our communication with, and our political efficacy within, the wider public arena. (pp. 2–3)

As Del Gandio describes, activist organizers are well versed in the discussions and debates about tactics, public texts, and local actions; however, much of the scholarly literature on activist and grassroots organizing focuses attention on the broader public impact of major texts and actions that critique hegemonic structures, speak truth to power, and keep institutions accountable. Indeed, Hauser and McClellan (2009) have noted how "studies of social movements have focused on the discourse of leaders, on single events, or on movement strategies" (p. 29), while scholarly attention has largely ignored the vernacular discourse of a social movement's rank-and-file members. For Hauser and McClellan, attending to the discourse and rhetorical processes of the vernacular provides a fuller understanding of how beliefs, values, and ideologies circulate and sustain across a movement.

Taking up that call, I endeavored to better understand the role of vernacular forms of writing assessment employed and structured among activists. How are these internal discussions structured? Who has or should have a voice in these discussions? How can we give voice to community stakeholders? How can organizational leaders structure discussions that reflect values of democracy, collaboration, and consensus?

This chapter explores the possibility of addressing these questions by using *vernacular writing assessment*: the structures of interpretation and judgment of everyday writing that sustain community discourses and that lead to decisions, actions, or changes in the discourse of that community. I focus this chapter on one particular community organization. I offer observations about the structures of assessment that are designed and implemented within and through The Plant, a volunteer-operated, community-driven creative space where "everyone is welcomed and empowered to organize, research, and encourage the free expression of others" (as stated in their description and mission statement). Community organizers in and around the Tallahassee, Florida, area have used The Plant as a gathering space and activist hub for a variety of causes. During my time talking with volunteers at The Plant, they were hosting monthly PFLAG Tallahassee meetings, a semiregular event called "Political Prisoner Letter Writing and Free Dinner," and a workshop titled "Radical Women's Liberation," among other events. The Plant gives activists and community organizers an opportunity to meet in a welcoming space—just as long as they align with The Plant's broader mission.

I observed the discursive activity of two of The Plant's key volunteer organizers—Ham and Billy—and discuss how they each use, design, implement, and navigate different kinds of writing assessment practices. These two volunteers offer a compelling foil in how they approach assessment activity: Ham focuses on the internal organization of The Plant community and attends to structures of assessment to sustain and negotiate the values of The Plant; Billy is centrally concerned with the public perception of local actions he has helped organize, and he seeks out and offers feedback for publicly circulated texts. For both volunteers, it is clear their assessment activity operates to exchange, sustain, and negotiate values for the organizations and communities they are involved with, whether The Plant or other grassroots organizations. Vernacular writing assessment appears integral to sustaining the activity of the various communities that intersect with The Plant: it can aid in building, understanding and maintaining social bonds among volunteers; create opportunities to disseminate and negotiate organizational values and expectations; and sustain the core mission and vision of The Plant through often very quick shifts in the makeup of volunteers.

In what follows, I provide background on how scholarship in writing studies has observed writing assessment as a structural means to sustain communities and then offer some observations about assessment from vernacular writing contexts as a point of departure to understand the assessment activity of The Plant. From there, I articulate observations from both Ham and Billy's discursive activity and how they consider and design the structures of assessment to sustain their own activism and community organizing. I conclude each case study with implications for grassroots activists. Namely, their assessment experiences offer grounds to consider goal-oriented discussions around written texts, democratically structured collaboration with members, matriculating newcomers, and benchmarking success for public audiences.

COMMUNITY AS CONTEXT FOR WRITING ASSESSMENT

Writing assessment involves these three basic components: (1) the interpretation or *judgment* of written texts based on a set of values, (2) the *articulation* of a judgment on those texts in the form of some response, and (3) the *impact* that the articulation has on some related exigence—such as the basis for a decision or the change in future writing activity. The components, when taken together as a whole, make up a social exchange by which participants of an assessment can negotiate—or at the very least make available—what they value in a given context about text, about a community, and about writing, generally. These components extend to school-based assessment practices and can likewise apply to writing assessment in vernacular contexts such as the exchanges of feedback and discussions involved in developing local actions among grassroots activist organizations.

I understand the impulse to resist assessment as a tool to support activist work. Educational and corporate institutions have historically relied upon assessment measures as means of identifying whether individuals are meeting the needs of the economy and as a means of justifying punishment when competencies are not met. However, to some extent, assessment is also inevitable for any organization that engages in textual discussions and discourse—to return to Huot (2001), assessment is, in fact, everywhere. Rather than seeking to ignore or avoid discussions of assessment, activists and grassroots organizers would be better suited to engage deeply and intentionally with assessment and design assessments that align with their values. Writing assessment researchers have long understood how assessments are social actions that define our textual realities. They are constitutive in, as Yancey (1999) writes, "the formation of the self and writing assessment, because it wields so much power, plays a crucial role in what self, or selves, will be permitted—in our classrooms; in our tests; ultimately, in our culture" (p. 144). Though referring primarily to institutional assessments, Yancey's articulation of the constitutive nature of assessment is relevant to grassroots activist contexts as well. The design and structure of writing assessment both represent and construct wider, systematic cultural values.

As a response to the corporate imperatives and psychometric measurement tradition that have historically framed the assessment of writing in support of educational institutions in the last century, writing assessment researchers in literacy studies have sought to explore the community contexts of writing assessment. Researchers like Adler-Kassner and Harrington (2010) and Gallagher (2011) have endeavored to articulate new frames to understand the function of writing assessment, frames that do not invoke the values of neoliberalism—efficiency, ranking, and competition. Rather, Adler-Kassner and Harrington offer a responsibility framework that, among the key ideas, includes building alliances with others, which necessarily involves "active listening and dialogue" (p. 87). Writing assessments should be engaging others "in the *full* process of assessment, thinking *with* them (rather than handing *to* them) about what 'good writing' means and looks like" (p. 88). And likewise, such a framework involves making changes and decisions based on dialogue with several constituents. This kind of democratic structure of assessment appears closely aligned with community-based assessment where values emerge from dialogue and interaction with multiple constituents within the community. In a similar way, Bob Broad's (2003) dynamic criteria mapping (DCM), a qualitative inquiry into writing programs' latent value criteria, frames writing programs as a space of communal writing values. DCM attends to these communal values and specifically invites teachers to participate as a community to articulate their often implicit values and develop a professional, disciplinary community. Broad's invocation of community for writing assessment recognizes the ways that facilitating community participation can socialize a group of people to articulate and generate common values and common practices in ways that go beyond the typical channels of a disciplinary community (such as conferences, books, journals, and so on).

These research perspectives from Adler-Kassner and Harrington (2010) and Broad (2003) draw attention to how fostering of community for an assessment context offers disparate individuals a structured way to better articulate their dynamic and implicit writing values and provides a means to involve the voice of multiple constituents, even those with the least power within the system. In other words, an assessment structure can reflect and reinforce democratic values—if designed and considered intentionally. Although much of the literature on writing assessment focuses on renewed institutional uses of assessment, such research offers a useful starting point to describe how the frame of community—and its emphasis on building alliances, dialogue, and shared meaning—could likewise be a point of departure to begin to understand assessment in vernacular writing contexts.

WRITING ASSESSMENT STRUCTURES
IN VERNACULAR CONTEXTS

Discourse within the realm of the vernacular is often defined by its position outside of or in opposition to an institutional context. Vernacular rhetoric, as defined in the work of Hauser (1999) and Hauser and McClellan (2009), describes the distinct language and performances that inscribe the everyday interactions of a counterpublic discourse community. I use the label of "vernacular" because of its relationship to community actions in, often, direct opposition to institutional contexts. Kynard (2013) explains that she sees vernacular discourse as "not only counterhegemonic, but also as affirmative of new, constantly mutating languages, identities, political methodologies, and social understandings that communities form in and of themselves, both inwardly and outwardly" (p. 11). Kynard's definition is particularly useful to build an understanding of vernacular writing assessment: how are communities enacting assessment practices for their own purposes and needs? And in a way that operates outside of (and often in direct opposition to) the neoliberal assessment practices of institutions?

Reading across activist rhetorical scholarship, allusions to potential assessment practices are often in service to internal processes of solidarity-building or solidification among activists. Solidification, defined by Bowers, Ochs, Jensen, and Schulz (2010), describes the means of cohering an agitating group around shared beliefs, values, and ideologies and uniting followers by "[creating] a sense of community" that "reinforces the cohesiveness of members" (p. 29). While Bowers, Ochs, Jensen, and Schulz attend to major art pieces— plays, songs, poems, art installations, and so on—as sources of solidification, I argue that solidification is also achieved through vernacular assessment practices. Kevin Mahoney (2020), for instance, alludes to processes of assessment and feedback built into the editorial process of the Raging Chicken Press, a progressive media outlet for local Pennsylvania causes. Mahoney describes the recursive process of matriculating new writers for the press and "breaking them of their neutral observer voice" that typically characterizes mainstream journalistic reporting. As he writes, "it takes a while for Raging Chicken writers to find their voice on our site and that is precisely the point. Raging Chicken provides a *place* to practice those skills in the world in a sustained way" (p. 123). While a deep description of the particular feedback processes is not provided, I would argue that Mahoney is engaging in a structured assessment practice: he makes reference to a recursive and sustained process to help new writers align with the genres, expectations, and values of the press. This structure of assessment serves the overlapping purposes of preparing writers for the outlet's reading audience as well as engaging in practices of solidification among the outlet's community of reporters.

A deeper descriptive analysis of matriculation and consensus-building in an activist context can be found in David Graeber's (2009) ethnographic research of New York City Direct Action Network (DAN), a network of anti-capitalist organizations and activist groups. Graeber demystifies the structures of feedback within DAN's internal processes by describing the consensus-building model employed by DAN members to discuss proposals and make collective decisions. Consensus is a model and process for discussion, developed by the Quakers and employed often as an alternative to *Robert's Rules of Order* among activist groups. Although DAN's use of consensus as a process is meant as a structure to organize and facilitate mass meetings, Graeber's recounting of DAN members' justification and purpose behind the consensus offers a compelling example of a kind of vernacular writing assessment. The consensus process (1) centers on members' proposals, sometimes verbal, sometimes textual; (2) is predicated on the assumption that members may have different perspectives and the consensus process provides a forum to engage those perspectives; (3) is goal-oriented and is a process that seeks to make decisions; and (4) is structured in a way that gives voice to members regardless of status within the organization. As one DAN member, Chris, reflects:

> Well, I guess the idea of consensus is that it's a way of seeking commonality. You start by assuming everyone in the room probably has a somewhat different perspective, and you're not trying to change that, you're trying to see if you can create some kind of common ground. (Graeber, 2009, pp. 304–305)

The recent shifts toward community-grounded and democratic assessment processes in the scholarly field of writing assessment resemble the foundation of assessment practices already in practice in activist communities. DAN, an activist network that is already grounded in anti-capitalism, rejects neoliberal imperatives—premised on surveillance, accountability, and punishment for inefficiency—in their assessment structures. Rather, the structures are put in place to engage individual disagreement and diverse perspectives, offering more equitable power to community members to contribute to the decision-making process.

DAN's decision-making structures are fairly stable and well-established for facilitating their mass meetings, but I seek to better understand more local, smaller-scale activist organizations. In the second half of this chapter, I provide a description of a research study that looks at the granular assessment practices and interactions that sustain the activist work at The Plant.

METHODS

To investigate the writing assessment activity from a vernacular community context, I implemented case study methods that sought to observe the literacy activity of writers in Tallahassee. Specifically, I contacted organizers or facilitators of groups who, in some way, participate in some kind of collective writing or composing. Among the groups I contacted were the organizers at The Plant, a community organization for a do-it-yourself community space that also functions as a site for local organizing. I was then able to solicit voluntary participation from two mainstay volunteers in the space:

Ham,[1] aged 39,[2] white, American woman. Ham often led meetings and scheduled events. At the time of the study, Ham was in her final year of a doctoral program in Art Education.

Billy, aged 32, white, American man. Billy took occasional responsibilities to schedule and vet events. Billy is also an active member of Students for Justice in Palestine (SJP)[3] and has experience coordinating rallies.

I approached the data collection using case study methodology, a descriptive empirical research design that attends to the particular, observable experiences of individuals (as in the case of this project) or a single organization, group, or program. Of importance to this study is observing how an individual operates within a given context—or in this case, how these two individuals navigate, construct, design, and facilitate different kinds of assessment activity within a community context. The participants engaged in three methods of data collection:

1. **Field observations** of community meetings (six in total) focused on participants' engagement within their community context. These observations provided some information about the community's exchange of writing, how such writing facilitates aspects of the community, and most importantly, how the participant interacts with such writing.

2. **Experience-sampling methods,** or ESM, which is "a research method in which participants are signaled at the occurrence of certain events or random intervals during a given time period to stop and record what they are doing and how they feel about what they are doing" (Addison, 2007, p. 176). I employed a time-use diary, a kind of ESM, to track the kind of everyday, vernacular writing activity that participants wrote and responded to, day-to-day, during the data collection period.

3. **Reflective text-based interviews** were conducted, where participants were invited to reflect on their diary responses. The interviews themselves were a means of describing the writer's rhetorical choices about their writing behaviors, focused specifically on discussing the role assessment played in their writing choices. Participants were invited to discuss how judgments, whether from others or from themselves, and evalua-

---

1. All names referenced are pseudonyms. Ham and Billy chose their own pseudonyms. All other pseudonyms were chosen by author.

2. Age at the time of data collection.

3. Billy is not currently enrolled as a student yet remains an active member in SJP (Students for Justice in Palestine).

tions impacted their writing choices. Two interviews were held with each
participant.

Through these methods, I sought to triangulate participants' accounts of their
literacy experiences, particularly the ways they interact with or constructed
vernacular writing assessment. Data collection occurred between August and
October 2017.

THE PLANT

The Plant refers to two interrelated entities: (1) the physical structure or space
to hold events and (2) the social, organizational structure made up of volunteers. The space is made available to any organizer who wishes to host an event
that reflects The Plant's values: all-inclusive, DIY, creativity, free expression,
and social justice. At weekly meetings, volunteers reflect upon the success
of events in the previous week, discuss proposals for upcoming events, and
schedule approved events. Although these are the central goals of each meeting, they also have a secondary function as a social gathering for some volunteers, who attend without proposing new events. The Plant facility is owned
by George, a retired university professor from the fine art department at the
local university, Gulf State University.[4] Although he owns the space, George
delegates the primary goals of the meeting to Ham and Billy. As leaders in the
space, Ham and Billy facilitate the meeting, including focusing on the agenda,
opening discussion on proposed events, and scheduling approved events. The
Plant's organizational structure places a lot of value on collaborative input of
its volunteers, even if some volunteers may not regularly attend organizational
meetings. The Plant's membership is constantly in flux, often with members
joining for a few weeks or a few months and then stopping their involvement,
often unannounced and without explanation. During my time with The Plant,
it was experiencing something of a transition, and both Billy and Ham were
involved in articulating a clearer structure moving forward. Billy mentioned
that such a structure could contribute, in part, to qualifying The Plant for
nonprofit status, while Ham saw the structuring as a means of mending some
of the issues she identified in organizing and facilitating events through The
Plant, especially given the turnover with members.

---

4. "Gulf State University" is used in place of the actual local university.

Ham

This first case study reports on Ham and her instrumental role in facilitating The Plant's event proposal approval process. The approval process functions as a structured vernacular writing assessment: volunteers who wish to host an event in The Plant draft an "event proposal agreement," a textual document where potential event organizers must articulate the specifics of their event. That document is then discussed during face-to-face meetings where volunteers in attendance evaluate the textual document to determine whether it reflects the space's values. This feedback-assessment leads to the approval of the event proposal, or not, and it also provides a means for the community to articulate what they value in the space.

Ham believed that a structured process of vetting proposals helps ensure The Plant is both a collaborative space that seeks the input of its members in a structured manner and a space with core values that sustain across a constantly changing community membership. In comparison with Billy, who is driven by The Plant's social activism, Ham's involvement and motivation with The Plant is to create a functional space for meaningful relationships and collaboration to flourish. Ham was instrumental in the development of the event proposals (along with George and Billy) and, during meetings, was often seeking to sustain the use of the event proposals to ensure events aligned with the values of the space.

Although I was unable to observe volunteers discussing an event proposal firsthand, I did observe Ham explaining this process to a newcomer, Harriett, who wanted to host an event. Ham highlighted the kinds of events that take place at The Plant. She alluded to the mission statement, which mentions that the space itself is a site for inclusion and social justice. To Harriett, Ham explained: "You don't have to make it a social justice theme. All are welcome. We encourage activities around art, talks, discussion. We've done all sorts of stuff—it's a safe space. As long as it's encompassed in our mission. Letting kids express themselves is welcome." Here, Ham outlines the expectations of the event proposal and values of The Plant, itself, to prepare Harriet for the writing task. Ham asked Harriett to frame her writing to fit generally within those frameworks. In my observations of meetings and interviews with Ham, it didn't seem likely that an event would be rejected if it didn't fit the mission of the space. Rather, it seemed more likely that volunteers might ask the proposal writer to adjust aspects of the event to more closely align with the space's values—though the "values" or "mission" of the space appear to be constantly negotiated depending on who is involved with the space at a given moment.

In our interviews, Ham mentioned that the values of The Plant are articulated in the description of the space in various pamphlets and social media ("an all-inclusive creative space, where everyone is welcomed and empowered to organize, research, and encourage the free expression of others"). More specifically, how some of these ideas are defined and understood rests on the consensus of the group through discussion. Ham lamented the challenge of having a "revolving community," since the members—and their values—are constantly shifting depending on who shows up to the meeting. Ham explains:

> The mission statement has been sort of on-again [off-again] because there's been so many different people from since we've had all these different goals. Like, we're going to go get a new mission statement and then the people that started saying they want to go work, then they don't come anymore.

Ham often identified the consistency of members as a challenge for The Plant, a particular challenge for defining what the volunteers at The Plant value. Defining these values appears particularly necessary for the event proposal assessment process.

Although this appeared to be a semiformalized process, Ham was frequently advocating for volunteers to write up proposals if they wished to use the space, and in some cases, she received pushback from regularly attending volunteers who saw the event proposals as unnecessary or unimportant. In one meeting, a regular attendee named Carl verbally proposed a Halloween event called the "Un-Condition-Lounge." The event would have the dual purpose of being a social get-together (as he remarked, "all the worst people at the best possible time") and a screening for local filmmakers, possibly involving students in the film and theatre departments at Gulf State University. As Carl proposed these events verbally, Billy and George began to offer some verbal feedback in response. However, Ham urged Carl to propose the event in writing before it could be put on the schedule of events. Their exchange is summarized in my fieldnotes:

> Ham asks Carl to write up his event in the proposal form so they can put the event on the books—that is, in the proposal's binder. Carl appears ambivalent to the proposal form, saying that they can put it on the books now: "it's going to happen." Ham pushes the point—she'd really like the form. Carl, appearing a little annoyed, says, "fine, give me a form." Billy hands him a form. Carl begins writing the form at the meeting table.

Although Carl laid out much of his proposal verbally and other members like Billy and George began to discuss the event, Ham was adamant that Carl follow the formal procedures of approval process and write his event proposal. Ham placed value on the use of written texts and documents to organize The Plant; indeed, during our interviews, Ham noted that generating textual documents is key to keeping The Plant cohesive and that she was often the only one to advocate for sustaining these writing practices. She worried that "if nobody does it, nothing gets done." Inviting volunteers to propose events through writing may lead to more concrete action, including keeping event hosts accountable.

Ham's insistence that members write the proposal form is similar to concerns raised by DAN members in Graeber's (2009) ethnography. Graeber recounts the concerns raised by Mark, a DAN member, who advocated that proposals be restated and repeated throughout the meeting: "I can't tell you how many times I've sat through a ten-, fifteen-minute argument and it turned out that the only reasons people were arguing is because they didn't understand what was actually being proposed" (p. 302). Although DAN does not ask members to write proposals, Ham similarly appears to invite written proposals as a way to ensure members know what the proposers are asking for and what members are discussing. And for Ham, establishing these protocols could also be a means of giving The Plant a higher profile. She commented, "I think it's important, if we're really trying to make progress with this organization and make it more well-known and to have people stay, [then] there needs to be some sort of protocol, and it didn't seem to have that."

She recalled in our interview that when volunteers at The Plant initially discussed ways to structure and streamline the meetings, she received some pushback on establishing some of the formal structures of documenting and vetting proposals. Specifically, Ham noted that Billy was initially hesitant to establish more structure for the organizational meetings; according to Ham, "Billy has actually come around a little more. Like in the very beginning, he was like 'just let things—you can't tell anybody [what to do]. We can't take any structure.'" According to Ham, Billy saw more structure, like the event proposal agreement, as a way to confine the decision-making process for the community. However, Ham sought more of a balance:

> And it ended up being that nothing gets done. If you are completely . . . loose and no direction or everybody gets a say, I mean it's basically like eight thousand Ronnies in one room, and you can't get anything done. Again, I say that out of the kindness—bless his heart, but he's long-winded, and we all can be long-winded, but I mean, we can make a decision.

Ham alluded to a regular member named Ronnie who is particularly loquacious and known to instigate arguments during (and after) meetings—some of which I witnessed firsthand during my field observations. Ronnie, and volunteers like Ronnie, can distract from the purpose of discussing The Plant and how it can facilitate events. Ham understood Carl similarly: he treats The Plant as a space for social interaction. "[H]e looks at it for maybe finding friends. Establishing, like, more real relationships." However, Ham underscored that while she saw The Plant as a place for building relationships, there were also goals to accomplish: "It's not social hour. We have things to accomplish, so that gets mixed. I think, like I said, Carl will come there and it's more social for him, but for us [Billy and Ham], we just want to get our stuff done and just move on." Given the concerns Ham raised about members like Ronnie and Carl, it appears that, for Ham, the use of the event proposal agreement also functions as a point of focus in the meeting: discussions center on the written event proposals, and if a volunteer has an idea without an event proposal, then it is set aside until it is articulated in the document.

ACTIVIST IMPLICATIONS:
ORIENTING TOWARD GOALS AND COLLABORATION

Though Ham's assessment practices are localized for the particular context and purposes of The Plant, her experiences provide some broader considerations that activists might consider as they seek to organize and facilitate community-engaged meetings. First, local organizers could reflect on how the production and discussion of textual documents can streamline and structure the decision-making process. For The Plant, the proposal functions as an externalized document, focusing discussion around whether the text aligns with the values of the space—and it keeps proposers responsible for what has been agreed upon. Second, such an assessment process can be a means of making legible and available the collective meaning of the values of the space. Ham recognized that The Plant operates with a set of values, some of which are represented in the broad mission statement, but those values and others may be more tacit and dependent upon the current membership iteration of The Plant. Facilitating a process to discuss a proposal's alignment with The Plant's values necessarily requires those values to be taken up, articulated, and defined among the collaborative membership.

In the next case study, Billy focuses his attention more on the public representation of the actions performed by the activist collectives with which he is involved. He both provides feedback to public texts and seeks out feedback to ensure that he can better anticipate different forms of representation that can happen.

Billy

The second case study reports on Billy, and I focus particular attention on his concern about the representation of his social activist community in public texts. The week prior to the start of the data collection period, Billy and Students for Justice in Palestine (SJP)—an antiwar and anti-racist organization—held a rally they organized in Tallahassee to support the counterprotests against white nationalists in Charlottesville, Virginia, in August 2017. Below, I discuss two kinds of writing assessment activity from Billy's experiences in relation to this rally: feedback he offered to a video of the rally that would be posted on YouTube and feedback he sought from a friend on responses he drafted to a reporter's questions about the rally. Neither of the writing and assessment contexts were centered at The Plant, per se. Rather, they were adjacent to The Plant: Billy was not operating in direct connection with The Plant, but I observed Billy and other members of SJP use The Plant's backroom as a space to plan and discuss ongoing demonstrations and store supplies related to those demonstrations.

First, as part of the rally, Billy invited a friend, Tiffany, to attend so she could collect video footage to edit and post online. Tiffany, as Billy explained in our interviews, had never attended a demonstration before, and Billy invited her in part to give her a reason to participate and in part to help produce a promotional video for the local chapter of SJP. The video would eventually be posted on the YouTube channels for The Plant and SJP. Toward the latter goal to promote the local SJP, Billy noted that the finished video was not fully aligned with how he'd like the group and the rally to be represented. Reflecting on the video initially, Billy commented that Tiffany wasn't given much direction on what was expected of her when editing the video, so he took the opportunity to offer feedback and edits. His feedback drew attention to several different components of the video he wished to see revised: particular phrasings and labels, the involvement of other local activist groups, and the relationship of the Tallahassee rally to Charlottesville. As he explains, he commented on

> the wording of it, and also making it not like, "Students for Justice in Palestine did this thing on this day. They were the ones that asked this group to speak and this." I was like, "Can we just say 'local organizers?'" I made sure it had all the groups that participated; all the people that spoke listed out.

The focus on phrasing was important for Billy, since such wording could frame the goals and nature of the rally itself for a public audience. He continued:

"For the rally, the thing we were protesting was an idea, so it wasn't like we were going to go to this place and make our demands. It was like, we're going to come together and strategize on how to move forward from this. I wouldn't say people are protesters, really." Each of these pieces of feedback seems to operate under an overall emphasis on how the rally will be represented in a public medium. For instance, rather than identifying the rally as an SJP-organized event, Billy sought to ensure that the other organizations were well represented; representing the rally in this way is important given the goal of the rally to allow various activist groups to interface and strategize on common ground.

The rally in August 2017 also garnered the attention of local Tallahassee reporters, particularly from the student-run local university newspaper at Gulf State University. After the rally, a reporter from Gulf State University's newspaper sent a series of questions to Billy about the nature of the rally, including how the rally was organized, who was involved with the rally, and how students were responding to it. In drafting his response to the questions, Billy drew upon a number of sources, including his prior knowledge and experiences with writing for newspaper publications and feedback from a friend who is aligned with him ideologically and who has experience as a journalist. His exchange with the reporter demonstrates the ways that vernacular writing assessment can help shape a message, as we will see through Billy's conceiving of the multiple ways his writing will be represented and interpreted by numerous audiences, including the reporter, his editor, and the reading public.

A large part of his thought process involved invoking prior experiences when working with reporters. He wanted to be sure that, despite the questions being open-ended and vague, "the answers are specific to messages we are trying to get across." He alluded to one particular instance during the rally itself that emphasized for him the need for care in drafting responses to reporters, generally. He recalled an instance when a reporter asked his friend Valerie if he could ask her a specific question for a live feed. Just prior to the filming, Billy and Valerie discussed what she could say, but during the interview, the reporter asked a different set of questions than initially promised. Billy recalled:

> They were like, "Hey, we're going to ask you this question." I was like, to my friend Valerie, "This is what they want to say." When it actually was a live feed, that's not exactly what he said at all. She was like, "I thought I was answering his stuff." She pre-arranged stuff. Being put on the spot doesn't look good.

In much of our discussion about this interaction with reporters, Billy noted his awareness that reporters approach these rallies with different goals, seeking to craft a narrative that may not be aligned with the narrative the rally organizers envisioned. Further, the stakes can be high when talking with reporters, since the quality of the rally organizers' responses can have an impact on the way the wider public perceives and reads the role of the rally and the organizations that organized it.

Because the goals of the activist organization and the news media reporting on demonstrators are not always aligned, Billy emphasized the need to be more deliberate in crafting the message to provide both substance to the cause that his organization was championing and to accurately representing their motives and values. Indeed, he noted that in the past, SJP has been featured in the newspaper with lukewarm results. He recalled, "We've been in the newspaper before as a group. I think people didn't have that idea [to have talking points]; I had to have sound bites and put in a message. They're just hanging out and talking, and there's not much content there." Billy sees the value of using vetted talking points with news media since it's more focused and deliberate. What was clear in my interviews with Billy is that he approached these public opportunities very intentionally, largely because of these experiences he's had with misrepresentations or lost opportunities.

In addition, not only has he had more exposure to these kinds of interactions with reporters, he also had access to friends, such as Paige, who are more familiar with genres of journalism. Billy described Paige as having experience as a copy editor for a newspaper, but potentially more important, she is also aligned with him politically. "I figured, politically, we're on the same page, so I didn't have to worry about her watering it down or make it more liberal sounding, which is an issue, especially with the media," Billy told me. Billy drew upon Paige because of her experience as a copy editor, her familiarity with journalistic reporting, and her ideology being aligned with his. Thus, for Billy, she operated as an ally in drafting the response. In Billy and Paige's exchange, she did offer some minor edits. Billy described it as follows:

Yeah. The question [from the reporter] was like, "Were you surprised by the number of protestors?" Or something like that. The answer was like, "It wasn't surprising that people feel that way." We were talking about the tragedy in the other half of the sentence. To be like, "We're not surprised someone got killed" looks bad if you don't take them out. She reworded it in a way that was like, "The tragedy was awful, but not particularly surprising," or something like that. I think that's how it went. "Someone died, but that happens, people are crazy."

With Tiffany, the videographer, Billy's concern about representation came across as he provided and designed feedback for Tiffany's video. In this instance of writing assessment with Paige, Billy sought feedback in order to help craft his writing so that his organization was not misrepresented through the reporter's article. Although Billy was not directly involved in the eventual drafting of the article, he was able to seek feedback from his journalist friend who was aware of the genre and rhetorical situation of such journalistic writing and had a familiarity with how source responses might be used in the drafting of an article. Billy was, however, able to read a copy of the article before it was sent to the editor of the newspaper and was ultimately able to judge for himself how his remarks were being framed in the article. Billy remarked he was pleased with the final product and how the rally was represented:

> I think he did a good job. The group came across exactly how I was hoping, not trying to look like a savior, just looking to be in solidarity in the allies, and not being the mouthpiece for an oppressed group, but also recognizing the responsibility to address it in your home community, not just tweet out snarky remarks or something.

ACTIVIST IMPLICATIONS: MATRICULATION AND BENCHMARKING

Like Ham, Billy's experiences in providing and soliciting feedback can provide implications for activists to consider, particularly as they prepare for public circulation of key texts, documents, and ideas. First, processes of assessment and feedback seem attached to procedures of matriculating newcomers. I was drawn to the ways Billy focused attention on preparing newcomers for public discourse. Certainly, representation appears to be of utmost importance for Billy—he is very much oriented to how he and his social activist community will come across to others. As such, we see Billy providing mentorship—in the form of direct feedback on Tiffany's video or in strategizing with Valerie before an interview—to help folks with less experience understand the implications of public circulation and framing of ideas. Second, in a vernacular context, activists need to find ways to benchmark expectations and success. Put another way, there are no rubrics that clearly explain and assess the value of a text. Billy was able to assemble a host of other resources to benchmark his success—that is, he was able to conceptualize the standards to which he would be writing, by invoking his prior experiences with reporters and the end result; seeking out and using feedback from Paige, who has more knowledge of journalistic practices; or reading the actual article to see whether he was pleased with the outcome. His process of benchmarking was connected to his interaction with assessment: he constructed his sense of the standards of the reporter specifically but also of newspaper media generally. Considering these standards, he strategized how to draft answers to produce an outcome with which he would be happy—in other words, a representation of the rally that keyed into his sound bites.

CONCLUSION

Reading across these case studies, we can describe the kinds of knowledge about vernacular writing assessment that can be gained from Ham and Billy's assessment experiences. Notably, components of assessment are intimately woven into the ongoing process of building consistent bonds of community, rooted in shared values. Ham insisted that event proposals be taken up during meetings in order to seek the input of all members in attendance rather than Ham herself or other key volunteers making unilateral decisions. Furthermore, the mission statement, although partly articulated in a description and partly upheld through ongoing discussions, is meant to operate as a guide to account for the revolving aspect of the community, where membership is constantly changing month to month, with new members joining who may bring different goals and values. The assessment process—via vetting event proposals—became a means of maintaining consistent values while also keeping them negotiable for the evolving membership. Likewise, Billy's feedback to Tiffany's video functioned to produce quality promotional materials while also functioning to matriculate a newcomer to these kinds of demonstrations. More broadly, Billy was particularly attuned to SJP's public messaging and sought to offer feedback and maintain consistent talking points to avoid being misrepresented.

A pattern emerges in these writing assessment practices: structured or semistructured feedback, and a means of articulating such feedback, manifests in vernacular contexts. And importantly, these assessment practices become a means to provide consistency in values. Structurally, both Ham and Billy demonstrate how the centering of certain values can still be predicated on negotiation, community- and alliance-building, and dialogue. In this sense, responding to certain texts—whether an event proposal, a promotional video, or responses to a journalist—is not simply about producing "good writing" but rather about negotiating values. Assessment practices in these contexts are also about engaging in dialogue about expectations, benchmarks for success, and values. In other words, expectations, benchmarks, and values are not always clearly defined or stable in these writing contexts. Rather, they are constantly being communicated and negotiated—and such negotiation is necessarily part of the process.

CHAPTER 18

Enacting Invitational Rhetorics

Leveraging Networks of Care in the US Asylum Process

MONICA REYES, RANDALL MONTY,
JORGE M. CAMARILLO, AND CINDY BERNAL

A person is eligible to apply for asylum in the United States if they are able to effectively persuade the United States Citizenship and Immigration Services (USCIS)—in written, narrative form—about the circumstances surrounding their escape from persecution in their home country. The process includes filling out an application (USCIS form I-589) in English, wherein asylum-seekers are asked to answer a series of detailed questions about their persecution in their home country. In some cases, individuals must appear before an immigration judge to recount the information in their asylum application. An appeal may take months, or even years, to get resolved, and even then, given the complexity of the process and the lack of professional and legal assistance accessible for immigrants, many appeals are rejected.[1] In 2019 only 31 percent of asylum cases handled by immigration courts were approved (Transactional Records, 2020), while a mere 16 percent of approved asylum cases were successful without help from a lawyer to navigate the process.

Asylum appeals narratives are vital, as they open opportunities for work, education, and a pathway to resettlement in the United States; however, these narratives are also dependent on a problematic ideology that centers on

---

1. For example, Migrant Protection Protocols, otherwise known as "Remain in Mexico," is a policy passed during the Trump administration that mandates that asylum-seekers must return to their country of origin, or to the last country they were physically in before entering the United States, while their claim is processed. This policy has resulted in thousands of people living on international bridges or in tent cities within Mexican border towns, where they can be victims of violence and have extreme difficulty accessing legal help.

hegemonic, dominant rhetorical traditions of whiteness and neoliberalism. This ideology is illustrated in the expectation that applicants tell a story that "predominantly conforms to the conventions of model narrative forms" (Vogl, 2013, p. 63). In other words, if an asylum-seeker struggles to articulate their experiences in accordance with the legalese and rhetorical expectations of the US asylum context, there is a high probability their claim will not be compelling enough to be approved.

The standardization of genre and form as a requisite for participation in the asylum process demands asylum-seekers retell and relive trauma, an expectation "that undermines narrative capacity" of the experiences themselves (Butler, 2004) and renders the asylum-seekers as those, "who are not persons or are not considered to be the kinds of beings with whom one can or must enter into an ethical relation" (Butler, 2012, p. 140). Through Butler's argument, we can view the United States' approach to the asylum process not only as an effort to control who is allowed into the country but as a process of determining who is human and who is deserving of protection. In doing so, the asylum process is designed to ignore the precarity inherent in sharing a planet with other humans. Further complicating the conditions of this grassroots initiative, although "retelling the trauma narrative is a way of claiming ownership of their experiences," Hesford and Shuman (2018) note that "for others, describing what they endured is retraumatizing" (p. 53). Taking these ideas together, by requiring every asylum-seeker to compose a written narrative to justify their claims, the US asylum appeals process flattens trauma and individual identity in service of a political and economic hegemony that renders all claims as comparable and in competition with each other (Lyon, 2018).

There are compelling arguments for why professionals associated with rhetoric and composition should leverage their expertise to support their communities in material ways (Cushman, 1996, 1999). For us, the border regions connecting Mexico and the United States bring the plight of refugees and asylum-seekers—including their difficulties navigating US immigration policy—to the forefront both liminally and materially. This context invokes Butler's (2012) concept of the precarity of cohabitation, the realization that our ethical obligations to one another emerge out of this "'up againstness'—the result of populations living in conditions of unwilled adjacency, the result of forced emigration or the redrawing of the boundaries of a nation-state" (p. 134). This "geographical proximity" reveals the precarity of human relationships and interconnectedness and calls to our attention the factors that contribute to the "glocal" conditions, including those we are culpable for, that cause other humans to migrate. This runs contrary to usual lines of thinking employed by nation-states, that interpersonal responsibility extends "only in the contexts of established communities that are gathered within borders" when humans "are

unified by the same language, and/or constitute a people or a nation" (Butler, 2012, p. 137). The existence of refugees and asylum-seekers, as well as the
global sociopolitical, economic, and environmental factors that cause people to
become refugees and seek asylum, reifies our obligations as cohabitants of our
world, to an extent well beyond regionality, linguistic affinity, and nationality.

In this chapter, the authors—a collective of shelter staff and volunteers—
discuss the development of a grassroots initiative, Retórica del Refugio (RDR),
whose name translates as "Shelter Rhetorics." This initiative was collaboratively designed by writing faculty at a large, public, Hispanic-Serving Institution (HSI), the University of Texas Rio Grande Valley (UTRGV), along
with staff and clients at an emergency shelter for displaced people in the Rio
Grande Valley border region of Texas, La Posada Providencia (LPP). Through
the initiative, volunteers, including faculty, staff, and students from UTRGV,
provide support and feedback for shelter staff on professional documents,
conduct professional writing workshops for clients seeking to enter the US
workforce, and at the core of RDR, provide writing consultation services for
shelter clients as they compose their asylum application narratives. To do this
work, it is essential that staff develop trust with each client, and one important
factor for developing clients' trust is effective communication.

Informed by tenets of "invitational rhetoric" (Foss & Griffin, 1995) as well
as critical new materialist theory (Clark, 2018; Coole & Frost, 2010), RDR
enacts the disciplinary expertise of rhetoric and composition to leverage and
diffuse asymmetrical networks of institutional, political, and individual power
to benefit asylum-seekers and the shelters as a whole, including helping to
ensure that individuals maintain agency and dignity throughout the writing
and appeals processes (Kreuter, 2018). In this way, the authors understand that
these networks of power, when enacted through an invitational rhetoric, must
be reimagined as networks of care.

In what follows, we—a team of coauthors consisting of public volunteers,
professional academics, and shelter staff—begin by outlining the networks for
care that were assembled to create RDR. Next, we detail the initiative's writing
consultation services and a pedagogy of writing consulting for working with
asylum applicants. We also point to systemic fissures of the initiative that help
us conclude with special considerations (and our recommendations) for rep-
licating such an initiative.

SHELTER PROFILE

LPP is a 15-minute drive from the international border connecting Mexico
and the United States. The shelter has helped over 10,000 asylum-seekers from

nearly 90 different countries around the world since 1989. In fact, during the late 2010s, there was an increase in families crossing to the United States from Africa. Often these families began their journey by flying or sailing to Brazil, then traveling (usually by foot) through Colombia, Panama, Costa Rica, Nicaragua, Honduras, Guatemala, and Mexico before finally reaching the United States. Many of these clients are asylum-seekers fleeing extreme poverty or persecution based on gender identity, sexual orientation, and political and religious beliefs.

The staff and volunteers of LPP are diverse and represent a variety of educational, political, and cultural backgrounds.[2] Staff work with clients to maintain a steady atmosphere of support. For example, many current clients assume chores such as cooking, laundry, and yard work, and three former clients are now employed at LPP. Volunteers are also involved in planning and carrying out LPP's mission.

Jorge, as LPP client coordinator, understands how the passion of the volunteers—many of whom are connected to UTRGV—makes the shelter's mission achievable. The shelter's mission statement explicates its religious motivation as follows:

> La Posada Providencia (LPP), founded and sponsored by the Sisters of Divine Providence, is a ministry for people in crisis from around the world, who are seeking legal refuge in the United States. The shelter staff provides a safe and welcoming home, mentors to promote self-sufficiency and cultural integration, and imparts values that witness God's Providence in our world.

One of the main differences between LPP and other organizations working in this area is that LPP is a long-term shelter that offers intensive case management to assist clients through the entire asylum-seeking process. Even though they can begin to feel a sense of peace upon arrival, asylum-seekers continue to experience traumatic stress and the effects of acculturated stress exposure. One of the many services LPP offers to clients is on-demand and on-call counseling as well as on-site medical services.

---

2. Volunteers come from nearby schools, churches, and other organizations, and the shelter also accepts charitable donations and facilitates philanthropic partnerships with local businesses. Therefore, because of this initially recognized exigence, volunteers for the initiative we outline here primarily, although not exclusively, joined the initiative through their connections to UTRGV. Most volunteers are faculty in UTRGV's writing and language department, while other volunteers include faculty from health sciences and political science departments, staff in the human resources department, undergraduate students in the biomedical sciences program, and independent counselors from the local community.

FIGURE 18.1. The interior of "Casa Carolina." Photo by Yazmin. Used with permission (IRB approval #18-024, Old Dominion University).

INITIATIVE DESCRIPTION

RDR offers writing support to clients who desire to talk and write about their experiences in service of their personal and professional goals. Pedagogical outcomes for the initiative include developing a protocol for tutoring asylum-seeking clients, designing reusable materials and resources for tutors, and analyzing asylum appeals as rhetorical genres. To these ends, RDR implements three main writing-focused activities: individual writing consultations, translation services, and professional writing workshops. Additionally, RDR coordinators have developed mental health support protocols for volunteers and counseling support for clients.

Writing consultations consist of faculty and student volunteers meeting with individual clients, typically at a round table (figure 18.1), to help them write their story about why they are seeking asylum in the United States. During these consultations, consultants help clients to generate and develop ideas, understand how content and structure are related, implement revision strategies for independent learning, and raise their confidence in writing and sharing stories. Obviously, the consultations function similarly to writing center tutoring sessions, although we are less strict with following disciplinary or local programmatic expectations, such as "the tutor doesn't write on the paper." This gives volunteers some leeway with helping clients to record their ideas, including transcribing while the client tells their story. Consultants are careful not to write or suggest anything on the client's behalf, because clients need to be able to articulate and support their narratives.

Although writing consultations are the galvanizing task of the RDR initiative and the focus of this chapter, varying client and shelter needs invoke different opportunities for collaboration and support. These include tasks like individual counseling services for vulnerable clients, technical writing feedback for documents written by shelter staff, translation services for shelter documents and client narratives, and professional writing workshops for clients who require support in finding work.

Assembling Networks of Care

By its nature as a shelter, LPP is developing "networks of care," which requires fostering the resources, personnel, and networks necessary to care for the needs of asylum-seekers. We understand "network" broadly as fluctuating connections made between a variety of human and nonhuman things in a rhetorical context; however, we also understand that networks often leverage power asymmetrically, impacting institutions, policies, and individuals (Clark, 2018). As such, we focus on the following primary networks of power that the authors worked to assemble and leverage for RDR in order to promote care for asylum-seekers: shelter rhetorics, expertise about the narrative demands of the asylum process, and writing tutoring.

Shelter Rhetorics

RDR builds on a larger study Monica had previously conducted that invited shelter clients, staff, and volunteers to share multimodal perspectives (through interviews, drawings, and photos) to understand the kinds of rhetorical support LPP provides clients to tell stories on their own terms. Monica learned that LPP provides opportunities for displaced communities to employ what she terms *shelter rhetorics*, distinct shared rhetorical practices of daily life—like silence and routine—that both safeguard vulnerabilities and enact agency for individuals within precarious spaces. By practicing shelter rhetorics, the shelter encourages clients to tell their unique stories in ways that help them to move forward as well as critique reductive dominant discourses about what it means to be an "asylum-seeker."

Shelter rhetorics at LPP rely on "invitational rhetoric" (Foss & Griffin, 1995), an alternative rhetoric that centralizes collaborative understanding instead of persuasion in order to "create an environment that facilitates understanding, accords value and respect to others' perspectives, and contributes to the development of relationships of equality" (Foss & Griffin, 1995, 17). Moreover, we see invitational rhetoric as closely tied with "rhetorical listening," articulated by Kristina Ratcliffe (1999) as a strategy of rhetorical invention, like reading, writing, and speaking, that leads to attuning oneself to "discursive intersections of gender and race/ethnicity (including whiteness) so as to help us to facilitate cross-cultural dialogues" of understanding (p. 196). Additionally, Ratcliffe's key ideas about the underlying rhetorical value of silence and listening coincide with work done within displacement contexts from the social sciences that ideologize silence as a strategy for displaced people to tell stories on their own terms and at their own pace (De Haene, Grietens, & Verschueren, 2010; McFadyen, 2018; Puvimanasinghe, Denson, Augoustinos, & Somasundaram, 2015).

Clients, staff, and volunteers saw cultural-rhetorical practices as ways to understand one another more deeply; this is a contrast to traditional models of rhetoric that focus on persuasion. Through shelter rhetorics, LPP strives to "create an environment that facilitates understanding, accords value and respect to others' perspectives, and contributes to the development of relationships of equality" (Foss & Griffin, 17).

One way that LPP illustrates invitational rhetoric is that there is no expectation for clients to share their story of persecution with anyone at the shelter unless they want to, because clients are not obligated to begin their official asylum application during their stay. Ayana, a participant in Monica's study, described from her own experience how this type of respect for silence is necessary for asylum-seekers. Although she didn't speak about her own past to other clients, Ayana did listen to others' stories at LPP, and this fostered a feminist materialist space of speaking, listening, and silence. Ayana captured a photo of the outdoor circular table, "la mesa redonda" (figure 18.2), to depict the space where she slowly built community with other women every day:

> In the evenings, after dinner, we have free time, some girls would gather there, and sometimes, I would join them. Little by little, I would join them, and all of them would start telling their story, what they used to do in their country or why they came here and things like that. I would listen. I wouldn't share my stuff, but I would listen. I liked to listen. It distracted me, listen-

FIGURE 18.2. Exterior photo of *la mesa redonda*. Photo by Ayana. Used with permission (IRB approval #18-024, Old Dominion University).

ing to it, each one's story, and it was always like that. We'd start—maybe, we didn't always talk about [the past] but also about our future and all that, so that was something really beautiful that we would do in the evenings, after dinner, there, at the table. (Ayana)

Ayana's initial hesitance to tell her story of persecution and suffering combined with her willingness to listen to others' stories demonstrates how LPP offers a reprieve to the accelerated, persuasion-driven demand for credibility narratives within the US asylum system that centers on criminalizing people who seek asylum.

First, the rhetorical intents of sharing a story of persecution are different at *la mesa redonda* than during a credible fear interview.[3] The former is based on "rhetorical listening" (Ratcliffe, 1999) and "invitational rhetoric" (Foss & Griffin, 1995), while the latter is based on classical rhetorical perspectives of persuasion. Ayana and the women she joined at the table are thus fulfilling

---

3. A credible fear interview is the first screening for a person seeking asylum at a port of entry, in which they justify their need for asylum in the United States. The screening is completed by an asylum officer with US Customs and Immigration.

their need for "adequate space to tell their stories at their own pace and in a manner most conducive to them" (Puvimanasinghe, Denson, Augoustinos, & Somasundaram, 2015, p. 70). This self-paced rhetorical exchange, this listening, is especially seen in Ayana's description of how she became part of the group "little by little." In this way, *la mesa redonda* is a critical part of the network of care at LPP for those seeking asylum, especially women, in that it offers a habitual meeting space for those who voluntarily desire to listen and speak among other displaced women, without the same bureaucratic high stakes of an asylum hearing.

Second, the community and storytelling that takes place here is in stark contrast to the storytelling that demarcates lines of difference between mainstream or bureaucratic audiences in the Global North and those who seek asylum. Instead, the outdoor round table allows Ayana to experience stories as empowering for refugee and immigrant women because they are "told among . . . friends" and "told in a language or talk style that is comfortable to them," and this provides Ayana and the other women "space to voice themselves" (Hua, 2000, p. 113). As a rhetor, Ayana has slowly been able to gauge the rhetorical possibilities at this table and make meaning at her own pace and in collaboration with women who may have faced similar circumstances. *La mesa redonda* is a space for Ayana and the other women to practice what Cheryl Glenn (2002) refers to as the "feminist rhetorical art" of silence that works to "resist" powerful bureaucracies that use the words of marginalized people to reduce and categorize them (p. 262).

Expertise about the Narrative Demands of the US Asylum Process

To add to the shelter rhetorics in place at LPP, RDR required expertise about the asylum process and the many struggles clients have when sharing their stories to make claims for their asylum case. While Cindy, an intern at LPP, was never a client, she has been through the immigration process personally. As a teenager, Cindy had to face immigration officials in the United States, with fear and uncertainty about her future; however, she attributes her own success in this problematic process to her faith and to her pro bono attorneys, who were willing to give her their time and resources to carefully guide her through her immigration process. Cindy was already a critical part of LPP's network of care, as one of her main roles during her internship as a UTRGV social work graduate student was assisting clients in drafting narratives that they could use on their asylum application.

A primary challenge clients face is the fear and anxiety about what information to include as part of their narratives. Immigrants and refugees are often skeptical of those offering help, due to the corruption existing in their home countries. People in authority positions, such as law enforcement officers, are known to be involved with gangs and criminal acts. Law enforcement officers and even government officials at all levels are often involved in extortions and other violent crimes to receive financial and political gains. Sometimes Cindy could sense the clients' inhibitions about sharing their stories with her.

Additionally, Cindy noted that many clients tended to summarize their stories because of how traumatic their experiences had been. At first, many clients refused to elaborate on details; not only because they were fearful of who the information would be shared with, but also because they had a difficult time recalling events and struggled with sharing their experiences in chronological order. It was common for them to not always remember dates, names, and details when describing traumatizing events that pushed them to migrate. If they were trying to write about an event, they would leave out details of who the perpetrator was, when the event happened, and the reason why they were being persecuted. While these challenges may have various explanations, one of the factors applicants struggled with was that by sharing their stories, they were reliving their experiences.

Also, and especially if a client had never before shared about their persecution, it was common for them to experience the trauma of those events again simply by telling their story. As an intern, it was important for Cindy to be mindful of this reality and learn how to assist them in narrating their stories in a way that made them feel safe. Even just writing these narratives, clients at LPP often experienced exhaustion and fatigue, either because they experienced storytelling as arduous and anxiety-producing or because writing their stories was a form of therapy in their process of healing.

Cindy helped us understand how asylum narratives function rhetorically as archives of evidence, which Rice (2020) defined as inclusive of "literal documents and records, cultural memories archived through multiple retellings, family stories, preserved media files, personal archives of experience, and so forth" (loc. 408). Further, narratives are an essential part of the appeals process, because they function as "tools for the construction of public memory" (loc. 444) and reflect "ordinary and extraordinary experiences in public life that leave lasting, palpable residues, which then become our sources—our resources—for public discourse" (loc. 430). However, asylum-seekers in the United States often encounter difficulty composing these necessary forms of evidence because of institutional expectations that narratives be written in the genre and vernacular English that the adjudicating parties recognize and prefer.

Complicating this evidentiary process are limitations and biases of those evaluating claims and documents, conditions Popescu (2019) identifies as owing to state actors that "have multiple and often conflicted responsibilities and limited understanding or knowledge of the context of forced migration" (p. 109). These conditions leave those seeking asylum at physical border crossings, notably the Mexico–US border, at the mercy and discretion of US Customs and Border Protection (CBP) officers (Musalo, 2019). What counts as evidence and archives varies greatly across contexts, audiences, and purposes, and what counts as evidence in US asylum courts—physical evidence, medical reports, and expert testimony—can be extremely difficult for asylum-seekers to produce. This difficulty is due to a number of factors: asylees typically leave previous locations under duress, physical items like papers and photographs may not travel well, the country of origin might not supply requested evidence, the receiving country's expectations might not be known before arriving, and some preferred documents can be expensive to procure.

This is why Reyes (2020) reframed these narratives as "accounts of asylum": because they "provide access within the globalized migration conversation, but also serve as a proof of authenticity for the displaced individual themselves." Before being presented to a judge, narratives are finalized with the help of an immigration lawyer, typically working pro bono, to ensure legal compliance. In the complex legal ecosystem that is the US asylum application process, narratives are essential forms of documentation that can become determining factors for whether an individual's claim is approved.

Writing Tutoring

With shelter rhetorics and expertise about the narrative demands of the asylum process in place, RDR required an assemblage involving willing and knowledgeable writing tutors to carry out the work. Early in the spring 2019 semester, Monica approached her departmental colleague Monty (then the associate director of the UTRGV Writing Center) to see if he could help expand the writing support offered at LPP. The network of care was growing. Importantly, contemporary writing center scholarship provided numerous touchstones of relevance for supporting LPP's mission: multilingual writing tutoring (Lape, 2013; Severino & Prim, 2016), using feminist (McNamee & Miley, 2017) and anti-racist (Faison, 2018) theory to support tutors and writers from vulnerable populations (Denny, 2010; Alvarez, Salazar, Brito, &

Aguilar, 2017), collaborative approaches to tutoring (Scharold, 2017), aligning tutor education with social justice missions (Godbee, Ozias, & Kar Tang, 2015) including specifically at Catholic institutions (Zimmerelli, 2015), and implementing effective tutoring in nonacademic and online spaces (Miller-Cochran, 2015).

A grassroots approach to community partnerships informed by rhetorical listening requires academics to diffuse the kinds of power they may be used to maintaining. Given the constant variability of LPP's needs, it was in the best interest of the clients and the shelter for the volunteers to follow and respond to their lead rather than preemptively developing initiatives or services. This dynamic played out in an unexpected but beneficial way with RDR as a kind of writing center initiated by an articulated praxis but flexible enough to modify according to individual needs.

Commonly in both composition and writing center studies, students, faculty, and (especially) other academic programs within the institution view writing and writing tutoring according to deficit models. That is, writing is something that is to be done "correctly," and the writing classroom or center is where students go to get their writing fixed, once and for all. While there was some deference to our professional status as writing teachers, interactions facilitated through RDR were marked by a noticeably different expectation on the part of our community collaborators and, as a result, our interactions enacted an idealized version of a collaborative, writer-centered consultation. There were fewer expectations about conventions (grammar, spelling, punctuation) and more of an immediate focus on developing ideas and conveying them with clarity, accuracy, and individual voice. This focus may have been due to the material consequences of the writing opportunity, and so the clients likely approached the consultations as part of the larger asylum-seeking process, resulting in more engaged consultations.

Empathetic and intentional listening is a key strategy of effective writing tutoring (Valentine, 2017) and is especially important when supporting students who are hesitant to write about complex and controversial topics (Draxler, 2017). Furthermore, discussing physical violence and other traumatic experiences of persecution can be consequential, both for the speaker and the listener. Internalizing this dynamic, the asylum-seeker might be hesitant to talk about their experiences because of personal trauma or out of concern for their listener. In addition, we acknowledge that clients who participate may experience discrepancies of power between themselves and the volunteers, because the questions we ask during individual consultations may mirror the credible fear interview that clients have endured. Similarly complicating the conditions of a consultation, asylum-seekers can be hesitant to report traumatic experiences because they may view their experiences as mundane, shared by families and neighbors who may not have been able to escape the violence at home. If everyone you know has had the same experience, what makes yours—or you—special? This is particularly problematic because expected traumatic stories represent the preferred evidence in appeals narratives. In response to these concerns, RDR employs tenets of safety, value, and freedom from Sonja K. Foss and Cindy L. Griffin's "invitational rhetoric" approach. Volunteers do this by assisting clients in composing authentic narratives that resist the rhetorics of dominance and persuasion inherent in USCIS asylum screenings and required storytellings and by providing peer counseling support for volunteers.

CONSIDERATIONS AND RECOMMENDATIONS

There are no tidy solutions; there is just continued work. While we acknowledge the systemic inequalities and racism in the US asylum process, we also understand that progressive change occurs slowly. In other words, we don't think advocating for systemic change and supporting people who are navigating the current system (like RDR does) are mutually exclusive. We do, however, offer guidance about the effects of storytelling for others who are inspired to take on work like that of RDR.

First, while RDR offers LPP clients opportunities to tell diverse stories on their own terms, it also supports clients who desire to tell their stories within the highly problematic, bureaucratic, and reductive rhetorical ecology that is the US asylum system. So the question must be asked: By helping clients write "compelling" public narratives of asylum for their applications (by hegemonic US asylum standards), is the initiative only perpetuating the binary-based, inflexible narrative standards of asylum experience that are already so difficult to navigate? A complicated answer emerges when we observe how LPP uses RDR to nurture clients, first, as human beings. RDR allows clients to tell stories, which fracture the "false sense of stasis" about identity, and encourages them to offer stories that highlight the "in-motion and in process qualities of the displacement where 'moving identities' are constantly in action" (K. Powell, 2015, p. 15). This is important, as Powell argues, for the act of being displaced impacts identity in profound ways, even in the opportunity for a displaced individual to "resist having a narrative identity imposed on them, and create subversive narrative identities as resistance to the subjectivities inscribed on them" (Powell, 2015, p. 13).

Second, the efforts the faculty and clients make toward collaborative storytelling is one way to resist reductive portrayals of the asylum experience. RDR is essentially advocating for more nuanced and meaningful representations of people who are marginalized and oppressed (Hesford, 2010, p. 55). By asking questions about their home communities and the specific types of persecution and layers of oppression faced, faculty volunteers and clients work together to put aside simplistic representations of displaced people and delve into the intricate networks and "political structures and processes, global economic systems, or colonial histories that imbricate systematic . . . violence against [marginalized populations]" that are often neglected (Dingo, 2013, p. 532).

Third, initiatives like RDR work best in concert with the organic invitational rhetoric practices such as those already at work in spaces like LPP, like the ones used at *la mesa redonda* that Ayana describes earlier. One way this is achieved is by expanding RDR to also support other stories that clients desire to tell, aside from stories of persecution. These stories may include listening to clients in their own languages (translation) or helping clients express their hopes for the future (resume writing). For example, LPP recently developed a series of educational initiatives for clients to complete in order to demonstrate to governmental authorities and agencies that the clients were prepared to enter into and contribute to the US workforce. To support this endeavor, RDR developed and led a resume-writing workshop where clients created their very first English-language resumes. Within a week of participating in the workshop, one client submitted several job applications along with the resume they had created with RDR's help.

And a final consideration is the consequence of physical and emotional harm suffered by refugees and asylum-seekers before, during, and after the transition process, which has been substantially and continuously documented (Berthold & Libal, 2019). Likewise, and without downplaying the severity of those experiences, the work of writing tutoring can be traumatic for tutors themselves when writers are writing about topics that are volatile, violent, and potentially triggering. This phenomenon is related to what professional counselors and therapists refer to as "vicarious trauma," wherein "the traumatic imagery presented by clients . . . may cause a disruption in the therapist's view of self, others, and the world in general" (Bober & Regehr, 2006). Early in the initiative, we experimented with different ways for volunteers to reflect and decompress after meeting with clients, such as through one-on-one meetings with initiative coordinators and through writing for a shared blog space.

As the first volunteer under the auspices of RDR to assist a client with a writing consultation, Maggie (a professional academic whose areas of specialization include carceral studies and community literacy) constructed her reflection as a narrative of her experience and a preview for fellow volunteers. The initial session lasted three hours, which included the consultation with the client and meeting with the client coordinator. Although her reflection ended on a positive note, looking forward to the next session, Maggie described the session as "a very intense few hours," noting that she, "was exhausted in every way" afterward. Maggie's feelings mirrored common sentiments across the volunteers' written and informal reflections: helping the clients write their asylum appeals narratives was difficult and stressful. Importantly, these challenges are not due to the clients' literacy skills, which vary widely from client to client, but rather because the personal experiences asylum-seekers are required to write about in their narratives are traumatic and violent.

As a result of vicarious trauma, it is common for counselors to feel pressure for their clients to make progress and achieve goals. This pressure can lead to feelings of burnout, a lack of self-esteem, professional isolation, compassion fatigue, substance abuse, apathy, and a need to save or rescue future clients (Glover-Graf, 2012; Lusk & Tarrazas, 2015). Without sufficient preparation and support, volunteer consultants and writing center tutors are also susceptible to these outcomes, especially given the material consequences of the asylum appeals process.

In response, volunteers with grassroots initiatives like this one can "take note of the consequences of working within a context filled with trauma and be prepared to be responsive to the needs of their staff" (Lusk & Tarrazas, 2015). For our initiative, training workshops to prepare volunteers for the content they will encounter and critical reflection opportunities allow for processes of resilience-building and consideration of programmatic assessment of our initiative. Critical reflection also validates the framings of invitational rhetoric and networks of care. Likewise, praxes recommended by recent and emergent writing center scholarship that support tutors' emotion and mental health (Giaimo, 2020), such as "giving consultants the space and time to process emotional issues they encounter in sessions" (Perry, 2016), practicing mindfulness meditation (S. Johnson, 2018), enacting trauma-informed practice and writing pedagogy (Krimm, 2020), and tutoring the whole person (Driscoll & Wells, 2020), can provide guidance for how to facilitate grassroots initiatives that ask individuals to enter into potentially traumatic writing tutoring contexts.

The asylum-seeking process is precarious, as policies are in flux, people are transient, and the diverse experiences and needs of asylum-seekers contradict the expected and preferred actions of international, neoliberal systems (Stenberg, 2015). For example, the Trump-era border policy Title 42, cynically activated to deny asylum-seekers from certain countries entry to the United States under the guise of preventing the spread of COVID-19, resulted in new concerns and working conditions for emergency shelters like LPP. As such, the embodied existence of asylum-seekers can be viewed as an act of resistance to hegemonic institutions and systems. These positive deviations from the norm provide valuable insights into how individual experiences can prove useful as replicable models for intervention and response (Durá, 2015). We understand that what is happening at LPP is not indicative of what is or can happen at other emergency shelters or nonprofits that support displaced communities, which is why our focus on methods and approach are emphasized. It is unrealistic to expect systemic change overnight, but as we move toward systemic change, we can look for immediate ways to help people navigate the system, and we can celebrate small glories.

A Counterstory Afterword in Vignettes

Quisieron enterrarnos, pero se les olvido
que somos semillas *[They tried to bury us.
They didn't know we were seeds.]*

AJA Y. MARTINEZ

JANUARY 21, 2017
WASHINGTON, DC
THE COLLECTIVE

What felt like a flowing river of humans moving together as one had led us to the newest Smithsonian on the mall, the National Museum of African American History and Culture (see in this volume Pittman; Mayberry).[1] Having marched for several hours, I spotted what resembled a Tetris-like assemblage of empty benches near the museum's impressive structure and decided this was as good a place as any to extract ourselves from the flow of humanity to catch our breath and rest our feet for a bit.

Our group was diverse. Sofi, my 14-year-old daughter, and I had driven down from Philadelphia. She cried the day Trump was elected, unable to comprehend how and why this country seemingly had no regard for the livelihood and future of her generation, Gen Z. We bought a kitten soon after the election, a sweet black female we named Helena—a nod to Helena Bonham Carter. She was our therapy kitten.

My cousin, Luis, and his partner, Gema, joined us from Chicago. Gema, born and raised in Phoenix, AZ, was the daughter of an American Indian

---

1. For more counterstory and composite counterstory characters, see Martinez (2020).

(O'odham) father and a mother from Guadalajara who had existed within undocumented precarity for much of her life and livelihood (see in this volume Whitebear, Pebbles, & Gasteyer; Conway; Reyes, Monty, Camarillo, & Bernal). Gema had a master's in public health and now worked at a community clinic in Chicago's Little Village (see Novotny in this volume). Gema's upbringing, along with her career path, opened her eyes and heart to the activist identity she passionately embraced as not a choice but a necessity in her line of work. To Gema, activism was a way of life.

Luis admired Gema's strength and fierce reactions toward injustice. He didn't think of himself as an activist. Although he was raised by Mexican American parents from the borderlands of Arizona, he was third generation and generally of the mind and spirit that all's well that goes well if folks would just go along to get along. While Gema's activist spirit was the beacon that attracted Luis to her flame, this activism in some ways also repelled him: he didn't always understand it—why was she so passionate, protesting *everything*? Why couldn't she "just get along?"

Bernie bro that Luis was, when Trump succeeded in securing the presidency, he realized that the social action networks that Gema was involved with throughout Little Village (public health workers, doulas, mutual aid groups, etc.) would very likely spring into action (see Novotny in this volume). He had been with Gema long enough to know something would be planned, and when he got wind through our familywide social media network (SMN) direct message (DM) (see Hallman Martini in this volume) that his cousin, Alejandra Prieto (me), was making plans to attend the postinaugural march on Washington and inviting anyone to come along and stay at the Airbnb I was renting in Baltimore, Gema said, "Absolutely, we're in. All our Little Village community health orgs are going anyway." Luis knew there was no other option.

"Who knows," he thought to himself, "it could be interesting."

Rounding out the group was our cousin Sol. Sol was an interesting and unexpected participant within the group. Having served in the US Navy for eight years, Sol, an out yet still very private and discrete gay man, was now employed by Homeland Security in a high-paying job with an even higher security clearance. Raised within the same Mexican American family system, by Boomer parents no less, we were all well versed in the "don't ask don't tell" culture of their generation. Admittedly, I didn't really know what my cousin Sol's political alignments and commitments were. All I knew was that when I extended the SMN DM to all family members about the Airbnb in Baltimore, Sol was the first to respond that he had just relocated to Baltimore to escape exorbitant Washington, DC, rent prices and that he'd see us there and would show us where to park for free in his old DC neighborhood before the march.

By the time our motley crew reached the National Museum of African American History and Culture, it was about three hours into our participation in the march and we needed a break. Hands linked, I led the five of us out of the fray toward the Tetris-shaped benches. We positioned ourselves to rest and reflect and, ultimately, time-travel backward and forward to points in our lives where we have sought "to better understand what drives people to get involved in activism on a personal level" (see Warren-Riley, Bates, & Phillips, p. 11 in this volume).

JULY 2014
TUCSON, ARIZONA
ALEJANDRA AND SOFI

Sofi and I were within the first year of having moved out east from Arizona to Philly. We had endured a colder winter than we'd ever thought possible—locals kept assuring us it was mild. We gladly met the strong summer sun and the expanse of blue sky that welcomed us back home in Tucson. Not long into that visit, I was contacted by my comadres Diana and Feliz, two Latine grad students from the program I had just graduated from (see Ribero & Arellano, 2019). Diana and Feliz said that leading up to June of 2014, ICE and the Border Patrol had been dropping off hundreds of Central and South American travelers, most of them asylum-seekers, at the Greyhound bus station in Tucson. A few people from the community and local churches were coming together to bring food to the bus station. Those efforts eventually became a formalized program at a large, welcoming shelter space with a house called Casa Alitas (Casa Alitas Program, 2020). Diana and Feliz had been volunteering for months now and wondered if 12-year-old Sofi and I would be interested in volunteering while we were in town.

"Do they welcome child volunteers?" I asked.

"Absolutely!" affirmed Feliz. "The house is all women and their children. La Migra locks up the men as soon as they get them at the border—separates the families, you know? So, the women and children get dumped at the bus station, the men get put in handcuffs and sent to some prison to await stream-line.[2] Anyway, the kids get bored and need new kids to play with, and the

---

2. Operation Streamline is a program under which federal criminal charges are brought against individuals apprehended crossing the border illegally. Created in 2005 as a joint initiative of the Department of Homeland Security (DHS) and the Department of Justice (DOJ), the program fast-tracks resolution of these immigration offenses, providing for mass proceedings in which as many as 80 unlawful border crossers are tried together in a single hearing, typically pleading guilty en masse (National Immigration Forum, 2020).

moms need a break to get a minute to meet with the legal advisors and such and don't need the kids distracting them 24/7. So yes, bring Sofi, it'll help a lot."

Sofi and I arrived at the address we were provided. The house was very nondescript and unassuming, within a university-area neighborhood of cute stucco and adobe single-family homes. As we approached the entrance to the house, the scent of fresh tortillas and clean laundry intermingled in the air, wafting out of the open front door where Feliz waited with a smile to welcome us. We walked through a tidy living room with mismatched and clearly donated or thrifted couches and armchairs. There were a couple women and children watching what looked like the Disney channel. The women and kids briefly looked up and over at the newcomers, but my guess was there were lots of newcomers in and out of that front door so their gazes didn't linger; Disney had much more enticing colors and sounds to offer.

As we made our way into the dining area and kitchen, we passed what looked like a pantry, but it was stocked full of backpacks that were stuffed full of Ziplock bags.

"What are those?" I asked Feliz, stopping to take a closer look.

"Oh!" she responded, "well, actually, come sit here at the table for a minute so I can further explain this house and the experience for those who stop here."

Feliz then gestured for Sofi and me to sit at the long rectangular picnic-style table that made a direct diagonal across the room from the backpack-filled pantry. There was already another woman sitting at the table, a towel turban wrapped around her freshly washed hair, quietly eating a bowl of fideo. When she saw us approaching to sit, she attempted to get up and leave, offering her apologies in Spanish, though clearly not done with her soup. Feliz, who as a child migrated with her family to the United States from Colombia, and whose Spanish is much better than mine, assured the woman that she had a place at the table and that she should continue her meal—which she did (see in this volume Wills; Novotny).

"So," Feliz began, "what was happening at the border was inhumane as shit, which I know I don't have to say, but then again, I do have to say, because that helps you understand the mission of this house. It's about conferring dignity unto migrants and asylees in their journeys" (see in this volume Conway; Reyes, Monty, Camarillo, & Bernal).

Sofi stifled a giggle at Feliz's cursing, but then solemnly nodded as Feliz continued.

"La Migra was basically rounding up people who have family sponsors around the country, like families in Chicago, Philly, Florida, sometimes close like Phoenix or Cali if they are lucky, but ICE and Migra were gathering up these folks whose families could send them a bus ticket and just dumping them straight from border detainment to the Greyhound station for, in some cases, a two- to three-day journey across the country, and with nothing! No food, no money, no hygiene supplies, nada!"

"Oh my God," I said exchanging a look with Sofi and then automatically shifting our gazes to the pantry of backpacks. "So those are the supplies." I surmised.

"Yep," nodded Feliz, "all donations of course, and pretty good stuff too, toothbrushes and paste, hair supplies, sanitary napkins, condoms, deodorant, wet wipes, granola bars, ramen, that kind of stuff. And that's just what they leave the house with. When they come here they get to rest, shower, and eat hot food, for the first time in who knows how long."

"All things for dignity in the experience," Sofi said, a bit under her breath, but Feliz heard her and exclaimed:

"See! You get it! A kid gets it! Why don't grown ass men?"

JANUARY 2020–FEBRUARY 2021
DALLAS, TEXAS
SOL

Fed up with life on the East Coast, fed up with DC and, frankly, fed up with working a government job under the Trump administration, Sol began searching for new employment closer to his Arizona roots at the start of 2020. Optimistic for this bright new year, Sol secured a great new position at Boeing, accompanied by an enormous raise and, to Sol's happy surprise, a much more affordable cost of living. A man of refined taste and reasonable means, Sol decided to take up residence in the Aster building at Turtle Creek in downtown Dallas. There he could get in his steps on the lovely winding nature pathways lining the creeks, and he was close, but not *too* close, to all the nightlife and best restaurants. It would suit him just fine. The best part was, he completed his final interviews and housing search visits in February when it was still horribly dreary and bitterly cold in Baltimore and DC but quite pleasant, quite sunny in Dallas—something to look forward to, if this is what Februarys in Texas were going to be like from here on out.

As if moving halfway across the country and starting a new job during a global pandemic isn't horrible enough, imagine the added horror of experiencing your first ever natural disaster.

On Valentine's Day 2021, Sol had set up a date with a guy he'd seen a few times at what had become his favorite brunch spot. Sol always looked at him, of course. This man was gorgeous, but was he a grad student? A professor? He was so studious, always with a book in hand, never eating, and only drank a tiny espresso. Apparently, he had seen Sol as well, because just last week he,

Cal, approached Sol himself, made his introductions, asked if he could sit, and initiated a conversation that went on for hours. They made plans for an official date on their only next free day, which was Sunday, and coincidently was Valentine's Day; they assured each other that was just a coincidence and that it was the free day that was the actual priority here.

Sunday, February 14, rolled around, and Cal, who it turned out *was* a professor of sociology specializing in critical race theory (if this works out, I'll need to introduce him to my cousin Alejandra, Sol thought—or maybe not, haha they might be insufferable together!) arrived at Sol's apartment to pick up Sol for their date. When Sol opened the door there were thick fluffy snowflakes stuck to every bit of Cal's ash blonde hair.

"What happened to you?" asked Sol, "You look like you walked out of a snow globe!"

Running his hand back through his snow-damp hair, Cal responded, "Have you looked outside today? I don't think we're going anywhere. I barely got here myself, it's really coming down and piling up. I can't believe it."

Sol and Cal walked briskly to the large floor-to-ceiling window in the center of the living room. Admittedly, Sol had not looked out of the window all day, because he'd been meticulously primping for the date in his room, with lights on and blackout shades rolled down. Sure enough, there was at least a foot of snow on the ground covering all roads, sidewalks, and surfaces—and not a shovel or snowplow or bag of salt in sight. Cal and Sol weren't going anywhere that night; for then, that inconvenience suited them just fine.

By the next morning, both Sol and Cal had received email and text alerts from their jobs, informing them all operations were canceled for the day due to power-grid stress and failure throughout Texas.

"What?!" exclaimed Cal. "The entire thing just failed? What does that even mean, how does something like that happen?"

Having been employed in DC as a government worker under Trump and seeing behind the curtain everything he had seen, Sol knew exactly how this sort of thing happened.

"Business deals and greed, it's big business and greed. And Texas likes to do things its own way, be its own self-reliant Republic within the country. ERCOT has all the political power, they are the group of folks with all the power here overseeing the system, the power grid this state runs on. But the problem here is that when it fails, it *really* fails" (see in this volume Olson Beal; Whitebear, Pebbles, & Gasteyer).

Both Sol and Cal were silent for a few moments, scrolling through their SMN feeds, seeing images of destruction and devastation in other parts of

Dallas and the state, cars crashed and buried, people's rooves caved in from the weight of snow and ice, huge fallen oak branches heavy with snow on cars and houses and other structures. A scraping sound resonating all the way up to Sol's twentieth-floor apartment grabbed their attention away from their screens. Sol padded barefoot to the living room window; he was surprised to see a work crew clearing the sidewalks with actual metal snow shovels, spreading out snow melt, and he heard in the distance the familiar whirring of the snowplow coming through the roads, well before he ever saw it. He realized that his neighborhood, his residential area of Dallas, would be just fine. The powers that be were making sure Sol and people at Sol's income bracket were taken care of. The environmental injustices were stark and couldn't be clearer (see in this volume Jones; Whitebear, Pebbles, & Gasteyer).

By Tuesday, February 16, the rolling blackouts had affected most of the Dallas–Fort Worth metropolitan area, and if people weren't experiencing a rolling blackout that lasted an hour or so, it was just a complete blackout with sustained freezing temperatures well below zero. People were dying. Literally freezing to death. But Sol's building had never faltered. There had never been a minute without power, without heat, without water, without a means to cook a meal, to stay informed, to stay clean. What had begun as a romantic adventure between Sol and Cal was becoming a desperate situation, because although the sidewalks and roads surrounding Sol's apartment were cleared, there was no indication that such was the case anywhere else in the city, and although Cal didn't live in a low-income neighborhood, his neighborhood SMN page kept him well informed that they were experiencing rolling blackouts and frozen pipes and that the roads were blocked and obstructed by broken tree branches and other debris from ice and uncleared snow. It was a disaster. Although by Wednesday the temperatures mercifully started to rise, frozen pipes began to burst all over the city, flooding homes, businesses, churches, and schools. As if the flooding weren't enough, the local water district announced that all tap water was now unsafe to drink until further notice.

"This is unbearable!" Cal exclaimed. He softened his tone when he saw the crestfallen look on Sol's face. "No, not my time with you, Sol. You're lovely, and my god, if you can be lovely within this, the very worst of circumstances, then I can't wait for time with you when we're not in the midst of a natural disaster."

Sol smiled a bit.

"What I mean," Cal continued, "is that I can't sit here any longer and just bear witness to this devastation, feeling like I'm doing nothing. There's only so much and so far SMN activism can go in moments like this. Yes, I've been sharing stories of the devastation. Yes, I've been sharing mutual aid pages and link trees. Yes, we've both even been donating. But we gotta *go*, *I've* gotta go, I have to get out there and *do* something, anything" (see in this volume Hallman Martini; Knievel; Whitebear, Pebbles, & Gasteyer).

"But where can we go and what can we actually do? All these mutual aid funds are asking for donations of supplies like water and food. The news is reporting repeatedly that the stores here in Texas are ransacked."

"Well," Cal replied, "I told you I'm a citizen of the Chickasaw Nation, right?"

"Yes," Sol answered, tentatively.

"I was born and raised in Oklahoma City, but most of my people live in Ardmore, Oklahoma, and that's just 30-some miles north of the Texas border, a straight shot up I-35. And guess what's great about Oklahoma?"

"They're not on the ERCOT power grid!" Sol guessed excitedly.

"That's right!" said Cal with a definitive nod, "The grocery stores will be open and well stocked. We can get stuff for ourselves and what they're asking for at the donation sites too. Skoden!"

JUNE 17, 2015
CHICAGO, ILLINOIS
GEMA

Even though it was the middle of the week and the week already felt long and tiring, Gema was really looking forward to tonight. Tonight was the first session of what she hoped would become a regular occurrence with her group of doulas, mothers, other community health workers, and community members. Gema did her best to spread the word about tonight's program through available SMNs, but she also made sure to print flyers and staple plenty of those to the announcement boards around the clinic and on many a light post to and from her walk to work. She wanted a good turnout. She titled the program "Telling Our Stories, Telling It Our Way: A Writing Workshop" (see Reyes, Monty, Camarillo, & Bernal in this volume).

Gema's exigence to craft this workshop was the stark reality of budget cuts her community health clinic was presently facing (see in this volume Appel, Decker, Herzl-Betz, Simpson, Durante, Flores, & Azab; Stone). Most of their operating budget depended on allocations from the city, decisions of course made by politicians, and most of these politicians didn't know the first thing about public health, community health centers, health disparities, the needs of low-income and migrant communities, and so on. It was exasperating. Gema resolved that if these decisions are being made for our communities, and about our communities, without knowing the first thing about these communities, then you know what, I think we can do something about that. We can tell them who we are. We can write our stories: "I can form those stories into a budget proposal, and then that can become the basis for how I'll make a case for this community, on this community's terms" (see Lukowski & Gross in this volume).

Gema wasn't alone in this work. While earning her master's in public health at University of Illinois, Chicago, she befriended a bad-ass Honduran rockabilly chica from Long Beach, CA, named Beatriz. "Bad Bea" was a writing studies PhD student, so she knew all the ins and out about writing workshops, and when Gema asked Bea if she'd consider cofacilitating the program and workshop with her, Bea responded with her typical "Bad Bea" bravado:

"Girl, I give all the shits about the work you do for your community. Of course, I'll do this, hellz yeah!"

Bea and Gema arrived at the El Centro community center 15 minutes early, giving themselves enough time to set out the galletas and pan dulce, start the giant carafe of coffee, and arrange water bottles, spiral-bound notebooks, and pencils on the long entryway table. As community members began to trickle in, Gema was thrilled to see five, then the group doubled to ten, then the group suddenly expanded to 30. Gema and Bea were anticipating no more than 25 as a best-case-scenario turnout for this first session, so they scrambled to the back room, where they knew there were additional stacks of chairs, and recruited some of the teenagers to help them. There were community members of all ages and genders, speaking English, Spanish, and every code-meshed version that falls in between. The group was clearly buzzing with energy, and after counting to 58, Gema stopped counting, lost count, she wasn't sure, she just felt Bea nudge her out of her distracted daze and hiss, "Hey chica, you're on! It's almost 7:15 and this thing was supposed to start at 7! Vamos!"

Startled back into action, Gema cleared her throat and then had to clear it again a bit louder to get everyone's attention. When that didn't work, Bea took it as her cue to stick her fingers in her mouth and loudly cattle-whistle. That did the trick, the room snapped into silence. "Hello everyone, bienvenidos a todos!" Gema began with a smile.

There were a few murmured hellos and smiles returned.

"We are so excited to have such an amazing turnout tonight for our writing workshop, where we will work on telling the stories of our community here in Little Village, from our lives and our perspectives, in our voices," Gema continued.

A hand in the sea of an audience shot into the air, and Gema said, "Yes, is there a question?"

A high-school-aged boy stood up and spoke. "But are we going to talk about Trump? About what he said about us yesterday on that escalator?"

The sea of heads began to nod, and the volume of the room turned back up from zero to 60 as the community members exploded into angry discussion of yesterday's events, events Gema admittedly hadn't yet caught up on because she had been so buried and distracted in her plan-making for this event. Mortified, Gema realized she had forgotten to watch the news, scroll her SMNs, or anything else. Turning as discretely as possible to Bea, Gema whispered, "What happened, what did he do?"

Bea clutched at her fake pearls, feigning shock, and replied, "Oh girl, you don't know? That orange foo descended those stairs, announced his bid for prez, and made sure to say Mexicans are criminals and rapists—among other things, but that's what's got your folks mad as hornets here tonight!"

"Oh my God," Gema mouthed, but then steeled herself, stood up straight, and faced her community. "Hey Bea," she hissed, "do that whistle again."

With the room now once again quiet, Gema proceeded: "This is exactly why we are here tonight. Because there are people like that man out there spreading mierda like that about our gente. And they don't know *our* stories."

Lots of murmurs and head shakes of no in agreement with her filled the audience.

She continued, "The only ones who *can* and *should* tell our stories is *us,* because it is *us,* in *our* voices, who know *our* stories. We are the carriers of our historias, our tradiciones, our cultura!"

Cheers resonated throughout the crowd.

Smiling and surveying one end of the filled room to the other, Gema concluded, "This is the space where we come together, to make our voices known and to decide together what is good, what represents us, and what our terms are. Let's get started, vamos!" (see Cirio in this volume).

MAY 5, 2010
TUCSON, ARIZONA
LUIS

It was May during Luis's senior year at Tucson High Magnet School (THMS), and campus was positively buzzing. The weather was perfect, prom was this coming weekend, and graduation was only a couple weeks away. What more could a guy ask for? Well, today was also Cinco de Mayo, so there's always that bonus of a guaranteed great night at whatever nearby house party Luis and the boys would end up at, sure to be well-stocked with booze, bud, babes. Life was good.

Making his way out of campus for the day, Luis rounded the corner of the main entrance to the school and heard what sounded like chanting (or was it shouting?) coming from the front side of the school that faced Sixth Street. Curious, as were many other students and staff, Luis and a growing group ventured to the front of the school to bear witness (see Knievel in this volume) to a group of THMS students (see in this volume Baniya; Kannan & Johnney) shouting and then, yes, chanting at times, "Our education is under attack, what do we do, FIGHT BACK!"

Many people held up painted signs that read "Save Ethnic Studies," "Stop the hate, Educate," "HB2281 is Racist," "Don't Hate Reinstate MAS," "Don't Criminalize Our Education," and "Honk for Ethnic Studies."

One of the student protesters had a bullhorn in her hand. She was leading the chants, shouting all sorts of things into the growing crowd as passing cars on Sixth Street honked. The whole sight was curious for Luis to behold. What was everyone so worked up about, he wondered? As if responding to his internal query, the student with the bullhorn began speaking: "We are gathered here today to take a stand, we are here today in defiance, and with demands. The Arizona legislature has finally secured Governor Jan 'La Bruja' Brewer's signature on HB 2281, which effectively bans our beloved MAS ethnic studies courses here at THMS and other schools in our city."

The crowd booed at this.

"But we are not going to take this lying down!" the student continued, to great applause and cheers. "When our education is under attack, what do we do?"

The crowd yelled: "FIGHT BACK!"

"That's right," the student nodded, a stern and determined look on her face.

Luis realized in that moment that he knew her. That was Natalia. They'd been in classes together since about fourth grade back at Lineweaver Elementary School. She was always so shy and never said anything in class, or at least that's how he remembered her—and now he was bearing witness to her doing this (see Knievel in this volume)? What had happened to her?

Natalia's impassioned speech continued, to a clearly enraptured audience, but Luis had to get a move on. He had big "Cinco de Drinko" plans for the night, and so he needed to get home to nap and eat whatever his mom made for dinner, then it would be time to party. He had a nagging curiosity at the back of his mind about Natalia though. What happened to transform the shy, silent little girl who used to hide in the back corner of the classroom to the front-and-center shouting activist with a bullhorn he saw today? But he had plenty of time to catch up with Natalia another day, another time.

EARLY SUMMER TO EARLY FALL 2020
NEW YORK, NEW YORK (SORT OF)
SOFI

Sofi's senior year had been blown to pieces. She was in the class of 2020, so Sofi's class got no prom, no real graduation ceremony, no true closure for the high school experience. The only two things Sofi had to look forward to in this otherwise horror show of a year were starting college (even if virtually at first) at the New School, which meant an eventual move to NYC, and the presidential election. Sofi was finally of voting age, and she *could not wait* to cast her vote contra to the orange menace.

Sofi was keenly aware of her intersecting identities—they were queer, nonbinary, in a queer platonic relationship but also interested in nonplatonic hookups. Sofi's pronouns are she/they, and although they are white-passing, they come from a very strongly identified Indigenous Mexican American family and background. An artist and animal-lover by nature, Sofi ran with a local group of activist-oriented theater and public art kids who believed art is and should be political (see Kannan & Johnney in this volume). Art is possible anywhere: on our bodies (Sofi's mom, Alejandra, cringed at the increasing number of tattoos Sofi kept coming home with), on public property, on a canvas, anywhere!

Sofi spent much of their summer protesting and marching for George Floyd and #blacklives. Hyperaware of their white-passing privilege, Sofi made sure they were one of the white bodies that formed the barrier line between riot police and fellow marchers and protesters of color (Martinez, 2020, p. 44; in this volume see Knievel; Olson Beal). As the summer ended and it was time to retreat back behind screens and into Zoom-confined "classrooms," Sofi did her best not to let the overwhelming depression she felt about the state of the world and society consume her. Sofi's generation was one born into the wake of 9/11, into national and international trauma and instability. Crisis and anxiety was all Gen Z had ever known, and some days, for Sofi, the weight of it all felt like too much. Her mom, a millennial, often said how bad she felt for Sofi's generation because of how much access and exposure they have to the news and media—to the atrocities of the world, the darkest corners of the web. It wasn't the childhood their mom had.

"We didn't care about anything," Sofi remembered her mom saying, "because we were insulated from many truths and led to believe there wasn't anything to care about. That racism was over. That everything was okay. That we had overcome."

Sofi's generation, on the other hand, cared about everything, probably too much, and they shouldered the seemingly universal Gen Z anxiety and depression as a result.

The one fall semester class Sofi was excited to begin was a course on political art and activist expression. As the course progressed, they began to learn about the history of graffiti in NYC, and the words of one author really resonated with Sofi (see Kannan & Johnney in this volume). Speaking on the question of art versus vandalism, especially in relation to protest (something Sofi and her friend collective back home engaged in regularly), the author confirmed, "In fact, it is their illegality that really defines them" (see Mitchell in this volume).

"Yes," Sofi thought, "that's exactly right!"

Continuing, the author said, "Regardless of any individual purpose, graffiti writers and vandal artists cut through the illusions that govern particular social systems. Their inscriptions work as disruptions to the spaces in which they write and to the powers that govern those spaces. It is my argument that protest graffiti writing and vandal art can create the opportunity to turn public spaces into contested places and allow discounted bodies to matter in those spaces" (see Mitchell, p. 151).

In that moment, Sofi felt seen. In that moment, with revelation and surprise, Sofi realized that she, too, is a counterstory activist. Just like her mom, Alejandra. But unlike her mom, Sofi's counterstories weren't written: they were visual, they were public art.

JANUARY 21, 2017
WASHINGTON, DC
THE COLLECTIVE

The five of us—Sofi, Luis, Sol, Gema, and me (Alejandra)—sat in contemplative silence for a few moments more, ruminating on moments past and moments yet to come. As we sat, the river of marchers continued to flow past us, and the clear presence and representation of collectives and organizations, national and transnational (see Baniya in this volume), were on display behind the many signs and banners the intersectional bodies held in coalition and solidarity with each other. It was a sight to behold.

I noticed a particularly well-drawn likeness of Stacey Abrams etched on a poster with the words "Abrams for Governor" written under it. The Black mother-daughter duo carrying the poster had dislodged from the river, seemingly needing a break too, and headed toward the benches our group was resting on.

I smiled as they approached, waved them over next to me as I scooted down the bench a bit toward Sofi to make more room. The mother looked to be about late-20s, and the daughter maybe 8 to 10 years old. They reminded me of me and Sofi in our early protest days.

"How you doing?" I asked, "We needed a break too!"

"Oh yes," the mother replied, "that crowd just moves you along, but Amaya here needed a break and I wanted to tell her about this museum anyway."

"Oh, hey Amaya," I said, "I'm Alejandra, and this is my daughter, Sofi," I said nodding over at Sofi.

Sofi waved and Amaya offered a smile and a wave but then hugged her mom's arm shyly.

"I'm Janet," the mom said, shaking my hand.

"And I take it y'all are from Georgia?" I asked, gesturing to the Abrams poster. "That's a gorgeous poster, by the way."

"Thanks," confirmed Janet, "and yep, we sure are. I'm a graphic artist, so I have some tools and skills at my disposal," she laughed. "But wait," Janet continued, now addressing Sol, Gema, and Luis as well. They had scooted closer to join the conversation.

"These are my cousins, Sol, Gema, Luis," I said, quickly eager to know what Janet was about to reveal.

Quick nods and hellos were exchanged.

Janet then flipped her poster around to reveal the other side; it was an even more stunning portrait of Fannie Lou Hamer with the words "From Hamer to Abrams, the vote is secured! Vote Abrams for Gov!"

"Whoa!" Gema and I said in unison, clearly impressed.

Janet smiled, pleased with our reaction. Sol, Luis, and Sofi had looks on their faces like they needed some more explanation, and Janet took the cue.

"Amaya, why don't you tell these nice people who Ms. Fannie Lou Hamer is."

Amaya continued to grip her mother's arm and although her mouth spread into a toothy grin, she tucked her head behind her mom's body, shaking her head no.

"Amaya Jervette Ross. You just did a report on Ms. Hamer for class. You know what to say. Now go on."

Emerging from behind her mom's arm, smiling but avoiding looking at any of our group, Amaya said, "Ms. Fannie Lou Hamer is a legend. She is a Civil Rights leader, she helped our people vote, she didn't care how long it took, or how much work she had to do. She just did it because she cared about us!" (see Pittman in this volume). Amaya ended with a giggle and hurriedly retreated behind her mother's arm.

"Very good, Amaya," Janet said, smiling and nodding with approval at her daughter, while the rest of us offered our praise and applause.

"Okay," Janet said, getting up from her seat, half-lifting Amaya with her, "we're going to go check out the museum, it was nice meeting you all. Don't forget Ms. Hamer, and *definitely* don't forget Ms. Abrams: she'll be President someday." She finished with a wink, picked up her sign in one hand, and offered the other hand to Amaya. Off they went toward the National Museum of African American History and Culture.

"Shall we rejoin the march?" I asked the group.

Everyone nodded. Then Sofi said, "Wait, there's a vendor over there selling some stickers and pins, can we check that out first?"

Sure, I said, shrugging and following her to the small table a few yards away. We all walked over and perused the various offerings displayed on the table, ranging from pussy hat iconography to rainbow flags to #blacklivesmatter options. Then my eyes zeroed in on one pin I knew I had to have. It was the pin that summed up the diversity of our collective activist experiences, those in the past and the present and those yet to come. It was a simple pin with a white background, displaying a mound of dirt and a green sprout springing from the dirt. The words overlayed on the image were the oft-quoted Zapatista words: *Quisieron enterrarnos, pero no sabían que éramos semillas.*

They tried to bury us. They didn't know we were seeds.

All of us, different as we are, are scattered across time, space, place. And like seeds, with our different lives and different paths, we make very different contributions and are moved by different exigencies. But we can all still contribute. Our activism can still count in the manifold ways of possible expression. Some approach their activism perceivably more engaged or passionately than others. Some come to their activist consciousness later in the game than others. But above all, I believe everyone has the potential of a seed, forming strong roots and bearing good fruit, growing strong and resourcing others along the way.

REFERENCES

Ackerman, J. M., & Coogan, D. J. (Eds.). (2013). *The public work of rhetoric: Citizen-scholars and civic engagement.* University of South Carolina Press.

Adamovic, E., Newton, P., & House, V. (2020). Food insecurity on a college campus: Prevalence, determinants, and solutions. *Journal of American College Health, 70*(1), 1–7. https://doi.org/10.1080/07448481.2020.1725019

Addison, J. (2007). Mobile technologies and a phenomenology of literacy. In H. McKee & D. DeVoss (Eds.), *Digital Writing Research* (pp. 171–184). Hampton Press.

Adler-Kassner, L., & Harrington, S. (2010). Responsibility and composition's future in the twenty-first century: Reframing "accountability." *College Composition and Communication, 62*(1), 73–99.

Agence France-Presse. (2019, October 9). Iranian women allowed to watch football at stadium for first time in decades. *The Guardian.* https://www.theguardian.com/football/2019/oct/09/iranian-women-allowed-to-watch-football-at-stadium-for-first-time-in-decades

Alexander, J., Jarratt, S., & Welch, N. (Eds.). (2018). *Unruly rhetorics: Protest, persuasion, and publics.* University of Pittsburgh Press.

Al-Haq. (2013, April 8). *Water for one people only: Discriminatory access and "water apartheid" in the OPT.* https://www.alhaq.org/publications/8073.html

Al-Haq. (2018, January 31). *Settling Area C: Jordan Valley exposed.* https://www.alhaq.org/publications/8057.html#:~:text=This%20report%2C%20Settling%20Area%20C,a%20legal%20and%20historical%20lens

Alvarez, N., Salazar, C., Brito, F. N., & Aguilar, K. (2017). Agency, liberation, and intersectionality among Latina scholars: Narratives from a cross-institutional writing collective. *Praxis: A Writing Center Journal, 14*(1), 9–14.

Alvarez, S. P., & Wan, A. J. (2019). Global citizenship as literacy: A critical reflection for teaching multilingual writers. *Journal of Adolescent & Adult Literacy, 63*(2), 213–216.

Appadurai, A. (2013). *The future as cultural fact: Essays on the global condition.* Verso.

Asante, M. K. (1998). *The Afrocentric idea.* Temple University Press.

Asen, R. (2000). Seeking the "counter" in counterpublics. *Communication Theory, 10*(4), 424–446. https://doi.org/10.1111/j.1468-2885.2000.tb00201.x

Asen, R. (2018). Public: A network of relationships. *Rhetoric Society Quarterly, 48*(3), 297–305. https://doi.org/10.1080/02773945.2018.1454216

Asen, R., & Brouwer, D. C. (2001). (Eds.). *Counterpublics and the state.* SUNY University Press.

Asher-Schapiro, A. (2015, March 11). NYU's graduate student union just won a historic contract. *The Nation.* https://www.thenation.com/article/archive/nyus-graduate-student-union-just-won-historic-contract/

Associated Press. (2015, October 14). Iranian filmmaker Keywan Karimi sentenced to 6 years in jail, 223 lashes. *CBC.* https://www.cbc.ca/news/entertainment/iran-karimi-keywan-jail-1.3270312

Atkinson, J. (2017). *Journey into social activism: Qualitative approaches.* Fordham University Press. https://www.jstor.org/stable/j.ctt1hfrork.3#metadata_info_tab_contents

Austin, J. L. (1962). *How to do things with words.* Harvard University Press.

Bacon, J. M. (2019). Settler colonialism as eco-social structure and the production of colonial ecological violence. *Environmental Sociology, 5*(1), 59–69.

Baniya, S. (2020). Managing environmental risks in the age of climate change: Rhetorical agency and ecological literacies of transnational women during the April 2015 Nepal earthquake. *Enculturation, 32.* https://www.enculturation.net/managing_environmental

Baniya, S. (2021). The implications of transnational coalitional actions and activism in disaster response. *Spark: A 4C4Equality Journal, 3.* https://sparkactivism.com/volume-3-call/transnational-coalitional-actions-and-activism-in-disaster-response/

Becker, L. L. (2016, June 6). *Adjuncts are unionizing, but that won't fix what's wrong in higher education.* Washington Post. https://www.washingtonpost.com/posteverything/wp/2016/06/06/adjuncts-are-unionizing-but-that-wont-fix-whats-wrong-in-higher-education/

Benjamin, W. (1968). The work of art in the age of mechanical reproduction. In H. Arendt (Ed.), *Illuminations: Essays and Reflections* (pp. 217–253). Houghton Mifflin Harcourt.

Berkeley Copwatch (2020a). *Mission.* https://www.berkeleycopwatch.org/about

Berkeley Copwatch (2020b). *People's Database.* https://www.berkeleycopwatch.org/people-s-database

Berthold, S. M., & Libal, K. R. (Eds.). (2019). *Refugees and asylum seekers: Interdisciplinary and comparative perspectives.* Praeger.

Biber, D. (2006). *University language: A corpus-based study of spoken and written registers.* John Benjamins Publishing.

Bista, H. (2018). अनलाइन क्रान्तिको बिगुल. (Online Krantiko Bigul; translation: Online Revolution's Roar). *Naya Patrika Daily.* Republished on Rage Against Rape website (2018, December 9). https://rageagainstrape.wordpress.com/

Black Hand. [@blackhand.streetart]. (2014, November 19). [Photograph of a depiction of a female football fan with dishwashing liquid]. Instagram. https://www.instagram.com/p/vkr__amB2c/%20%20?utm_medium=share_sheet

Black Hand. (2018, October 1). *Please read to the end, and do not just like. Talking about women's rights is upsetting for me. Not because* [Photograph]. Instagram. https://www.instagram.com/p/BoZKv3WjTpf/?utm_medium=copy_link

Blain, K. N. (2021). *Until I am free: Fannie Lou Hamer's enduring message to America.* Beacon Press.

Blair, K. L., & Nickoson, L. (2018). *Composing feminist interventions: Activism, engagement, praxis*. WAC Clearinghouse; University Press of Colorado. https://wac.colostate.edu/books/perspectives/feminist/

Bober, T., & Regehr, C. (2006). Strategies for reducing secondary or vicarious trauma: Do they work? *Brief Treatment and Crisis Intervention, 6*(1), 1–9.

Bock, M. A. (2016). Film the police! Cop-watching and its embodied narratives. *Journal of Communication, 66*(1), 13–34.

Bohman, J. (2004). Expanding dialogue: The internet, the public sphere, and prospects for transnational democracies. In N. Crossley & J. M. Roberts (Eds.), *After Habermas: New perspectives on the public sphere* (pp. 131–155). Blackwell.

Bollier, D. (2008, June 26). Using sousveillance to defend the commons. *On the Commons*. https://onthecommons.org/using-sousveillance-defend-commons/

Bowers, J. W., Ochs, D. J., Jensen, R. J., & Schulz, D. P. (2010). *The rhetoric of agitation and control* (3rd ed.). Waveland Press.

Boyle, C., & Rivers, N. (2018). Augmented publics. In C. G. Brooke & L. Gries (Eds.), *Circulation, writing, and rhetoric* (pp. 83–101). Utah State University Press.

Brighetti, A. M. (2010). At the wall: Graffiti writers, urban territoriality, and the public domain. *Space and Culture, 13*(3), 315–332. https://doi.org/10.1177/1206331210365

Broad, B. (2003). *What we really value: Beyond rubrics in teaching and assessing writing*. Utah State University Press.

Brock, Pauline. (2018, June 20). Manu or Mr President? Macron's double standards show his lack of cool. *The Guardian*. https://www.theguardian.com/commentisfree/2018/jun/20/president-macron-double-standards-france

Brooke, C. (2013, April 13). Social media win: University online petitions win teachers a fair wage. *Business2Community*. https://www.business2community.com/social-media-articles/social-media-win-university-online-petitions-win-teachers-a-fair-wage-0463978?fbclid=IwAR3qfJoNSWizaV7U6U6DqkPQIc8vjsegzAmwrYbik4NjvWpC1445uDJnCys

Brooks, M. P. (2011). Oppositional ethos: Fannie Lou Hamer and the vernacular persona. *Rhetoric and Public Affairs, 14*(3), 511–548.

Brooks, M. P. (2014). *A voice that could stir an army: Fannie Lou Hamer and the rhetoric of the Black Freedom Movement*. University Press of Mississippi.

Brooks, M. P. (2020). *Fannie Lou Hamer: America's freedom fighting woman*. Roman & Littlefield.

Brooks, M. P., & Houck, D. W. (Eds.). (2011). *The speeches of Fannie Lou Hamer: To tell it like it is*. University Press of Mississippi.

B'Tselem. (2017, November 11). *The Jordan Valley*. https://www.btselem.org/jordan_valley

Burke, K. (1969). *A rhetoric of motives*. University of California Press.

Burton, Z. (2013, April 4). Fellows fighting for funds. *The Daily Cougar*.

Butler, J. (1997). *Excitable speech: A politics of the performative*. Routledge.

Butler, J. (2004). *Precarious life: The powers of mourning and violence*. Verso.

Butler, J. (2012). Precarious life, vulnerability, and the ethics of cohabitation. *The Journal of Speculative Philosophy, 26*(2), 134–151.

Butler, J. (2015). *Bodies that matter*. Taylor & Francis.

Butler, J. (2020, July 3). Performativity and Black Lives Matter. *IAI News, 89*. https://iai.tv/articles/speaking-the-change-we-seek-judith-butler-performative-self-auid-1580

Butts, S., & Jones, M. (2021). Deep mapping for environmental communication design. *Communication Design Quarterly, 9*(1), 4–19. https://doi.org/10.1145/3437000.3437001

Caldwell, G. (2005). Using video for advocacy. In S. Gregory, G. Caldwell, R. Avni, & T. Harding (Eds.), *Video for change: A guide for advocacy and activism* (pp. 1–19). Pluto Press. https://www.jstor.org/stable/j.ctt183q4hn

Calhoun, C. (1992). Introduction. In E. Calhoun (Ed.), *Habermas and the public sphere* (pp. 1–48). MIT Press.

Campaign for a Healthy CUNY. (2011, April). *Food insecurity at CUNY: Results from a survey of CUNY undergraduate students.* https://food.ucsb.edu/docs/default-source/default-document-library/foodinsecurity-cuny-copy.pdf?sfvrsn=a5af4669_0

Carastathis, A. (2013). Identity categories as potential coalitions. *Signs: Journal of Women in Culture and Society, 38*(4), 941–965.

Carney, P. A., Hamada, J. L., Rdesinski, R., Sprager, L., Nichols, K. R., Liu, B. Y., Pelayo, J., Sanchez, M. A. & Shannon, J. (2012). Impact of a community gardening project on vegetable intake, food security and family relationships: A community-based participatory research study. *Journal of Community Health, 37*(4), 874–881. https://www.ncbi.nlm.nih.gov/pmc/articles/PMC3661291/

Casa Alitas Program. (2020). *Info: Our history.* https://www.casaalitas.org/info

Castells, M. (2010). *The rise of the network society* (2nd ed.). John Wiley & Sons, Ltd.

Chávez, K. R. (2013). *Queer migration politics: Activist rhetoric and coalitional possibilities.* University of Illinois Press.

Chávez, K. R. (2021). *The borders of AIDS: Race, quarantine, and resistance.* University of Washington Press.

Cho, S., Crenshaw, K. W., & McCall, L. (2013). Toward a field of intersectionality studies: Theory, applications, and praxis. *Signs: Journal of Women in Culture and Society, 38*(4), 785–810.

Chun, J. J., Lipsitz, G., & Shin, Y. (2013). Intersectionality as a social movement strategy: Asian immigrant women advocates. *Signs: Journal of Women in Culture and Society, 38*(4), 917–940.

Cizek, K. (2005). Storytelling for advocacy: Conceptualization and preproduction. In S. Gregory, G. Caldwell, R. Avni, & T. Harding (Eds.), *Video for change: A guide for advocacy and activism* (pp. 20–73). Pluto Press. https://www.jstor.org/stable/j.ctt183q4hn

Clancy, J. L., & Pierson, B. L. (2020, March 17). Indian nations law update. *National Law Review, 13*(186). https://www.natlawreview.com/article/indian-nations-law-update-march-2020

Clark, N. (2018). The limitations of choice: Toward a new materialist reading of "mommy war" rhetorics. In J. Rice & B. McNely (Eds.), *Networked Humanities: Within and Without the University* (pp. 157–181). Parlor Press.

Clarke, B. (2012). "The poor man's club": The middle classes, the public house, and the idea of community in the nineteen-thirties. *Mosaic: An Interdisciplinary Critical Journal, 45*(2), 39–54. https://www.jstor.org/stable/44030680

Claus, L., and Tracey, P. (2020). Making change from behind a mask: How organizations challenge guarded institutions by sparking grassroots activism. *Academy of Management Journal, 63*(4), 965–996.

Collins, P. H. (2019). *Intersectionality as critical social theory.* Duke University Press.

Coole, D., & Frost, S. (Eds.). (2010). *New materialisms: Ontology, agency, and politics.* Duke University Press.

Cooper, B. (2021). Foreword. In K. Schuller (Ed.), *The trouble with white women: A counterhistory of feminism* (pp. 1–13). Bold Type Books.

Cooper, M. (1986). The ecology of writing. *College English, 48*(4), 364–375. https://doi.org/10.2307/377264

CopBlock. (2020). *About.* https://www.copblock.org/about/

Copwatch Brooklyn [@CpuBrooklyn]. (2020, August 9). *#PoliceBrutality in Mount Vernon* [Tweet; video]. Twitter. https://twitter.com/CpuBrooklyn/status/1292633833574105088

Copwatch Patrol Unit–Brooklyn. (2020, September 27). *#defundthepolice* [Video]. Facebook. https://www.facebook.com/CopWatchBrooklyn/videos/3474209065973529/?__so__= channel_tab&__rv__=latest_videos_card

Corral, O. (2021). To 'the fellowship of the springs,' Florida is selling out an environmental treasure. *WUSF Public Media.* https://wusfnews.wusf.usf.edu/environment/2021-04-17/ to-the-fellowship-of-the-springs-florida-is-selling-out-an-environmental-treasure

Crary, J. (2014). *24/7: Late capitalism and the ends of sleep.* Verso.

Crenshaw, K. (1991). Mapping the margins: Intersectionality, identity politics, and violence against women of color. *Stanford Law Review, 4*(6), 1241–1299.

Crenshaw, K. (2006). Intersectionality, identity politics and violence against women of color. *Kvinder, Køn & Forskning,* 2–3. https://doi.org/10.7146/kkf.v0i2-3.28090

Cruz, D. (2020, February 13). NYBG enters residential housing market. *Norwood News.* https:// www.norwoodnews.org/wp-content/uploads/2020/02/Norwood-News-Vol.-33-No.-4.pdf

Cull, I., Hancock, R. L. A., McKeown, S., Pidgeon, M., & Vedan, A. (2018). *Pulling together: A guide for front-line staff, student services, and advisors.* Creative Commons Attribution-Noncommercial 4.0 International License. https://opentextbc.ca/indigenizationfrontlineworkers/

Cushman, E. (1996). The rhetorician as an agent of social change. *College Composition and Communication, 47*(1), 7–28. https://doi.org/10.2307/358271

Cushman, E. (1999). The public intellectual, service learning, and activist research. *College English, 61*(3), 328–326.

Cushman, E., Powell, K. M., & Takayoshi, P. (2004). Response to "accepting the roles created for us: The ethics of reciprocity." *College Composition and Communication, 56*(1), 150–156.

D'Angelo, F. J. (1974). Sacred cows make great hamburgers: The rhetoric of graffiti. *College Composition and Communication, 25*(2), 173–180.

Dadas, C. (2017). Hashtag activism: The promise and risk of "attention." In D. M. Walls & S. Vie (Eds.), *Social writing / social media: Publics, presentations, and pedagogies* (pp. 17–36). WAC Clearinghouse; University Press of Colorado. https://doi.org/10.37514/PER-B.2017.0063.2.01

Davis, A. Y. (1990). *Women, culture, & politics.* Vintage Books.

Davis, D. (2007). *Inessential solidarity: Rhetoric and foreigner relations.* University of Pittsburgh Press.

Davis, J. (2012). *The first generation student experience: Implications for campus practice, and strategies for improving persistence and success.* Stylus Publishing.

Dean, J. (2003). Why the net is not a public sphere. *Constellations, 10*(1), 95–112.

Dean, J. (2009). *Democracy and other neoliberal fantasies: Communicative capitalism and left politics.* Duke University Press.

De Haene, L., Grietens, H., & Verschueren, K. (2010). Holding harm: Narrative methods in mental health research on refugee trauma. *Qualitative Health Research, 20*(12), 1664–1676.

Dehghan, S. K. (2014, August 6). Interview: Street artist Black Hand tells *The Guardian* how Banksy has inspired a new set of graffiti on Tehran walls. *The Guardian.* https://www. theguardian.com/world/iran-blog/2014/aug/06/iran-banksy-street-graffiti-tehran-black-hand-interview

DeLanda, M. (2016). *Assemblage theory.* Edinburgh University Press.

Deleuze, G., & Guattari, F. (1987). *A thousand plateaus: Capitalism and schizophrenia* (B. Massumi, Trans.). University of Minnesota Press.

Del Gandio, J. (2008). *Rhetoric for radicals: A handbook for 21st century activists*. New Society Publishers.

DeLuca, K. M. (1999). *Image politics: The new rhetoric of environmental activism*. Routledge.

DeLuca, K. M., Lawson, S., & Sun, Y. (2012). Occupy Wall Street on the public screens of social media: The many framings of the birth of a protest movement. *Communication, Culture, & Critique, 5*(4), 483–509.

Denny, H. (2010). *Facing the center: Toward an identity politics of one-to-one mentoring*. Utah State University Press.

Devins, N. (1994). Philadelphia plan. *Faculty Publications*. https://scholarship.law.wm.edu/facpubs/1637/

DeVoss, D., Haas, A., & Rhodes, J. (2019). Technofeminism: (Re)generations and intersectional futures. *Computers and Composition, 51*. http://cconlinejournal.org/techfem_si/00_Editors/

Dich, L. (2016). Community enclaves and public imaginaries: Formations of Asian American online identities. *Computers and Composition, 40*, 87–102. https://doi.org/10.1016/j.compcom.2016.03.012

Ding, H. (2009). Rhetorics of alternative media in an emerging epidemic: SARS, censorship, and extra institutional risk communication. *Technical Communication Quarterly, 18*(4), 237–350.

Dingo, R. (2012). *Networking arguments: Rhetoric, transnational feminism, and public policy writing*. University of Pittsburgh Press.

Dingo, R. (2013). Networking the macro and micro: Toward transnational literacy practices. *JAC, 33*(3/4), 529–552.

Dingo, R., Riedner, R., & Wingard, J. (2013). Toward a cogent analysis of power: Transnational rhetorical studies. *JAC, 33*(3/4), 517–528. http://www.jstor.org/stable/43854566

Dixon, K. (2014). Feminist online identity: Analyzing the presence of hashtag feminism. *Journal of Arts and Humanities, 3*(7), 34–40.

Dobrin, S. (2015). An American beach. In J. Rice (Ed.), *Florida* (pp. 212–230). Parlor Press.

Dobrin, S., & Morey, S. (Eds.). (2009). *Ecosee: Image, rhetoric, nature*. SUNY Press.

Draxler, B. (2017). Social justice in the writing center. *The Peer Review, 1*(2). https://thepeerreview-iwca.org/issues/braver-spaces/social-justice-in-the-writing-center/

Driscoll, D. L., & Wells, J. (2020). Tutoring the whole person: Supporting emotional development in writers and tutors. *Praxis: A Writing Center Journal, 17*(3), 16–28.

Druschke, C. G. (2013). Watershed as common-place: Communicating for conservation at the watershed scale. *Environmental Communication, 7*(1), 80–96. http://dx.doi.org/10.1080/17524032.2012.749295

Druschke, C. G. (2019, February 20). A trophic future for rhetorical ecologies. *Enculturation, 28*. http://enculturation.net/a-trophic-future

Druschke, C. G., & McGreavy, B. (2016). Why rhetoric matters for ecology. *Frontiers in Ecology and the Environment, 14*(1), 46–52.

Druschke, C. G., & Seltzer, C. E. (2012). Failures of engagement: Lessons learned from a citizen science pilot study. *Applied Environmental Education & Communication, 11*(3–4), 178–188. http://dx.doi.org/10.1080/1533015X.2012.777224

Duarte, M. (2017). Connected activism: Indigenous uses of social media for shaping political change. *AJIS. Australasian Journal of Information Systems, 21*. https://doi.org/10.3127/ajis.v21i0.1525

Dunlap, A. (2020). The politics of ecocide, genocide and megaprojects: Interrogating natural resource extraction, identity and the normalization of erasure. *Journal of Genocide Research, 23*(2), 212–235. https://doi.org/10.1080/14623528.2020.1754051

DuPont, D. (2019, July 5). *La Conexión to plead detained immigrants case with Latta*. BG Independent News.

Durá, L. (2015). What's wrong here? What's right here? Introducing the positive deviance approach to community-based work. *Connexions International Professional Communication Journal, 4*(1), 57–89.

Dyehouse, J. (2011). "A textbook case revisited": Visual rhetoric and series patterning in the American Museum of Natural History's horse evolution displays. *Technical Communication Quarterly, 20*(3), 327–346. https://doi.org/10.1080/10572252.2011.578235

Edbauer, J. (2005) Unframing models of public distribution: From rhetorical situation to rhetorical ecologies. *Rhetoric Society Quarterly, 35*(4), 5–24. https://doi.org/10.1080/02773940509391320

Edmonds, D. (2015, May 28). More than half of college faculty are adjuncts: Should you care? *Forbes*. https://www.forbes.com/sites/noodleeducation/2015/05/28/more-than-half-of-college-faculty-are-adjuncts-should-you-care/?sh=864701316005

Edwards, M., & Andone, D. (2017, December 7). Ex-South Carolina cop Michael Slager gets 20 years for Walter Scott killing. CNN. https://www.cnn.com/2017/12/07/us/michael-slager-sentencing/index.html

El Grito de Sunset Park. (2020). *About the Project*. https://elgrito.witness.org/about-the-project/

Elmusa, S. (1996). The land-water nexus in the Israeli-Palestinian conflict. *Journal of Palestine Studies, 25*(30), 69–78.

Eodice, M., Geller, A. E., & Lerner, N. (2017). *The meaningful writing project: Learning, teaching, and writing in higher education*. University Press of Colorado.

The Executive Committee of Tenure for the Common Good. (2020, April 30). A very stable and secure position? *Inside Higher Education*. https://www.insidehighered.com/views/2020/04/30/covid-19-shows-how-precarious-positions-contingent-faculty-actually-are-opinion

Faison, W. (2018). Black bodies, Black language: Exploring the use of Black language as a tool of survival in the writing center. *The Peer Review, 2*(1). https://thepeerreview-iwca.org/issues/relationality-si/black-bodies-black-language-exploring-the-use-of-black-language-as-a-tool-of-survival-in-the-writing-center/

Feleb-Brown, V. (2020, October 26). Not dried up: US-Mexico water cooperation. *Brookings*. https://www.brookings.edu/articles/not-dried-up-us-mexico-water-cooperation/

Fields, G. (2017). *Enclosure: Palestinian landscapes in a historical mirror*. University of California Press.

Fiore, F., & Gollner, P. (1991, March 5). Video showing beating by L.A. officers investigated. *Los Angeles Times*. https://www.latimes.com/local/california/la-me-video-showing-beating-by-la-officers-Investigated-19910305-story.html

Fishman, J., & Rosenberg, L. (2018). Guest editors' introduction to Community Writing, Community Listening. *Community Literacy Journal, 13*(1), 1–5.

Flores, G. M. (2017). *Latina teachers: Creating careers and guarding culture*. NYU Press.

Florida Springs Institute. (n.d.). *FSI Story Map*. https://floridaspringsinstitute.org/story-map/

Foss, S. K., & Griffin, C. (1995). Beyond persuasion: A proposal for an invitational rhetoric. *Communication Monographs, 62*(1), 2–18.

Foust, C. R., Pason, A., & Zittlow Rogness, K. (Eds.). (2017). *What democracy looks like: The rhetoric of social movements and counterpublics*. University of Alabama Press.

Franklin, M. I. (2013). *Digital dilemmas: Power resistance and the internet*. Oxford University Press.

Fraser, N. (1992). Rethinking the public sphere: A contribution to the critique of actual existing democracy. In C. Calhoun (Ed.), *Habermas and the public sphere* (pp. 109–142). MIT Press.

Fredlund, K. (2018). Feminist activism in the core: Student activism in theory and practice. In K. L. Blair & L. Nickoson (Eds.), *Composing Feminist Interventions* (pp. 475–500). WAC Clearinghouse.

Fredrickson, C. (2015, September 15). There is no excuse for how universities treat adjuncts. *The Atlantic.* https://www.theatlantic.com/business/archive/2015/09/higher-education-college-adjunct-professor-salary/404461/

Freire, P. (2000). *Pedagogy of the oppressed* (M. Bergman Ramos, Trans.). Continuum. (Original work published 1970)

Freudenberg, N., & Steinsapir, C. (1992). Not in our backyards: The grassroots environmental movement. In R. E. Dunlap & A. G. Mertig (Eds.), *American environmentalism: The U.S. environmental movement 1970–1990* (pp. 27–35). Routledge.

Fricke, P. (2015, August 25). *Mizzou profs. cancel classes to support grad student protest.* Campus Reform. https://campusreform.org/article?id=6756

Gabel, A. (2013, April 10). Social media: A powerful protest tool at the University of Houston. *Social Media Today.* https://www.socialmediatoday.com/content/social-media-powerful-protest-tool-university-houston

Gallagher, C. W. (2011). Being there: (Re)making the assessment scene. *College Composition and Communication, 62*(3), 450–476.

Ganz, M. (2010). Leading change: Leadership, organization and social movements. In N. Noria & R. Kuhrana (Eds.), *Handbook of leadership theory and practice.* Harvard Business Press.

Gates, H. L. (1988). *The signifying monkey: A theory of Afro-American literary criticism.* Oxford University Press.

Gershenson, S., Hart, C., Hyman, J., Lindsay, C., & Papageorge, N. W. (2018). The long-run impacts of same-race teachers (No. w25254). *National Bureau of Economic Research.*

Giaimo, G. N. (2020). Laboring in a time of crisis: The entanglement of wellness and work in writing centers. *Praxis: A Writing Center Journal, 17*(3), 3–15.

Gilio-Whitaker, D. (2019). *As long as grass grows: The Indigenous fight for environmental justice, from colonization to Standing Rock.* Beacon Press.

Gilson, O. (2021). An intersectional feminist rhetorical pedagogy in the technical communication classroom. In R. Walton & G. Y. Agboka (Eds.), *Equipping technical communicators for social justice work: Theories, methodologies, and pedagogies* (pp. 178–196). Utah State University Press.

Gilyard, K., & Banks, A. J. (2018). *On African American rhetoric.* Routledge.

Gladwell, M. (2010, October 4). Small change: Why the revolution will not be tweeted. *The New Yorker.* http://www.newyorker.com/magazine/2010/10/04/small-change-malcolm-gladwell

Glenn, C. (2002). Silence: A rhetorical art for resisting discipline(s). *JAC: A Journal of Composition Theory, 22*(2), 261–291.

Global Witness. (2020). *Enemies of the state? How governments and businesses silence land and environmental defenders.* https://www.globalwitness.org/en/campaigns/environmental-activists/enemies-state/

Glover-Graf, N. M. (2012). Ethical responsibilities in working with persons with disabilities and our duty to educate. In I. Marini, N. M. Glover-Graf, & M. Millington (Eds.), *Psychosocial aspects of disability: Insider perspectives and strategies for counselors.* Springer.

Godbee, B., Ozias, M., & Kar Tang, J. (2015). Body + power + justice: Movement-based workshops for critical tutor education. *The Writing Center Journal, 34*(2), 61–112.

Gogan, B. (2014). Expanding the aims of public rhetoric and writing pedagogy: Writing letters to editors. *College Composition and Communication, 65*(4), 534–559. https://www.jstor.org/stable/43490872#metadata_info_tab_contents

Gonzales, L., Walwema, J., Jones, N. N., Yu, H., & Williams, M. F. (2021). Narratives from the margins: Centering women of color in technical communication. In R. Walton & G. Y. Agboka (Eds.), *Equipping technical communicators for social justice work: Theories, methodologies, and pedagogies* (pp. 15–32). Utah State University Press.

Good Shepherd Collective. (2020). *Our Olive Trees*. https://goodshepherdcollective.org/olive-tree-planting/

Graeber, D. (2009). *Direct action: An ethnography*. AK Press.

Gray, L. (2013, April 3). UH fellows up in arms on stipend. *Houston Chronicle*.

Greene, D. M., & Walker, F. R. (2004). Recommendations to public speaking instructors for the negotiation of code-switching practices among Black English-speaking African American students. *Journal of Negro Education, 73*(4–11), 435–442.

Grewal, I., & Kaplan, C. (2001). Global identities: Theorizing transnational studies of sexuality. *GLQ: A Journal of Lesbian and Gay Studies, 7*(4), 663–679. http://muse.jhu.edu/article/12186

Gries, L. (2015). *Still life with rhetoric: A new materialist approach for visual rhetorics*. University Press of Colorado / Utah State University Press.

Griffin, A. (2018). Our stories, our struggles, our strengths: Perspectives and reflections from Latino teachers. *Education Trust*. https://files.eric.ed.gov/fulltext/ED588864.pdf

Gross, J. & Lukowski, A. (2020). Writing for advocacy: DREAMers, agency, and meaningful community engaged writing (course profile). *Reflections: A Journal of Community Engaged Writing and Rhetoric, 19*(2), 130–139.

Haas, A. M. (2012). Race, rhetoric, and technology: A case study of decolonial technical communication theory, methodology, and pedagogy. *Journal of Business and Technical Communication, 26*(3), 277–310.

Haas, A. M. (2020, June 2). *ATTW president's call to action to redress anti-Blackness and white supremacy*. ATTW. https://attw.org/blog/attw-presidents-call-to-action/

Haas, A. M., & Eble, M. F. (Eds.) (2018). *Key theoretical frameworks: Teaching technical communication in the twenty-first century*. Utah State University Press.

Hallman Martini, R. (2021). When things fall apart: A story about graduate student labor. In R. Jackson & J. G. McKinney (Eds.), *Self-culture-writing: Autoethnography for/as writing studies* (pp. 57–70). Utah State University Press.

Halsey, M., & Young, A. (2006). Our desires are ungovernable: Writing graffiti in urban space. *Theoretical Criminology, 10*(3), 275–306. https://doi.org/10.1177/1362480606065908

Hamer, F. L. (1963). "I don't mind my light shining," speech delivered at a freedom vote rally in Greenwood, Mississippi, fall 1963. In M. P. Brooks & D. W. Houck (Eds.), *The speeches of Fannie Lou Hamer: To tell it like it is.* (pp. 3–6). University Press of Mississippi.

Hamer, F. L. (1964). "We're on our way," speech delivered at a mass meeting in Indianola, Mississippi, September 1964. In M. P. Brooks & D. W. Houck (Eds.), *The speeches of Fannie Lou Hamer: To tell it like it is* (pp. 46–56). University Press of Mississippi.

Han, H. (2014). *How organizations create activists: Civic organizations and leadership in the 21st century*. Oxford University Press.

Hands, J. (2011). *@ is for activism: Dissent, resistance, and rebellion in a digital culture*. Pluto Press.

Hao, K. (2020, June 10). How to turn filming the police into the end of police brutality. *MIT Technology Review*. https://www.technologyreview.com/2020/06/10/1002913/how-to-end-police-brutality-filming-witnessing-legislation/

Hardy, M. (2013, April 3). Teaching for peanuts: UH creative writing graduate students stage a sit-in to protest 20 years without a raise. *Houstonia.*

Harlow, S., & Johnson, T. (2011). Overthrowing the protest paradigm? How the *New York Times, Global Voices* and Twitter covered the Egyptian revolution. *International Journal of Communication, 5,* 1359–1374.

Hauser, G. A. (1999). *Vernacular voices: The rhetoric of publics and public spheres.* University of South Carolina Press.

Hauser, G. A. & McClellan, E. D. (2009). Vernacular rhetoric and social movements: Performances of resistance in the rhetoric of the everyday. In S. M. Stevens & P. Malesh (Eds.), *Active voices: Composing a rhetoric of social movements* (pp. 23–46). SUNY Press.

Hawk, B. (2007). *A counter-history of composition: Toward methodologies of complexity.* University of Pittsburgh Press.

Hayes, L. L. (1997). Support from family and institution crucial to success of first-generation college students. *Counseling Today, 40*(2), 1–4.

Healthy CUNY & CUNY Graduate School of Public Health and Health Policy. (2019, March). *Q&A on food insecurity as a barrier to academic success at CUNY.* https://sph.cuny.edu/wp-content/uploads/2019/03/Report_02_Food-Insecurity_Final.pdf

Helms, J. (2017). *Rhizcomics: Rhetoric, technology, and new media composition.* Sweetland Digital Rhetoric Collaborative. https://www.digitalrhetoriccollaborative.org/books/rhizcomics_drc/

Helsel, P. (2015, April 8). *Walter Scott death: Bystander who recorded cop shooting speaks out.* NBC News. https://www.nbcnews.com/storyline/walter-scott-shooting/man-who-recorded-walter-Scott-being-shot-speaks-out-n338126

Heneiti, A. (2016). Bedouin communities in greater Jerusalem: Planning or forced displacement? *Jerusalem Quarterly, 65,* 51–69.

Hesford, W. S. (2010). Cosmopolitanism and the geopolitics of feminist rhetoric. In E. Schell, K. J. Rawson, & K. Ronald (Eds.), *Rhetorica in motion: Feminist rhetorical methods and methodologies* (pp. 53–70). University of Pittsburgh Press.

Hesford, W. S., & Kozol, W. (Eds.) (2005). *Just advocacy?: Women's rights, transnational feminism, and the politics of representation.* Rutgers University Press.

Hesford, W. S., Licona, A. C., & Teston, C. (Eds.). (2018). *Precarious rhetorics.* The Ohio State University Press.

Hesford, W. S., & Schell, E. E. (2008). Introduction: Configurations of transnationality: Locating feminist rhetorics. *College English, 70*(5), 461–470.

Hesford, W. S., & Shuman, A. (2018). Precarious narratives: Media accounts of Islamic state sexual violence. In W. S. Hesford, A. C. Licona, & C. Teston (Eds.), *Precarious rhetorics.* The Ohio State University Press.

Hill, M. L. (2018). "Thank you, Black Twitter": State violence, digital counterpublics, and pedagogies of resistance. *Urban Education, 53*(2), 285–302.

Hogan, K. (2019, April 22). What OFA has accomplished, and the fight ahead. *Medium.* https://medium.com/allontheline/what-ofa-has-accomplished-and-the-fight-ahead-2c319oo6of8c

Holt, L. J., & Fifer, J. E. (2018). Peer mentor characteristics that predict supportive relationships with first-year students: Implications for peer mentor programming and first-year student retention. *Journal of College Student Retention: Research, Theory & Practice, 20*(1), 67–91.

Holzhausen, J., & Grecksch, K. (2021). Historic narratives, myths and human behavior in times of climate change: A review from northern Europe's coastlands. *WIREs Clim Change, 12*:e723. https://doi.org/10.1002/wcc.723

Howard, S. (2016, April 25). 1968 Phila. (Rizzo) proclamation targeting protesters. *My Auction Finds and the Stories behind Them*. https://myauctionfinds.com/2016/04/25/1968-phila-proclamation-targeting-protesters/

Howard-Pitney, D. (2005). *African American jeremiad rev: Appeals for justice*. Temple University Press.

Hua, A. (2004). Travel and displacement: An (ex)refugee and (ex)immigrant woman's tale-tell. *Canadian Women's Studies, 19*(4), 110–114.

Huot, B. (2001). *(Re)articulating writing assessment for teaching and learning*. Utah State University Press.

Hussain, S. (2020, February 28). UC Santa Cruz fires 54 graduate student workers striking for higher pay. *Los Angeles Times*.

Ingraham, C. (2018). Energy: Rhetoric's vitality. *Rhetoric Society Quarterly, 48*(3), 260–268. https://doi.org/10.1080/02773945.2018.1454188

Iranian director sentenced to six years and 223 lashes for film that insults religious sanctities. (2015, October 21). *Art Forum*. https://www.artforum.com/news/iranian-director-sentenced-to-six-years-and-223-lashes-for-film-that-insults-religious-sanctities-55697

Itchuaqiyaq, C. (2020). *MMU Scholar List*. Itchuaqiyaq.com. https://www.itchuaqiyaq.com/mmu-scholar-list

Jackson, S. J., Bailey, M., & Welles, B. F. (2020). *#HashtagActivism: Networks of race and gender justice*. MIT Press.

Johnson, S. (2018). Mindful tutors, embodied writers: Positioning mindfulness meditation as a writing strategy to optimize cognitive load and potentialize writing center tutors' supportive roles. *Praxis: A Writing Center Journal, 15*(2), 24–33.

Johnson, T. R., Letter, J., & Livingston, J. K. (2009). Floating foundations: Kairos, community, and a composition program in post-Katrina New Orleans. *College English, 72*(1), 29–47.

Jones, M. (2018). Writing conditions: The premises of ecocomposition. *Enculturation: A Journal of Rhetoric, Writing, and Culture, 26*. http://enculturation.net/writing-conditions

Jones, M. (2019). (Re)placing the rhetoric of scale: Ecoliteracy, networked writing, and MEmorial mapping. In S. I. Dobrin and S. Morey (Eds.), *Mediating nature: The role of technology in ecological literacy* (pp. 79–95). Routledge.

Jones, M., Beveridge, A., Garrison J. R., Greene A., & MacDonald, H. (2022). Tracking memes in the wild: Visual rhetoric and image circulation in environmental communication. *Frontiers in Communication, 7*, Article 883278. https://doi.org/10.3389/fcomm.2022.883278

Jones, N. N. (2014). The importance of ethnographic research in activist networks. In M. F. Williams and O. Pimentel (Eds.), *Communicating race, ethnicity, and identity in technical communication* (pp. 45–59). Baywood Publishing Company.

Jones, N. N. (2016). Narrative inquiry in human-centered design: Examining silence and voice to promote social justice in design scenarios. *Journal of Technical Writing and Communication, 46*(4), 471–492. https://doi.org/10.1177/0047281616653489

Jones, N. N. (2020). Coalitional learning in the contact zones: Inclusion and narrative inquiry in technical communication and composition studies. *College English, 82*(5), 515–526.

Jones, N., & Walton, R. (2018). Using narratives to foster critical thinking about diversity and social justice. In A. Haas & M. Eble (Eds.), *Key Theoretical Frameworks: Teaching Technical Communication in the Twenty-First Century* (pp. 241–260). Utah State University Press.

Jones, N. N, & Williams, M. F. (2020, June 10). The just use of imagination: A call to action. *ATTW*. https://attw.org/blog/the-just-use-of-imagination-a-call-to-action/

Jones, R. (2020). Rhetorical activism responsibility in the ivory tower. In J. Lee & S. Kahn (Eds.), *Activism and Rhetoric: Theories and Contexts for Political Engagement* (2nd ed., pp. 26–37). Routledge.

Jones, S. (2020). #BlackStudy the past to find hope in the future. *Spark: A 4C4Equality Journal, 2.* https://sparkactivism.com/volume-2-call/vol-2-intro/blackstudy/

Jordan Valley Solidarity. (2020). *Planting olive trees: resisting annexation and the wall.* https://jordanvalleysolidarity.org/news/planting-olive-trees-resisting-annexation-and-the-wall/

Jue, M. (2020). *Wild blue media: Thinking through seawater.* Duke University Press.

Kativa, H. (n.d.). *What: The Columbia Avenue riots (1964).* Civil Rights in a Northern City: Philadelphia. http://northerncity.library.temple.edu/exhibits/show/civil-rights-in-a-northern-cit/collections/columbia-avenue-riots/the-columbia-avenue-riots—196

Kennedy, G. (1992). A hoot in the dark: The evolution of general rhetoric. *Philosophy and Rhetoric, 25*(1), 1–21. https://www.jstor.org/stable/40238276

Kennedy, S. (1983, May 29). James Tate of Philadelphia; Held mayor's post in 1962–72. *New York Times.* https://www.nytimes.com/1983/05/29/obituaries/james-tate-of-philadelphia-held-mayor-s-post-in-1962-72.html

Kilby, T. (2020, June 15). *Robert E. Lee Monument: 6.15.2020.* https://terrykilby.com/portfolio/robert-e-lee-monument-6-15-2020/

King, W. A. (2004). Through the looking glass of Silver Springs: Tourism and the politics of vision. *Americana: The Journal of American Popular Culture (1900–present), 3*(1). https://www.americanpopularculture.com/journal/articles/spring_2004/king.htm

Kinnard, M. (2017, December 8). Video key in ex-officer's stiff sentence for killing. *AP.* https://apnews.com/article/14bd2518f6ed42608acb8bf5c5f6b59c

The Kino-nda-niimi Collective. (2014). *The winter we danced: Voices from the past, the future, and the Idle No More Movement.* ARP Books.

Kirkness, V. J., & R. Barnhardt. (2001). First Nations and higher education: The Four R's— respect, relevance, reciprocity, responsibility. In R. Hayoe and J. Pan (Eds.), *Knowledge across cultures: A contribution to dialogue among civilizations.* Hong Kong, Comparative Education Research Centre, The University of Hong Kong.

Klein, M. (2020, January 25). Hunter college students protest campus Starbucks. *New York Post.* https://nypost.com/2020/01/25/hunter-college-students-protest-campus-starbucks/

Knoblauch, A. A. (2012). Bodies of knowledge: definitions, delineations, and implications of embodied writing in the academy. *Composition Studies, 40*(2), 50–65.

Kreuter, N. (2018). Network asymmetry and survivability in the digital humanities. In J. Rice & B. McNely (Eds.), *Networked humanities within and without the university.* Parlor Press.

Krimm, A. (2020, Aug. 17). Writing center research in a time of trauma: Strategies for tutors. *Connecting Writing Centers Across Borders.* https://www.wlnjournal.org/blog/2020/08/writing-center-research-in-a-time-of-trauma-strategies-for-tutors/

Krupanski, M. (2012, March). *Policing the police: Civilian video monitoring of police activity.* Global Minds. https://www.theglobaljournal.net/article/view/643/

Kynard, C. (2013). *Vernacular insurrections: Race, Black protest, and the new century in composition-literacies studies.* SUNY Press.

La Conexión. (2020). *Programs.* https://laconexionwc.wixsite.com/laconexion/programs-community

La Conexión Immigrant Solidarity Committee. (2018, March 25). *Dreamer, artista, y miembro de La Conexión Federico Cuatlacuatl diseña nuevo logo para celebrar el 5th aniversario* [Video]. YouTube. https://www.youtube.com/watch?v=8hcIDfEx6mg&t=0s

Lang, H. (2019). #MeToo: A case study in re-embodying information. *Computers and Composition, 53*, 9–20. https://doi.org/10.1016/j.compcom.2019.05.001

Lape, N. G. (2013). Going global, becoming translingual: The development of a multilingual writing center. *The Writing Lab Newsletter, 38*(3–4), 1–6.

Latour, B. (1999). *Pandora's hope: Essays on the reality of science studies.* Harvard University Press.

Laungaramsri, P. (2012). Frontier capitalism and the expansion of rubber plantations in southern Laos. *Journal of Southeast Asian Studies, 43*(3), 463–77.

Ledbetter, L., & Vaccaro, N. (2019). Cultivating intersectional awareness through the #performanceartselfie: A creative multimodal pedagogy. *Spark: A 4C4Equality Journal, 1.* https://sparkactivism.com/volume-1-coda/performanceartselfie/

Ledesma, A. (2017). *Diary of a reluctant dreamer: Undocumented vignettes from a pre-American life.* Ohio State University Press.

Lefebvre, H. (1991). *The production of space* (D. Nicholson-Smith, Trans.). Blackwell. (Original work published 1974)

Lee, J., & Kahn, S. (Eds.). (2010). *Activism and rhetoric: Theories and contexts for political engagement.* Routledge.

Lee, J., & Kahn, S. (Eds.). (2019). *Activism and rhetoric: Theories and contexts for political engagement* (2nd ed.). Routledge.

Libal, K. R., & Berthold, S. M. (2019). Supporting refugees and asylum seekers in an era of backlash: An introduction. In S. M. Berthold & K. R. Libal (Eds.), *Refugees and asylum seekers: Interdisciplinary and comparative perspectives.* Praeger.

Lieberman, P., & Murphy, D. (1992, May 2). King case aftermath: A city in crisis. *Los Angeles Times.* https://www.latimes.com/local/california/la-me-king-case-aftermath-a-city-in-crisis-19920502-story.html

Ludwig, D. (2015, April 15). Why graduate students of America are uniting. *The Atlantic.* https://www.theatlantic.com/education/archive/2015/04/graduate-students-of-the-world-unite/390261/

Luft, R. E., & Ward, J. (2009). Toward an intersectionality just out of reach: Confronting challenges to intersectional practice. In V. P. Demos & M. T. Segal (Eds.), *Perceiving gender locally, globally, and intersectionally* (pp. 9–37). Emerald Group Publishing Limited.

Lunsford, A. (2015). Performative writing. In L. Adler-Kassner & E. Wardle (Eds.), *Naming what we know: Threshold concepts for writing.* Utah State University Press.

Lusk, M., & Tarrazas, S. (2015). Secondary trauma among caregivers who work with Mexican and Central American refugees. *Hispanic Journal of Behavioral Sciences, 37*(2), 257–273.

Lynch, T. (2014). "Nothing but land": Women's narratives, gardens, and the settler-colonial imaginary in the US West and Australian Outback. *Western American Literature, 48*(4), 374–399. http://doi.org/10.1353/wal.2014.0024

Lyon, A. (2018). Precarious narratives: Media accounts of Islamic State sexual violence. In W. S. Hesford, A. C. Licona, & C. Teston (Eds.), *Precarious rhetorics* (pp. 41–61). The Ohio State University Press.

Mahoney, E. (2020, March 5). UC Santa Cruz fires over 70 striking graduate teaching assistants. *National Public Radio.*

Mahoney, K. (2018). We are not all in this together: A case for advocacy, factionalism, and making the political personal. In J. Alexander, S. Jarratt, & N. Welch (Eds.), *Unruly rhetorics: Protest, persuasion, and publics* (pp. 146–161). University of Pittsburgh Press.

Mahoney, K. (2020). Raging media: Investing in an infrastructure for resistance. In J. Lee & S. Kahn (Eds.), *Activism and rhetoric: Theories and contexts for political engagement* (2nd ed., pp. 113–127). Routledge.

Mann, B. W. (2018). Rhetoric of online disability activism: #CripTheVote and civic participation. *Communication, Culture, and Critique, 11*(4), 604–621.

Marcus, E. (2020, October 8). Will the last confederate statue standing turn off the lights? *New York Times.* https://www.nytimes.com/2020/06/23/style/statue-richmond-lee.html

Marder, M. (2017). *Energy dreams: Of actuality.* Columbia University Press.

Martín, C. S., Hirsu, L., Gonzales, L., & Alvarez, S. P. (2019). Pedagogies of digital composing through a translingual approach. *Computers and Composition, 52,* 142–157.

Martinez, Aja Y. (2020). *Counterstory: The rhetoric and writing of critical race theory.* NCTE.

Matheny, K. (2019a, August 13). Michigan agency held meeting with Upper Peninsula mine applicant to avoid public records. *Detroit Free Press.* https://www.freep.com/story/news/local/michigan/2019/08/13/michigan-upper-peninsula-mine/1969243001/

Matheny, K. (2019b, August 13). Upper Peninsula mine approved despite major concerns from DEQ and EPA staff, records show. *Detroit Free Press.* https://www.freep.com/story/news/local/michigan/2019/08/13/back-forty-mine-menominee-river-upper-peninsula/1935792001/

McAuley, J. (2019, November 6). Yellow vest anniversary: What happened to the movement that shook France. *Washington Post.* https://www.washingtonpost.com/world/europe/yellow-vest-anniversary-what-happened-to-the-movement-that-shook-france/2019/11/15/3ef43c98-0570-11ea-9118-25d6bd37dfb1_story.html

McConnell, P. J. (2000). ERIC review: What community colleges should do to assist first-generation students. *Community College Review, 28*(3), 75–87.

McCorkle, B., & Palmeri, J. (2014). Putting our bodies on the line: Towards a capacious vision of digital activism. *Harlot, 11.* http://harlotofthearts.org/index.php/harlot/article/view/213/147

McDorman, T. F. (2001). Crafting a virtual counterpublic: Right-to-die advocates on the internet. In R. Asen & D. Brouwer, *Counterpublics and the state* (pp. 187–209). SUNY Press.

McFadyen, G. (2018). Memory, language and silence: Barriers to refuge within the British asylum system. *Journal of Immigrant & Refugee Studies, 16*(1), 1–17.

McKenna, E., & Han, H. (2014). *Groundbreakers: How Obama's 2.2 million activists transformed campaigns in America.* Oxford University Press.

McLaughlin, E., & Vera, A. (2020, August 24). Wisconsin police shoot a Black man as his children watch from a vehicle, attorney says. *CNN.* https://www.cnn.com/2020/08/24/us/kenosha-police-shooting-jacob-blake/index.html

McLaughlin, J. L. (2020, August 31). La Conexión to help forgotten essential farm workers during a pandemic. *BG Independent News.*

McNamee, K., & Miley, M. (2017). Writing center as homeplace (a site for radical resistance). *The Peer Review, 1*(2). https://thepeerreview-iwca.org/issues/braver-spaces/writing-center-as-homeplace-a-site-for-radical-resistance/

Mead, N. (2020, May 4). Teaching assistants plan a "sick-out" strike. *Washington Square News.*

Menominee Tribal Legislature. (2020, January 16). *Resolution No. 19–52: Recognition of the rights of the Menominee River. Citizens for Safe Water around Badger.* https://cswab.org/wp-content/uploads/2020/02/Menominee-Tribe-Resolution-19-52-Recognition-of-the-rights-of-the-Menominee-River-16-Jan-2020.pdf

Mexican farmers, troops skirmish over La Boquilla dam water in Chihuahua. (2020, September 9). *El Paso Times.* https://www.elpasotimes.com/story/news/2020/09/09/mexico-farmers-troops-clash-over-la-boquilla-dam-water-chihuahua/5762578002/

Michel, C. (2013, April 4). Forced to work at waffle bus, Rice English Ph.D. students lodge stipend complaints. *Houston Press.*

Middleton, M., Hess, A., Endres, D., & Senda-Cook, S. (2015). *Participatory critical rhetoric: Theoretical and methodological foundations for studying rhetoric in situ.* Lexington.

Milioni, D. L. (2009). Probing the online counterpublic sphere: The case of Indymedia Athens. *Media, Culture & Society, 31*(3), 409–431.

Miller-Cochran, S. K. (2015). Multilingual writers and OWI. In B. L. Hewett & K. E. DePew (Eds.), *Foundational Practices of Online Writing Instruction* (pp. 297–314). WAC Clearinghouse / Parlor Press.

Mills, S. (2018, January 5). Wisconsin's infant mortality for African-Americans highest in nation. *Wisconsin Public Radio.* https://www.wpr.org/wisconsins-infant-mortality-african-americans-highest-nation

Milner, H. R. (2006). Preservice teachers' learning about cultural and racial diversity: Implications for urban education. *Urban Education, 41*(4), 343–375.

Mohanty, C. (2003). *Feminism without borders: Decolonizing theory, practicing solidarity.* Duke University Press.

Morey, S. (2014). Florida econography and the ugly cuteness of econs. *Journal of Florida Studies, 3*(1), 1–25. http://www.journaloffloridastudies.org/files/vol0103/03EcoSEAN.pdf

Movement 4 Black Lives. (2022). *Vision for Black lives.* https://m4bl.org/policy-platforms/

Mulhere, K. (2014, October 9). Strike for better benefits. *Inside Higher Education.* https://www.insidehighered.com/news/2014/12/03/u-oregon-grad-students-strike-better-benefits

Musalo, K. (2019). Evolution of refugee and asylum law in the United States. In S. M. Berthold & K. R. Libal (Eds.), *Refugees and asylum seekers: Interdisciplinary and comparative perspectives* (pp. 17–43). Praeger.

Mutnick, D. (2018). Answering the world's anticipation: The relevance of Native Son to twenty-first century protests. In J. Alexander, S. Jarratt, & N. Welch (Eds.), *Unruly rhetorics: Protest, persuasion, and publics* (pp. 209–227). University of Pittsburgh Press.

Nash, J. C. (2008). Re-thinking intersectionality. *Feminist Review, 89*, 1–15.

National Immigration Forum. (2020, September 1). *Fact sheet: Operation Streamline.* https://immigrationforum.org/article/fact-sheet-operation-streamline/

National Literacy Directory. (2022). *Lehman College Adult Learning Center (Bronx).* https://www.nld.org/page/lehman-college-adult-learning-center

Nelson, S. (Director). (2016). *The Black Panthers: Vanguard of the revolution* [Film]. PBS.

Newman, D. (1984). Ideological and political influences on Israeli rurban colonization: The West Bank and Galilee mountains. *Canadian Geographer / Le Géographe canadien, 28*(2), 142–155.

Nixon, R. (2011). *Slow violence and the environmentalism of the poor.* Harvard University Press. http://www.jstor.org/stable/j.ctt2jbsgw

Norris, C. (2002). *Deconstruction* (3rd ed.). Routledge.

North Bronx Collective. (2020, October 14). *Reimagining food justice in an uprising.* Verso. https://www.versobooks.com/blogs/4875-hot-city-reimagining-food-justice-in-an-uprising

Odum, H. T. (1957). Trophic structure and productivity of Silver Springs, Florida. *Ecological Monographs, 27*(1), 55–112. https://doi.org/10.2307/1948571

Odum, H. T. (1973). Energy, ecology and economics. *AMBIO, 2*(6), 220–227.

Olschki, L. (1941). Ponce de León's fountain of youth: History of a geographical myth. *The Hispanic American Historical Review, 21*(3), 361–385. https://doi.org/10.2307/2507328

Onishi, N. (2019, December 11). France announces tough new measures on immigration. *New York Times.* https://www.nytimes.com/2019/11/06/world/europe/france-macron-immigration.html

Oregon Cop Watcher. (2017, July 12). *Illegally detained and quick ID refusal* [Video]. YouTube. https://www.youtube.com/watch?v=j2hIlczDnzU

Organizing for Action. (2019a, December 16). *Effective conversations.* https://ofalegacytrainings.com/ofa-trainings-effective-conversations/

Organizing for Action. (2019b, December 16). *OFA trainings.* https://ofalegacytrainings.com/home/

Ouellette, J. (2018). The viability of digital spaces as sites for transnational feminist action and engagement: Why we need to look at digital circulation. In K. L. Blair & L. Nickoson (Eds.), *Composing feminist interventions: Activism, engagement, praxis* (pp. 275–296). WAC Clearinghouse / University Press of Colorado. https://doi.org/10.37514/PER-B.2018.0056.2.14

Palczewski, C. (2001). Cyber-movements, new social movements and counterpublics. In R. Asen & D. Brouwer, *Counterpublics and the state* (pp. 161–186). SUNY Press.

Papacharissi, Z. (2015). *Affective publics.* Oxford University Press.

Paramo, A. (2014, June 9). Pipas venden de modo indebido 40% de agua completan abasto de agua. (Pipes improperly sell 40% of water completes water supply.) *Excelsior.* https://www.excelsior.com.mx/comunidad/2014/06/09/964082

Parker, A., & Sedgwick, E. K. (1993). *Performativity and performance.* Routledge.

Parks, S. J., & Hachelaf, A. A. (2019). Of rights without guarantees: Friction at the borders of nations, digital spaces, and classrooms. *Literacy in Composition Studies, 7*(1), 90–113.

Patel, R., & Moore, N. (2017). *The history of the world in seven cheap things: A guide to capitalism, nature, and the future of capitalism.* University of California Press.

Patton, S. (2013, April 4). U. of Houston teaching fellows protest two decades without a stipend increase. *Chronicle of Higher Education.*

Payne, C. M. (2007). *I've got the light of freedom: The organizing tradition and the Mississippi freedom struggle.* University of California Press.

Peace and Justice Works. (2017, May 2). *Portland police manhandle copwatcher—May Day 2017* [Video]. YouTube. https://www.youtube.com/watch?v=FanI9V9wB2I&feature=youtu.be

Peaceful Streets Project. (2016, August 10). *By kicking woman, Austin police officer demeans entire community.* http://peacefulstreets.com/?s=By+kicking+woman%2C+Austin+police+officer+demeans+entire+community

Pearson, T. (2017, August 14). Is water the new drug for Mexico's cartels? *New Internationalist.* https://newint.org/web-exclusive/2017-08-14/mexico-water-cartels

Penney, J., & Dadas, C. (2014). (Re)tweeting in the service of protest: Digital composition and circulation in the Occupy Wall Street movement. *New Media & Society, 16*(1), 74–90.

Pérez, W. (2015). *Americans by heart: Undocumented Latino students and the promise of higher education.* Teachers College Press.

Pérez, W., Cortés, R. D., Ramos, K., & Coronado, H. (2010). "Cursed and blessed": Examining the socioemotional and academic experiences of undocumented Latina and Latino college students. *New Directions for Student Services, 131,* 35–51.

Perry, A. (2016). Training for triggers: Helping writing center consultants navigate emotional sessions. *Composition Forum, 34.* http://compositionforum.com/issue/34/training-triggers.php

Peterson, C. L. (1995). *"Doers of the word": African-American women speakers in the North (1830–1880).* Oxford University Press.

Pettman, D. (2016). *Infinite distraction.* Polity Press.

Pezzullo, P. C. (2009). *Toxic tourism: Rhetorics of pollution, travel, and environmental justice.* University of Alabama Press.

Pidgeon, M., Archibald, J., & Hawkey, C. (2014). Relationships matter: Supporting Aboriginal graduate students in British Columbia, Canada. *Canadian Journal of Higher Education, 44*(1), 1–21.

Pigg, S. (2014). Coordinating constant invention: Social media's role in distributed work. *Technical Communication Quarterly, 23*(2), 69–87. https://doi.org/10.1080/10572252.2013.796545

Popescu, M. (2019). Migration policies in Europe and the United States: Securitization, safety, and the paradox of human rights. In S. M. Berthold & K. R. Libal (Eds.), *Refugees and asylum seekers: Interdisciplinary and comparative perspectives.* Praeger.

Portland Copwatch. (2020). *Welcome to the Portland copwatch web page.* http://www.portlandcopwatch.org/

Potts, L. (2014). *Social media in disaster response: How experience architects can build for participation.* Routledge.

Powell, K. M. (2015). *Identity and power in narratives of displacement.* Routledge.

Preston, J. (2015). Project(ing) literacy: Writing to assemble in a postcomposition FYW classroom. *College Composition and Communication, 67*(1), 35–63.

Prohibiting Non-State Identification, H.B. 2312, 110th General Assembly State of Tennessee. (2018). https://legiscan.com/TN/bill/HB2312/2017

Prohibiting Sanctuary Policies, H.B. 2315, 110th General Assembly State of Tennessee. (2018). https://legiscan.com/TN/bill/HB2315/2017

Puvimanasinghe, T., Denson, L. A., Augoustinos, A., & Somasundaram, D. (2015). Narrative and silence: How former refugees talk about loss and past trauma. *Journal of Refugee Studies, 28*(1), 69–92.

Rainey, S. A., & Johnson, G. S. (2009). Grassroots activism: an exploration of women of color's role in the environmental justice movement. *Race, Gender & Class, 16*(3/4), 144–173.

Rape cases in Nepal peaked in past two months. (2020, September 27). *Republica.* http://myrepublica.nagariknetwork.com/news/99641/

Ratcliffe, K. (1999). Rhetorical listening: A trope for interpretive invention and code of cross-cultural conduct. *College Composition and Communication, 51*(2), 195–224.

Read, J. (2014, December 18). Distracted by attention. *New Inquiry.* https://thenewinquiry.com/distracted-by-attention/

Rendleman, J. (2020, June 5). [Photograph of dancers in front of a monument of Confederate general Robert E. Lee, in Richmond, VA]. *Reuters.* https://richmond.com/entertainment/how-a-photo-of-young-ballerinas-at-the-lee-statue-became-an-iconic-image-of/article_69ab8776-bae6-511f-b5e3-e57ac1bc1b8a.html

Rendleman, J. (2020, June 18). [Photograph of artist Dustin Klein's projection of an image of George Floyd onto the statue of Confederate General Robert E. Lee in Richmond, Virginia. *Reuters.* https://www.reuters.com/news/picture/top-photos-of-the-day-idUSRTS3EF3G

Reyes, M. (2020). Accounts of asylum: A call toward transnational literacies of displacement. *Enculturation: A Journal of Rhetoric, Writing & Culture.* https://www.enculturation.net/accounts_of_asylum

Rhodes, D. (2019, March 9). Teaching assistants go on strike at University of Illinois at Chicago: "We have to fight for the school to care about us." *Chicago Tribune.*

Ribero, A. M., & Arellano, S. C. (2019). Advocating *comadrismo:* A feminist mentoring approach for Latinas in rhetoric and composition. *Peitho, 21*(2), 234–256.

Rice, J. (2012). *Distant publics: Development rhetoric and the subject of crisis.* University of Pittsburgh Press.

Rice, J. (2016). *Craft obsession: The social rhetorics of beer.* Southern Illinois University Press.

Rice, J. (2020). *Awful archives: Conspiracy theory, rhetoric, and acts of evidence.* The Ohio State University Press.

Rice, J. E. (2008). The new "new": Making a case for critical affect studies. *Quarterly Journal of Speech, 94*(2), 200–212. https://doi.org/10.1080/00335630801975434

Rickert, T. (2013). *Ambient rhetoric: The attunements of rhetorical being.* University of Pittsburgh Press.

Rios-Aguilar, C., & Deil-Amen, R. (2012). Beyond getting in and fitting in: An examination of social networks and professionally relevant social capital among Latina/o university students. *Journal of Hispanic Higher Education, 11*(2), 179–196.

Rios-Aguilar, C., Kiyama, J. M., Gravitt, M., & Moll, L. C. (2011). Funds of knowledge for the poor and forms of capital for the rich? A capital approach to examining funds of knowledge. *Theory and Research in Education, 9*(2), 163–184.

Rivers, N. A., & Weber, R. P. (2011). Ecological, pedagogical, public rhetoric. *College Composition and Communication, 63*(2), 187–218.

Robinson, C. J. (1983). *Black Marxism: The making of the black radical tradition.* University of North Carolina Press.

Rojas-Flores, L., Clements, M. L., Hwang Koo, J., & London, J. (2016). Trauma and psychological distress in Latino citizen children following parental detention and deportation. *Psychological Trauma: Theory, Research, Practice, and Policy, 9*(3), 352–361.

Rose, E. J., & Cardinal, A. (2021). Purpose and participation: Heuristics for planning, implementing, and reflecting on social justice work. In R. Walton & G. Y. Agboka (Eds.), *Equipping technical communicators for social justice work: Theories, methodologies, and pedagogies* (pp. 75–97). Utah State University Press.

Royster, J. J., Kirsch, G. E., & Bizzell, P. (2012). *Feminist rhetorical practices: New horizons for rhetoric, composition, and literacy studies.* Southern Illinois University Press.

Ryder, P. M. (2010). *Rhetorics for community action: Public writing and writing publics.* Lexington Books.

Salvo, M. (2001). Ethics of engagement: User-centered design and rhetorical methodology. *Technical Communication Quarterly, 10*(3), 273–290. https://doi.org/10.1207/s15427625tcq1003_3

Sanburn, J. (2014, July 23). Behind the video of Eric Garner's deadly confrontation with New York police. *Time.* https://time.com/3016326/eric-garner-video-police-chokehold-death/

Save KCC Urban Farm. (2020). *Say NO to budget cuts at the urban farm!* https://actionnetwork.org/petitions/say-no-to-proposed-budget-cuts-to-kingsborough-community-colleges-urban-farm

Scharold, D. (2017). Challenge accepted: Cooperative tutoring as an alternative to one-to-one tutoring. *The Writing Journal, 36*(2), 31–55.

Schell, E. E. (2013). Transnational environmental justice rhetorics and the Green Belt Movement: Wangari Muta Maathai's ecological rhetorics and literacies. *Journal of Advanced Composition, 33*(3/4), 585–613. http://www.jstor.org/stable/43854569

Schmidt, W. (2004). Springs of Florida. *Florida Geological Survey Bulletin, 66.* http://publicfiles.dep.state.fl.us/FGS/WEB/springs/bulletin_66.pdf

Schuller, Kyla. (2021). *The trouble with white women: A counterhistory of feminism.* Bold Type Books.

Schneider, G. (2020, December 11). Northam proposes major effort to reimagine public space around Robert E. Lee statue in Richmond. *Washington Post.* https://www.washingtonpost.com/local/virginia-politics/northam-proposal-lee-statue-richmond/2020/12/10/10018a1c-3a3a-11eb-98c4-25dc9f4987e8_story.html

Seattle Cop Block. (2014, November 24). *Seattle police use explosives again* [Video]. Facebook. https://www.facebook.com/watch/?v=402428866571969

Severino, C., & Prim, S. (2016). Second language writing development and the role of tutors: A case study of an online writing center "frequent flyer." *The Writing Center Journal, 35*(3), 143–185.

Shaw, T. C. (2009). *Now is the time!: Detroit Black politics and grassroots activism.* Duke University Press.

Simonson, J. (2016). Copwatching. *California Law Review, 104*(2), 391–445. https://www.jstor.org/stable/24758728#metadata_info_tab_contents

SisterSong. (n.d.). *Reproductive justice.* https://www.sistersong.net/reproductive-justice

Sivils, M. W. (2004). William Bartram's travels and the rhetoric of ecological communities. *ISLE: Interdisciplinary Studies in Literature and Environment, 11*(1), 57–70. https://doi.org/10.1093/isle/11.1.57

Smith, L. (2012). *Decolonizing methodologies: Research and Indigenous peoples* (2nd ed.). Zed Books.

Smitherman, G. (1977). *Talkin and testifyin: The language of Black America.* Wayne State University Press.

Soliman, M. (2022). *Resource mobilization in Palestinian nonviolent campaigns.* ICNC Press. https://www.nonviolent-conflict.org/wp-content/uploads/2022/08/Soliman_Resource-Mobilization-in-Palestinian-Nonviolent-Campaigns.pdf

Soto Vega, K., & Chávez, K. R. (2018). Latinx rhetoric and intersectionality in racial rhetorical criticism. *Communication and Critical/Cultural Studies, 15*(4), 319–325.

Speer, P. W., & Christens, B. D. (2014). Community organizing. In V. Chien & S. Wolfe (Eds.), *Foundations of community psychology practice* (pp. 220–236). Sage.

Spinuzzi, C. (2008). *Network: Theorizing knowledge work in telecommunications.* Cambridge University Press.

Squires, C. R. (2002). Rethinking the Black public sphere: An alternative vocabulary for multiple public spheres. *Communication Theory, 12*(4), 446–468. https://doi.org/10.1111/j.1468-2885.2002.tb00278.x

Staples, L. (2016). *Roots to power: A manual for grassroots organizing.* Praeger.

Stenberg, Shari J. (2015). *Repurposing composition: Feminist interventions for a neoliberal age.* Utah State University Press.

Stokes, A. Q., & Atkins-Sayre, W. (2018). PETA, rhetorical fracture, and the power of digital activism. *Public Relations Inquiry, 7*(2), 149–170.

Stone, E. M. (2018). The story of Sound Off: A community writing / community listening experiment. *Community Literacy Journal, 13*(1), 16–22.

Strayhorn, T. L. (2007). Factors influencing the academic achievement of first-generation college students. *Journal of Student Affairs Research and Practice, 43*(4), 1278–1307.

Tatarchevskiy, T. (2011). The "popular" culture of internet activism. *New Media Society, 13*(2), 297–313.

Taylor, D. (2003). *The archive and the repertoire: Performing cultural memory in the Americas.* Duke University Press.

Tennessee Education Equity Coalition. (2018). *Our partners.* http://tnedequity.org/national-partners/

Terruso, J. (2015, January 20). Tasco looks back as she prepares to leave city council. *The Philadelphia Inquirer.* https://web.archive.org/web/20150320152607/http://articles.philly.com/2015-01-20/news/58235672_1_tasco-marian-b-city-council

Tessier, B. (2018, December 2). [Photograph of police at work near graffiti reading "the yellow vests will triumph," sprayed on the Arc de Triomphe]. *Reuters*. https://www.theguardian.com/world/gallery/2018/dec/02/the-aftermath-of-the-gilets-jaunes-riots-in-paris-in-pictures#img-2

Toch, H. (2012). *Cop watch: Spectators, social media, and police reform*. American Psychological Association.

Transactional Records Access Clearinghouse of Syracuse University. (2020, January 28). *Record number of asylum cases in FY 2019*. https://trac.syr.edu/immigration/reports/588/

Travers, A. (2003). Parallel subaltern feminist counterpublics in cyberspace. *Sociological Perspectives, 46*(2), 223–237.

Trottier, J., Leblond, N., & Garb, Y. (2020). The political role of date palm trees in the Jordan Valley: The transformation of Palestinian land and water tenure in agriculture made invisible by epistemic violence. *Environment and Planning E: Nature and Space, 3*(1), 114–140. https://doi.org/10.1177/2514848619876546

Tuck, E., & Yang, K. W. (2012). Decolonization is not a metaphor. *Decolonization: Indigeneity, Education & Society, 1*(1), 1–40.

United States Department of Labor. (2021, January 14). *Unemployment insurance weekly claims* [Press release]. https://www.dol.gov/ui/data.pdf

University of Houston. (2014). *University of Houston-Tier One FAQs*. uh.edu.

Valentine, K. (2017). The undercurrents of listening. *The Writing Center Journal, 36*(2), 89–115.

Vander Lei, E. & K. D. Miller. (1999). Martin Luther King Jr.'s "I have a dream" in context: Ceremonial protest and African American jeremiad. *College English, 62*(1), 83–99.

Veracini, L. (2015). *The settler colonial present*. Palgrave Macmillan.

Vickers, L., & Wilson-Graham, C. (2015). *Remembering Paradise Park: Tourism and segregation at Silver Springs*. University of Florida Press.

Vie, S., Carter, D., & Meyr, J. (2018). Occupy rhetoric: Responding to charges of "slacktivism" with digital activism successes. In I. Management Association (Ed.), *Media Influence: Breakthroughs in Research and Practice* (pp. 64–78).

Vogl, A. (2013). Telling stories from start to finish: Exploring the demand for narrative in refugee testimony. *Griffith Law Review, 22*(1), 63–86.

WAFA News Agency. (2020, October 16). *Israel confiscates 11,000 dunums of Palestinian land in Jordan Valley*. https://english.wafa.ps/Pages/Details/120596

Walls, D. M., & Vie, S. (Eds.). (2017). *Social writing / social media: Publics, presentations, and pedagogies*. WAC Clearinghouse / University Press of Colorado. https://wac.colostate.edu/books/perspectives/social/

Walsh, L. (2015). The visual rhetoric of climate change. *WIREs Climate, 6*(4), 361–368.

Walsh, P. (2020, June 11). Teen who recorded George Floyd video wasn't looking to be a hero, her lawyer says. *Star Tribune*. https://www.startribune.com/teen-who-shot-video-of-george-floyd-wasn-t-looking-to-be-a-hero-her-lawyer-says/571192352/

Walton, R., & Agboka, G. Y. (2021). *Equipping technical communicators for social justice work: Theories, methodologies, and pedagogies*. Utah State University Press.

Walton, R., Moore, K. R., & Jones, N. N. (2019). *Technical communication after the social justice turn: Building coalitions for action*. Routledge.

Wang, B. (2013). Comparative rhetoric, postcolonial studies, and transnational feminisms: A geopolitical approach. *Rhetoric Society Quarterly, 43*(3), 226–242. https://doi.org/10.1080/02773945.2013.792692

Wang, Z. (2020). Activist rhetoric in transnational cyber-public spaces: Toward a comparative materialist approach. *Rhetoric Society Quarterly, 50*(4), 240–253. https://doi.org/10.1080/027 73945.2020.1748218

Ward, E. G., Thomas, E. E., & Disch, W. B. (2014). Mentor service themes emergent in a holistic, undergraduate peer-mentoring experience. *Journal of College Student Development, 55*(6), 563–579.

Warner, M. (2002). *Publics and counterpublics*. Zone Books.

Warren-Riley, S. & Verzosa Hurley, E. (2017). Multimodal pedagogical approaches to public writing: Digital media advocacy and mundane texts. *Composition Forum* 36. http://compositionforum.com/issue/36/multimodal.php

Williams, M. F., & Pimentel, O. (Eds.). (2014). *Communicating race, ethnicity, and identity in technical communication*. Baywood Publishing Company.

Wimmer, J. (2012). The times they are a-changin': The digital transformation of "classic" counterpublic spheres. *Communication Management Quarterly, 23*, 5–22.

Wisconsin Department of Health Services. (2018, April). *Wisconsin maternal mortality review: Recommendations report*. https://www.dhs.wisconsin.gov/publications/p02108.pdf

Wittig, M. A. (1996). An introduction to social psychological perspectives on grassroots organizing. *Journal of Social Issues, 52*(1), 3–14.

Woke Foods. (2020). *Our story*. https://wokefoods.coop/our-story/

Wonneberger, A., Hellsten, I. R., and Jacobs, S. H. J. (2020). Hashtag activism and the configuration of counterpublics: Dutch animal welfare debates on Twitter. *Information, Communication, and Society, 24*(12), 1694–1711.

Wourman, J. J., & Mavima, S. (2020). Our story had to be told! A look at the intersection of the Black campus movement and black digital activism. *Spark: A 4C4Equality Journal, 2*. https://sparkactivism.com/volume-2-call/vol-2-intro/our-story-had-to-be-told/

Wright, R. (2003). The word at work: Ideological and epistemological dynamics in African American rhetoric." In R. L. Jackson J. II & E. Richardson. (Eds.), *Understanding African American rhetoric: Classical origins to contemporary innovations* (pp. 85–97). Routledge.

Yancey, K. B. (1999). Looking back as we look forward: Historizing writing assessment. *College Composition and Communication, 50*(3), 483–503.

Yomtov, D., Plunkett, S. W., Efrat, R., & Marin, A. G. (2017). Can peer mentors improve first-year experiences of university students? *Journal of College Student Retention: Research, Theory & Practice, 19*(1), 25–44.

Zimmerelli, L. (2015). A place to begin: Service-learning tutor education and writing center social justice. *The Writing Center Journal, 35*(1), 57–84.

CONTRIBUTORS

MOLLY APPEL, PhD, is an assistant professor of English at Nevada State College and has been a K–20 educator for 15 years. Through the co-formation of her research and teaching, she examines how Latinx and Latin American literature are a space of pedagogical praxis for human rights and social justice.

MARIAN AZAB is an immigrant, disabled, Arab woman. She is a lecturer of sociology at Nevada State College. She received her PhD in sociology with specializations in inequalities and social movements from the University of New Mexico. Marian's goal is to empower minority students to achieve higher career aspirations.

SWETA BANIYA is an assistant professor of rhetoric and professional and technical writing and an affiliate faculty of the Center for Coastal Studies at Virginia Polytechnic Institute and State University. Through a transnational and non-Western perspective, her research focuses on transnational coalitions in disaster response, crisis communication, and non-western rhetorics. She is working on her first book-length project, *Transnational Assemblages: Social Justice Oriented Technical Communication in Global Disaster Management,* where she explores transnational activism in the April 2015 Nepal Earthquake and 2017 Hurricane Maria in Puerto Rico.

JULIE COLLINS BATES is an associate professor of rhetoric, composition, and professional writing at Millikin University. She also directs Millikin's university writing program and is the book review editor for *Rhetoric Review.* Her scholarship bridges environmental rhetoric, intersectional feminism, community literacy, and technical and professional writing. Her research has appeared in *Enculturation, Reflections,* and

Computers & Composition Online, and her dissertation was awarded the 2019 Conference on College Composition & Communication Outstanding Dissertation Award in Technical Communication.

CINDY BERNAL is a director at a non-profit agency specialized in providing legal services to immigrants in South Texas. She has been working with this population for the past ten years, developing special expertise in working with children and their families. Cindy served as an intern at La Posada Providencia while earning a master's degree in social work from the University of Texas Rio Grande Valley.

JORGE M. CAMARILLO is the case manager at Refugee Services of Texas—Rio Grande Valley, founded in 1978. Refugee Services of Texas (RST) is a social-service agency dedicated to providing assistance to refugees and other displaced persons fleeing persecution. RST provides services to hundreds of refugees, asylees, survivors of human trafficking, and related vulnerable populations from over 30 different countries of origin each year.

JOE CIRIO is assistant professor of writing and first-year studies and convenor for the writing-across-the-curriculum program at Stockton University. He teaches courses on rhetorical memory, professional writing and design, and race and gender in American Society. His research focuses on community literacy and, in particular, the functions of everyday and vernacular literacy activity within community contexts.

APRIL CONWAY holds a PhD in English with a specialization in rhetoric and writing and a women's, gender, and sexuality studies graduate certificate. Her research and writing interests include community literacies, alternative assessment practices, creative writing, and rhetorics of motherhood. She is a lecturer at the University of Michigan.

LAURA DECKER teaches and researches composition, writing studies, and literacy at Nevada State College. She holds an MFA in creative writing from Texas State University and a PhD in Literacy Education from UNLV. She is a native Texan and enjoys being outdoors the most, especially hiking and camping with her family in the beautiful wild spaces Nevada has to offer.

KATHERINE A. DURANTE, PhD, is an assistant professor in the department of sociology at the University of Utah. Her research centers around incarceration, race and ethnicity, and families.

ROSEMARY Q. FLORES is Nevada State College's Teacher Academy Pipeline Project (TAPP) Coordinator. At UNLV's College of Education, she was a co-PI for the Abriendo Caminos/Opening Pathways project and the family engagement specialist overseeing the MESA Family Network. She received her MPA at UNLV and is now pursuing her doctoral degree. She holds a bachelor's degree from UNR in STEM Secondary Education. She is a National Hispana Leadership Institute 2004 Fellow and received the Executive Program Certificate from Harvard University's JFK School of Government.

STEPHEN P. GASTEYER is an associate professor of sociology at Michigan State University. His research focuses on community and environmental justice—specifically food, water, and land—and strategies of community building and resistance to extractive capitalism in the US and the Middle East.

JEFFREY GROSS is an associate professor of English at Christian Brothers University. He teaches courses in American cultural studies and American and African American literature. His research examines inequity, democracy, and literary and cultural representations of the persistence of the antebellum in US politics and culture.

REBECCA HALLMAN MARTINI is associate professor of English at the University of Georgia where she also serves as the director of UGA's Writing Center. Her book, *Disrupting the Center: A Partnership-Based Approach to Writing in the University* (Utah State University Press, 2022), establishes an administrative, strategic partnership model for writing center and writing across the curriculum collaborations. Her work has been published in or is forthcoming from *WPA, The Writing Center Journal, Across the Disciplines, WAC Journal, Praxis,* and *Computers and Composition.*

RACHEL HERZL-BETZ, PhD, is an assistant professor in the department of humanities at Nevada State College. She is also the director of the Writing Center. Dr. Herzl-Betz earned her BA in English from Carleton College (2008) and both her MA and PhD from the University of Wisconsin-Madison (2017). Dr. Herzl-Betz's research focuses on the interplay between writing spaces and accessibility, particularly as it impacts multiply marginalized communities.

LEAH LILLANNA JOHNNEY earned a BA in English/professional writing from Lehman College and has lived in the British Virgin Islands, New York, Texas, Florida, and Trinidad. She is passionate about serving her community, from addressing food insecurities to fighting for an inclusive curriculum. She plans to pursue an MA in intercultural communication and education.

MADISON JONES is an assistant professor in the departments of writing and rhetoric and natural resources science at the University of Rhode Island. His research forges connections between ecology, space/place, advocacy, and emerging technologies and has appeared in *Kairos, Rhetoric Society Quarterly, Enculturation,* and elsewhere.

VANI KANNAN, PhD, is an assistant professor of English at Lehman College, CUNY. Vani's research interests include social justice-oriented writing pedagogies, community literacies, and Asian/American rhetorics. Her work has appeared in journals including *Women's Studies Quarterly, constellations, Present Tense, enculturation, Writers: Craft & Context,* and *Studies on Asia.*

MICHAEL KNIEVEL is an associate professor of English at the University of Wyoming, where he teaches undergraduate and graduate courses in composition and technical and professional communication. His current research focuses on the rhetoric of policing, as well as on ways that citizens engage with policing as an institution.

ALISON A. LUKOWSKI is an associate professor at University of Wisconsin-Stout, where she teaches courses in first-year composition and gender studies. Her research focuses on the intersection of gender and digital media; in particular, the ways mothers use social media to create, distribute, and seek knowledges about their own bodies.

AJA Y. MARTINEZ is associate professor of English at University of North Texas. Her award-winning scholarship, published nationally and internationally, makes a compelling case for counterstory as methodology through the well-established framework of critical race theory (CRT).

KALIE M. MAYBERRY is a civic and community leader who has worked at the intersection of community development and social impact for over a decade. As a researcher and instructor at Harvard University's Berkman Klein Center, Kalie explores communication and strategic actions of social movements and corporate social responsibility.

ANGELA MITCHELL has been a WPA in some form or other for most of her career and is currently the director of first-year writing at the University of North Carolina Charlotte (UNCC). Angela is currently working on analyzing qualitative data on underrepresented minority students' experiences in first-year writing at UNCC. Her other research interests include work on programmatic assessment, transfer, and placement issues for first-year writing. She is also interested in exploring feminist administrative perspectives and approaches in WPA work and has a particular interest in investigating the rhetorical and aesthetic contexts of graffiti and street art.

RANDALL MONTY is an associate professor of rhetoric, composition, and literacy studies at the University of Texas Rio Grande Valley, where he teaches classes on professional and technical writing, rhetorical theory, historiography, and literacy. His scholarship focuses on political and educational discourse, particularly in writing centers. With his service work, he partners with refugee and asylum shelters and nature centers in the Rio Grande Valley.

MARIA NOVOTNY is an assistant professor of English at the University of Wisconsin-Milwaukee. Her research focuses on health activism, rhetorics of reproductive justice, and feminist rhetorics. As a community-engaged scholar, Maria advocates for improving access to fertility treatment options as steering committee member of the Building Families Alliance of Wisconsin with Sara Finger.

HEATHER K. OLSON BEAL is a professor of education studies at Stephen F. Austin State University. She teaches courses in educational foundations, family and community engagement, and educational policy and advocacy. Her scholarship examines the issues of school choice and the experiences of women and mothers in academia. She has three feisty and bighearted children who guide and shape her scholarship and teaching.

KENLEA PEBBLES (Cherokee/Choctaw/German/English descent) is a PhD candidate at Michigan State University. Her work on water focuses on cultural rhetorics, environmental rhetorics, and technical writing in communities (such as Native American and immigrant communities), science, and policies and legislation.

LISA L. PHILLIPS is an assistant professor of English in the technical communication and rhetoric program at Texas Tech University. She conducts research and teaches graduate and undergraduate courses on environmental issues, intersectional feminisms, technical communication, and sensory rhetoric.

OCTAVIO PIMENTEL joined the department of English at Texas State University in 2005. He has taught various classes in the technical communication and rhetoric and composition fields, including first-year composition, advanced composition, technical writing, as well as critical graduate courses that encompass issues of minority languages, rhetoric, and writing. Critically trained in rhetoric, writing, and education, Dr. Pimentel combines these fields to address critical issues pertaining to minoritized individuals in the rhetoric, composition, and technical communication fields.

CORETTA M. PITTMAN is an associate professor in the English department at Baylor University who teaches courses in the professional writing and rhetoric major. Her current book, *Literacy in a Long Blues Note: Black Women's Literature and Music in the Late Nineteenth and Early Twentieth Centuries,* focuses on the intersections of literacy, literature, music, race, and class. Future work will continue to focus on Black women's literacies and rhetorical practices.

MONICA REYES is an assistant professor in the writing, rhetoric, and discourse department at DePaul University. Her research interests include cultural rhetorics; critical refugee studies; and transnational feminist rhetorical literacies. Her work has been featured most recently in *enculturation* (2020) and *Postcolonial Text* (2019). She has been a volunteer with La Posada Providencia since 2014.

JOLLINA SIMPSON is a mother of three, midwife, reproductive rights activist, and lover of musical theatre.

ERICA M. STONE is a content designer and researcher with experience in both academia and industry. She works at the intersection of technical communication, public rhetoric, and community organizing. Contact Erica via email (erica.m.stone@gmail. com).

SARAH WARREN-RILEY is an assistant professor of rhetoric, composition, and literacy studies and coordinator of professional and technical writing at the University of Texas Rio Grande Valley, where she teaches courses in rhetoric and professional/ technical writing. Her research interests lie at the intersection of public, digital, and cultural rhetorics with technical/professional communication, focusing particularly on rhetorics of advocacy and activism. Her work has been published in *Composition Forum, Computers & Writing Online, Technical Communication Quarterly,* and *Citizenship and Advocacy in Technical Communication.*

LUHUI WHITEBEAR (Coastal Band Chumash of the Chumash Nation) is an assistant professor in the school of language, culture, and society (Indigenous studies) at Oregon State University. Her research focuses on California Indigenous studies, Indigenous feminisms, Indigenous rhetorics, Indigenous activism, MMIW, national law and policy, and Indigenous land and water rights. Luhui is a mother, poet, and Indigenous activist.

MIRIAM F. WILLIAMS is professor of English and associate chair of Texas State University's department of English. Her books and articles focus on public policy writing, social justice, and archival research. She is a fellow of the Association of Teachers of Technical Writing, SIGDOC's 2022 Rigo Award Winner, and Editor-in-Chief of the Society for Technical Communication's journal, *Technical Communication*.

ERICKA WILLS is a labor educator, researcher, and activist for workers and their unions, ranging from steelworkers and miners to teachers and flight attendants. Her work implements both place-based and global approaches to building worker power, promoting union inclusivity, cross-border solidarity, and internal organizing. Dr. Wills is an assistant professor at the University of Wisconsin-Madison School for Workers.

INDEX

coalitions: concept of, 4; copwatching and, 47; definitions of, 10, 47; intersectionality and, 10–11; La Conexión and, 145; Organizing for Action and, 189–90, 194; #RageAgainstRape and, 178–81, 183; Tennessee Educational Equity Coalition (TEEC), 196, 199–200, 206, 207; Urban Affairs Coalition, 166–71

Coleridge, Samuel Taylor, 130

Collins, Patricia Hill, 177

colonialism, settler, 107–9, 117–20

community control, 124

community gardening, 122–27

community listening, 191–92

community organizing, 12–13, 56–57, 189–94. See also Plant, The

community-driven approach, 99–100

Complete Tennessee, 202

Conexión Américas, 196, 207

confederate statues, 160–64

consensus, 221–22

Cooper, Brittney, 6–7

Cooper, Marilyn, 35

CopBlock, 37–38

Copwatch Brooklyn, 42

copwatching activism: about, 31–34; coalitions and, 47; digital archiving, 42–43; ecological model, 35–36; embodied agonistic participation, 34–35; online work, 41–42; organization, goals, and activities, 36–38; rhetorical work of video in, 43–46; on the streets, 38–41

Council of Federated Organizations (COFO), 62

counterpublics. See publics and counterpublics

COVID-19 pandemic: food insecurity and, 123, 126–27; La Conexión and, 148; Nacogdoches Accountability Coalition and, 51–52, 54

Crenshaw, Kimberlé, 10, 132, 177

culture making, 205

Customs and Border Protection (CBP), US, 245

Dakota Access Pipeline, 19, 111–12

D'Angelo, Frank, 162

databases, 42–43

Davis, Angela, 12

Davis, Diane, 134n3

Davis, Robert, 107n1

Dean, J., 84

Decker, Laura, 211–12

Declaration of Independence, 153

Deferred Action for Childhood Arrivals (DACA) program, 147, 196, 200–201, 204n3, 205

Deil-Amen, R., 202

Del Gandio, Jason, 216–17

Democratic National Convention, 55–56, 70

Dich, Linh, 178

Ding, H., 20

Direct Action Network (DAN), New York City, 221–22, 227

Dobbs vs. Jackson, 96

Dobrin, Sid, 140

domestic violence shelter (La Conexión), 146–47

Dreamers, 147, 200–201. See also Deferred Action for Childhood Arrivals (DACA) program

Druschke, Caroline Gottschalk, 133, 135, 138

Duarte, M., 113, 120

Dunlap, A., 107n1, 108

Durante, Katherine A., 213–14

dynamic criteria mapping (DCM), 220

Eble, M. F., 21

ecological model of writing, 35–36

"econs," 140, 143

"ecosee," 140

Edbauer, Jenny, 36, 46, 142

Educate-Organize-Advocate (EOA) conference, 192

Ejército Zapatista de Liberación Nacional (EZLN), 114

El Grito de Sunset Park, 42–43

Emancipation Proclamation, 153

embodied activism: copwatching and, 34–35, 43–46; graffiti and, 151–52, 158; Lefebvre on bodies in space, 151; rhetorical energy of place and, 136

INTERSECTIONAL RHETORICS

KARMA R. CHÁVEZ, SERIES EDITOR

This series takes as its starting point the position that intersectionality offers important insights to the field of rhetoric—including that to enhance what we understand as rhetorical practice, we must diversify the types of rhetors, arguments, frameworks, and forms under analysis. Intersection works on two levels for the series: (1) reflecting the series' privileging of intersectional perspectives and analytical frames while also (2) emphasizing rhetoric's intersection with related fields, disciplines, and research areas.

www.ingramcontent.com/pod-product-compliance
Lightning Source LLC
Chambersburg PA
CBHW020337270326
41926CB00007B/218